# HIS NAME WAS JOHN

The Life Story of an Early Mennonite Leader

By Barbara F. Coffman

*Wipf and Stock Publishers*
EUGENE, OREGON

Wipf and Stock Publishers
199 West 8th Avenue, Suite 3
Eugene, Oregon 97401

His Name Was John
The Life Story of an Early Mennonite Leader
By Coffman, Barbara F.

ISBN: 1-59244-312-5
Publication date 8/18/2003
Previously published by Herald Press, 1964

# FOREWORD

I never saw my Grandfather Coffman. He died before his second son, my father, was married. But for some years I have been living very close to J. S. Coffman, sharing his experiences, delving into his thought life, watching with awe his spiritual growth. In writing this biography I feel I have come to know most intimately a truly devoted servant of God.

To understand the life and work of J. S. Coffman it is first of all necessary to have some knowledge of the time in which he lived. Changes which have affected all phases of living since Coffman began his ministry a century ago have been especially significant in the Mennonite Church. Our young people today may have some difficulty in trying to visualize a church without Sunday schools, with no evening meetings, no youth activities, and a preaching service only once or twice a month. Besides, there was very little Christian literature at that time, the *Herald of Truth* being the only Mennonite publication. Missions were nonexistent as far as the Mennonite Church was concerned.

Change came slowly, and not without great struggle. John S. Coffman was in the midst of this struggle, along with a few other men of vision who saw the need for prompt and aggressive action if the church was to survive.

Although I have written this biography in the style of fiction, it is by no means fictitious. All the incidents are true, and are based on the wealth of material I had at my disposal. Conversation necessarily was invented, but it, too, is based on documented material. I have used conversation liberally in order to add variety in telling the story, to bring out thoughts and ideas expressed in letters and diaries, and to help portray character.

By telling the story in this manner I have endeavored to bring the inspiration of this nineteenth-century man of God to a greater number of readers. I have tried to show the great needs of the church of that period through the eyes of J. S. Coffman, in order that the reader might share in the struggle to bring about the change and rejoice with Coffman as he sees a gradual awakening and signs of life and growth.

In his short lifetime J. S. Coffman's influence was felt throughout the entire church in the United States and Canada. His ministry was a blessing to thousands, both young and old. It is my prayer that through the story of his life his influence may continue.

Most of the material for this book came from the pen of J. S. Coffman himself in the form of diaries and letters. The quotations from these are verbatim. I am deeply grateful to my Virginia relatives, the Heatwoles and Coffmans, who furnished me with letters written by J. S. Coffman to his parents, brothers, and sisters back home in Virginia after he moved to Indiana. I am also grateful to members of the J. S. Coffman family who carefully preserved the large file of letters Coffman received from relatives, friends, and church workers from all parts of the United States and Canada.

I am also indebted to a warm personal friend of J. S. Coffman, the late M. S. Steiner, who wrote a short biography of this Mennonite evangelist which was published in 1904 by the Mennonite Book and Tract Society. Much of the material concerning his early life was drawn from this book.

Another important source was verbal information—family stories and reminiscences of J. S. Coffman's sons and daughters, and others who worked with him and knew him well.

I have used the *Mennonite Encyclopedia,* H. A. Brunk's *History of Mennonites in Virginia,* and many other books, periodicals, and manuscript sources, including family and institutional records.

Without the help and inspiration of my father, S. F. Coffman, I probably would not have attempted this work. He not only furnished me with much information and encouragement, but was my main critic and adviser until his death in 1954. Invaluable assistance also came from other members of the J. S. Coffman family: the eldest, William, who gave a critical reading to the completed manuscript before his death, only a few months before the publication of this biography; Fannie, Mrs. J. C. Landis, who died in 1961; and the youngest member of the family, Mrs. Dilman Gingrich, still residing in the old home town of Elkhart.

Among those who told me of their association with J. S. Coffman, I particularly want to mention J. S. Hartzler, a co-laborer during the early years of the Elkhart Institute; Eli Hallman, who became acquainted with him during his first series of meetings at Berlin (now Kitchener), Ontario; and J. B. Smith, who was among his converts in Waterloo County, Ontario.

I am also indebted to a number of historians and writers who kindly read the manuscript and offered helpful advice and criticism. These include the late Dr. Harold S. Bender, Dr. J. C. Wenger, Dr. Melvin Gingerich, Dr. John A. Hostetler, Dr. Harry A. Brunk, and the book editor for Herald Press, Paul Erb.

Special thanks are also due a native Virginian, Miss Nellie Coffman, who helped her Canadian cousin with dialect and the correct usage of Virginian colloquialisms. According to this authority the term "right smart" which appears a number of times in the book has no remote relationship to the word "smart" found in the dictionary. It means "a large quantity." And in spite of common belief among northerners, "you all" is not approved in the best Virginian society unless used in the plural form.

## Dedication

To four Coffman men who with zeal and devotion have served God and the church over four generations; Samuel Coffman, a bishop in Virginia; John S. Coffman, evangelist; Samuel F. Coffman, a bishop in Ontario; and my brother, John E. Coffman, now serving in England.

## Dedication to

## John S. Coffman

*By J. S. Shank*

Man of great heart whose noble thoughts have made
That life a grand example, pure and strong;
Not stained with acts of selfishness and wrong;
Not scarred in soul, but of ignoble deeds afraid;
Those benign lips have spoken words of balm,
When hearts 'neath sorrow's burden drooped forlorn;
Those piercing eyes, like burning stars, could warm
The soul, giving it courage new, and calm.
To childhood's heart, his manly purpose shone
Like the golden orb that brings the summer day;
To youth's ambitious hope, he gave the one
Great gift—an ear of sympathy;
On human hearts where'er his life was known,
A sweet and holy benediction lay.

From the first volume of the Goshen College *Maple Leaf:* "Dedicated to J. S. Coffman, pioneer in the educational work of the Mennonite Church, whose abiding love for men and whose practical application of the truth teach us to avoid clouded thinking and hesitating action, to live simply and sincerely, and to work devotedly in this world of men."

*Dig deep into the lore of other years*
*And make the dead past speak again,*
*That saints today betoken with their tears*
*May sympathize in sad refrain.*
*In living tongue tell deeds of noble dead,*
*How they for Christ the world forsook;*
*And may thy life as pure as theirs be read*
*Translated in God's heavenly book.*

Tribute by J. S. Coffman to Joseph Sohm, translator of *Martyrs' Mirror.*

# 1

"You know, Sam, I can't rightly believe he's ourn. Just look at him. Isn't he beautiful?"

Propped up with pillows Frances gazed with awe at her newborn son cuddled tightly in her arms. Almost like a madonna, Samuel thought, with her brown hair slicked back under her white cap, and her clear-cut features radiant in the candlelight as she smiled on her babe.

Samuel shook his head silently, not knowing what to say as he carefully set the candle on the table by the bed and turned to look at his wife and son.

"Why don't you hold him?" Frances suggested as he bent awkwardly over the bed for a closer peek at the squirming little figure in her arms.

"Hello, little John," he said, gingerly touching a tiny hand.

Frances looked up in surprise. "John, did you say?"

"Why, sure. Don't you mind? We talked some of callin' him John if he was a boy."

"Yes—I reckon we did. But now it's so right, Sam, so right! John!" she breathed softly. "His name is John."

"Why, Franey, what do you mean?" Samuel asked wonderingly. "There's nothin' so special about it."

"Oh, but there is, Sam. There is. If only I could tell you right."

Laying the baby tenderly on the bed beside her, Frances leaned back on her pillow, a rapturous faraway look in her shining brown eyes.

"Well, can't you tell me?" he asked gently, reaching for her hand.

"It was this morning, Sam," Frances began, "just before he was born. While I was layin' here in all that misery I was prayin'—prayin' hard for the child I was abringin' into the world."

"Go on," Samuel urged, pressing her hand reassuringly.

"It's so hard to explain," she continued, gazing fixedly at the ceiling. "You mind how we've been aprayin' for this child. How we gave him to God just as soon as we knew about him. Well, all at once it seemed an answer come. A strange feelin' come over me, and I knew—just as plain as if I'd heard the words, that God had accepted our gift—that the child belonged to Him and He would use him for some special work."

The stern gray eyes under the bushy brows grew suddenly misty as Samuel glanced tenderly from mother to child. "And what about the name?" he asked.

"Why," Frances said, "right away I had to think of Elisabeth and her son, there in the first chapter of Luke, and the special work God had for him to do. And I thought of that verse there, 'Thou, child, shalt be called the prophet of the Highest: for thou shalt go before the face of the Lord to prepare his ways.' And there's something more about salvation."

" 'To give knowledge of salvation unto his people by the remission of their sins,' " Samuel finished the verse.

"Well," Frances sighed, "I reckon this boy won't be a John the Baptist, but God will use him in some way. He has some special purpose for him."

"And what about a second name for him?" Samuel asked.

Frances smiled. "Well, since you called him John, I'll give him another. It's Samuel. John Samuel Coffman. A right big name for such a little boy."

Stepping softly from the tiny bedroom curtained off from the rest of the cabin, Samuel stirred up the fire in the crude fireplace. It was only October (the sixteenth, 1848, the calendar said), but it was a chilly, rainy evening, and a fire felt good. Seated in the splint-bottom armchair Frances' father had made for them, he watched the flames dreamily. There were so many things to think about—events of the past—his new status as a father—and great new responsibilities. Such a variety of thoughts came crowding into his mind.

It seemed only yesterday, but actually a year and a half had gone by since he had crossed the Alleghenies from Greenbrier County to start a new life in the beautiful Shenandoah Valley. It had been hard to leave his father and mother, Christian and Anna Wenger Coffman, and his nine brothers and sisters. But he was now twenty-five years old. Several of his older brothers were already established on farms of their own, and he decided it was time he, too, should be looking out for himself.

Ever since his visit to Rockingham County the previous summer Samuel had dreamed of living in the lush green valley with the wooded mountains and gently rolling hills. It would be good to be able to go to church every Sunday and to associate with the young people of Mennonite background like himself. There were so few Mennonites in Greenbrier, and church services were held only on the rare occasion when a minister from the valley made the long, tedious trip across the mountains on horseback.

There was also another drawing power back there in the valley, a beautiful young woman with dark brown hair and dreamy brown eyes. He had met her once at a singing. Some friends had pointed out Frances Weaver, subtly suggesting that she would be a fine wife for him.

Somehow, he couldn't keep thoughts of her from coming to his mind, her trim little figure and capable, gracious manner. He had made up his mind that as soon as he got back to the valley he would call at the Weaver home. He had a good excuse, for Mrs. Weaver had sent a length of linsey as a gift to the Coffmans with one of the ministers who came to preach one Sunday. Maybe it wasn't intentional, but he looked directly at Samuel when he explained that the work had been done by Frances. He also added Frances' message that she could do much better. Samuel could still feel his face turning red. He had left quickly to finish his chores at the barn. Yes, duty demanded that he visit the Weavers to thank them for the gift.

After his arrival Samuel spent many interesting hours at the Weaver home. He had hired himself for the season to a farmer nearby. He also enjoyed many cross-country rides with Frances, their horses trotting agreeably side by side when he was her privileged escort from a meeting or a bee of some kind, or maybe a singing.

Knowing that Samuel, like most young people of that time, had given little thought to religion, Frances frequently steered their conversation to a discussion of Christian principles. She herself was a devout believer, and had been baptized at the unusual age of sixteen. As a rule, such a step was taken only after marriage. It was something new for Samuel to be discussing religion with a girl like Frances. To her, Christ was not only a divine Being, but a personal Saviour and precious Friend. Her sincerity and interest made a great impression on Samuel, and it was not long before he, too, was searching the Scriptures and taking more interest in the Sunday morning preaching. Suddenly he found himself able to take part in the conversation around the dinner table at the Weaver home when the sermon was discussed. It was a delight to Samuel Weaver to watch the spiritual development of this fine young man who apparently was soon to become his son-in-law.

The wedding date was set for November 11. When Samuel went to see the minister about performing the ceremony, he was also able to inform him of his decision to live a Christian life. Arrangements were made to have him join the class to be received into the church by baptism the following spring.

After the wedding, the bride and groom packed their few possessions and rode off to their new home near Burketown. Samuel was to be a hired hand on the farm of J. R. Keagy. The little old cabin they were to occupy as tenants was far from being a dream house, but it soon became a cozy home and the young people were content.

But now—now that he had a son, Samuel suddenly felt the weight of many new problems and responsibilities. Rousing himself, he added a few more sticks to the fire and again sat back in his chair to do some hard thinking. A decision which must be faced soon was whether or not to stay on at the Keagy farm. True, he made a living for himself, but with wages what they were, it would be years before he could save enough for a farm of his own.

Also to be considered was the distance from church. Before her marriage Frances had lived almost next door to Weavers Church. And on the Sundays when there was no service there she could easily ride over to the Pike. But since the move to Burketown they both had missed many services. And now with a baby to care for, Frances would miss even more. But could they afford to miss so many? With a son dedicated to the service of Almighty God, they would need all the spiritual help and teaching they could possibly receive.

John Samuel was over two years old and the population of the little cabin had increased to four before the first moving day arrived for the Coffman family.

It was a balmy day in early spring, 1851, when they finally set out to begin life on a farm near Spring Creek. Little John made the trip on horseback with his father, while Mother and baby Jacob came with the wagonload of furniture. Since the roads were rough and heavy with mud at that time of the year, it was a good half day's drive from the Keagy farm to Spring Creek.

Samuel met his wife at the front door and ceremoniously led her into the main room of the large, old farmhouse, where a fire burned cheerily in the fireplace. Young John was already racing and shouting through the empty rooms, investigating every nook and corner.

After the tiny cabin to which they had become accustomed, this house seemed alarmingly large. But Frances sighed contentedly as she warmed herself at the fire and looked thoughtfully about her.

"You know, Sam, I reckon we'll like it right well here," she said. "There's right smart room, with the big kitchen and all. Like as not we won't need to use the upstairs, not this spring anyway."

"But I fear we're agoin' to need more chairs and things," Samuel said ruefully, thrusting his hands deep in his pockets.

"Oh, well, there's bound to be a sale hereabouts someday, and we can get a couple chairs, and mebbe a bed for the boys. But we ain't aneedin' much. I could do with a good loom most of all. It's agoin' to keep a body busy makin' pants for them two," she added, watching the boys clambering up and down the stairsteps.

Eight years were spent on the little farm at Spring Creek, eight happy years of growing, learning, working, and playing for the lad marked for special service. John grew rapidly and learned quickly. In a few years he became a big help to both Father and Mother. Little sister Lizzie arrived in February, 1852, and as she grew older it was John who minded baby sister when Mother was busy.

Watching the children at play, Frances often wondered about her first-born. Never could she forget that experience at his birth. He was an exceptional child, but sometimes the thought troubled her. Was it fair to the other children to consider him in any way special? Discussing the matter with Samuel, they wisely decided to train all their children alike, and not to mention the revelation to John until he had made his own commitment and dedicated himself to the service of his Lord.

John enjoyed life on the Spring Creek farm. He loved to play outdoors, to ramble through the wood lot and splash in the little stream that ran through the farm. But his favorite occupation was helping Mother in the house. He liked to be with his mother, for she talked to him more, and didn't seem to mind answering questions.

"It's a right nice day, boys," Frances said one bright spring morning. "You all had better be out helpin' your father plant those taters."

"Ah, Jake can go. I want to stay and help you," John said, watching as she rolled her sleeves to her elbows preparing to knead the bread rising in the dough tray beside the fireplace.

"Well, then, you see to Lizzie while I'm a kneadin' down this bread," Frances said, removing the clean piece of woolen blanket that covered the rising dough. "Mind that she don't get into nothin'."

But John was soon oblivious to everything as he watched his mother deftly pummeling and punching the soft, spongy dough.

"But where did it all go, Mother?" he finally asked as Frances gave the dough a final pat and pinched off a piece to start forming a loaf.

"Why, it's all right there," she said.

"But there's only a little left, and it was full right up to the top."

"I know," Frances replied slowly, "but you see it had a lot of air holes, and when I punched and poked it around, all the air went out. But it'll come in again, I reckon, before I bake the loaves. It's the holes as makes the bread light and easy to chew on."

John peered thoughtfully into the dough tray as Frances started on another loaf.

"But what makes the holes, Mother?"

Frances heaved a sigh. "It's the yeast, son. Mind how I put

that crockful of stuff in the tray last evening, and mixed the flour in it? Oh, look, there's Lizzie climbin' up on the table after the crock. Grab her before she spills the bit that's left, or I won't have any more for Friday."

"Do you always have to leave some for next time?" John asked, hauling Lizzie to the floor.

"Yes, in a way I do, but I make more too— Oh, it's so hard to explain," she ended lamely. "Just wait till Father comes in. Mebbe he can tell you better about yeast. Now be sure and watch Lizzie better while I go out to see how the fire's comin' in the oven."

Day after day John's insatiable curiosity continued to stump his father and mother. Both could read and write, but their education was meager, and books were scarce. So many of John's questions received only vague replies.

"If ever anybody needed schoolin', it's that boy of ourn," Frances said one evening, discussing the day's problems with Samuel after the children were in bed. "I declare I couldn't think up all them questions if I sat and thought for a year."

"I'd sure be glad if he could go," Samuel replied, tilting his chair back from the table where he had been sitting to read his Bible. "But there ain't none close enough, and anyway it costs right smart to send a child to school."

"If only we lived a little closer, we could send him to the school at Weavers Church in the winter," Frances suggested.

"Yes, he could at least get a start in the three R's, I reckon," Samuel said, "but it is too far from here."

For a moment Frances' knitting needles stopped clicking as she sat gazing at the fire. "But there must be some way, Sam, sometime. This boy is different, mind? God gave him an uncommon good mind and all for a purpose. And He's aholdin' us responsible for his learnin'."

Samuel nodded. "I know. And I've been thinkin' about it plenty. But there's another thing to think about still."

"And what's that?"

"I'm a minister now, you know."

"Of course," Frances replied in surprise. "But what's that got to do with it?"

"Mebbe not much," said Samuel slowly, "but I reckon there'd be a good many who'd have plenty to say if a minister started sendin' his children to school."

Frances shrugged. "If there's them as thinks it wrong to learn a little bit 'bout this wonderful world we're livin' in," she said heatedly, waving a knitting needle for emphasis, "all I say is let 'em talk. There ain't nothin' wrong with a little learnin' as far as I can see."

"It's just that they're afraid of pride, Franey," Samuel answered softly, "most of 'em anyway. They're afraid if a body knows a bit more than they do, he'll be proud. But I reckon we'll have a little time to think about it, and we'll see. We'll see."

It was July, 1852, when Samuel Coffman was called to the ministry. After the Virginia Conference sanctioned a request for the ordination of a new minister for the middle district, three men had received votes in the district churches. One was excused from the lot, claiming inability to sing and lack of general knowledge. And so Samuel was one of the two whose names were in the lot that Sunday morning.

It was a solemn hour for both Samuel and Frances. They had prayed a great deal during the few weeks that had elapsed since the vote. Samuel felt keenly his lack of training and knowledge of the Bible. How could he expound to others the Holy Scripture which he himself had begun to study only four short years ago? But he had faith, and a desire to serve God, and so resigned himself completely to His leading in the important decision.

"You won't feel bad if I don't go to church this morning, will you?" Frances asked, taking five-month-old Lizzie from the cradle and commencing to dress her.

"Why, I reckon we'll have plenty of time to get ready. We're early, and I'll hurry with the chores so I can give you a hand."

"No, Sam, it's not that. I could get ready. It's just that I want to stay here and pray. It—it's so important. I must pray."

It was late when Samuel finally came riding down the lane from church. With him came a visitor, his cousin, Martin Burkholder, bishop of the middle district.

"Here comes Father. Here comes Father," cried John and Jacob, rushing into the house. "And there's someone with him."

Frances walked anxiously out to the lane with the boys and soon recognized the visitor. One glance at Samuel's face as he dismounted at the gate, and she knew instantly how the lot had fallen. There was no need for the announcement Burkholder made as he solemnly shook her hand. Even though her heart was pounding and she was seized with an overwhelming desire to rush back to her room to pray, Frances listened politely. Then clasping Samuel's hand she led the way into the house where dinner was waiting.

Somehow they got through that meal. Burkholder did most of the talking. Even the children seemed to sense the solemnity of the occasion and were quieter than usual. That afternoon Samuel and Frances enjoyed a season of prayer and worship with Burkholder which would linger long in their memories. Together before God they poured out the pent-up feeling of their hearts. Once more they dedicated themselves, their home, their children to His service and sought His wisdom and guidance in their increasing responsibilities.

*The Christian parent should show his children that he is a praying Christian; and teach them that it is their duty to pray daily, and never to be ashamed of this duty no matter who is in their company.*—Diary.

# 2

"It's school time, John," Frances ordered. "Get your slate and get busy."

John was now six and his education had begun. The kitchen table was his desk, his parents the teachers, and an A B C book, a Bible, and a slate his equipment.

"But I want to watch the snow," protested John, fascinated by the sight of the huge flakes falling fast that October afternoon.

Standing at the window with John and Lizzie, Frances, too, was fascinated. Snow never was too plentiful in Virginia and snow in October most unusual.

"Pretty soon you can look again," she said. "But first you're to write a whole slateful of B's."

"Mebbe I should go out and help Father a while," John suggested hopefully. "Mebbe he and Jake won't get all the taters dug before they get all covered up with snow."

Frances laughed. "Not likely. I reckon it'll stop pretty soon. It's only October, you know. If you get your lessons done quick, you and Jake can play outside a while."

"Oh!" John exclaimed excitedly. "We'll get our sled and play in the snow."

Again Frances laughed. "In October? You'll be lucky if you can use it in January."

But the snow that day broke all precedents. Faster and faster it fell, quickly covering the ground with a thick, white carpet. After finishing his B's, John again joined his mother and sister at the window and together they admired the beautiful tracing of white on the leaves and branches of the old apple tree and the rows of miniature igloos in the vegetable garden.

Soon Father and Jacob came stamping into the kitchen, shaking the wet snow from their coats and hats. Their job in the potato patch had become quite impossible. John noticed the anxious look exchanged by his parents, but he also spied several beautiful snowflakes on his father's dark coat. School resumed then, with a nature study lesson on the subject of snow.

October 26, 1854, was long remembered by Virginians as the day of the big snowstorm. All afternoon and evening and all night long the snow continued to fall, gently and steadily. But frequently during the night the stillness was broken by the sound of a terrible rending, followed by a crashing thud.

"Another branch of the apple tree," Mother would say in a loud whisper. Or, "Sounds like the big maple out front this time."

A sight both beautiful and terrible met their gaze next morning. The earth lay buried under a twelve-inch blanket of gleaming white snow. But the trees, still in full foliage, had paid a heavy toll for their brief hour of ultra glory, and the loss in timber and orchards was very heavy through the entire valley.

In the education of the Coffman children religious instruction was considered of utmost importance. But this training was not formal. John listened to his father read the Bible and pray during daily family worship. When anyone asked for stories, it was usually a Bible story they heard. Both Father and Mother were good storytellers and instilled in their children a love and appreciation for the Word of God that was lasting.

"Mother, what is Good Friday?" John asked one day, overhearing a discussion regarding plans for that day.

"Why, John, you know. It's the day Jesus died. Don't you mind?"

"But why do they call it good? It should be bad Friday."

"No, we call it good, for it was good for us. If He hadn't died, we couldn't go to heaven, you know."

John thought about this a while and then said, "Tell me about it again, won't you, please. About how Jesus died."

This was John's favorite story. He both loved and dreaded it, for it made him feel so very, very sad.

Leaving her ironing for a few minutes in order to give full attention to the story, Mother sat in the rocker cuddling baby Anna, who had joined the family in October, 1855. Once again she recounted the sad, tragic story of the crucifixion. John listened with rapt attention, feeling in his own heart the dishonor, disloyalty, and agony endured by the Saviour. Finally he could control himself no longer. Running to his mother, he buried his head in her lap and sobbed bitterly.

"Why, John, what's wrong? Ain't you feelin' well?" Frances asked anxiously.

"Oh, those men, those men," sobbed John. "They shouldn't have done it. They were bad."

"Yes, they were bad," soothed Mother, stroking the lad's head tenderly. "But listen. I haven't told the best part yet. They killed Him, but He didn't stay dead, you know." And Frances continued with the glorious account of the resurrection, and the discomfiture of the guards and soldiers when they had to admit the tomb was empty.

But the agony of the cross lingered on in the sensitive soul of the child, on and on into the years of manhood, never failing to fill him with the deepest emotion.

Music also had a place in the informal curriculum. A love for music seemed to be a family trait; so it was only natural that singing and practice in reading notes should become part of the regular routine.

"Ut re mi fa so la si ut," sang John as he worked or played around the house. A favorite pastime was playing singing school. Jacob and Lizzie, John's pupils, were carefully corrected whenever they failed to sing the right tone. John had a lovely, clear treble voice which developed later into a rich baritone.

From his father John also caught his first glimpse of the world beyond the lofty horizons of their valley home. Stories of boyhood days in Greenbrier County, which later became a part of West Virginia, and accounts of his trips on foot and horseback across the mountains always delighted the children. But the greatest story of adventure and an all-time favorite was the story of great-great-grandfather Andrew Kauffman who came with his family across the great ocean from Switzerland in 1717.

There were so many intriguing things about that voyage that Samuel was always deluged with questions. How could a boat keep on a straight path on a big ocean with no land in sight? What made the boat go? John felt little chills running up and down his spine when he thought of the storms. What kept a boat from sinking when waves were higher, even, than a house?

And then there was the question, "But why did they come here, Father? Why didn't they stay in their own country? Didn't they like it there?"

"Why, I reckon they did, son," Samuel replied, stroking his chin thoughtfully. "Andrew Kauffman had a right good business in Steffisburg, Switzerland. A hosen-streicher, or trouser maker, they called him. And Switzerland is right nice, they say, with lots of high mountains. But there was one thing he didn't like, and that was war. It seems there was nearly always fightin' goin' on somewheres, and they made all the menfolk take trainin' so they could fight. Well, Andrew didn't believe it was right to fight, and he didn't want his boys to take the trainin'; so he decided to come over to this country where he could live like he wanted."

Then followed the story of the arrival of the Kauffmans in Pennsylvania, where Andrew purchased a 200-acre farm near Philadelphia. In 1741 his twelfth child, Isaac, was born. Isaac became a minister in the Mennonite Church in the community. After his marriage he purchased a small piece of land from his brother, who had inherited a part of the expanded home farm. But after the arrival of several sons in his family Isaac decided to move into a less populated district where there would be more opportunity of providing farms for his growing family. A number of Pennsylvanians were moving to Shenandoah County, Virginia, and so Isaac and his wife Esther decided to join the trek.

Christian Coffman, Isaac's third son and Samuel's father, was born in 1780 in Virginia. When he was eight years old, the family decided on another move, this time to the western part of the state. Hearing stories of rich, fertile land which could be obtained at low prices across the Alleghenies, they decided to see what Greenbrier County had to offer.

Here Christian Coffman grew to manhood, helping to clear the acres which comprised his father's farm and later hewing out field after field of his own little farm where he raised his family of six sons and four daughters. Samuel was the seventh child of this family, and the fifth son.

* * *

One fall evening, just after John's eighth birthday, Samuel sat with the boys at the kitchen table helping them with simple sums. Suddenly he put down the slate, tilted back in his chair, and cleared his throat to make a tremendous announcement.

"Well, boys, how would you like to start to school on Monday?"

"To school?" John's eyes were wide with surprise. "Y—you mean a real school—all day long?" he stammered in his excitement.

"Hooray, school!" shouted Jacob, jumping to his feet and dancing around the room.

"Shush, Jake, sit right down and be quiet. You'll wake up Anna," Samuel commanded.

"Yes, boys, please be quiet," added Frances, who sat stitching away on a pair of sturdy homespun trousers. She watched John's expression closely as Samuel broke the news. Oh, how much it means to him, she thought, noting the set lips and small clenched fists of the lad as he waited breathlessly for further explanation.

Then Samuel told them of a school being held in an old log building several miles away by a Mr. Whitehair. His fee would be one dollar a month for each pupil. Since the outside work was pretty well finished that fall, they had decided that John and Jacob could go to school for at least a month or two.

John could scarcely get to sleep that night, and all day Saturday and Sunday he went about as in a dream, thinking of nothing but school. How slowly the hours dragged by!

But Monday morning finally arrived and the boys were up early. They were both too excited to eat breakfast properly, but Father said "Eat," and obediently they crammed down their corn bread, bacon, and sweet potatoes.

Samuel went with the boys that first morning, in order to meet the teacher and make the necessary financial arrangements. Off they started, with the boys seated behind their father on the horse, and the lunch basket and new slates carefully stowed away in a saddlebag. Frances stood with the little girls at the doorway, waving good-by to her men and silently breathing a prayer for the blessing of God upon the new venture.

Arriving at school the boys shyly hung their coats and hats on a peg by the door and hand-in-hand began to look around. One glance was enough for Jake, and John, too, had sudden misgivings. It wasn't just the menacing fists of several big boys showing off in a corner, nor the giggling girls seated at the end of one of the long benches. But the teacher!

"I thought he'd have white hair," whispered Jake.

"So did I," replied John, clutching Jake's hand a little harder.

Fearfully they eyed the man, taller and heavier even than their father, who seemed to have shrunk a bit as he stood talking to him. His thatch of long, black hair, trailing mustache, and heavy black eyebrows all tended to give a fierce look to the beady eyes which kept darting to every corner of the room. But most alarming of all was the sight of the stout birch switch hanging most conspicuously beside the fireplace at the front of the room. Designed to discourage any possible misdemeanor it struck terror in the hearts of the younger children.

When the boys came trudging home that evening, Frances walked down the lane to meet them, eager to hear their report. But to her surprise she was greeted by a quiet, almost listless pair of little boys. Neither mentioned school as they sauntered up the lane.

"Tired, John?" she asked, as an opening to her investigation.

"Oh, tolerable," replied John.

"A good many at school?"

"Thirteen," said Jake, "nine boys and four girls."

"And what did you learn, Jake?" Frances continued.

"Nothin'," exploded Jake. "Not a single thing. Just a lot of baby stuff that I knew already: A-B ab, E-B eb, I-B ib, O-B ob, and U-B ub."

"What, no numbers?" queried Frances, trying desperately to keep her voice calm.

"Well, I had to write a few one's and two's about fifty times. Wasn't a bit of fun."

"And what about you, John? What did you learn?"

"A-B ab, E-B eb, I-B ib, O-B ob, and U-B ub," echoed John tonelessly.

"Oh, no!" exclaimed Frances. "Not you too. Why, you already read right good. Didn't he put you in a different class?"

"No, he just asked if we'd ever been to school, and them that hadn't went in the A B C's."

"Didn't you say you could read?"

"Sure, but he said I'd have to start at the beginnin' just like the rest."

"Did he read to you or tell you any stories?"

"Humph!" said Jake. "He tried to, but he can't read nearly as good as you and Father."

"He didn't get some of the words right when he was reading the Bible," added John.

"Well, like as not things'll be better in a day or two," Mother said cheerfully. "Just wait and see."

But things did not improve. And at the end of a month a halt was called to the formal type of education and lessons were continued at home.

* * *

It was a cold morning in February, 1857. Clattering downstairs for breakfast the boys were surprised to find Grandmother Weaver bustling around the kitchen, and still more surprising, Father was helping her get breakfast. Mother was nowhere in sight.

"Where's Mother?" John asked anxiously.

"Why, she's still in bed," answered Grandmother. "She ain't feelin' too good this morning." There was a strange look on Grandmother's face, and both she and Father appeared to be covering smiles.

"B—but you're smilin'," observed John, greatly perplexed.

"Come and see," said Father, leading the way into the bedroom.

Mother did look pale and tired. But she, too, was smiling. And in each arm she held a queer-shaped bundle.

"A baby!" exclaimed John.

"Two of 'em!" shouted Jake, climbing quickly on the bed to get a good look. "What are they, boys or girls?"

"Both," said Father, beaming proudly. "A brother for you boys and a sister for the girls. So everybody should be happy."

Naming the twins required many family consultations until finally they agreed on Joseph and Mary.

* * *

With the arrival of a new teacher in the district that fall, Frances insisted that the boys should have another chance at school. Their disappointing experience under Mr. Whitehair troubled her, and she felt keenly the need for better instruction than they could get at home.

The new teacher, John H. Moore, called to see them one evening. He was young and well-educated and seemed to understand children. He listened to the boys read, praised the progress they had made, and before he left two little boys were once more eagerly looking forward to going to school.

Back in the old schoolroom the same old benches were again filled with boys and girls of all sizes, most of them their friends of a year ago. The same old table stood at the front of the room, but it looked different under the pile of books the new teacher brought. A blackboard hanging on the wall beside the fireplace also gave the room a different appearance. But one of the greatest changes was the absence of the old birch rod. The big boys speculated about the matter, but the little ones took it only as a happy omen.

It soon became evident that Mr. Moore could handle a switch when occasion demanded, but his young pupils were happy to discover that it wasn't, after all, essential to the learning process. John developed rapidly under his instruction and soon discovered the enjoyment of a good book. Mr. Moore had a fine supply which he lent to the children and during the winter many of them were carried home and enjoyed by the Coffman family as they took turns reading aloud, Father, Mother, and John. Both boys enjoyed several fall and winter terms under Moore's instruction.

* * *

The second moving day for the Coffman family came in the spring of 1859. The move this time was not so far. For some time Samuel had been looking for a larger farm nearer the Weaver and Bank churches where he now preached quite regularly. Eventually he decided to buy the farm of the late Henry Heatwole near Dale Enterprise.

The Heatwole house was a large stately building of red brick with tall white pillars on the front porch. Besides the large kitchen, dining room, and living room on the first floor there were two bedrooms downstairs and five upstairs, also a large basement and attic. There was plenty of room for the family of six children as well as a spare bedroom for guests. Several weeks after the move, son Daniel joined the family.

That spring young John and Jacob became full-time farm hands. This farm was considerably larger and Samuel needed all the help he could get. It was a busy season for the entire household, and for a time there was no thought of school for anyone.

But John's busy mind, stimulated by the months of instruction under Mr. Moore and the few books he had read, refused to take a holiday. He had caught a glimpse of the vast world of the unknown and was not to be satisfied until he had learned more of its secrets. Father and Mother Coffman were no longer able to cope with his innumerable questions or to satisfy his thirst for knowledge.

Fortunately there were a few individuals in the community who understood the predicament of young lads like John. One of these was David A. Heatwole, a man interested in the welfare of the community and of the church. Realizing that many of the young people had little opportunity to attend school, he had organized evening classes for their benefit.

But a great hindrance to education in the district at that time was the school building itself. A small, dilapidated, log building only 12 by 14 feet, known as Walnut Grove school, was far from adequate for the needs of the community.

Calling at the Coffman home one day Heatwole found that Samuel was out, and so he discussed the situation with Frances.

"There are lots of children around here that should be in school," he pointed out. "But if only a quarter of them came, the old building wouldn't hold them all."

"No," Frances agreed, "I reckon it wouldn't. We'd sure send our boys if Sam didn't need 'em so bad, no matter what kind of building it was. But mebbe more would come if we had a better place."

Heatwole nodded thoughtfully. "That's what I've been thinking. If folks see that we think education is important enough to put up a new building, mebbe they'll want to get in on it too. If I thought enough folks'd help, I wouldn't mind going round trying to raise money for it. That's why I come over today, to see what Sam thought about it."

"Well, it's too bad he ain't here, but I'm sure he'd say go ahead. And I'm sure he'd want to give something toward it."

Samuel headed the list of subscribers for the new school with a donation of twenty dollars. His cousin, Bishop Martin Burkholder, contributed an equal amount. After that the necessary amount was quickly raised. A piece of land about half a mile east of Walnut Grove was donated for the building and with labor donated as well, Fairview school was ready for use that fall. John enrolled for the evening classes, and also enjoyed several months at day school during the winter.

The winter term at Fairview was very well attended. Having invested in the new building many parents decided to reap some benefit. The slack winter season seemed to be a good time to send their children. A large percentage of the winter termers were big boys and girls from twelve to sixteen years of age. For many of them it was their first experience in school.

Things were a bit dull for John one afternoon as he sat with the big boys on the long bench at the back of the room. He had finished his sums and there was nothing new to read. Nor was there anything to interest him in the monotonous recitation of the second-grade reading class in progress at the front of the room. To talk or write notes to a neighbor was, of course, strictly forbidden. And so there was nothing to do except recount the rafters on the ceiling or gaze at the formidable backs and hairdos of the big girls on the bench in front of him. Such a wide variety of shades in blue, gray, and brown in the row of frocks, he noticed. And for contrast each girl wore a colorful apron with a big bow tied in the exact center of her back.

The biggest bow of all that day was right in front of him. It belonged to Bettie Heatwole, one of the big girls, about three years older than himself. Her apron strings were not only the widest but the longest of any in the whole row. Quite unnecessarily long, he decided, reaching nonchalantly into his pocket for his penknife. Without stopping to think of possible consequences he neatly lopped off several inches from each of the trailing ends and stuffed them in his pocket. Feeling the tug on the strings Bettie quickly discovered the vandalism.

When school was out, Bettie waited outside with a group of friends planning how to discover the culprit and avenge the deed. But a plot wasn't necessary. Seeing Bettie talking with the other girls, John walked boldly up to the group and meekly handed over the two little pieces of cloth.

"Wh—why you, John Coffman," stammered Bettie. "I reckon I'd of never thought it was you."

"Why not?" John asked calmly. "I've got a right sharp knife."

Bettie was practically speechless with surprise. Young, innocent-looking John, always so well behaved, boldly owning up to such a crime! The whole school had gathered around John and Bettie, and all were enjoying the scene.

"B—but why did you do it?" demanded Bettie, her eyes flashing and her lips set tight in exasperation.

"Well," said John, looking very serious even though his eyes were laughing, "the preachers say anything unnecessary like that is pride. And so I thought I'd help you get rid of some of it."

*Hatred and revenge and retaliation are as far below the true ideal of progress as when Christ said, "Love your enemies, . . . pray for them which despitefully use you, and persecute you." These are doctrines that must be taught.*

—Elkhart Institute Address.

# 3

History began to come alive for John and his night school chums during the winter of 1859 and '60. Stories of ancient civilization, discoveries, and conquests always fascinated him. But suddenly they began to be more than stories. Government wasn't just something he read about in a book. It was something that actually made a difference in everyday life. It touched even the families in his own quiet little community in the lovely Shenandoah Valley.

John was only eleven when events began to take shape that caused the great upheaval in the United States of America. Virginians talked politics that year as they never had before. John listened, and he asked questions. It seemed as if the boys at night school were constantly arguing.

"Ah, Lincoln'll never be elected," some of the big boys contended. "Why, hardly anybody knows him."

"And what is he? A rail splitter, that's what," others would volunteer. "How could a man without much schoolin' hope to be president?"

"But he's got a big idea that they like right well in the North," came the reminder, over and over again. "And if he gets to be president and tries to force abolition, there'll sure be trouble."

John always felt a chill at the thought of possible consequences should Lincoln be elected. In his heart he felt sympathy for the man who had educated himself, and he couldn't help admiring the spirit of one who had been so successful over circumstances. What if he should go on to bigger successes?

As to the abolition issue, wasn't it a good thing? Wasn't Lincoln right in wanting to free the slaves? The controversial matter had bothered him ever since the John Brown episode at Harpers Ferry. Trouble was pretty close that time, and everybody felt relieved when the uprising failed and Brown was captured. But why should a man be condemned to die when his crime was such a just one, he wondered. All he wanted was to free human beings from slavery.

Patiently Father Coffman tried to explain to his young son that it wasn't for his ideals that Brown had died, but for the ill-advised method he had chosen to carry out his purpose. Evil cannot be conquered by evil, he pointed out.

"But could the slaves be freed without fightin'? Would there have to be war if Lincoln got in and tried to do it?" he wanted to know.

"There wouldn't have to be," Samuel replied. "But more'n likely there would be."

"But why?" John persisted.

"Just because every slaveholder in the South'd stick up for his rights," Samuel answered. "They ain't agoin' to let no young president suddenly rob them of their property."

"But slaves aren't property; they're people," John protested.

"No, they paid for 'em, and they consider them property just the same as land or livestock or anything else they own. And remember this, those big landowners couldn't raise no crops without 'em. If they suddenly lost their slaves, they'd be helpless, ruined! Folks in the North can't quite understand this, and that's what's causin' so much trouble and hard feelin,' They're really gettin' fired up and I'm afeared our troubles are just astartin'."

Samuel's fears were substantiated shortly after the announcement of Lincoln's victory on the morning of November 7, 1860. John never forgot the shock of hearing the news.

It was noon, and the family was already seated at the dinner table when someone spied the neighbor come riding up the lane. There was an immediate rush out to the gate, for he had promised he would bring them news on his return from town. John could feel his heart thumping. He looked hopefully for a smile on the neighbor's face as he drew near, but there was none, and his heart sank.

"It's Lincoln," he said, and without another word he turned and was off down the lane. The Coffmans stood as if stunned until horse and rider finally disappeared behind a knoll. Little Joe at last broke the silence. "Let's eat, Mother. I'm hungry," he said, tugging at her apron and pulling toward the house.

"Yes," said Frances, taking the little ones by the hand and trying to speak naturally. "Come in, everybody. No use standin' out here while our dinner's gettin' cold."

John hung back for a word with his father, who still gazed

motionlessly out over the valley. "Does it really mean war, Father?"

"I don't know. I really can't say," he replied slowly, "but we can always hope, lad, and pray."

After the election the country moved rapidly toward a state of war. Each time Samuel rode into town he came home looking more troubled. Soon came the news that South Carolina was seceding. Then it was Florida, with Alabama, Georgia, Louisiana, and Texas following in quick succession.

"It won't be long now," Samuel observed. "Lincoln won't sit back and let that happen without doin' something. We can be glad Virginia voted to stay with the Union."

But Virginia was soon to change sides. Samuel was shocked by the angry mood of a mob of men and women who had gathered in Harrisonburg from miles around one morning to demand another vote. The war was now on, Fort Sumter marked the beginning, and Lincoln was demanding Virginia's quota of 75,000 volunteers to help "whip the seceding states back into the Union." Virginia was in no mood to take orders of that nature.

On the seventeenth of April, 1861, Virginia voted to secede, and immediately all men between the ages of 18 and 45 were called for military duty to help "whip" the North instead of the South. A fine would be imposed on anyone failing to report for training at the drilling stations.

Military training was nothing new to the Mennonite men in the valley community. Four times a year all able-bodied men were required to report for a period of training, but a muster fine of fifty to seventy-five cents excused those not wishing to take the training.

But now the situation was different. They were at war. Although they realized that the Mennonite Church had stood for the principles of peace and had taken no part in warfare for over 300 years, this was their first personal experience in applying the doctrine in time of war.

"What shall we do?" they asked, coming to Coffman for advice. Since the death of Bishop Martin Burkholder in December, 1860, members of the middle district congregations were looking more and more toward Samuel Coffman for leadership. His ordination as bishop was to take place within a few weeks.

Without hesitation Samuel replied to their question. "Do just like you done before. Pay your fines and stay home. We can have no part in war, especially this one with brother fightin' brother."

But the problem was not so easily settled. Officials soon found that too many men were paying fines instead of reporting for duty. And so a draft bill was passed by the Confederate government permitting no exemptions.

Ignoring the new order, the Mennonite men continued their usual routine, putting in crops and cultivating their farms until one day the blow fell. It was a Sunday John would never forget.

He had accompanied his parents to church that day. As a rule, children didn't go to church. But John was now twelve and both Father and Mother agreed that he was old enough now to get some benefit from the services.

Weavers Church was crowded that morning. Looking over the congregation John saw a few other boys, not much older than himself, sitting uncomfortably beside their fathers or big brothers. Everyone looked very grave and serious. Too bad they couldn't be happy on such a glorious June morning. The windows were open and John could hear the happy twittering of the birds in the grove beside the church. The soft spring breeze was tantalizing and made him long to be outside instead of sitting on a hard church bench. With a tremendous effort he tried to put his heart into the service and concentrate on the sermon as his father rose to address the congregation.

About halfway through the sermon he was suddenly distracted by the sound of hoofbeats slowing down and turning into the churchyard. The congregation stirred uneasily, and many heads turned as the door swung open and two uniformed men entered. One was an officer.

A gasp of fear swept over the crowd as he marched to the front of the room where he seated himself and listened to the remainder of the sermon. Although surprised, Samuel did not become flustered, but continued for a few more minutes on his theme. Then calling for a hymn he sat down.

Immediately the officer was on his feet. Turning to face the congregation he delivered his message, brief but emphatic. A draft bill had been passed, he reminded them, and it was not to be ignored. Every man between the ages of 18 and 45 was to report immediately for military training. That was the law, and the law would be strictly enforced. That was all. Without more ado he marched down the aisle and out the door to the accompaniment of stifled sobs. The hymn Samuel Coffman had called for never was sung. No one could sing now. Samuel rose again, pale and trembling, his voice choking as he faced the weeping congregation.

The time of conflict for his people had arrived, a conflict of spiritual forces, involving right and wrong, and calling for action. For each man of military age a choice would have to be made immediately. He prayed in his heart for grace and guidance, that each one might make the right choice. It was no time for a long discourse on the doctrine of peace and nonresistance. Most of his men understood that. All he could do now was to encourage them by reminding them that as children of God they were subject to a higher law than that of man, and that God would be with them to help them.

That evening and all next day many of the drafted men called at the Coffman home to say good-by. John watched them come and go and over and over again heard the pledge never to shoot or take any part in the destruction of human life.

John worked long hours that summer. Everybody did. But there was always Sunday to look forward to, and Sunday afternoon was usually a time to relax and visit. John's frequent guest was Peter Hartman, a boy several years older than himself. The two got together as often as possible either at John's home or Peter's.

"Did you see the comet the other evening?" Peter asked as they were walking home from Weavers Church one Sunday. It was a hot day in early July, and the boys made slow progress as they shuffled down the road trailing sticks in the dust and occasionally aiming a stone at some fence post.

"Sure I saw it. Wasn't it wonderful?"

"Pretty terrible, I thought," Peter said. "I was scared."

"Well, mebbe I was too, just a little," John confessed. "But Father said it was just something natural. But all those balls of fire shootin' off. I never saw the like."

"My pa said it means something," Peter offered, his voice sounding ominous, "and something not too good. He called it a sign. And did you see how funny the sky was all afternoon?"

"You mean part dark and part sunny and bright?"

Peter nodded. "That's what I mean. Did you see which was the dark part?"

"Well," John replied thoughtfully, "the south part, I reckon."

"Right over the Mason-Dixon line is where it divided, my pa said. And that's a sign too. It don't look good for the South. There's bad times ahead."

"And that was the very day they were supposed to be tryin' to see if they could find a way of settlin' things and stop the fightin', wasn't it?" John added.

Again Peter nodded wisely. "Pa knew it wouldn't work. The sky was a sign they had failed."

"I sure wish it'd be over soon," John said, "so the men could come home again. It just don't seem right without 'em at church. And everybody havin' to work so hard. Do you s'pose they really don't shoot?"

"We had a letter from cousin Simon," Peter replied, "and he said as how they tried to make 'em aim right and shoot, but some of 'em just shoot straight up or in some direction where they can't hit nobody. Nas Heatwole, he said, found he could take the balls out of the cartridges with his teeth and so he fires duds. They threaten to court-martial all of them, but they keep on just the same."

"I wonder if I could be that brave?" John pondered. "Could you?"

Peter shrugged. "I reckon we just don't know what we would do, if we had to. But I do know this—" Peter's voice grew very solemn. "I never, never could kill a man."

John shuddered. "Nor me. It's bad enough even to have to help when Father's stickin' a pig."

Early in the fall the Mennonite draftees came straggling home, to the delight of their surprised families. Since their questionable assistance could easily be spared at a time of relative inactivity, they had been granted leaves to visit their homes and help with fall planting.

Eager to hear a firsthand account of war experiences John and friend Peter cut across the fields one Sunday afternoon to visit the Heatwoles and hear what Manassas would have to say.

Bettie met them at the door. She always pretended to be frightened when she saw John, and quickly grabbed her apron strings.

"Don't worry," John assured her. "I don't have my knife with me today. Where's Nas?"

"Oh, he's out with Pap lookin' over the farm," she said, her eyes twinkling. "But he ate so much dinner I reckon he won't go far. Like as not you'll find him asleep by a straw stack."

All afternoon the boys listened spellbound to Manassas, as he described life in the army camp—the long marches—the places they saw—the skirmishes with the enemy as they moved north toward Washington—the evening sing-songs when the men from the valley got together—the ingenious methods they devised to keep from harming their fellow men, while giving strict obedience to their officers.

"At last they gave up," Manassas said, "and put most of us to work on the side lines, lookin' after the horses or the sick and wounded, or workin' in the kitchen."

"It must have been pretty hard lookin' after the wounded, specially after Bull Run," John suggested.

For a moment Nas didn't reply. His face suddenly turned gray as well as grave, as he finally made the solemn declaration, "If there is such a thing as hell on earth, that was it. I never seen nothin' like it, and I never hope to agin. Over 2,000 killed or wounded and that was only our side. The other had even more. It was—ghastly!"

"But you will see more of it, I reckon," said Peter.

"Mebbe—mebbe not," Manassas replied ambiguously.

"But—but your leave will soon be up," added John.

Manassas nodded. "I know."

"But—"

"There are ways," said Manassas.

And then one Sunday most of the drafted men were again absent from the Sunday service.

"Where were all the men today, Father?" John asked as they rode home from church. "Gone back to the army?"

"I don't rightly know, son; their leaves are up. Mebbe some of 'em went, but most of 'em, I reckon, ain't agoin' back."

"Then what are they goin' to do?"

"Hide. Or mebbe go north, some of 'em."

"But wouldn't it be easier just to go back?"

"Sure, a heap sight, I reckon," Samuel replied. "But I talked to a lot of 'em and they feel it's all so wrong that they can't even help on the side lines. They'd rather die, they say, than have the guilt of war on their souls."

That was the winter of the big hunt in the valley, with men and boys in the role of the hunted and armed scouts the hunters. From the first it was a fruitless task, but the scouts stuck doggedly to their job tracking down the deserters to try to return them to the army.

Occasionally John caught sight of Manassas Heatwole, and though he sometimes talked to him or to Bettie, he didn't know until after the war that he had a hiding place under the house. It was reached by means of a trap door in a small closet under the stairway. The closet was usually strewn with laundry so that the searching scouts never noticed the telltale cuts in the floor boards. A careful watch was kept and a signal given whenever anyone spied soldiers.

Peter Hartman had an exciting story to tell John one day, and he had something to show him, too—a big silk handkerchief that cousin Simon had given him. A soldier had dropped it when he was out at the Burkholder place looking for him.

"And he nearly got him this time," Peter said. "He shot at him."

"Whew!" said John. "Did he get hit?"

"No. Simon saw him in the nick of time and dropped just as the gun went off. He crawled on his hands and knees for a ways through a cornfield and then got up and run as fast as he could."

"I reckon an angel was guarding him," John said, "and Potter John too. Did you hear about him?"

"No," replied Peter. "What about him?"

"Why, they found out about his hide-out in the cave up the mountain."

"Oh!" gasped Peter. "They didn't get him, did they?"

"No, someone managed to warn him. But what do you think he did?"

"What?"

"Well, there was snow on the ground last week, you know, and he knew they could track him; so he simply walked backwards up the mountain. Likely he's in West Virginia somewhere now."

As the weeks went by, more and more of the men chose the risk of crossing the line into northern territory rather than continue to live like hunted animals, in danger both day and night. Singly and in groups many men of nonresistant faith, Mennonites, Dunkards, and Quakers, made their way across the Alleghenies into West Virginia or down the valley into Maryland and Pennsylvania. Here they were free, for they knew they could not be forced into either the Confederate or the Federal army.

John was out in the garden helping his father plant some early potatoes one March morning when suddenly they saw Bettie Heatwole come running across the field.

"Something wrong?" Samuel asked gently as she approached. They could see she had been crying.

"It—it's Nas," Bettie replied, breaking into fresh sobs. "He—he's been took—and Uncle Gabe, too."

"Why, I thought they was agoin' north with the big group the other night," said Samuel.

"They did go," sobbed Bettie, "but—but they got all of 'em."

"The whole seventy?"

Bettie nodded. "All but two."

"All but two!" exclaimed John. "And they came and told what happened?"

Again Bettie nodded. "They just come and told us this morning! They said they heard 'em say they'd bring 'em to the jail in Staunton."

"But how did they get 'em?" John asked. "A cavalry unit or something?"

"No, just five men," Bettie replied, dabbing furiously at her eyes with a corner of her apron. "They just ordered 'em to stop and hand over their arms, and that was all."

"But—but none of 'em had guns, did they?"

Bettie smiled through her tears. "No, but a lot of 'em did hand over something."

"What?" Samuel asked.

"Bibles. They said the soldiers were right smart surprised."

From Staunton the seventy were taken to Richmond, where they were kept in Libby prison while officials decided what to do with them.

Later that spring Samuel himself was forced to make a difficult decision. It was a drizzly morning. He was working with John, piling wood in the woodshed, when suddenly he said, "Sit down, lad. Let's rest a spell. I been wantin' a little talk with you."

John glanced uneasily at his father seated on a block of wood, mopping his forehead with a big red handkerchief. He had been unusually quiet and thoughtful that morning. In fact, he had seemed worried for several weeks.

"I—I don't rightly know how to say this," Samuel began. "But—well, could you and Jake get along alone on the farm for a spell?"

"Alone? Wh—why, Father, what's wrong? Are you sick?" John sounded alarmed.

"Oh, no, not sick. Only I fear it'd be better for me to go north too, for a little while anyways."

John gasped. "You go north? But why? You're a minister. The army can't take you."

"Yes, yes, I know, son. They can't take me, but I reckon they can make it purty warm for us all. There's been some nasty things said lately. They know I've been helpin' our men. I don't want to scare you, but you might as well know there was quite a crowd followin' me in town yesterday, yellin' about the Mennonite cowards and their coward preacher. One loud-mouthed officer boasted he'd get me and every Mennonite man in the valley into the army."

"But he couldn't really, could he?" exclaimed John.

"Of course not. But for the good of everybody I reckon it'd be good to go away."

"Was it last Sunday's sermon that did it?" John asked after a brief silence.

"Well, mebbe it had something to do with it," replied Samuel thoughtfully, "if they got wind of it."

"It was a good one, Father. I think I understand things better now."

"I'm glad if you do, John. I reckon mebbe it wasn't too wise to preach so straight agin' war just now. But I had to do it. It's all so wrong, and they been apressin' so hard for men lately. Our older men understand purty good, but it's the young men I'm thinkin' about. They'll like as not be called up soon, and I felt they had to get things straight."

For a few minutes both man and boy sat lost in thought. Samuel gazed fondly at his son, sitting there on the woodpile making little circles in the sawdust with the toe of his boot. He was tall for his age, but looked much too young and slight for the big job he was asking of him.

"Well, what do you say, boy?" he asked gently. "Can you look after the farm for me, you and Jake?"

"Why, yes, Father, I reckon we can," John replied, rising slowly to his feet and throwing his shoulders back. "I'm thirteen now, and Jake will soon be twelve. We can handle the horses, and have helped with nearly everything. Anyway we can try."

A few mornings later John and Jacob were awakened a little earlier than usual. Rubbing their eyes sleepily, they heard Mother say, "Come on, boys, get up. You all got work to do today. Father's gone. He left last night."

At breakfast that morning John sat in Father's chair. And when he read the chapter from the big family Bible, it seemed as if his voice took on a new manliness.

Soon after this came the alarming news of the approach of the northern army under General Banks. Meeting little resistance he came up the valley and made camp near Harrisonburg during the last week of March.

Having experienced some plundering from their own men, and hearing stories of ransacking in Winchester, everyone was surprised to find Banks' men well disciplined and courteous. Instead of looting, they paid for produce from the farms, and frequently lingered for a friendly chat. The singing of these valley folk fascinated them. Everywhere they went, it seemed they heard singing. One evening a singing was arranged for the benefit of a group of Banks' men. It was held at Peter Hartman's home.

John enjoyed the singing that evening. He observed the surprise and pleasure of the soldiers as they listened, or joined in the singing of a well-known hymn. But these men, he suddenly realized, were their enemies. These were the men that their government would have them kill. He shuddered at the thought of aiming a gun at any of them. And yet these same men would be firing on Virginians as soon as the opportunity arrived. War was so bewildering! How much better and easier it would be for folks simply to be friends! With a sudden flash of insight came the thought that that was the way it had to be for the Christian. Had not Christ said to His followers, "Love your enemies"? He could understand that now. And then he thought of the seventy in prison at Richmond. Was the southern army their enemy as well? Could he really love those five men who had taken them prisoner, or those responsible for keeping them in jail? He wished his father would be home so that he could talk to him about some of these things.

After about two weeks Banks suddenly withdrew from Harrisonburg, taking his men once more down the valley. But a short time later another contingent of bluecoats appeared. This time it was General Fremont with his 45,000 men sent to intercept General Jackson, who had caused Banks' retreat. These men proved to be quite different in temperament. They had come not only to fight but to replenish their dwindling supplies.

Coming up to the house for a drink one afternoon, John was surprised to see several soldiers lurking around the yard. His first impulse was to bolt back to the potato patch or rush to the house to call his mother. But that would be cowardly. He was the man of the place now. And so, even though his knees were trembling, he greeted the men politely.

"Is—is there something I can do for you, sir?" he asked the captain.

"Why, yes, son," replied the swaggering young officer with a smirk. "Ya might show us where yer smokehouse is."

"Why—er—it's right over there," stammered John, pointing hesitantly toward the small whitewashed building near the house.

"Got any hams or bacon?" asked the officer.

"Uh—m—mebbe a few," John replied slowly, "but I don't think there's any to sell. I'll run to the house and ask my mother."

"No, no, never mind. We won't bother her. We weren't aimin' on buyin' anyway," laughed the officer. "Let's go and take a look."

A few minutes later the group emerged from the building, each with a bacon skewered fast to a bayonet, or a ham tucked under an arm.

"And now for some nice fresh bread," said the officer, following a tantalizing scent which led him straight to the open kitchen door. In spite of Frances' protests the soldiers demanded that the entire batch of bread be handed over, along with a crock of homemade butter.

It was a subdued group that sat around the supper table that evening.

"It was a good thing you'd left that one loaf in the oven," said John, spreading the last crust for little Joe. "I reckon we should have a place where we could hide some things. Like as not there'll be plenty more times like this."

"I been thinkin' that too," Mother agreed thoughtfully as she slowly nibbled at a thin slice of bread spread sparingly with molasses. "Oh, if only I had a bit of salt fer in my bread. Everything tastes so flat these days."

"Someone said there's to be a load comin' into Harrisonburg one of these days," observed John. "We'll have to be there to get our share."

"A load of salt?" exclaimed Jake. "Why, where's it comin' from?"

"West Virginia," said John. "They're diggin' it out of a roadbed."

Mother looked horrified. "Not a roadbed, John, surely? How could they get salt out of a road?"

"Just because they put it there," he replied matter-of-factly. "It comes from a factory. The salt forms in the bottom of some big boilers and they use the stuff in building roads."

"B—but we ain't agoin' to use that dirty stuff," sputtered Frances.

"Sure we are," asserted John. "We need salt and we should be glad for it. You'll have to clean it and pound it fine. A nice job for the girls, I reckon."

When word reached the community that Jackson and his men were heading back, they knew there would be a clash with Fremont, perhaps right there on their own green fields and hills. Fremont was jubilant. "We've got Jackson in the jug now," he boasted. "All we need to do is put the stopper in."

It was a Saturday evening when the first battle took place. Although they had been listening all day for the sound, John felt suddenly ill when he heard that first shot. It was such a balmy June evening, now suddenly made hideous by the sound of gunfire. In the distant haze they could see puffs of smoke followed by the dull boom of cannon. In his mind John followed the shells to their human targets and sickened at the thought of the death and agony men were bringing



2

upon each other out there on the beautiful hillside. Why did it have to be? And the winning side, he suddenly realized, would be the side that could kill off the most men. Somehow, it didn't seem reasonable. But it was actually happening right there—almost in their own back yard. Would it never end?

It did end. In a brief half hour, which had seemed a day, the shooting ceased. Fremont's men yielded their hillside position in the preliminary skirmish to retreat to a new and better position for the main combat next morning. This took place at Cross Keys, about eight miles southeast of Harrisonburg.

John stayed at home with his mother all day that Sunday. It was an anxious day as they waited for some news of the battle. Toward evening neighbor Heatwole, Bettie's father, came riding up the lane. He had been to town and stopped by to see how his neighbors were faring.

Frances noticed how pale and tired he looked.

"Won't you set up and have a bite with us?" she offered. "Supper's just ready, and I reckon it's been a while since you et dinner."

"I'm much obliged," said Heatwole, "but I couldn't eat a thing right now."

"Why—you—you ain't ailin', are you?" asked Frances.

"Oh, no, I'm fine. It's jest the things I seen today. This war! I know now what Nas meant when he said it was hell on earth. It's true. I seen it with my very own eyes."

"Surely you wasn't out there where they're fightin'?" Frances said.

"No, I didn't have to go that fur. I seen enough right there on the streets of Harrisonburg. They been bringin' 'em in this afternoon, cartload after cartload—some dead—some dyin'—some shot half to pieces—hundreds and hundreds of 'em. It was enough to turn anybody's stomach."

"But what are they doin' with all of 'em?" Frances asked.

"I helped lay some of the poor fellows on straw in the schoolhouse. They're usin' schools, churches, any buildings they kin get a hold of. A lot of the town women were out with hot soup and bandages doin' all they could. But by tomorrow there'll be hundreds more and they won't have half enough stuff. We'll all have to pitch in and help."

"I reckon we can all spare some food and bedding," Frances said. "If only Sam was home."

"Well, we'll just have to do without him," Heatwole said. "I'll stop at some more of the neighbors on my way home and see what they kin do."

Next morning a number of Mennonite farmers collected supplies and hauled them to town, where every public building had been turned into an emergency hospital.

All summer the war dragged on with terrible losses reported

on both sides, but never a decisive victory. But for one whole month that fall Virginia had a rest. Peace reigned in the valley while they harvested a bountiful crop and prepared for winter.

Then one day in October, 1862, came a joyful announcement. The Confederate Congress had passed a new bill granting freedom from military service to Mennonites, Quakers, and Dunkards upon payment of a tax of $500, or hiring a substitute. Faced with the problem of what to do with the seventy objectors lodged in Libby prison, they made a careful study of their case, examining the Mennonite Confession of Faith carried by some of the men. Sydney Baxter of the War Department interviewed each of the prisoners, and finding them sincere in their belief he recommended their release upon payment of the required fine.

Although the news brought joy to the valley community, there was also sorrow in many homes. Five hundred dollars seemed an impossible sum to many, especially when there were two or more men in the family to release. But a subscription was started immediately to help those who couldn't pay. It seemed as if everybody was happy to contribute to this cause, for in a short time enough money was raised to bring home the imprisoned men and also to pay the fee for those who had been in hiding.

In the Coffman home there was another reason for rejoicing. Father came home, arriving as unobtrusively as he had left. He was in time to help raise the enormous sum to be paid into the Confederate treasury in return for the freedom of the men in his district. But there were some families who also needed consolation, among them neighbor Heatwoles. While Uncle Gabe was permitted to return home, Manassas had been forced back into army life. He had not been a member of the church at the beginning of the war and therefore did not qualify for exemption.

*Just thirty years ago this Fourth of July I was baptized in Muddy Creek at Jacob Heatwole's ford, east of the Bank Church. What years have these been, not all spent holy before God. But God be praised for the grace that saves. Those baptized at the same time were Peter Hartman, Abram Weaver, John Bell, and others. How quickly these years have passed. I may sleep long ere another thirty years pass by.*—Diary.

# 4

"Well, how do I look? Is my tie straight?" John turned from the little mirror on the kitchen wall above the washstand. He had spent an unusually long time smoothing his hair and adjusting his tie.

"You look right nice," Mother said, smiling fondly at her tall son as she tugged at the ends of the long, string tie. "Now be good tonight. Remember you're a young man now."

"You better wear a warm cap," Jake snickered. "With all that water plastered on your hair you'll like as not catch cold."

John scowled at Jake and turned to give one more pat to his hair before donning his coat and hat.

"O—oh, won't you have a good time!" said Lizzie. "Wish I was old enough to go to an apple schnitzing. Why can't we have one here just for the young people?"

"We will sometime," Mother said, "now that John's old enough to go."

"I'm nearly old enough, too," said Jake, drawing himself to his full height.

"Yes, next year it'll be your turn," Mother agreed, going to the table drawer for a knife. "Here's a knife for you, John. Now don't lose it. And you'd better hurry. You don't want to be late for your first schnitzing."

The apple schnitzing that night was at Peter Hartman's home. It was the first of a series of parties designed to turn work into fun as bushels of apples were peeled, cored, and prepared for drying. Bees of this nature, combining work with pleasure, were an important part of the social life of the Mennonite community.

John felt a bit shy at this introduction into the young people's group. But the worst was to come, he realized, as he surveyed the roomful of young women. They would soon be drawing partners and he would be stuck with one of them for the rest of the evening.

With great relief he saw he had drawn the name of his neighbor, Bettie Heatwole. And if Bettie felt any disappointment in discovering that her partner was a mere fifteen-year-old boy, she didn't show it.

"So it's you," she teased, as they seated themselves with a big pan of apples balanced between them on their knees. "Reckon I'd better tuck in my apron strings."

"Oh, I wouldn't bother trimming off the skimpy bows you're wearing now," laughed John. "The war's made a big change in apron styles around here. How'd it be if I'd core and you peel?"

"Good," said Bettie. "I'd much rather peel. My, I'm glad I got you," she confided, lowering her voice to a whisper. "I was afeared it'd be Abe again. I—I just can't talk when I'm with him. He makes me feel so dumb."

But she could talk to John, she found, and the evening passed swiftly and gaily. John was surprised to find her so witty, and he was also surprised to find himself drawn into discussions of a more serious nature. Yes, the evening had been enjoyable, he decided as he rode slowly homeward. It was an evening to be remembered for a long, long time.

"Did you have fun last night?" Lizzie asked next morning.

"Best time I ever had," he replied quickly.

"Who was your partner?"

"Why, Bettie Heatwole," John replied with a dreamy look in his eyes. "You know, Lizzie, she's nice. I never knew she could be so lively. And she's got such bright eyes. They're so—so twinkly when she laughs."

Somehow John managed to contrive that the lively woman with the bright eyes was his partner at another schnitzing or two that winter. She was different from other girls. He enjoyed being with her so much that he began inventing excuses for going to the Heatwole farm. There was always a chance that he might catch a glimpse of her.

Sometimes on a Sunday afternoon he and Peter would walk over to Heatwole's to talk to Manassas, who was once more in hiding at home. They never tired of hearing his army experiences or of the terrible months in Libby prison. He enjoyed watching Bettie's face while Nas talked. How her eyes twinkled when something amused her, and how quickly her expression changed when her sympathies were aroused!

"I never in all my life was so hungry as I was in that jail," Nas said. "I didn't know a body could be so hungry and still live."

"Why? Didn't they give you three meals a day?" John asked.

"They mighta fed us three times, but they weren't no meals," Nas said. "Nothin' but a few slices of moldly bread and thin, tasteless soup that smelled even worse than your pap's swill barrel. I tell you, I'd gave anything for a good drink out o' one of them there barrels. It'd tasted jest as good and been a heap more nourishin', I reckon."

Bettie shuddered, and John shuddered with her.

Swinging the ax at the woodpile one day John was startled when he suddenly realized that he had been thinking about Bettie practically all morning. In fact, she had been on his mind most of the time for several days and he had held many imaginary conversations with her. If only he could really talk to her! But that was impossible. His youth was against him. Fifteen-year-olds did not go calling on young ladies, and so all conversation with her would have to be limited to a few casual words whenever they happened to meet.

And then came the inspiration. The idea popped into his head so suddenly that he almost dropped the ax. There was a way of conversing with absent friends. For years he had been writing occasional little notes to friend Peter. Why not put his silent discourses with Bettie on paper and send them to her? His heart pounded at the thought. Why shouldn't he write and tell her some of the things he thought about? And then maybe—just maybe—she might write a note to him. For the rest of the day his mind was busy planning the letter he would write and dreaming of the note he might possibly receive in return.

That night he began his letter, but not until the entire family had gone to bed. Mother tried to send him upstairs when she went to bed, but he begged to be allowed to study a little longer. Finally, when the house was quiet, he stealthily produced his paper, pen, and ink and set to work. He had to write fast, for there wasn't much left of the candle. He lighted an extra fat lamp to throw a little more light on his paper, for this was one occasion when his writing had to be his very best.

The words came fast after he got started. He couldn't, of course, tell her how much he thought of her. That wouldn't do for the first time. He just wanted to tell her some of the interesting things he had thought of lately—just wanted to talk to her, and have her talk to him.

It took several evenings to finish the letter, and then came the question of how to deliver it. Since he couldn't risk being seen slipping a note to the young lady, he decided to take friend Peter into his confidence and entrust him with the precious missive. Peter was trustworthy, and Peter had a good head on him. The very next Sunday he contrived a means of quietly slipping her first billet-doux into the hands of a surprised Bettie.

Although she was thrilled and delighted to be the recipient of a letter, Bettie also was worried. Did this mean that the lad had taken a special liking to her? He was so young, much younger than herself. Should she encourage him in any way? He was a fine boy, an exceptional one, and she admired him a great deal. But would it be proper for her to answer that wonderful little letter? Well, maybe once wouldn't hurt. It would be interesting to get at least one more letter from him, and yes, she had to admit it, she did like him! She had often thought about him since that first apple schnitzing.

But for Bettie, letter writing was more than a task. It was an ordeal. Like John, she could write only after the rest of the family had gone to bed. Unlike John, she was a very poor writer. Her schooling amounted to only a few short terms at Fairview. Reading was fairly easy, but spelling so difficult.

"Oh, but he'll think I'm dumb," she moaned to herself, "and he writes so—o beautifully!"

Another difficulty was finding suitable paper to write on. With all the available paper in the community carried off by the Confederates to make shells and gun wads, writing paper had become exceedingly scarce and practically unobtainable in local stores. But Bettie managed to find one sheet, slightly soiled, which she hid away until she was ready to use it.

Seated at the kitchen table late one evening, Bettie carefully ruled off the unlined paper, then thoughtfully toyed with the feather of the old quill pen before finally dipping in the ink to commence her tedious task.

> April 10th—
>
> Dear friend. I now take my pen in hand to drop yo a few lines that I am well at present and hope yo are enjoying the same blesing. Dear friend, the times are hard indeed, as yo say, but I hope that they won't stay hard all the time. I have enjoyed myself wright well so far. I was very much pleased with your singing the other night. I thought they sung wright well. I hope they can all stay together. I wish they Yankys would come and stay, and chase the rebbles off so that we wouldn't see them any more. I want yo to let nobody see this scribbly wrighting for I had a very bad chance to wright. The old folks was in my way all the time I could'nt wright half, and I had just half paper to wright on. I reckon yo think this is poor paper, and I think so myself. The rows are so grum and cripply. I had to rule it myself. Oh the paper is scairce in the confederacy, and so cracky. I believe this is all for this time and not much at that. I must come to aclose for the time is ageting short.
>
> Now I will commence again. Please let nobody see this but that person that helped yo get your letter to me, P. S. H. I was agoing to give this to yo one time, but I had no chance.
>
> I will give my love and best respect to yo all. To J. S. C.
>
> from E. J. H.

John rejoiced when he received the missive delivered to him by his trusted agent. Eagerly he read it and read it again, looking for some word or phrase showing that she might care. Did she mean that last sentence, "I will give yo my love and best respect," or was it merely a formal way of ending a letter? Anyway, she thought enough of him to write, and as he saw the "grum and cripply" lines and the sometimes almost illegible writing, he realized what a tremendous effort the letter had cost Bettie. Carefully he hid it away with his greatest treasures. He knew now what she did think of him. He had established communication and he was content. He would write many more letters in the future, he decided, if she would continue to accept them. But he would not press her for answers.

That spring an event of much greater import and consequence came into the life of John S. Coffman. Perhaps it began at the Good Friday service when he heard once more the moving story of the crucifixion and felt again the burning tears well up within him. Being a young man now, he fought hard to keep back the tears, blinking and turning to look out the window in a desperate effort to turn his thoughts to something else. But this time there was a compelling force behind the voice from the pulpit which gave him no choice but to listen. And this time he understood as never before why it was necessary for Christ to die. "The Son of God came into the world for one purpose only," Samuel Coffman explained, "and that was to die for sin—your sin, my sin." He seemed to be looking straight at John as he said this, and the words burned deep into his consciousness.

For the first time his beloved story took on a personal significance for John. "He died for my sin—my sin!" Over and over the phrase kept running through his mind. But what was his sin? Did he have any particularly great sin that needed to be forgiven?

And so began a long struggle in the heart of the lad whom the Lord was calling to a special service. Like many other young people of Christian parentage, John's problem was not one of knowledge. He knew a great deal about the Bible. He loved the stories about Jesus and believed in Him as the Son of God. But sin was the stumbling block—to see himself as a sinner and to acknowledge his guilt before God.

Day after day he found himself thinking about that Good Friday sermon. At night, as he lay in bed, staring into the darkness, a great uneasiness came over him. He tried hard to forget the matter, telling himself severely that religion was only for grownups, that he would have plenty of time when he was older to think about such things. But still the serious thoughts persisted, and the harder he tried to ignore them, the more they seemed to press upon him.

Although he was shy about mentioning his struggle to anyone, John realized that help could be found in the Word of God and eagerly searched for the light. It was with a start one day that he came across the verse in Romans, "For all have sinned, and come short of the glory of God." There was his answer; "All have sinned." Evidently then he, John Coffman, had sinned and before God he was guilty and needed forgiveness.

But a new problem now troubled his mind. Did that mean that in God's sight sin was sin, regardless of how great or small it might be? Did God not recognize degrees of sin? And what was sin—merely the breaking of the Ten Commandments? As far as he knew, he kept the commandments. At least he tried hard.

Questioning his father on this matter, John received the help he needed.

"It's right there in the Bible, plain as can be," Samuel pointed out. " 'The wages of sin is death.' Does it say a big sin? No, it don't matter if it's big or little; any sin has to be paid for—with death. But the bill's been paid, you know. Christ did the dying. And before God we're free *if* we believe and accept these facts."

"B—but sin, Father, what is it? Just breaking the commandments?" John asked.

"No," Samuel replied thoughtfully, "I'd say it's anything that displeases God—anything agin' His will. Just thinkin' something wrong is sin, same as doin' it. Or not doin' something we know we should. That's the only rule we can go by."

John now had a great deal to think about. He had sinned, he had to admit it. Therefore he was under guilt, and therefore he was lost! The thought came as a shock, and he was frightened. But he was not yet ready to do anything about it. In his mind salvation was somehow connected with baptism and joining the church. A fifteen-year-old boy couldn't very well ask for baptism, he decided. It simply wasn't done.

But the crisis came at last. It was a balmy spring evening. John was restless and decided to take a walk. With soldiers once more overrunning the countryside, he couldn't go far from home. And so, grabbing his hat, he slipped quietly out the back door and started on a walk around the farm.

Once away from the chatter of the children, he found his thoughts slipping again into the old groove, but he checked himself quickly. No, he couldn't permit himself to be miserable, not tonight. It was such a glorious evening, an evening to be happy. If only Bettie could be with him so that they could enjoy together the beauty of the sunset, the bright green of the rustling leaves, the soft cooing of the doves, and the happy trills of the cardinals. How good God was to make everything so beautiful, and yet how terribly man was spoiling it!

Why did there have to be such things as wars, he wondered, his thoughts again becoming serious. He knew the answer. It was sin. Sin alone had changed a beautiful world into a chaos of destruction.

It was man taking things into his own hands, contrary to the will of God. It was hatred filling hearts where there should be only love. But what about himself? Was he any better in God's sight than the men carrying out this work of destruction all over the country? Sin was sin, he suddenly remembered, and he was equally as guilty as they. "The wages of sin is death." He could hear the words ringing in his ears. Like a crushing weight the enormity of his sin seemed suddenly to overwhelm him, forcing him to his knees, crying to God for mercy.

There under the trees in the old apple orchard, with no thought now for the beauties of nature—no thought for anything but his own sin—John Coffman poured out his soul in an agony of grief and shame. For a long time he remained on his knees, confessing his sin and humbly seeking forgiveness.

Gradually a feeling of peace stole into his heart as he realized the significance of the words he had read and thought about so frequently; "If we confess our sins, he is faithful and just to forgive us our sins." He had confessed and now he knew he was forgiven.

"Thank you, Lord, for dying for me," he breathed. "And thank you, Father, for forgiving my sins," he added as a sense of his new relationship with the divine Being now dawned upon him. He was forgiven! Truly now he had been born again and was a son of the heavenly Father.

Rising to his feet, John breathed deeply the fragrant air. It was as if he were looking on an entirely different world. "Ah, now I know what it means to be born again," he thought, strolling once more through the orchard. How good it was to be alive! How wonderful to be relieved of that terrible weight—to be free! I must tell the folks right away, he thought, walking a little faster as he neared the house.

John told friend Peter of his sacred experience the next Sunday afternoon as the two were rambling through the wood lot at Peter's home. Peter was greatly surprised at the confession, and then it was John's turn to be surprised. Peter, too, had found his Saviour under similar circumstances out under the stars one night.

"Are you going to be baptized?" asked Peter, seating himself on a stump to think the matter over.

"Yes, I reckon I am," John replied resolutely. "But that's one thing that's been bothering me. Folks hardly ever get baptized in our church before they're married. But the Bible says we should, and—well, I reckon I want to do what's right."

"Me, too," said Peter. "But did you—eh—ever think mebbe of joinin' some other church?" Peter spoke slowly, looking at his friend.

John blushed. "We—ell, I can't say I've thought much about it. I like our church, and I know my father and mother would feel bad if I left."

"Have you ever gone to any other?"

Again John blushed. "Not very often, I reckon."

"Then how do you know you like ours best?" persisted Peter. "Now take me—I've been around, and I'm thinkin' some of mebbe joinin' the Presbyterians or the Methodists. They're good churches, and do a lot more for their young folks than the Mennonites. Nobody should join a church just because his father did."

"Of course not," John agreed. "But it's something that takes a lot of thinkin'."

"That's what I mean," answered Peter. "We should look around—go to other churches and find out about 'em before we decide which one to join. Why don't we go to the Methodist meetin' tonight? They're havin' a candlelight service. Then mebbe next week we can go to the Presbyterian if your father'll let you."

"There's the Dunkards, too," said John. "I've been there sometimes with Father."

"Yes, and they're pretty good," said the experienced Peter, "but the trouble is they make so much of baptism."

For a few weeks the boys made a real effort to learn what they could about the teachings and practices of other denominations. It was the doctrine of nonresistance, however, that finally won them over and held them to the faith of their fathers. It was going a bit too far, they decided, when they heard other ministers pray from the pulpit for the destruction of the enemy. It didn't seem quite in accord with Christ's command to love your enemy.

On the Fourth of July, 1864, John S. Coffman was baptized and became an active member of the Mennonite Church. Since the class chose to be baptized in a stream, the ceremony was scheduled for Monday afternoon, at Jacob Heatwole's ford in Muddy Creek, near the Bank Church. Even though the day was hot and the country again infested with soldiers, quite a number gathered on the river bank for the solemn occasion.

John's mother sat with bowed head during most of the service. To her this hour was most sacred. It was the beginning of the fulfillment of her vision. Her eldest son, her John, had found Christ, and was dedicating himself to His service. Silently she prayed that he might be a faithful servant, and that God might accomplish His purposes in his life.

Samuel shared this feeling. As he questioned the candidates, his heart was stirred when he came to his son, and listened to his reply. There was no doubting the intense earnestness and dedicated purpose of the lad. It was expressed both in the clear strong voice, and in the gleam of the serious gray eyes which seemed to have caught a vision of the future.

For John, this was the most important day in his life. Although he did not understand fully the significance of the rite of baptism, nor realize the extent of service which would be demanded in his promise of faithfulness, yet he did feel that a new life was beginning for him. He realized he was following a new and great Master. A thrill went through his being as, kneeling in the shallow stream with the rest of the candidates, he felt water being poured on his head and heard the benediction being pronounced upon him by his father. He had been obedient to God and was now a member of His big family, the church. "God bless you, my son," Samuel whispered as he received him with a kiss into the brotherhood.

* * *

"Oh, soldiers, Mother, look! A whole lot of 'em comin' up the lane!" shrieked Molly, rushing into the house. It was a hot summer morning. The twins were playing in the yard with David, Daniel, and one-year-old baby Sarah. The big girls were helping Mother in the kitchen while John and Jacob were with Samuel in the hayfield.

"It's all right," soothed Frances, hurrying outside to gather up her baby. "They ain't agoin' to hurt you; so don't be afraid."

"Will they take away all our bread and our meat again?" grumbled Joe.

"I can't say. But you all stay right here in the shade and be quiet. I'll go see what they want."

Frances trembled as she noted the grim expression of the officer and listened to the curt command to ransack the house. While he stood guard at the doorway, the men entered, spreading through the entire house from cellar to attic.

"Just what are you all alookin' for?" asked Frances, addressing the captain as she sank into the small rocking chair by the kitchen window.

"Anything, Ma'am, anything we can find," came the reply.

"But—but why can't you ask for what you want and let me get it?" she spluttered. Out of the corner of her eye she caught a glimpse of wild confusion in the living room, and listened with a sinking heart to the thumps, thuds, and hurried footsteps overhead.

"Orders, Ma'am," snapped the captain and relapsed into silence.

The next few minutes seemed like hours to Frances. She sat rocking her baby, and seeing in her mind's eye the havoc being created in her orderly rooms. Through the living room door she now caught sight of a small cloud of feathers floating from the bedroom. Oh, no! Surely they couldn't be ripping open the pillows or the feather ticks! But they could. And they did.

Soon the men started to reappear to report their booty to the captain.

"Find anything?" he asked as the first two men appeared.

"Not much. A little silver and a few pieces of clothing."

Frances' agitation increased as more men reported and the list grew. There wasn't much in the line of clothing that could be of use to the Federals, but there was some precious bed linen and a few good blankets. It was the kitchen and cellar, however, that again suffered most. Helplessly she watched her breadbox being emptied, pies, butter, eggs, and potatoes carried up from the cellar, and the smokehouse looted once more by the ruthless brigade. Listening to their footsteps as they set off down the lane, Frances was about to give way to tears when suddenly she heard a rifle shot, followed by a scream from the back yard. Terrified, she rushed to the door.

"Mother, Mother," shrieked Molly, "they shot our cluck hen."

With a sigh of relief Frances looked toward the spot where little Joe was already hovering over the feathered body of the ill-fated red hen. Lizzie and Anna were trying to round up her frightened chicks.

"Is she dead, Joe, or just hurt?" asked Mother, still dazed from the shock, and gratefully thanking God that her little brood was safe in spite of the afternoon's havoc.

"I—I reckon she's dead," choked Joe. "She don't move none."

Molly was crying. "What'll the peepies do without a mamma?"

"Don't cry; we'll take care of 'em," Frances replied, gently stroking the little head. "We'll put 'em in a box and take 'em in the house tonight. Joe, you run to the barn and see if you can find something that will do for a pen for a while."

For weeks, Hunter's raid held top rank as conversational material, especially among the outraged housewives of the valley. Very few homes, it seemed, escaped the havoc. Disgruntled by minor defeats at the hands of the Confederates, and the constant annoyance of bushwhackers, Hunter apparently ordered the nuisance raids as a form of retaliation. Sometimes he even ordered a burning to revenge some personal slight or stubborn resistance.

This was the spring of 1864, a crucial period in the course of the war. Although the Confederate cause looked more and more hopeless, especially in the West and in the South, the valley forces still showed plenty of spirit and remained a constant thorn in the flesh to the Federals.

In order to continue their resistance, however, reinforcements as well as provisions were urgently needed. And so once again the valley communities and farms were combed by Confederate scouts in a final desperate attempt to build up strength. Ignoring the substitute exemption law and certificates proving payment of commutation fees, some officials took into custody a number of the Mennonite young men, forcing them into the army.

In September the need for men was so acute that the Confederate Congress voted to abolish the law which had provided exemption for the conscientious objectors. At this time they called up all men between the ages of 17 and 60. The news was received with consternation in the valley community. It meant hiding again for most of the men, or a long, dreary trek over mountain trails into safe territory.

With a shock John S. Coffman realized one day that within a few months he would be sixteen. Being tall for his age he might well be taken for seventeen and might have a hard time convincing scouts that he was not old enough for service. Was it time he, too, should start looking for a good hide-out?

Discussing the matter with Peter Hartman one day, John discovered that Peter had been a draft dodger ever since the new law had come into effect. In November he would be eighteen. But Peter wasn't as tall as John, and looked even younger. The situation was dangerous, they realized, and it was most essential they should start planning immediately. Since the idea of hiding was repulsive to both of them, escape into Federal territory seemed to be the best plan.

For some reason the thought of leaving home troubled John. He should have been excited, like Peter, who eagerly looked forward to a new adventure, seeing new country, meeting new people. But he wasn't. Trying to analyze his feeling, John discovered that it wasn't simply the thought of leaving his father and mother that worried him. There was also Bettie. True, he didn't see her very often, but what if he should come back after a year or more and find her engaged, or maybe even married? With the war still raging they might not be able to write very often, and she might forget a mere boy like himself. The very thought frightened him. No, he couldn't leave Bettie, at least not without some kind of understanding between them.

Before starting a letter to Bettie one evening, John picked up her last note and reread it eagerly, feeling again the glow of pleasure he had experienced when he first read it. Of course it was no literary masterpiece, but his heart leaped at the message conveyed by the simple words and phrases:

> Yo think yo haint welcome, but yo are quite welcome, my dear John. . . . I received your kind letter and was glad to hear from yo. I was glad that yo wrote without telling me to wright. I love to hear from yo. It does me a great deal of good. I would like to wright iff I could as well as yo can. It would be no hard matter to wright then if I had the paper plenty. I enjoyed myself wright well last Sunday. I think yo are as friendly and as good a company as ever I was with. But that haint very often. . . . I will try and do a little better this time for this is my last paper and my pen is agiving out too. I think there is no paper to get nor anything else. I was sorter bashful when I wrote the other time, and this wrighting is very bad. I am almost ashamed to send it. Meby yo can make out what it is. Still try and try again. I must come to aclose with this and commence something better. "The rose is red—the vilet blue—shuger is sweet—and so are you—and sweeter too." Wishing yo all the good I posably can, I will give yo all my love and best respect.

No, there was no mistaking the fact that she did care for him, and that his letters and little attentions were welcome. But more of an assurance of fidelity to himself would be necessary before he could leave with an easy mind. The candle burned low before he finished his letter that night. It was a long letter in which he poured out his heart as he had never done before. Impatiently he awaited the reply. It was a letter which thrilled and satisfied him completely.

> Dear friend, I once more take my pen in hand to informe yo that I am well at this present time and hope yo are enjoying the same blessing. I received your kind letter and was glad to heare from yo againe. I cant see well to write. I was at the wake last night and did not sleep a drop. Dearest friend, yo dont imagine how much pleasure it affordes me to heare from yo. Still I did not think yo loved me so much, but I dout not in my hearte but what yo do love me as well as I love yo. Do not think I am agoing to forsake yo, for I am not. I reckon yo thought I wasn't agoing to wright any more, but the paper is most to scarse with me to write. Still I got som againe that does first trate. The paper does better than the wrighting. I recking I have to go to school after while to write well, and must not talk so much and lurn.
>
> Do not think I care not for yo because I don't wright very often. I write as often as I can and have the chance. I have such bad chance to write. Now I will commence something good. I love yo with all my heart and still more, for I think yo are so lovely and so good company. Do not think that I care not for yo for I think of yo every day and still more. Yo said I cant well think of yo more than yo think of me. I reckon we think alike. Yo said yo are so bashful. Just so am I iff I haint with cusent M. H. Then we can help ourselves when we are together. Then we can have all the fun. Dear friend, I must bring my letter to aclose for this time by wishing yo the grace of God. Many are lovely, but yo excell all. I give my love and best respect. To J. S. C. from E. J. H.

With this important matter settled, John felt much easier in his mind. He could leave now, suddenly, if need be, and have no worry about the bright-eyed Bettie. She had confessed her love for him and promised that she would not forsake him. He was content.

In August the report reached the community that Grant, the great northern general, had consolidated the forces of the Upper Potomac, putting General Sheridan in charge. Sheridan! How would he treat them, they wondered? Would he be like Banks or like Hunter?

Within a few weeks Sheridan made his way in triumph up the valley. It was early one Sunday morning in September when he reached the town of Harrisonburg. There was no service that day.

Folks waited trembling at home wondering what the new order would bring.

They had not long to wait. Camp was quickly set up and all public buildings and churches taken over by the army. Before the day was over, hundreds of blue-coated soldiers had spread out over the countryside, bent on carrying out destructive orders far beyond the fears of the most pessimistic.

The Coffmans were all at home that day. Samuel and Frances were sitting on the porch steps watching the little ones play on the lawn while the older boys played catch with their homemade yarn ball. John was stretched out under a shade tree with a book. Suddenly Samuel noticed a company of soldiers riding swiftly down the road. Both he and Frances shivered as they saw a detachment turning in the lane.

"Better take the children to the house," Samuel said, turning quickly to Frances. "I'll see what they want this time." John and Jacob walked slowly to the gate with their father, while the rest disappeared quickly inside.

Without pausing to speak, the soldiers made straight for the barn and the pasture field. Soon shots began to ring out from every direction. A pig in the barnyard was the first victim. And then another and another dropped dead in their tracks. Next it was a young heifer in a field that the horrified spectators saw topple over. John's knees suddenly felt weak. Seeing him turn pale, Samuel tried to send him to the house.

"No, I'm all right," John protested. "But can't you do something? Can' you make 'em stop? Look, they're even shootin' the sheep and there's some goin' to the chicken yard. At least go and talk to 'em!"

"No use," sighed Samuel. "I reckon they know what they're doin' even if we don't. We can just pray that they'll show a little mercy."

"But we won't have nothin' left," wailed Jacob.

"No, I'm afeared we won't," said Samuel quietly. "See, here come a couple of 'em with Prince and Judy, our best team. At least they didn't shoot 'em."

"And here comes another with Nell, our rider," groaned John. "They can't take her. They just can't!"

Samuel hailed the men as they passed with the horses. "Good day, sir," he called. And the men stopped. "You've got a fine team there."

"Yes, sir," replied the young lieutenant, stroking Judy's neck. "They look mighty fine. Been well cared for."

"Just see that they still are," said Samuel. "Mind tellin' us what this's all about?" Samuel's lip trembled, and there was such a huge lump in John's throat that he thought he would choke.

"Orders, sir, that's all we know," replied the lieutenant, not unkindly. "Can't leave anything that might be useful to the enemy."

"Or anything that might feed innocent women and children?" Samuel asked tartly.

Without replying, the lieutenant mounted his horse and set off down the lane leading Judy. A second soldier followed, riding Nell and leading Prince.

Then from the field came a small herd of the best cattle. Taking their cue from their father, the boys stood in stony silence watching the strange parade of cattle, sheep, and a few pigs being driven down the lane by the soldiers.

It seemed like hours, but in less than an hour the first onslaught was over. As soon as the last soldier had galloped down the lane, Samuel and his sons made a melancholy tour of the premises, taking stock of the remains.

In the fields and stable lay dead cattle, although a few milch cows had mercifully been left. "Thank God for that," breathed Samuel. Also surviving were a few scrawny sheep and pigs, while in the chicken yard and orchards several hens straggled from hiding places.

"Likely ran out of ammunition," suggested Jacob, bitterly, noticing the dead birds scattered all around.

Almost every day that week the men returned, raiding house as well as barn and carrying off wagonloads of wheat and oats from the granaries and hay from the well-filled mows.

"Oh, well," Samuel observed philosophically, "we won't be aneedin' it all anyway, with all our stock gone."

After one of these raids a family conference was held. Samuel had heard in town that Sheridan was offering transportation north for anyone desiring to leave the ravished state. While creating a famine in the valley, he was at the same time mercifully and hopefully offering a means of existence to the suffering people.

The question of whether Frances and the children should go with the refugees to Pennsylvania was soon settled. If Samuel felt it his duty to stay, it was hers to stay with him. They would manage somehow to find food for the children. "God will take care of us," Frances asserted.

"But what about you, John?" Samuel asked. "You have been thinkin' of the north. Don't you think this'd be a good chance for you?"

"Yes, I reckon it is," John replied. "I've been thinkin' about it quite a while. Maybe the Confederates won't be back, but I have a feelin' they will, and if they do, they'll grab every man they can find. I reckon I'd better go while I can."

"And what about Peter Hartman? Has he made his plans?" Samuel asked.

“Likely he'll go if I do. We've been talkin' about it all summer. And there's cousin Chris Brunk and three or four others that'll want to go.”

“Well, mebbe we'd better ride over to Hartman's first thing in the morning if we can borrow a horse somewhere. Sheridan wants all those who want to go to report in a few days; so we better get our plans made. We'll miss you, son, but it's best you should go.”

*The occasional World's Peace Congresses in recent years, where representatives of all the civilized nations are pleading for the beating of "swords into plowshares," for the settling of all disputes between nations by arbitration for the reign of universal peace, are but an enlarging of the cloud of witnesses which has been hanging as a "man's hand" in the religious sky for centuries. May it soon break upon the nations with a deluge of love.*—Elkhart Institute Address.

# 5

John's heart thumped as he stood waiting in an anteroom at Sheridan's headquarters. Along with Peter Hartman, Chris Brunk, and three other Mennonite boys, he had come into town that Sunday afternoon ready for the journey north next morning. They were immediately taken into custody by the Federals and were quite surprised to learn that they would have to appear before the general himself.

"Who've you got there?" snapped Sheridan, when they were finally ushered into his office. His fierce, almost savage expression as he surveyed the group nearly paralyzed them with fear.

"Some men who've come into the line to go north, sir," replied the guard.

With great relief the boys saw the grim expression relax, while the shadow of a smile crossed his lips.

"Sit down, lads, and tell me who you are," he ordered.

While the questioning was in progress, another guard appeared with two more men. Again the savage look and the harsh question, as the general's piercing eyes took in the new arrivals.

"Two men taken back in the woods bushwhacking our soldiers," was the reply this time.

"Take them down and show no mercy," growled the general.

After finishing his examination and filling in passes, Sheridan turned to the boys and said gruffly but kindly, "If any of you can find horses that we've taken from your folks, you have my permission to get them and take them north with you."

"I know where there are two of ours," exclaimed Peter quickly.

"Fine," said the general. "You may take one, but you'll have to come back and get a pass for your horse too."

Several of the boys found horses, but John's search was fruitless.

Wrapped in a blanket and lying under a wagon for shelter, John experienced his first pangs of homesickness that night.

Peter lay beside him. For a long time they talked, trying to keep up their courage, but the unyielding ground didn't feel much like a bed, and both turned and tossed uncomfortably.

"If only that soldier in the wagon would stop groaning and go to sleep," suggested Peter. "Do you s'pose he's hurt bad?"

"I don't know," replied John, "but I saw a doctor looking at him while you were out home getting a saddle. He sounds bad. But maybe we'll soon get used to it."

"I certainly hope so," yawned Peter.

For a few moments the lads were quiet and Peter began to think that John had dropped off when suddenly he heard a whisper, "Peter, you still awake?"

"I reckon so," grunted Peter, tiredly. "Whatcha want?"

"Do you think they'll do any—any worse things than they've already done around here?"

"Hard to say," yawned Peter. "They couldn't do much more, unless—Why? What makes you ask?"

"Oh, I've just been thinkin' of yesterday," said John. "A real mean officer was out at our place. Said he'd do all kinds of things when he found a loaf of bread in the clock that Mother had been hiding from him. She tried to make him take it, but he wouldn't, and said he'd get even."

"Well, don't worry. Like as not it was just talk."

"No," sighed John, "I have a feelin' something dreadful will happen. I hate to leave the family, not knowing what might happen."

"There ain't much you could do anyway," consoled the practical Peter; "so quit thinkin' about it. I reckon God can look after them all right, even if you are away."

"I know," John agreed, "but I still hate to go." A moment later he added sleepily, "Wouldn't it be awful, though, if we didn't have a God to look after things?"

After a night of fitful sleep, John and Peter were roused at daybreak by several men who had come to transfer the wounded soldier to a makeshift hospital.

"Here you," shouted one of the men, prodding Peter with his foot, "give us a hand, will you?"

Peter willingly came to their aid, but one look at the ghastly features of the wounded man was all he could take. He felt his knees give way, and the earth sway around him. Seeing his predicament, John quickly stepped up to take his place.

"Whew! That was bad, wasn't it?" exclaimed Peter, wiping the cold sweat from his forehead as the ambulance wagon drove off. "No wonder the poor chap groaned all night. Reckon I'm not cut out for a doctor."

John, too, was mopping his face. "Oh, this insane war!" he murmured thoughtfully. "There goes another proof that we simply can't have anything to do with it. Suppose one of us had shot that poor man!"

In a short time the whole camp was astir and officers were shouting commands to the teamsters in preparation for the start of the journey.

The six boys ate a cold breakfast from the baskets of lunch their mothers had provided. Then Peter went off to feed his horse while John sauntered through the camp and talked to a number of Mennonite families who were also making the trip. There would be 400 wagonloads of refugees, someone informed him.

Soon the order was given and the long train of wagons began to roll down the valley toward the Maryland border. What a sight it was as they wound their way along the valley pike—wagons as far ahead and as far behind as the eye could see. Total caravan, an officer informed him, amounted to 1,600 wagons, stretching out along the road for sixteen miles.

All day long and until late that night they kept up a steady pace, stopping only at noon for a short rest. Although John envied the riders their unhampered view of the glorious mountain scenery, his soul thrilled to the continuous panorama of changing views unfolding through the open back of the wagon.

By the time the caravan halted for the night, most of the travelers were suffering from thirst. The small water bottles the boys had brought were soon emptied and they hadn't been able to refill them. But when they started to look for water, there wasn't a stream, a spring, or a well in sight. Soon, however, someone discovered a pond about a quarter of a mile farther on.

"Doesn't sound too good," said Peter, "but we must have water and so must my horse. Let's go."

It wasn't so bad drinking from the pond in the dark, and so they drank eagerly and thirstily. The bank was soon lined with refugees drinking, washing themselves, and filling pails and water bottles for use in camp. Next morning, when the wagons rolled past the little pond, the boys were horrified to see several dead mules lying in the shallow water.

For five long, weary days the journey continued. At last, on Friday night, the wagon train arrived at Martinsburg, on the border of Maryland. Here the free transportation ceased, and next morning the boys set out for Hagerstown.

At Hagerstown the boys located a Mennonite Church on Sunday

morning and attended their first church service in a number of weeks. John felt strangely moved as he worshiped for the first time away from home. He felt so alone, sitting in this church filled with strangers. Even though he tried to concentrate, his thoughts kept going back to the folks at home. Last night at the tavern they had heard rumors of the burning in the valley. Had they burned his father's barn too? Was the family safe? Would they be at church that morning or were the soldiers still quartered at Weavers?

If the service would only be in English, he thought, trying once more to get into the spirit of worship. Back home they occasionally had a service in German, but not often. But here even the singing was different. Everyone sang the melody instead of harmonizing in three parts as they did in Virginia. Well, might as well get used to it, he decided. But as he listened to the sermon, intoned in a monotonous singsong fashion, he found his thoughts drifting again and again to more familiar scenes.

The next day arrangements were made among some of the farmers, and the boys were hired to help with the fall work. But by February they realized there wasn't too much work for them in this community, and they decided to try Cumberland County, Pennsylvania.

The train trip to Pennsylvania, their first train trip, didn't quite meet expectations. A snowstorm almost halted rail traffic, and time and again the boys were called on to help shovel big drifts from the tracks so that the train could get through. Eventually they arrived in Shiremanstown, where they were taken to the home of George Rupp, a Mennonite bishop.

Here they soon found work as farm hands. John was hired by Preacher Samuel Zimmerman. He felt quite at home in the minister's family. Samuel, Jr., Leah, and little Sarah reminded him much of his own brothers and sisters. Leah was quite an attractive young woman. He frequently found himself comparing her with Bettie. But, then, no one could be compared with Bettie, he decided. She was in his thoughts a great deal. Once he had a letter from her which she managed to send through the lines with someone coming north. It was a brief letter, written on a small, torn piece of rough wrapping paper. But how he treasured it! She still loved him and was eagerly awaiting his return.

A few letters also came through from the home folks. The first, from Lizzie, told of the terrible burnings in the valley shortly after the boys left.

"It's like I thought," John said, discussing the letter with Peter. "That mean officer got even, all right."

"Why, what'd he do?" asked Peter.

"Scared 'em half to death. Just listen." And Peter listened while John read of the ordeal his family endured during the terrifying days when the northern army was carrying out its scorched earth policy in the valley. Arriving at the Coffman home one morning, the spiteful officer smilingly informed Frances that he intended burning her house but would mercifully grant her exactly one-half hour to get out anything she wanted to save.

They worked like mad, Lizzie said, and got out everything, even to the last crock of apple butter, when the officer, still smiling, informed them that he had changed his mind and they could now lug it all back again. They sat and watched while the barn went up in flames, but it didn't seem nearly so bad now that they knew their house was safe.

"Whew!" exclaimed Peter, "that was close. I reckon there ain't too many barns left in the valley."

"Lizzie says they didn't burn Heatwole's."

"That's funny. I wonder why."

"Mrs. Heatwole wouldn't let 'em. She said they started a fire on the barn floor several times, but she stood right there and raked it out every time. Not many women would have that much nerve."

During their stay in Maryland and Pennsylvania the boys followed closely the progress of the war through the columns of the small weekly newspapers. At first it seemed strange to hear the outspoken sentiment and to listen to the general abuse of the southern rebels. But gradually they became accustomed to this line of thought. It was a relief that among the Mennonites a greater understanding existed.

All winter long, as one Confederate stronghold after another fell into the hands of the Federals, the northerners kept saying it was only a matter of time. But still the army called up more and more men as well as more supplies. When finally Sheridan joined Grant in an all-out attack to break the stubborn resistance of Petersburg, there was great rejoicing in the North, even though they knew there was still tough, bitter fighting ahead.

In the North, the boys discovered, exemption from military service could be secured upon the payment of a much smaller fee than in the South. The required sum was $300 instead of $500. This amount could be paid by anyone desiring exemption and was used by the army for the purpose of hiring substitutes. Because of the strong opposition of Mennonites and Quakers and other nonresistant bodies to this use of the money, a new act was passed in February, 1864, recognizing conscientious objectors and specifying three alternatives to military service: (1) assignment to duty in hospitals for care of sick and wounded soldiers; (2) assignment to duty in the care of freedmen; (3) payment of a commutation fee of $300 to be applied to the benefit of sick and wounded soldiers.

In the little church in Cumberland County, Pennsylvania, there was joy and a deep feeling of gratitude on the morning when the new act was explained to the congregation. They could feel now that their money would not be used to employ others to carry on the work of destruction they could not do.

News of the fall of Petersburg on April 2, 1865, spread rapidly through the country, both north and south. In the North there was great jubilation and John was surprised at the sense of relief which it brought to him. Perhaps he would get home sooner than he expected. Several days later, when the weekly paper arrived, they read with great excitement the account of the Confederate defeat at Five Forks on the first, and then of the tremendous assault which forced the surrender of the weary defenders of Petersburg. For a week the entire nation waited, expecting momentarily news of Lee's surrender. Then on the ninth of April it came. The famous southern gentleman and soldier gave up the struggle at Appomattox Courthouse.

It was hard to grasp the concept of peace—hard to realize that the bloodshed was over and that friendly relations would once more be restored throughout the nation. It was especially hard for John and his Virginian friends who came together for a private celebration of their own during the rejoicing of their northern associates. They could scarcely recall a peaceful mode of life, free from gnawing fear and apprehension. Five years was a long stretch of time in their young lives.

"I just can't believe it's true," John was saying for about the tenth time as the three sauntered along the street in Shiremanstown on Saturday afternoon. They were enjoying the holiday atmosphere and the happy expression on the faces of the crowds which filled the streets. The whole country, it seemed, was in town that afternoon.

"It's almost too good to be true," Peter observed cautiously. "Do you suppose something might still go wrong? There might be more trouble somewhere?"

"I reckon there'll be plenty of trouble," Chris Brunk remarked, "but the shooting's done. The South is licked all right, but I reckon she's agoin' to have to pay for it."

"There's one thing sure," put in John, "things can't be much worse at home than they are now. My, how happy they'll be that it's all over. Do you think they'll let us go home soon or will we have to wait till our time is up? How long did you sign up for, Brunk?"

"Only a couple of months," replied Chris. "I reckon I can leave all right by the end of the month."

"My time won't be up till the end of May," sighed John.

"And I hired out to Henry Zimmerman for all summer," groaned Peter.

"Well, we can at least talk it over with them," John suggested. "They've been good to us. I'm sure they'll understand how anxious we are and be considerate."

One afternoon about a week later, on April 15, 1865, Peter came riding up Zimmerman's lane posthaste. John, who was plowing near the lane, recognized him immediately and hurried to meet him.

"Have you heard the news?" shouted Peter, dismounting and tying his horse to a fence post.

"No," yelled John, "what news?"

"Abe Lincoln's dead," called Peter, panting for breath as he came running toward John.

"Lincoln? The president?" exclaimed John unbelievingly.

"Yes, the president," replied Peter gravely. "He was shot last night, by some kind of a madman at a theater."

John was speechless. "B—but how did you find it out so soon?" he finally asked.

"The boss saw the flag at half-mast in Harrisburg this morning. So he went in to see what was wrong. Just got back a while ago."

"Well! Too bad," sighed John. "He didn't even live to enjoy the peace. He'd like as not have been a pretty good president."

"He said they're goin' to bring his body to Harrisburg tomorrow and we'll all be goin' to town to see him. Can you come with us?"

"I'll see," said John.

From miles around people poured into Harrisburg next day and the three Virginians as well as their employers were among the 45,000 individuals who filed past the flag-draped coffin at State House. They remained until evening and witnessed the procession as the hearse bearing Lincoln's body slowly made its way along Main Street. Slowly, very slowly, past thousands of sorrowing spectators, the procession moved toward the depot, while bands played stately, solemn hymns. In the distance the boom of cannon reverberated through the city at five-minute intervals. John was strangely moved by the spectacle, which left a lasting impression on all three of the teen-aged lads from Virginia.

*The storm ceased before sunset. The sun came out in all his splendor, presenting a scene most beautiful to the admirer of natural phenomena. The vivid rainbow in the east, the long dark shadows of the hills, the bright fields on which the sun cast his luminous rays, the sky being yet overspread with clouds, the bright streak of clear sky in the west, and the raindrops hanging tremulous on bush and tree, glistening in the sunbeams, fill the heart with emotions that will last almost while memory serves me. With every pleasing sight in nature, with every great truth of the Gospel that is unfolded to him, the heart of a Christian is filled with praise to God.*—Diary.

# 6

It was Molly who first spied John trudging up the lane. Pausing only long enough to shout the good news in the general direction of the house, she rushed to meet him, with Daniel and David in close pursuit. Then from the house came Mother and Anna and two-year-old Sarah. A lump came into John's throat and his eyes grew misty as he bent to embrace his little brothers and sisters. And then his mother! Her eyes were misty too, and for a moment neither could speak. It was Mother who spoke first.

"My, how tall you're agettin', John. But I see they ain't fattened you any."

"That's just what I've been thinking of you all," said John. "Why, I hardly knew the boys, they've grown so. And little Sarah—she was just a baby!" Sarah clung shyly to her mother's skirts and looked with big blue eyes at the tall stranger. "But—but you're all so thin. Have you been sick?"

"No," said Mother, "not particularly. You just don't get too hearty on the stuff we been eatin' since you left."

"Oh, I forgot," said John, adding hurriedly, "and where are the rest?"

"Jake and Joe are out in the field with Father," Mother replied. "Dan, you run and tell 'em we got company, but don't say who it is. It's nearly suppertime; so they might as well come in now anyway."

"And Lizzie?" asked John.

"Oh, she's at Brunk's. She's been workin' out some this spring.

But we'll bring her home for supper tonight too. We'll have a real celebration."

As they sat down to supper that night, John realized for the first time the extent of the hardship his family had endured that winter.

"Molasses!" shouted Joe as soon as they sat down to the table. "Look, everybody, molasses!"

There it stood in the center of the table, one little pitcher of molasses. All eyes were glued on that pitcher, and as soon as Father had asked the blessing, the children immediately started clamoring for a taste. At one end of the table was a plate of corn bread, and at the other a plate of little green onions from the garden. Beside the children's plates sat small mugs of milk, while the older ones had big cups of chickory-root coffee.

And this, John realized, was supposed to be a special meal—a celebration! A small spoonful of molasses added to the regular fare! No wonder the children were pitifully thin. No wonder Father and Mother began to look haggard and gray. He suddenly felt as if he couldn't choke down his piece of corn bread. As to the molasses, he couldn't touch it. He felt ashamed as he realized how hungry his little brothers and sisters were for something he had literally grown tired of in Pennsylvania.

But for the rest of the family this was truly a happy occasion, not marred by talk of hardships. Instead, John was encouraged to talk about Pennsylvania and Maryland. The children listened wide-eyed as he told about the train rides. He tried to avoid talking about food, but it was impossible. Somehow they seemed to draw some satisfaction in just hearing what folks in the North had to eat.

And then after supper John went to his bag and brought out the surprise. How thankful he was now for the gift which had been pressed upon him in Pennsylvania. At first he was inclined to think of it as a bit burdensome, those two bulky lengths of linsey. Now, seeing his family almost in rags, he was most grateful for the thoughtfulness of those who had sent it.

"Here, Mother," he said, handing her first a small white bag and then the pieces of heavy, dark homespun. "A present for you from the folks in Pennsylvania."

"Oh, linsey! Thank God, thank God! We need it so bad." Mother's voice shook, and she quickly dashed a tear from her eyes as she examined the two pieces and felt the firm texture of the cloth. "And what's this?" she asked in a teary whisper, untying the little white bag. "Oh, not salt! It can't be!" But it was salt, a whole pound of it. To John's surprise, this time, Mother completely broke down and cried.

Quickly the girls crowded around the bolts of new cloth, feeling the texture and admiring the rich shades of blue and brown.

"I need a new dress awful bad," said Lizzie.

"Me, too," chimed in Anna.

"You girls needn't think you're goin' to get it all," said John brusquely. "One of those pieces is for Mother."

"No, John," Mother said, hastily wiping her eyes. "The girls need it worse than me. They've both grown so. My Sunday dress is tolerable good, but if Lizzie gets a new one we can fix up her old blue for Molly. I reckon we can mebbe get two out of the big piece for Anna and Molly both."

"What about me? I sure need new trousers," exclaimed Joe.

"Yes, I know," sighed Mother. "Every last one of you needs a lot of things. But we'll just have to wait till we get more sheep and a good crop of flax."

As he looked around the countryside, John was shocked at the extent of the damage caused by Sheridan. In Rockingham County alone, he was told, Sheridan had destroyed more than $2,000,000 worth of property, burned some 2,000 barns, and 120 flour mills. Since he had carried off tons of flour as well as grain, white bread had become exceedingly scarce and a great luxury on valley tables.

"But what did you all live on all winter?" John asked his mother one day.

"Well," she said, "we hid some flour and corn meal and a bit of dried corn under the house. And Father had some garden things buried in a big pit. But it wasn't near enough. Mostly we had one or two small meals a day. Thank God we had some milk or the children wouldn't have lived."

"Things are gettin' a little better now, aren't they?" he asked.

"Yes, there's more to be had in the stores, but it takes money. And that isn't plenty, you know. They're sendin' grain and stuff in from the North, specially seed."

"If only there'd be some way of earning a little money," John sighed. "Everything is so high!"

Frances sighed too. "Yes, a lot of things we can't even think of. Bacon was a dollar a pound a couple of years ago already. I reckon it's a lot more now."

"Whew! at that rate what would a whole pig cost?" John wondered. "We have to get a few little ones somehow, and a horse and some more cows."

"I reckon we'll wait a while for another horse," Frances said. "A neighbor had to pay $1,000 for one not too long ago."

Samuel and his sons worked harder than they ever had that summer, planting more acres of grain and corn for cash crops. After the crops were in, they spent their time in the wood lot cutting timbers for a new barn and helping neighbors in the same job.

One winter evening cousin Chris Brunk came over to see John. They were pretty close friends now, those boys who had been in Pennsylvania together. Since his return Chris had been working at the building trade. Realizing the tremendous demand for builders in the community, a plan began to take shape in his mind. Why not get a gang to work together as a unit, putting up barns, mills, and other buildings? Teamwork meant faster work.

He proposed the plan to John that evening as they sat toasting their toes at the kitchen fireplace, then surprised him by adding, "How about joining the gang if we get one up?"

"Who, me? A carpenter?" John gasped. "Why, I—I wouldn't be much good. I've never done anything like that."

"Well, you could learn, couldn't you? Any carpenter has to learn. It really isn't so hard, and besides, there's so much to be done. We'll never get all the barns up unless we get some new hands on the job."

"I know," John answered slowly, "but—but I never even thought of it. Besides, Father needs me so bad."

"Mebbe he needs cash even more than he needs you," suggested Chris. "Anyway, that's what my pap said when he let me go. You could earn a nice bit this summer if you'd stick to it. Enough to buy a few cows mebbe, or some sheep, or to help pay to get your lumber worked up for the barn."

"Well, I can see what he says," John replied. "Mebbe it would be an interesting job after all."

Early that spring John started work with a building crew. He soon found he had an aptitude for handling tools and enjoyed the change in occupation, taking a personal pride in the work the gang turned out.

It was not only through their workmanship, however, that the boys found favor with their patrons. They gave more than service. As they worked, they sang. They couldn't help it. It was part of their nature. There were enough of them to sing parts and so they sang wholeheartedly, the notes ringing out above the noise of the hammer and saw.

"My, that was good singing you boys done this morning," said a farmer's wife one day as she served their dinner. "I just wish I could have heard the words. Couldn't you sing a while before you go back to work?"

"We'd like to oblige," said Chris, "but we're in a hurry to get this job finished. There are so many others waiting. Maybe we could come in and sing tonight, though, after work."

"Wonderful, just wonderful," sighed the woman after they had sung for her and her husband that first evening. "It makes one feel there's something worth livin' for after all. I just wish you'd sing for the neighbors next door. They're so discouraged. They lost several boys in the war, and what with the burnin' and everything I know you'd do 'em a lot of good."

They sang for these neighbors and for other neighbors. Night after night all summer long the boys took upon themselves the job of bringing cheer and comfort through their songs. Soon they became known as the singing carpenters.

John also found some time for his books that spring, as well as an occasional evening for Bettie. He was older now, and felt he could visit her now and then without causing too many lifted eyebrows. During his absence their love had matured and increased their respect and appreciation for each other. One memorable evening when John called at the Heatwole home he found the whole family seated in the kitchen. Bettie was seated behind the kitchen stove carding wool, an empty chair beside her. Suddenly developing an intense interest in wool carding, John went over to examine her work. Then with inner quaking but with outward calm he casually seated himself on the empty chair. Soon, one by one, first Manassas, then Susanna, then Father and Mother, all seemed to find interests elsewhere or decided it was time for bed.

Discovering himself alone with Bettie, John felt a blush creeping over his face.

"Well, I—I—" he stammered, realizing he should say something. Then he glanced toward Bettie and saw her shyly observing him out of the corner of a bright eye. They both began to laugh.

"Does this mean that they don't care for my company?" he chuckled. "Or maybe that I have at last been accepted?"

"I reckon it means something," replied Bettie, smiling. "Anyways, they don't always go to bed so early. Not when I want to write letters anyways."

After that John considered himself quite grown up and free to occupy the chair behind the stove beside Bettie.

"This is where Chris Good used to sit when he came to see Anna," Bettie confided to him one evening. "And Dan Good when he was a courtin' Maria. But don't think they're agoin' to leave us alone very often. It's only once in a long, long time."

It mattered little to John and Bettie that they shared the kitchen with the rest of the family. They could converse quite companionably and cozily behind the old stove, and they were satisfied. On warm spring evenings they moved their chairs to the porch. Sometimes, too, they would ride together over the countryside just like their parents before them.

* * *

John had become quite proficient as a carpenter when suddenly his new career ended. It happened one day when he was high up on the scaffolding helping to put some timbers in place.

"Look out there, that hand spike's slippin'," someone shouted. But it was too late. The spike struck John. He lost his footing and went hurtling thirty feet to the ground below.

In a twinkling the men were all beside him, loosening his shirt, chafing his hands, and rubbing his legs. But he lay there limp and unconscious, pale as death.

"Can you feel a pulse?" someone asked in an undertone as Brunk groped clumsily and frantically for the artery in his wrist.

"N—not yet," stammered Brunk, "b—but I'm not much good at this sort of thing. Do you think he's breathing?"

One of the men put his ear to his chest and another held a hand close to his mouth and nose. But they both shook their heads, slowly, bewilderedly.

"Here, one of you men jump on a horse and go for a doctor quick," ordered Brunk, jumping suddenly to his feet. "And someone go to the house for a pitcher of water."

"Shouldn't we carry him in?" one of them asked.

This matter was settled by the farmer's wife who came running from the house.

"What's all this? What happened?" she panted as she dropped to her knees and began examining the limp body. "Like as not he's just fainted," was her verdict. "He don't seem to be turning cold. Bring him to the house and I'll see to him."

Tenderly they carried the seemingly lifeless body to the house where they laid him on a couch in the kitchen. By the time the doctor arrived, John was showing signs of returning consciousness and commencing to groan as he became aware of the sharp, stabbing pain in his left arm.

That was the beginning of a long, enforced holiday for John S. Coffman. But as soon as he was able to sit up and take an interest, he began asking for his books. His only serious injury was a fractured wrist. He could now study and read to his heart's content for hours at a time. Neighbors were glad to lend him books and periodicals from their small supplies.

Knowing that it would be a long time before his weakened wrist would permit either carpentry or heavy farming, John was frankly worried. What else could he do? Deep in his heart he knew what he preferred, but he dared hardly admit, even to himself, that he longed to be a teacher. A teaching certificate seemed practically unattainable for one with such a limited education.

But it wasn't impossible, he decided with grim determination one day. If he set his mind to it, he could do it, and he would! From that day on, a teaching certificate became his goal, and he borrowed books, read and studied for a purpose as well as pleasure.

A book on the subject of painting and interior decoration gave John an idea one day. Painting would be easier than farming and might be the answer to his problem. As he read and studied the illustrations, the subject fascinated him, especially the chapter on graining. As soon as he was able, he purchased some brushes and graining tools and began practicing on the scuffed woodwork at home.

Soon he was working for neighbors, and as his fame spread, young Coffman found plenty of work during the next few years.

* * *

Tragedy struck the Coffman home during the winter of 1868. A cold snap and snowstorm in January brought with it the delight of coasting down little hills and sliding on the frozen creek.

One Saturday morning Daniel, David, and Sarah were playing on the ice when suddenly Daniel came rushing to the house shouting that David was hurt.

"Why, what happened?" cried Mother, hastily tying a kerchief on her head and throwing a shawl around her shoulders.

"He just fell, but he won't talk or move or anything," said Dan. Mother turned pale as she rushed out the door toward the creek, ordering Daniel to run quickly for his father.

David was unconscious when they reached him and he remained unconscious through several long days and nights. The doctor from Harrisonburg said there was nothing he could do. He had fractured his skull and might regain consciousness, or he might not.

John took his turn sitting beside his little seven-year-old brother. He had sat at bedsides like this before when a neighbor was ill. He had even seen death lay a chilling hand on the form of a friend and his heart had gone out in most sincere sympathy. But it—it wasn't like this, he thought. Never had he experienced such heart-rending agony as watching his own little brother growing weaker and weaker—bright, lively, happy little David. Surely it couldn't be that he should die so soon!

"Why, why?" his soul cried out. "Please, God, please, if it is not against Thy will, heal the little body."

Young David died early one morning without regaining consciousness. Although John could read their grief in the eyes of his father and mother, they did not give way to overwhelming sorrow such as he frequently witnessed. Speaking calmly to the children at family worship that morning, Father vividly portrayed the beautiful, happy home to which God had called their brother. Sadly John helped his father take David's measurements and then rode to town to order the plain little wooden coffin in which he would be laid to rest.

That night friends and neighbors from miles around came to the house to express their sympathy. John knew their feelings were genuine, but never before had he realized how utterly impossible it was for one human heart to touch another. And then like a flash came the thought: But God can. Through His Spirit He shares human sorrow and gives peace and comfort to troubled hearts. How he longed to get away from the crowd for a little while to ponder this new and wonderful truth!

There was a wake that night. A number of young people remained to look after the lifeless body in the little wooden coffin.

Every half hour or so they laid a fresh cold cloth over the little face so that it wouldn't turn dark before the funeral next day. John heard them moving about downstairs all night long. He thought of the many times he had done similar service, never thinking it would be necessary at their home so soon. Every once in a while someone started a tune and the rest joined in, softly and sadly. It sounded eerie in the dead of night and John shivered. But it was also comforting.

They buried little David in the cemetery at Weavers Church next day. As they lowered the tiny coffin into the grave in the snowy cemetery, John was so powerfully gripped with a sense of the uncertainty of life that the feeling never left him. The thought colored his thinking, his teaching, and his preaching through all his life.

This personal experience with sorrow enabled John to help Bettie when her father died the following year. Although she was very fond of her stepmother, Bettie had always felt very close to her father and felt the separation keenly. She was grateful for the comforting spiritual truths John shared with her, and through this mutual experience they were drawn still closer to each other.

Several months before his death Father Heatwole had given his consent to the marriage of his daughter to John S. Coffman. He had great respect and appreciation for the young man who was to become his new son-in-law, and happily gave his blessing to the betrothal. No date was set for the wedding, but John hoped that it might take place soon after his twenty-first birthday in October. After her father's death, however, Bettie felt that they should wait a while longer.

"I don't see why we should wait, Dear," John said, as they sat on the porch steps one June evening.

"Well, Mam feels so bad. We all do. A—a weddin' just don't seem to be fittin' now."

"I know," John said tenderly. "It's been hard for all of you. Even young Susanna isn't herself. We don't hear her sing any more when she goes out milking."

"But she does sing, only not so loud. She had to. The cows wouldn't give their milk till she did. But really, John, I—I just couldn't go through with a weddin'. I love you so much, but—"

"Well," said John, "we can put it off till, say, November. That's five months away. You'll feel different by then, I'm sure. We needn't have a big wedding, just the family."

"Well—mebbe that'd be all right. We'll see." The loving look from the soft hazel eyes, and the faint semblance of a smile were more reassuring to John than the words.

"I'm sure I'm agoin' to have the nicest, kindest husband in the whole world," she whispered as John drew her close.

That spring John had his first taste of schoolteaching. He was



3

quite surprised when the Fairview teacher called one evening to see whether he wouldn't take over the summer term for him.

"Oh, I couldn't; I don't have a certificate," John protested. "And I couldn't get ready for the examination in such a short time."

"Don't worry, you can do it," answered the teacher. "You won't need a certificate for just one term. There aren't many in the summer term anyway, just a few in the younger classes."

"Well, if you think I could, I might try. It sounds interesting."

"Good. I'll talk to some of the patrons and let them know. It will only be for a few months and I'll be there for a day or two to help you get started."

At first John felt a little shaky as he faced his young pupils the first morning. Then remembering his early experience and the monotonous A-B ab's, he took courage and threw himself wholeheartedly into the job. These children were expecting something of him. He couldn't fail them. Now was his chance to test some of the theories he had evolved through days and nights of study and dreaming.

The experience was a satisfying one. John found that he enjoyed teaching even more than he had expected. To work with people, to reach their minds and hearts, was of much greater importance, he decided, than merely wielding a paint brush or hammer or hoe. Although he was keenly conscious of his weaknesses and lack of training, this did not cause him to give up but rather to work a little harder for that coveted certificate. He knew now that he would have to press on toward a higher form of service for mankind.

*The season appears very late—vegetation was just as far advanced March 16 last year as now. But the Lord will no doubt give us just such a season as we need, probably not as we want. There is a great difference between our wants and our needs. Our wants gratified might externally ruin us. God knows best.*—Diary.

# 7

There was a frosty nip in the air, John noticed, as he made his way to the barn to help with the chores that November morning in 1869. But the sun shone brightly and he whistled and sang alternately as he helped his father and brothers with the regular work.

It seemed strange to be helping at home again. For about six months now he had been living over at the widow Rhodes farm, working it on a share basis. A hired boy was looking after the chores over there for a few days until he returned with his bride.

Dressed in their Sunday best, the Coffmans set out for the Heatwole home right after dinner. John felt stiff and uncomfortable in his new outfit. His father had bought him a new suit for his twenty-first birthday, a good black, tailor-made suit that fitted him neatly. Lizzie had made his new shirt and was especially proud of the fit of the stiffly starched collar. Jake teased, as usual. He had caught him rubbing his new shoes a little extra hard to bring out a shine. But he ignored him. He knew that for Mennonite men a dull look was preferred in shoes, but in John's eyes it was merely a careless look.

Frances could scarcely take her eyes off her eldest son, looking so manly and graceful in the new suit. It was hard to realize that her little boy was now a man and about to set up a home of his own. As the wagon jogged along, she didn't say much, but in her heart she communed with her Lord, imploring His divine blessing upon her boy and the home he was about to establish. For one fleeting moment John was her little boy again. As they climbed out of the wagon and started toward the house, he turned to her shyly.

"H—how do I look, Mother? Is my tie straight?" he asked, making a frantic attempt to smooth back a stubborn lock of hair.

"Why, you look right nice," Frances smiled as she brushed a few specks of dust from his coat and adjusted the tie. "God bless you, my boy," she whispered in a tender farewell embrace to his boyhood days.

The wedding ceremony was short and simple. John and Bettie stood in front of the glowing fire in the large parlor of the Heatwole home, while members of the two families sat stiffly on high-backed chairs arranged along the walls. Mother held her youngest daughter, twenty-month-old Rebecca, while Lizzie kept an eye on little Fannie.

The ceremony ended, John looked at his little bride as if he had never seen her before. How beautiful she seemed at that moment, so slender and shapely in the soft gray dress, her dark brown hair brushed smoothly back under her little white prayer covering. Her bright eyes, those compelling hazel blue eyes, shone even brighter as he clasped her hands tightly between his own and bent to kiss those full red lips.

John and Bettie arrived early at the Coffman home next day to help with the preparations for the infare, a dinner given at the groom's home the day after the wedding. There was lots to do—potatoes to peel, several big hams to slice, chickens to get ready for the stewing pots, and numerous last-minute jobs. The baking had been finished several days before. Frances gazed with satisfaction at the long line of pies on a shelf in the cellar and once more checked the contents of the well-filled breadbox. Yes, there should be plenty for everyone.

Molly and Sarah were given the job of setting the long tables arranged in the dining and living rooms. Planks and trestles served for makeshift tables, while tablecloths and dishes were borrowed from the neighbors. Frances kept glancing admiringly at the bride's table. The gleaming white porcelain looked beautiful against the red cloth. She was using her new set of dishes for the first time. It was a much-needed set for which she had saved butter and egg money for some time.

Dinner over, the main entertainment of the evening began. It was singing. John's heart was overflowing with happiness. With Bettie at his side and a room filled with his closest friends, singing was the most natural release for his emotions. The singing was exceptionally good that evening. It was hard to quit when some of the women began looking at the clock and suggesting it was time to get the children home to bed. But gradually the group broke up and while a few still sat singing in the living room, the new bride and groom stood at the door graciously bidding farewell to their guests.

Early next day several wagonloads of furniture moved from the Coffman and Heatwole homes to the John Coffman home on the

Margaret Rhodes farm. There was nothing new or luxurious in those loads—just articles that their parents could spare, plus a few essentials bought at recent sales. But Bettie, like her mother and mother-in-law before her, had a big chest filled with bedding and homespuns. And there was a good pile of new rag carpets that would help to make the little house cozy and comfortable.

John and Bettie were completely happy that first winter. The fact that John's income was meager didn't bother them unduly, for there was a good store of food in the cellar and several fat hogs to butcher. Bettie was kept busy fixing up the little home while John managed the farm and looked after the needs of the two households. In the evening he spent much time studying. A new subject added to his curriculum that year was agriculture. Occasionally bits of literature fell into his hands and he began with his usual enthusiasm to make plans for improving his methods of farming.

It was that winter, too, that John began to take a keener interest in Bible study. The incentive was a Sunday school which they planned to organize in the district that summer.

For several years the question of Sunday school had been under consideration in Virginia. It was brought before conference a number of times, but no action was taken. At the last fall conference, however, Samuel Coffman had again raised the issue. To him the subject was of vital importance, and he spoke so forcefully in favor of Sunday schools that a resolution was finally passed permitting schools to be established. Since this action was subject to the approval of individual congregations, the matter had been brought up and sanctioned at both churches—Weavers and Bank.

Enthusiasm was high at first, especially at Bank. Quite a few families in this vicinity had been sending their children to other Sunday schools, among them the Coffman children. Samuel himself had gone to Sunday school when he was a boy, and fully realized the benefit of formal, regular Bible teaching for children. His children attended the Presbyterian school at New Erection. Others went to the Methodist school at Trinity.

"If we want to keep our children in our own church," he warned conference, "we must start schools of our own."

The day for the opening of Sunday school finally arrived. It was a warm Sunday afternoon in July, 1870. The little group that had planned so long for the school was not disappointed. A good crowd had arrived and joined lustily in the opening songs. With the help of a few teachers from the Methodist and Presbyterian schools they were able to divide the group into classes and provide each with a competent instructor.

John's heart glowed with a deep sense of satisfaction as he rode home from church that afternoon. How wonderful to have a part in such an important work!

He stopped for a few minutes at his old home to give a firsthand report to his father and mother. Frances listened silently. The gleam in his eyes was reflected in hers as he launched into an enthusiastic account of this first Sunday-school session. Surely God was beginning to use her boy. This was perhaps a small beginning of some special service. Silently she breathed a prayer that his service might always be so wholehearted and willing.

Samuel, too, listened with intense interest. "Well," he said as John finished his report, "I'm right glad it went so good. But remember," he warned, "it ain't agoin' to be all clear sailin'. There's bound to be some trouble ahead and you'll have to go pretty careful."

"I know," John agreed. "We've got opposition, all right. But we're hoping we'll be able to show them what a good thing it is."

"One thing that they won't like," Samuel cautioned, "is havin' those teachers from the other churches. If only we had enough of our own!"

"It's just too bad we haven't," John said. "We've got plenty of folks that should be teaching, but they need teaching themselves. We should have had Sunday schools years ago. But we'll get there someday, I hope."

* * *

The farm prospered that summer. The season had been good and by the first of September the grain had been harvested, showing good returns for the summer's work. John had begun to cut corn and had made a fair start on his fall plowing when the heavy rain began.

For nearly a week the rain continued steadily. John kept watching the little creek that ran through their farm. It cut across the yard between the Rhodes house and barn. Finally one evening he saw that it was rising rapidly. Bettie noticed it too, when she went out to feed the hens. She looked worried when John came in for supper.

"Is this rain agoin' to last much longer, do you think?" she asked as she ladled out bowls of noodle soup and carried them to the table.

"I can't say, Dear," John replied quietly. "There are some signs of clearing. It didn't seem to be raining quite so hard when I came in. But it's hard to say. I'm no weather prophet."

"If it—it don't stop soon, do you reckon the creek'll flood?" she asked anxiously. "It's tolerable high right now."

"Well, I shouldn't wonder if it overflowed a bit. But it's been high before, and I reckon it won't do too much damage."

But the next morning John and Bettie awoke to the sound of rushing water. Running quickly to the door, John saw that the creek had risen to within a few feet of the Rhodes house and was already lapping at the barn foundations. Beyond that, where the banks were not so high, he could see that his cornfields were flooded and the shocks of corn which had stood so proudly in rows yesterday were down, and being carried off by the strong current.

During the next few days John learned that his loss in corn was small indeed compared to what many valley farmers suffered. The flood was one of the worst in the history of the state, with all the streams and rivers in the valley going on a rampage, destroying crops, wrecking houses and newly built barns and mills for miles around. In Rockingham County, where the farmers had just nicely recovered from the effects of the war, the blow was felt most keenly. Damage was estimated at one million dollars. As much damage in one night, some said, as in a whole year of war.

One cold January evening of the following year, 1871, John hastily saddled his mare, Duck, and rode at top speed to his father's home returning in a remarkably short time with his mother. A few hours later he sat in a kind of daze by the fire in the kitchen, watching with awe and wonder while his mother bathed and dressed a tiny, squirming little being, his son—his own little son.

"So, I have a son!" he said, gazing almost reverently at the babe as Frances placed him in his arms. "It's a sobering thought, isn't it, Mother?"

"Yes, John," his mother replied softly, sitting beside him to rest for a minute. "I know how you feel."

"Yes, I reckon you do. About twelve times over."

Frances nodded, looking dreamily into the fire. "But you know, I remember best the first time. When I held you in my arms, John, just like you're aholdin' your son now."

"But—but why should you remember that best?" John wondered. "That was over twenty-two years ago."

"Well, there's something about the first time—something you don't forget. And for me there was something very special about it. I've never told you, and I can't tell you even now. But someday I will."

Several days later when John was in town he bought a little red diary. As head of a family he felt he should now begin to keep track of events. Leafing back to January 13 he made his first entry in his very best writing: "William Coffman born." The main event of the next day was also entered: "Went for Susanna Heatwole." For the next few weeks Bettie's sister was a member of the household, helping to look after the baby and keep the home running smoothly until Bettie was again able to take over.

John's interest in school was heightened by an impromptu visit to Fairview one snowy morning in February. But the incident very nearly got him in trouble with his employer.

At the request of Mrs. Rhodes, or Aunt Peggy as they called her, John hitched the team to the sleigh and took the Rhodes children to school. Since he had nothing special planned for the morning, he stayed a while to warm up and have a little chat with the teacher. Then the bell rang and as the children trooped in, he felt a strong urge to stay a little longer and observe proceedings. He intended to listen to only one or two recitations, but before he realized it, recess time arrived. Then came another discussion and some more observation, so that by the time he arrived home it was after twelve. He found Bettie greatly agitated when he came in for dinner.

"It's about time you showed up," she scolded. "Where were you all morning anyways?"

"Why," exclaimed John in surprise, "I was just at school. You knew I took the children. I thought I might as well stay a little while and see how Minnich's getting along. I heard some real good recitations."

"But you didn't hafta stay so long," persisted Bettie. "And you didn't tell Aunt Peggy you was aimin' to stay either. She was over here half a dozen times awonderin' what was keepin' you."

"Well, I hadn't intended to stay, really, but I just couldn't help it. School is always so interesting."

"I know it is. And I really didn't mind myself. But Aunt Peggy did. She had a lot of things for you to do this morning. I'm afraid you're in for a scolding."

"Yes, I reckon I am. But just the same it was worth it. You should have heard some of those children spell, Bettie. And read!" John walked silently to his place at the table. "Do you s'pose I'll ever get my teacher's certificate?" he added as he sat down opposite Bettie.

"Of course you will," Bettie replied confidently. "You kin do it easy. But right now just remember you're still a farmer."

About once a week that winter he spent an evening at Fairview attending spelling school. Spelling bees proved to be a popular pastime in the community that season, and John took advantage of the splendid opportunity to improve himself in one of his most difficult subjects.

The first bee he was able to attend came on February 10. Before he went to bed that night he ruefully wrote in his diary: "Went to spelling school. Daniel Rhodes and Samuel Parret were captains. Rhodes beat. I was on the looseing side."

With Aunt Peggy's permission John spent quite a few days later that spring substituting for Mr. Minnich, the teacher at Fairview. The necessary study and the experience brought him a little closer to his goal.

In May the Sunday school was reorganized for the second summer season. There had been a heavy rain the day before and the roads were muddy.

"I'm doubtful whether there'll be many out this afternoon," John said as he discussed Sunday school with Bettie at the dinner table. "There's been so much talk against the Sunday school lately that I'm afraid it won't take much to discourage a lot of folks."

But to his surprise a good crowd was already on hand by the time he reached the church. Interested parents as well as children were there, eager to commence a new term of school. Leaders of the school were encouraged by the response and determined to make the course even more interesting and helpful.

In discussing ways of increasing interest with his fellow teachers one day, John suggested books. From his own experience he knew the value of good literature. And he also knew that books were very scarce in most homes. A few volumes of simple Bible stories would be of great interest to the children, he suggested, while the teaching staff could also benefit greatly from fresh, stimulating ideas readily available in book form.

Most of the teachers agreed with John. But the great drawback to the idea was lack of funds. To take an offering in the church or to ask the children to bring money to buy books would be to add more fuel to the smoldering opposition. The problem was finally solved when someone suggested using money from their own pockets. To this a number agreed, and John was appointed to select and order suitable books.

Several weeks later the books arrived. After looking through them and getting them ready for use, he recorded the event in his diary:

> Got the library that was sent for by the company consisting of A. C. Fishback, Joseph Heatwole, E. Suter, D. A. Heatwole, Sam Brunk, Chris Brunk, A. Weaver and myself.

Although the Sunday school commenced energetically that summer, opposition to the work was also energetic and feeling among the opposing faction mounted high. So strong did it become that a special meeting was called to discuss the matter once more. It was held late in May at the Bank Church. John attended the meeting and listened attentively as the ministers voiced their opinions pro and con. His father spoke eloquently of the need of special instruction for children, to give them a keener appreciation for God's Word and to instill in their minds the great principles of Christianity. Such teaching, he explained, would benefit not only the children but the entire church. Preachers Joseph Driver and Jacob Hildebrand were present from the upper district and D. H. Landis of the middle district. Several bishops were almost equally eloquent in their condemnation of the new venture. To them it was setting a precedent of bringing something new into the church, opening the door for many new practices. In organizing Sunday schools, they contended, the Mennonites were merely following the example of fashionable or "worldly" churches who were fast losing the faith and practices of their godly forefathers. "The same thing will happen to us," they warned, "if we permit these schools to continue."

No action was taken at the meeting, however, and the school continued. In July an attempt was made to organize a school at Brenneman's in the lower, or northern district. John and Bettie rode over to Brenneman's that afternoon in order to give the venture as much support as possible. But foes as well as friends were present and the opposition was so great that the matter was dropped. John was deeply grieved at this setback, and greatly feared the consequences in their own district. But the school continued without incident to the close of the season.

One fall evening Samuel Coffman rode over to his son's home. His face looked grave as he entered the cheery kitchen. He had a smile for his little grandson, who lay kicking and cooing in his cradle, but John noticed that his eyes remained troubled and unsmiling.

Reaching into his coat pocket he drew out a sheaf of papers and handed them to John.

"Here, did you get one of these?" he asked brusquely.

"Why, no," John replied. "What is it?"

"Read it and see. I reckon they only sent it to us preachers. It beats all what some folks won't think up."

John quickly unfolded the letter and read the heading aloud. "Objections to the Sabbath school of the Mennonite Church in Rockingham County."

"Whew!" he exclaimed, "and there are twenty-six of them, I see."

"Yes, and not one of the twenty-six as'd hold water. Read them," Samuel ordered.

John took the papers and sat down at the table. Drawing the candle a little closer, he commenced reading aloud so that Bettie could hear too:

1. We object to it because it was introduced into the church by one-sided representations and unfair means.

2. We object to it because it is not in accordance with the old order creed of our church in allowing any member to teach publicly in our church.

3. —because persons not members are publicly allowed to teach in our church.

4. —because women are allowed to teach publicly in our church.

5. —because it is in style with the Sunday schools of the highest class in our country.

6. —because it is become a fashion amongst the proudest and dressiest classes of our community to have such school. Romans 10:11, 12.

7. —because by the use of it we follow after some things in the highest repute by the world at large. James 4:4.

8. —because it is represented as teaching of our youth the sacred Scriptures only, while there is a mixture of other books of

subject matter used along with it gotten up by societies not opposed to war, bloodshed or imposing cost and inconveniences by suing at law.

9. —because it is giving our youth and nature the rein as may be seen from the following: Bishop Coffman stood up in conference on the 27th day of September, 1869, at Trissels church and said our children go to the Sunday school of other societies and we cannot keep them from it. We must organize Sunday school ourselves to keep them from going to those of others. On Sunday, July 16, a brother came to meeting at Weavers church from the lower district and said I am as much opposed to Sunday school as anybody, but our children go to Edom to Sunday school and we must organize a Sunday school at Brennemans church to prevent them from going to Sunday school at Edom. May it not be said from this that the fathers have become children and the children fathers as respects rule and subjugation? I Timothy 3:4.

10. —because a spirit of pride and exaltedness is being cultivated by it in giving the most progressive of the scholars marks of honor, etc.

11. —because cunning means are made use of to absorb the opposite party such as offering to them the office of teacher, etc.

12. —We object to it because it is something new.

13. —because the bishop (Coffman) openly declared to the church on the 19th day of October, 1869, at Weavers church that they do not want any other book than the Bible and Testament. But no sooner than the school was fully organized a host of other books were introduced thus playing false the church.

14. —because it is represented to our youth as a way better than that practiced by our forefathers.

15. —because our youth are by it shown to other societies as lights, examples, forerunners, rather than to our forefathers and who have almost a world-wide way to heaven.

16. —because Sunday school is a something that was instrumental in banishing the Bible and Testament from the weekday school to a considerable extent.

17. —because other books than the sacred Scriptures are used.

18. —because private council meetings were held of Sunday school teachers in our churches including persons not members of our church, while regular members are excluded.

19. —because the statement made to the church by Bishop Coffman on the 18th of October, 1869, that the Sunday school should be under the control of the church is no more respected.

20. —because our Confession of Faith is not used while the Question Books of other societies are.

21. —because it curtails the attention to our regular meetings.

22. —because the Mennonite was to be a people of God separate from the rest of the world, having close communion; and whereas

the present Sunday school is a mixture of other societies and the world generally, we consider it our duty to oppose it as a demoralizing evil in our church.

23. —We object to it on account of Sunday Christianism as there is a very large class of people in this country who make the Sabbath almost their whole Christianity and their conversation on religious matters is little else but of keeping the Sabbath Sunday school, and whilst nearly every other Christian duty is neglected by them and their pomp and show of fashion shows that their religion is vain. See Amos 5:21. Nearly all the destructive battles of the late war were fought on Sunday from which it may be inferred that the way of keeping the Sabbath in this country, making an idol of it in preference to all other commandments in the greatest display of pride and fashion was not pleasing to the most High. See Malachi 2:3.

24. —because it may serve as a means to corrupt the more orderly Sunday schools of the Mennonite communities within the United States.

25. —because there is no other Mennonite community from what we can learn on the continent of America that would allow such a Sunday school as this is.

26. —because we think it is carried on in a way that must in course of time bring our children to a level with the highest and dressiest and most warlike and worldly minded churches of our country and the world at large.

A demand. To our ministering brethren. According to our limited understanding the present so-called Mennonite Sunday school here is unscriptural the way it is carried on and conducted. We therefore demand of our ministers that they do show us direct Scriptural authority for such a Sunday school system, cite the passages by which such organizations are ordered or commanded. If they cannot do it, we demand that these Sunday schools be laid aside as an unscriptural passion of the latter days.

P.S. Read this, copy it and pass it round in the church. Why shall we stand still and fold our arms and look on this sad corruption in our own Mennonite church? Remember the zeal of our forefathers.

"Well, what do you think of it?" Samuel asked as John silently folded the paper and handed it back to him.

"The same as you do, I reckon," John replied with a big sigh. "It's just too bad, too bad! I hope it doesn't mean the end to our Sunday school. But I'm afraid it will do a lot of harm."

Samuel looked almost fierce as he shoved the letter back in his pocket. His bushy eyebrows fairly bristled above the steel-blue eyes.

"It's done harm already," he replied warmly. "Not only to the school but the whole church, and we'll feel it more very soon. We've got two kinds of Mennonites right now, the Sunday-school folks and the 'anti-Sunday-school party,' as I hear they call themselves."

"I know. I hear them talking. They've been working pretty hard lately, but I never suspected all this. We don't have to give up, do we?"

"Give up?" exploded Samuel, "No, sir. Not yet. Remember the zeal of our forefathers, as they say. But I reckon we'd better go a little easy," he added a little more calmly.

The school carried on, but on a reduced scale, for several more terms. Opposition, however, continued mounting and when finally the anti-Sunday-school party refused to take communion with the rest, the schools closed. Between the years 1873 and 1882 there were no Mennonite Sunday schools in Rockingham County.

John felt the defeat keenly. To be frustrated in an effort which was so obviously in the best interests of the church was a trying experience. He determined, however, never to give up the struggle, but to work with all his might to get the schools re-established. Was the work of the church always to be hampered by a few nearsighted members? he wondered.

* * *

"Well, that's the second wedding in the family," John said as he and Bettie were riding home from Father Coffman's home that February evening. It was Lizzie's wedding they had attended. There had been consternation at first when she insisted on marrying Wallace Minnich, a former quartermaster in the southern army, but everyone hoped for the best.

"Do you s'pose they can really be happy together, not believing quite alike?" Bettie wondered.

"Oh, I reckon so," drawled John. "They love each other, but it can't be quite the same. We can pray that he'll see things differently after a while. At least he's not taking her away from the church."

"He's right gentlemanly, too," added Bettie, "and a good talker. I like to listen to him."

"You're not trying to make me jealous, are you?" teased John.

"Land sakes, no," replied Bettie with fervor, "There ain't nobody half as good as my man."

"But he's a good businessman. And I reckon he'll be able to provide for his family better than I can."

"Humph!" exclaimed Bettie. "We have enough. And just wait till you get your certificate and start teaching. I reckon we'll have more then."

"Not much more, I'm afraid," John replied. "Teachers don't get much in these parts. But I think I'll try the examinations this spring and see what I can do. I can always try again if I don't make it the first time."

To his joy John was successful in the examinations and at last became the proud owner of a permit to teach. But as long as he was running the farm for Aunt Peggy Rhodes, he realized he would not be able to take a regular teaching position. He was, however, officially appointed as assistant to J. W. Rhodes at Fairview in the fall of 1872.

Another important event of 1872 was the birth of a second son, occurring on June 11.

"I'm going to call him Samuel," John told his father when he and his mother came over to see their new grandson. "You can give him a second name if you like."

Father Samuel looked pleased at the suggestion. "Well," he said, taking the child in his arms and gazing proudly at his namesake, "he's already got a preacher's name; so I reckon he might as well be named after a deacon too. It'll be Frederick, after my good friend Frederick Rhodes."

Upon the arrival of a third son, Jacob Manassas, in August of the following year, John began to think seriously of buying a farm of his own. They were quite crowded now in the little tenant house and needed larger quarters. Also he felt that if he were on his own, he could probably teach during the winter months to supplement the meager earnings from a farm.

After looking around he finally found a place that he considered quite suitable. It wasn't the quality of the land that made it suitable, but rather the size and the price.

"I'm afraid it's not much of a place, really," he told Bettie, "but I can get it for a little over $1,100, and will only have to pay about $500 cash. It's out on Gravelly Hill."

"Oh!" exclaimed Bettie. "Then I reckon it's—it's—"

"Yes, it's gravelly all right. It'll take years, I reckon, to clear it of rocks and stones, but it will grow a few things, I hope."

"It's all right, John," said Bettie. "If it suits you, it'll suit me. Is the house big enough?"

"Well," John hesitated, "it isn't much of a house either, come to think of it. It's bigger than this one, but pretty old and dilapidated."

"I reckon we kin manage," Bettie assured him. "Just so the roof don't leak. Is there an upstairs?"

"Ye—es," John replied, "but it's pretty rough. And I'm not too sure the roof doesn't leak. It'll take a lot of fixing up."

"Well, once we get livin' in it, we'll get it fixed. I reckon it'll soon look like a different place."

"You're a good little wife, Dear," John said, taking her in his arms. "I really shouldn't ask you to move into such a shack after what you've been used to. But don't worry. Someday you may have a good house of your own. A brand-new one, I hope."

*The fine spring air and the pleasant sunshine fill the Christian not only with the pleasure that others feel, but they cause him to praise the Giver of all good. The Christian feels thankful under all circumstances, but he feels especially thankful while enjoying special blessings.*—Diary.

# 8

It was a lovely April evening—too nice to stay inside, Bettie decided, as she cleared away the supper dishes. Slipping jackets on the little boys, she went out to the barn to help John finish the chores. Since the big move to Gravelly Hill she had been too busy to spend much time outdoors, and her fingers fairly itched to get started on a garden.

"Oh, you've finished the milkin'," she said as John started toward the house with a bucket of milk.

"Yes, I finally got it done, but I spent nearly an hour looking for that old cow. She was 'way back in the woods this time."

"Mebbe we'd better get a dog," Bettie suggested. "How's Milly doin'? Have you seen her lately?"

"No, not for several days. Likely she's back in the woods, too, somewhere."

"I don't think I ever seen a wilder heifer," laughed Bettie. "I can see her yet sailin' over the hedge the day we moved. But she'll tame one of these days."

"If she doesn't, we'll just have to make roasts out of her," John said, taking the milk into the springhouse.

"When are you agoin' to get my garden plowed?" Bettie inquired as he came out.

"Why, I think I can do it yet this evening, and maybe we can get some planting done tomorrow."

"Well, it's high time," said Bettie. "But you ain't too tired, are you, after haulin' all those rocks today?"

"Oh, I think I can do it. I got most of the stones off the garden spot today. And see that field over there by the wheat? I've got that all ready for corn."

"So that's the cornfield!" Bettie remarked. "My, the wheat's comin' up good. It looks so nice and green. And what are you agoin' to have there next to the barn?"

"More grain, I reckon," said John. "But do you know, Bettie, I've been thinking of going in more for fruit. We've got the little orchard over there that John Bell planted a few years ago, and it should have some good apples this fall. Some of the trees died, but the rest are growing well. I aim to make it a big orchard with all kinds of trees—peaches, cherries, plums, as well as a lot more apples."

"But, John, are you sure fruit will do good? There ain't much grown around here."

"I know there isn't, but I don't see why. I've been studying about it, and this climate should be all right. Of course I'd have to get the right fertilizers and learn how to prune, and all that."

"I hope you're right. It'll be nice to have lots of fruit."

"Well, we should have plenty of grapes this fall, too. Bell put in quite a big vineyard. I'll add a few new varieties to that too, I expect. I think in time fruit should pay better than grain around here. But we'll see."

"Don't you think it'll be more work though?" Bettie suggested. "If you're agoin' to start teaching this fall—"

"Oh, I don't think so. I'll manage," John replied.

Harvest was ended and most of the fall work completed when John began his first term of teaching. He had been accepted at Montezuma, a little one-room school several miles from home. He felt slightly unnerved as he started out that first morning. But the walk to school was delightful and his soul thrilled to the beauty of the purple mountains and the colorful wooded hillsides. As he entered the school, however, the immensity of the task suddenly swept over him. This time he was alone on the job and the responsibility was all his. And then came the comforting thought that he was not alone. A higher Power was directing him and would not fail him as long as he continued to seek God's help and guidance.

He was suddenly appreciative, too, for the bit of human help he had recently received. Tucked in a notebook were some precious lesson plans that his friend Lewis Heatwole had assisted in drawing up. Lewis, a son of D. A. Heatwole, was gaining quite a reputation in the teaching profession and had spent a number of evenings with John giving him helpful advice and assisting him with his curriculum.

As days went by, school became more and more interesting to John. The job meant long hours of preparation besides all the chores at home every night and morning. But the winter months passed swiftly and enjoyably. In his visits the county superintendent, Joseph

S. Loose, was both understanding and helpful, and commended his work highly.

All too soon winter was over, and by the middle of March, John had completed his first term of teaching. Although he was glad to be able to give more time to spring work on the farm, he realized more keenly than ever that his heart was much more in the teaching profession than in farming.

One evening that spring, 1875, John was surprised to see a stranger approaching on horseback. He was out examining his young apple trees when he saw him turning in the lane, and hurried to the gate to meet him.

"Good evening, sir," said the gentleman as he dismounted. "I guess I'm a stranger to you. My name is Bucher. I'm a teacher at Bridgewater."

"Oh, Dr. Bucher," exclaimed John, eagerly shaking his hand. "I'm glad to be able to meet you. Won't you please come to the house? I've been hearing something about a normal course that you're starting at Bridgewater this summer."

"Yes," said Bucher, following John across the yard, "we've been planning a short course for teachers for some time and hope to get going in June. In short, that's what I came to see you about this evening."

"Oh!" John's eyes widened in surprise and he looked questioningly at the doctor as he offered him a chair in the little living room.

"You see, I've heard your name mentioned favorably a number of times," Bucher continued slowly. "Mr. Loose gave a very good report of your work at Montezuma last year. So I thought perhaps you might be interested in the summer course we're planning."

"Interested, yes!" gulped John. "And I'd be delighted to take the course, but—"

"But you think you can't?" asked Bucher.

John shook his head regretfully. "I don't see how I could. I admit I haven't had much regular schooling. And what I did manage to learn was through private study. But I'm afraid I'll just have to keep on that way."

"Are you quite sure that a short course is impossible?" suggested Bucher quietly. "It's for only six weeks, you know, and it would be invaluable to you if you plan to continue teaching."

"Oh, I know it would be," John agreed heartily. "I expect to teach again this fall, and there's nothing I'd appreciate more than a good course in methods. It would be such a help."

"Then why not make up your mind to take it?" urged Bucher.

"For several very good reasons," John replied, carefully choosing his words. "You see I just bought this place last spring and so far have had barely enough off it to keep us in food. Besides, I have a family of four boys, the youngest only a few weeks old. My first responsibility is to them. There's a lot to do on a farm in the summer, you know, and I can't see how I could possibly get away even for a few weeks."

"I see your point," Dr. Bucher said kindly, "but I still think there must be some way you could manage. You're the kind of man that we need in our schools, and out of fairness to yourself as well as your pupils I think you should make every effort to get a little more training. As far as fees are concerned—well, forget them. Just come."

For a moment John was speechless. The words of commendation and the kind offer had taken him completely by surprise. But they also awoke a new sense of obligation toward his chosen profession.

"Thank you, Doctor, thank you," he finally murmured. "I appreciate your offer—more than I can ever express. Maybe—well, maybe by working hard mornings and evenings I could manage. Come to think of it, it is sort of in between planting and harvest times."

"Fine," said Bucher, rising and moving toward the door. "Just keep on thinking about it a while. We'll be looking for you at eight o'clock the first Monday in June."

For the rest of the evening John felt as if he were walking on air. And far into the night he lay wide-awake mentally rehearsing the surprise conversation with Bucher and reveling in an imaginary normal school course. But it was too much to hope for. The impossibility of the situation rose before him like a nightmare time and time again. With his mind in a whirl of alternate hope and despair he finally fell into a fitful sleep.

Bettie was quite sympathetic with the idea. "Of course you can do it," she said without hesitation. "Where there's a will, there's a way."

"Yes, that's a pretty saying," John said, "but think of all the work in June and July—haying, cultivating, hoeing, and even some harvesting. It—it's just impossible."

"No, John, it ain't. You must go. If you don't, you'll always be awishin' you had. This time of the year it's light early and the evenings are long. It will be hard work, but we can do it."

"That's just what I'm afraid of, Bettie—that 'we.' You can't be working outside too much this summer. With the babies to look after you have more than you can do in the house. And what will people say if I go to school and leave you at home with the work?"

"Who cares what they say!" replied Bettie stoutly. "I reckon Anna Sauers will stay to help me, and she can help outside too. So you just make up your mind you're agoin'."

Those weeks at Bridgewater Normal were sheer delight to John. He thoroughly enjoyed the lectures. Many of them opened up entirely new fields of thought to his eager mind. Psychology was fascinating.

Even the old friends, the three R's, took on new glamour as he reviewed them from a teaching angle. Eagerly he worked, taking home extra books to read as well as long assignments to be done by lamplight at the close of a long evening of work in the field. The need to buy new textbooks posed a financial problem to John—one he had not foreseen. Thinking he might be able to borrow or rent the texts, he discussed the problem with Dr. Bucher, who immediately offered him the use of any of the books in his well-stocked library.

But a much greater avenue of service also opened up before John S. Coffman that summer. Even while he was preparing to "feed the lambs," the call also came, "Feed my sheep."

Feeling the need of more ministerial help in the middle district, Bishop Samuel Coffman had asked conference for permission to ordain two new ministers that spring. The request was granted and the votes of the congregations taken. Among the twelve names presented as possible candidates was that of John Coffman.

Bettie was surprised when John told her he had received a vote. Somehow, she had never thought of him as a minister. He seemed so different from most of them.

"You're more of a teacher than a preacher, don't you think?" she suggested. "You—you don't feel you should be a preacher, do you?"

"I don't know, Bettie," John said, seating himself on a low stool beside her. "To tell the truth, I'm not quite sure how I do feel. It's been a surprise, and I haven't had much time to think about it, really. I do know that these things are in God's hands. If He wants me to be a teacher-preacher and if I'm chosen, I'll try my best to fill the place."

"Then you'll let your name stand?"

"Why not? The bishops will examine me. I don't know whether I'll pass their inspection or not. I know one of them thinks I'm getting too much education, and I reckon Brother Hildebrand remembers how I helped fight for Sunday schools. But we'll see what happens."

The date for the ordination was set for July 18, and the service was at the Bank Church that morning. Although the day was hot and the children were restless, Bettie decided to accompany John to be near him in this important hour. They had been praying very definitely about the matter and both felt entirely resigned to God's will. John wasn't surprised that his mother wasn't at church. He had heard his father tell how she had stayed at home to pray when he was ordained. So he knew that even now she was alone in her room praying that God would again accomplish His purposes in this hour of decision.

Sitting on the front bench with the other nominees, John tried to analyze his feelings as he waited for the service to begin. To be a minister of the Gospel, he realized, would require the highest type of service of which man was capable. Was he ready for it? He was a little disturbed that he felt no definite conviction about the matter. Was this a sign that God had not chosen him, or could it be that he had not prayed enough, or perhaps was not fully committed to Christian service? Maybe he had set his heart too much on teaching or planning how differently he would preach and conduct services if the lot fell to him. With a silent prayer for forgiveness and a complete surrender of his will to God, he reverently joined in the worship as the service began.

The three bishops of the Virginia Conference were present that morning—old Brother John Geil of the northern district, Jacob Hildebrand of the southern district, and Samuel Coffman, bishop of the middle district. All three took part in the service and it was during the long prayer just before the lot was taken that conviction suddenly came to John. Clear and distinct came the divine summons to serve God and the church in this special capacity. And immediately he knew that he was to be one of the two men chosen. As he rose from his knees and looked once more at the hymnbooks to be used in drawing the lot, now set up in a row on the pulpit, the awful truth dawned on him that he even knew in which book lay the slip of paper designating the one chosen. The suddenness and the seriousness of the revelation overwhelmed him for a moment, and he felt almost too weak to stand. But as he continued to commune in his heart with his Lord, he remembered the promise of divine help and felt a new strength flow through him.

One after another the candidates were asked to step forward and select a book from the row in front of them. When it was John's turn, he held back, choosing rather, because of the revelation, to wait until last. If the book was left, then he could be certain that the revelation and the call was truly of God. With outward calm but with a fast beating heart, he then walked up to the pulpit to pick up the one remaining book—the one he knew held the decisive slip. In his mind he could plainly see the words, "Brother, you have been called of God to the high office of minister of the Gospel."

As his father went down the line opening the books, looking for the slips, he found one in the book selected by Solomon Beery. The other candidates resumed their seats as their books were found empty. And then he came to his son and his face glowed while his eyes grew misty. The other slip, he realized, must be in his book. And there it was, just inside the cover. Surely God was bringing to pass His purposes in the life of his first-born.

A hush fell over the congregation as the two men knelt. Then through the laying on of the hands of the bishops they received their divine commission. In her seat Bettie wept silently. She, too, felt the burden of the responsibility which had come to her young husband.

That afternoon Father and Mother Coffman rode over to

Gravelly Hill for a visit. John wondered at the rapt, almost ecstatic expression on his mother's face as she greeted him. Humbly he bowed his head to receive the blessing of both parents.

"Now, John," Frances said, "now I can tell you what's been on my heart ever since the day you was born."

A feeling of awe came over him as he listened to the recital of that sacred experience. Added to his own experience of the morning it was just too much. An agonizing feeling of utter inadequacy once more overwhelmed him. For several long moments he sat with his head bowed in his hands, unable to say a word.

"I can't, I just can't," he whispered. finally raising his head. Beads of perspiration glistened on his forehead and his face was drawn as if in intense pain. "My name might be John, Mother, but I can never live up to it."

Frances smiled tenderly, covering his tightly clenched hand with her own. "Not of yourself, you can't, my son. It's just if you let God use you as He wants."

The words struck home. Immediately the worried lines on his face relaxed. But he shook his head as he solemnly looked at both parents. "But it—it's such an awful responsibility for an unlearned farmer like me."

"I reckon that other John didn't get too much schoolin' either out there in the wilderness," Samuel suggested thoughtfully. "But God gave him a mighty message, and he was willin' to deliver it. That's what counted."

There were other visitors, too, that afternoon—a number of friends who came to encourage him and some whom John had not expected. He soon realized, however, why these had come.

"Well, brother," said one man bent on performing his duty as soon as possible, "now that you've been ordained, I reckon you'll be givin' up this notion about schoolin'."

"You mean quit my normal school course at Bridgewater?"

"Well, yes, if that's what you call it. *'Wie gelehrter, wie verkehrter,'* you know."

"That rhymes in German," John replied, "but in English it's neither rhyme nor reason. It's wrong to think that knowledge confuses. In fact, it helps one to think more clearly. And as to the normal school, well—I made arrangements to take this course before I was ordained. Now that I am ordained I feel I need the training more than ever."

John trembled a bit when he went to church the following Sunday. A testing time had come. During the week he had given serious thought to the work of a minister. Since it was his duty now to proclaim the Word of God, certainly it was up to him to do it to the best of his ability. Why should he not put as much thought and preparation into a sermon as he would put into lessons for the children at school? How much more important to make plain the way of salvation than to explain an arithmetic problem? It would mean a break from the old way of more or less extemporaneous preaching, but he decided to do it right from the beginning.

He arrived early that morning, but as he entered the building he saw that his father and one of the other ministers were there before him. Would they ask him to take part in the service—to read the opening lesson, to pray or maybe preach? No doubt he would be called on for something. He had a brief outline of a sermon tucked in his Bible, just in case. But all the same his knees shook, and he had a sinking feeling in the region of his stomach as he thought of the possible ordeal before him.

"Well, John," Samuel said as he quietly entered the front door and hung his hat on a peg above the benches in the amen corner, "you might as well get started in this work; so we'll let you open the service and also preach this morning. I'll read the lesson."

"Very well," said John, drawing a deep breath as he followed his father into the pulpit.

John felt very self-conscious as he rose to announce the first hymn. Then amid the flutter of turning pages and clearing of throats he began to read the hymn. Immediately all sounds ceased and every eye rested on him in surprise and wonder. Not that the reading of a hymn was new, but the way he read it! "Why, it was just as if he was atalkin'," someone said later. "It was an old hymn, but it seemed almost like new. He made it mean something."

The sermon he preached was not long. He trembled at first, but he soon forgot himself; and as he warmed up to his subject, his thoughts came clearly and easily. Right from the first the congregation was wide-awake, listening attentively and expectantly. John saw appreciation expressed on many faces, but he also saw a number of frowns. He had expected this and prayed for a true spirit of love toward those who would criticize.

This service caused no small flurry in the district. Opinion was divided as to the merits of the new minister. It was the reading of the hymn that had caused the greatest offense. It showed pride. "He just wanted to show off how well he could read," some said. But others saw in it the dawning of a new day for the church in the valley. They foresaw new life and interest in the services, and looked forward to the days when young Coffman would take his turn in the pulpit.

Several weeks elapsed before John was again asked to preach. But as the summer and fall wore on, he had a number of opportunities of assisting with the opening or preaching, or giving testimony to the message of a fellow minister. He never knew, of course, when he would be asked to preach, and so usually went prepared.

One hot Sunday in August, Bettie suggested that they should all go to church again. It was a chore to take the four little boys, but she hated to ask Annie to stay home with the older ones too often. She herself had to miss services frequently.

"Well, get them ready," said John. "It's a nice day and nobody's sick; so let's go."

"But who will look after William and Samuel?" asked Bettie. "I'd ask Annie, but she likes to sit with the girls."

"Well, I can take them," John said.

"What, right up there in the pulpit?" protested Bettie.

"No, just to the front seat. I'll sit with them for a little while. They'll be good up there, and I can keep an eye on them from the pulpit. I don't think I'll be preaching, for I had it last Sunday. Maybe it'll be Sol Beery's turn. I haven't heard him preach yet."

At first four-year-old William and three-year-old Samuel F. were intrigued with the new seating arrangement. From this vantage point they had a good view of the congregation and found many interesting things to watch. Even when their father left them to take his place with the other ministers on the long pulpit bench, they didn't mind. There was still plenty to see.

As John had surmised, Beery was elected to preach that morning. In his mid-forties when he was ordained, Beery was considerably older than John and commenced his ministerial career in a more conservative manner. Copying the preaching style of some of the older ministers he spoke in a singsong fashion, frequently interjecting a long-drawn-out "ah." John was slightly amused at the surprised expression on the boys' faces as Beery began his talk. But gradually they lost interest in the droning voice and for a time gave their attention to the rhythmic fanning going on all about them. On the corner benches directly across from them even the young men were producing fans from their pockets and creating cooling breezes.

It was getting hotter and hotter in the church and the boys wiggled uncomfortably on the hard bench. Suddenly Samuel Fred began to cry. "Sh—sh," whispered William, putting his arm around him. "Don't cry. Father won't like it." Whereupon the tears flowed faster and the sobs grew louder. Finally John slipped out of his seat to try to comfort the lad.

"What's the matter, Samuel?" he asked gently, only to be answered by fresh sobs.

"Come now, dry your eyes and tell me what's wrong," he urged, pulling a handkerchief from his pocket to dry the tears.

No answer. But by now the sobs were more subdued; so John decided to take the boy with him as he returned to the bench behind the pulpit.

A few minutes later, seeing no hope of a letup, John once more turned to the lad. "Now listen, Samuel, you must tell me what's wrong," he ordered sternly. And then the answer came, one word at a time, interspersed with great heaving sobs:

"I—I'm—so—tired—of—hearing—that—man—grunt!"

Trying his best to suppress a smile, John again dried the teary eyes while he whispered the comforting words, "Never mind, he'll soon be finished." The incident left a deep impression on both father and son.

The summer of 1875 passed swiftly and busily. The six weeks of summer school came to an end, regretfully for John. It had been one of the happiest and most satisfying experiences of his life. The professors, Alcide Reichenbach and Dr. Bucher, had been very kind and helpful.

Returning the borrowed textbooks, John tried to pay Dr. Bucher a small fee for their use.

"No, Coffman, no," Bucher said, waving him away. "I don't want a cent. I take no favors from a man who gets his lessons on the plow handle while his horses are resting. I was glad to lend you those books. And if ever you can use more, just let me know."

With tears in his eyes, John turned away. He tried to thank the doctor, but there was such a lump in his throat that the words wouldn't come. Never had he received such encouragement from anyone.

That fall John looked forward with confidence and pleasure to the opening of school. He was eager to test the new theories and methods he had learned that summer. He had agreed to teach at Montezuma again, for a salary of $25 a month plus an additional monthly fee of 25¢ per pupil, to be paid by the parents.

Bettie had two men to get ready for school that first morning. William was now considered old enough to commence his formal education. Since Montezuma was outside their school district, William went with the neighbor's children to Narrow Gauge school, taught by Miss Susan Keagy.

Three more weddings in the Samuel Coffman family broke into the busy routine that fall. Anna's was the first. The man who won her affection was John S. Swartz, a cooper who had a nice little business in Rushville. A week later Jacob was married. His choice was Sarah Showalter, a pretty young Dunkard girl. Although Father Coffman regretted another marriage outside his own church, his chief concern was the spiritual welfare of his second son, who had not yet made a profession of Christianity.

Then came the marriage of one of the twins, Mary, or little Molly, as John usually thought of her. She became the bride of his fellow teacher, and good friend, Lewis Heatwole, son of David A. John was happy to attend this wedding. Lewis was a clever young man and a fine Christian. He knew it would be a happy marriage. The wedding took place on November 11, the anniversary of his own wedding, as well as that of his father and mother.

After all these festivities John settled down into the routine of teaching and farming without too many interruptions until the short break for Christmas. With the new year he again commenced making daily entries in a diary which furnish a good account of school activities:

> Jan. 3, 1876—After one week's vacation for the holidays I again return to the duties of the school room at Montezuma. Twenty-nine pupils were in attendance, three of them new ones. The pupils had sadly neglected their studies and were careless and inattentive the whole day. They were noisy and idle and showed a disposition to play rather than study.
>
> Jan. 5—Today I started the pupils in drawing pencil sketches.
>
> Jan. 13—I have the mental class divided and by that means keep up interest. The class is very critical and every word must be exactly correct. . . . The longer I teach mental arithmetic, the more I am convinced that it is an excellent thing to cultivate the memory and advance pupils in all the common branches.
>
> Jan. 17—Today I resorted to the self-reporting method to prevent communication. Quite a number reported imperfect this evening. We commenced writing in the copy books. The pupils are very particular with their copy books. They wrap them in paper and try to keep them as new. One reason is that I have offered a prize for the nicest one at the close of school.
>
> Jan. 20—This morning at eight the county superintendent of schools, Mr. Hawes, came to the school house. He took part in the religious exercise and singing. Examined the grammar class, made some commendatory remarks on the morning exercises. He witnessed a class drill in penmanship, listened to a reading by F. McKay and made some remarks on the object of education and left by 10:15.
>
> Jan. 27—Today one of the pupils refused to read. She said she could not read and that the others would laugh at her. I insisted gently and after hesitating a long time she rose, but losing confidence she again sat down. Patience was almost exhausted just then but I kept cool and insisted with determination but very gently. When she saw that I was determined and would not give up nor scold she rose and read. I dismissed two pupils from class for laughing, something I had not yet done in this school. The tune turned.
>
> Feb. 4—This morning the ground is covered with snow about three inches thick, the first snow this winter. Reports of guns were heard in all directions and number of rabbits were caught. Some of my pupils staid out of school to hunt. I held an oral examination in arithmetic and grammar and geography. Many of the pupils are interested in and love these examinations.
>
> March 9—I had a written examination in school today in grammar and arithmetic. I got some very excellent papers. I think

written examinations occasionally are very excellent helps to incite to diligence and they are a great help to composition.

Late one night John sat at the table staring moodily at a row of figures scribbled on the back of an old envelope. He had been out that evening to a meeting of the Teachers' and Patrons' Union at Rushville. Bettie, who had spent the evening with her mending basket, was still busy darning little boys' socks.

"Ain't you about done there?" yawned Bettie. "It's high time you was in bed."

"I know. I just want to finish some figuring here."

"What is it you're aworkin' at? Something for school?"

"No, it's not schoolwork. I'm just trying to figure out how much we've been spending this winter and how much we owe."

"Hm!" commented Bettie. "It's pretty bad, I reckon."

"Not too good, anyway," answered John, biting the end of his pencil. "Twenty-five dollars a month for teaching sounds pretty good, but it doesn't seem to go very far."

"Well, it's better than nothing," said Bettie. "I don't know where we would be if you didn't have the job."

"I don't know either. But I don't see how we can keep on like this unless crops are a lot better than last year."

"Well, don't worry. Like as not they will be. But what are those figures you've got there?" Bettie had laid aside her mending and stood looking over John's shoulder.

"This month's expenses," John replied, checking over the items with her. "This is what we owe Wallace Minnich for things we got at his store. I sent him this month's voucher for $25, but we still owe him about six dollars more. This $2.25 is what I paid Hiram Coffman for shoeing Duck and some other blacksmithing; and I sent three dollars to Timothy Funk for a subscription to *Harper's Weekly.* I ordered some *Harmonia Sacras* from him, too, for the singing in Augusta County, but of course I'll sell them and maybe get a little commission. But right now I'm afraid we're penniless till next month's pay, and no telling either when we can collect those school vouchers."

"Well, we can hope for the best," comforted Bettie.

"And here's a bill from John Funk at Elkhart, Indiana, for two dollars for the *Herald of Truth,"* John continued. "And I'd like to subscribe to a music magazine. I'm thinking that might be a little extravagant, though. I know I shouldn't get so many periodicals. I could save a little that way."

"And what if you could?" piped up Bettie. "It ain't much, and if you need 'em in your work, I think you should get 'em. It's part of your education and cheap at that."

"Yes, I reckon you're right," smiled John. "I know we'll get by some way, but—"

"No but's about it," stated Bettie. "Of course we'll manage. We always have a few eggs to sell and sometimes butter. That takes care of most of the store things. I got sugar and soda today for a dozen eggs. But let's get off to bed. You're tired and so am I."

"I am tired," yawned John, laying down his pencil and settling back in his chair for a good stretch. "Seems as if I'm always tired."

"How can you help but be, with all the things you're tryin' to do? First thing you know you'll be sick and won't be able to do anything."

"But what could I give up? Everything I do is important."

"All those meetings and spelling bees and things?"

"Yes, all of them. They're part of my schoolwork and are very important. The Teachers' and Patrons' Unions, and the district institutes—of course I have to be there. I'm to give a talk at the Ashby district meeting next month."

"Couldn't you have said no?"

John shook his head. "I can't refuse when I'm asked to do something like that. Besides, it helps me, personally. Like the Education Union at Bridgewater every two weeks. It's helpful, sort of like a continuation of my normal course. And I must do my part. I'm to prepare a talk for that by the end of the month on Phenomenal Geography. I'm to prove that the earth is round and travels around the sun."

"Another talk," sighed Bettie.

"I know. But I'll manage."

"Then how about giving up the singing school in Augusta? That takes too much time—the whole day every other Saturday and most of Sunday with three hours comin' and three goin'. It's just too much. Surely somebody else could do that."

"Yes, I reckon they could," John agreed. "But that's another job that's important to me. I feel it's part of my calling as a minister. A part of my service to the church. Of course I enjoy it, too, and the $40 subscription they've raised for me will help a bit with our finances. I'm sorry, though, that I have to leave you alone with the chores and all, so often. But it will be finished by spring."

"Well, let's get to bed," sighed Bettie, "or you won't be fit to teach tomorrow. It's a good thing you ain't asked to preach every Sunday, so you can get a bit of a rest now and then."

"Oh, I forgot to tell you I'm to go to Sangersville in Augusta County this Sunday. It's too bad it couldn't have been on a Sunday when I'm there for singing school anyway. But I'll be home all day on Saturday and leave early Sunday morning."

*Today was gloomy so far as the weather is concerned, but otherwise I cannot say so as we are all well and enjoying ourselves well, though for the last few months I have been laboring under a consciousness of increasing responsibilities on church matters. Responsibilities seem to increase faster than years.*—Diary.

# 9

"I think I'd better stay home today," John announced at breakfast one Sunday morning in September.

"Well, it does look like rain," Bettie said, glancing out the window. "Mebbe you'd better not venture."

"It's not just that," John said, "but there's no service at the Bank, and if I'd go 'way over to Timber Ridge, it would be so late by the time I got back."

"It generally is," commented Bettie.

"I know. But this grape season—I reckon we'll have just about as much company as we had last Sunday. And I'd hate to leave you alone."

"It would be nicer if you could be here," Bettie said wistfully. "How many did we have last week? It must've been over twenty."

"Let's see," said John, commencing to tick them off on his fingers, "there were Jake and Sally, Lewis Whitmore and wife, Switzer's four girls—"

"Wait," said William, running for his slate, "let me add them."

"Fine," said John. "Put down two two's and a four, and now go on: Jennie Miller, three of Mary Young's children and their cousin Eddie Earman, two of John Long's boys, two Earharts, two Garbers, two Wrights, Joseph Glick, and two of Roadcap's children."

"Exactly twenty-five," announced William. "My, it was fun. Will there be that many again today?"

"We don't know," replied Mother. "Uncle Wallaces said they'd be over and William Messersmiths thought they might come; so like as not there'll be a dozen for dinner. There's no tellin' how many might turn up since there's no preachin' at the Bank. I've got enough bread, I reckon, and there's a ham for slicin', but my lard is nearly all; so I only baked half a dozen pies on Friday."

"Don't worry," comforted John. "They'll all fill up on grapes."

Soon after breakfast John's brothers, Joseph and Daniel, arrived. Wallace and Lizzie came next, followed soon by the Messersmiths. While the women helped Bettie in the kitchen, the men headed for the grapery. Wallace was not only interested in the grapes but was glad for a chance to talk to his brother-in-law.

"You're planning to teach again this fall?" he asked, sampling a nice bunch of Concords.

"Yes," John replied. "I'll be at Bowman's this year. That's a little nearer home. I got my certificate again the other day; so I reckon I'm all set."

"How did you make out in the exams this year?" Wallace asked.

"Oh, tolerable!" John replied. "My best marks were in spelling and poorest in writing, much to my surprise. Ninety-eight and eighty."

"And what did you get in arithmetic?"

"Ninety, and eighty-five and eighty-six in grammar and geography."

"Not bad," Wallace declared. "Everyone is saying the exams were pretty tough."

"The hardest I've ever tried," John said. "They say they gave us the same tests the normal students had to take. I got a grade two certificate; so I'm quite pleased."

"Will you be getting more pay at Bowman's?" Wallace asked.

"No, I'm afraid not. I tried to make a better deal—30¢ per pupil plus the county wage, or a straight $35. But they voted me down until I lowered the rate to 25¢. So I reckon I won't be any better off financially, unless I have a lot more pupils."

"Well," said Wallace, helping himself to another bunch of grapes, "I reckon you won't be much worse off than most of us. Times seem to be getting harder for everybody around here, farmers and all. And when the farmers don't have cash, it certainly hits us storekeepers."

Like the Sunday before, the Coffmans had an unusual number of visitors that day, and as Bettie anticipated, most of them stayed for dinner. During the afternoon, in spite of rain, more friends arrived and between showers were able to satisfy their appetites for the sweet, juicy grapes in the little vineyard. After the last group left, John and Bettie tucked four tired little boys into their beds and finally settled down for a quiet evening of reading. Before going to bed, John wrote sleepily in his diary:

> We were at home all day. Wallace Minnich and William Messersmiths were here today and about twenty others who came for

grapes. I caught several persons, one my neighbor, in the grape patch. They dodged out and slunk away very sheepishly. I learn who of my neighbors are true gentlemen.

Before starting to teach again in October, John decided to take Annie Sauers back home for a visit with her folks in Hampshire County, West Virginia. She had been with them now for almost two years and was getting anxious to see her family again.

Since the route would take them through Hardy County, it was decided that John should help with weekend services at several places in the county. For a number of years ministers from the valley had been crossing the mountains to preach in localities where churches were scarce. Although Hardy County was usually visited by the ministers of the lower or northern district, sometimes middle district preachers were called to help. John's father was quite faithful in making the circuit of preaching points in Pendleton, Randolph, and Tucker counties, and occasionally helped in Hardy. Since this was John's first trip, it was arranged that he should be joined by Samuel Shank, who was well known to the Hardy County folks. John eagerly looked forward to the new experience. His diary tells the story of the trip:

Oct. 5, 1876—Started away from Dan'l Good with Anne Elizabeth Good and Annie Sauers at 2 o'clock. Near Armentrout's shop the bolt that holds the doubletree to the tongue broke. Stopped at the shop and got one made, 12 cents. Got to Jacob Good's after dark on account of being delayed on the road. Nellie works fine in the wagon.

Oct. 6—This morning I drove to Coote's store. Left the wagon and walked down to Uncle George Brunks and got instructions concerning the road. By request of John Good I left an appointment for preaching at the school house near his home when I return. As we drove through Brock's Gap I was struck with the grandeur of the cliff that overhangs the river on the south side, also the spar that stands a little further west. Stopped for dinner just below the forks of the Shenandoah River. Got to the Dunkard church on Lost River at 4 P.M. Went up the cove to Mr. Jenkins. They are clever [generous] people.

Oct. 7—We were well treated at the Jenkins. There was an appointment at the school house nearby. There I met Samuel Shank. The congregation was small but very attentive. Text—Matt. 22, "Thou shalt love the Lord thy God with all thy heart." Drove down Lost River to the widow Millers. We got an excellent dinner. We then drove to the Lower Cove Creek and filled the appointment at the Baptist church. The congregation was again small and attentive. Text—Luke 18:1-8, "The Unjust Judge." Went down Lost River six miles to Oliver Millers and put up for the night. We were cordially received.

> Oct. 8, Sunday—Mr. Miller's folks are clever, fine people. He is a well-to-do farmer. This morning Miller, Shank and I went to an appointment at a school house called Job's school, four miles west. Shank preached. The girls stayed at Millers and we got our dinner there. Went to an appointment at Bachman's school house. Text—Matt. 3:1-3. The congregation was large and appreciative. The people here appear intelligent and hospitable and a little more refined than in some parts of Hardy county. We went to Abram Barbs to stay all night. These are certainly Christian people.

A thirty-mile journey next day brought them to Annie's home and a joyful welcome. Annie spent three happy days with her family and friends. On the second evening there was a gay party at the Sauers home—a little too gay, John thought, and he was glad that Annie would be returning to the valley with him. He also encouraged the suggestion that her sister Martha accompany them and find employment in Virginia. Concerning the Hampshire young people he wrote:

> The young people here are very gay. They do not profess religion and their morals are not of the highest excellence. The young men seem characterized for rough and profane language. They seem to have but little conscientious scruple with regard to drinking intoxicating liquors.

Monday morning, October 16, found John back in the schoolroom with a new group of pupils to work with. Eighteen were present that first morning, some of them "bold and almost impudent." For these he prophesied "trouble." By the end of the week he summarized the situation:

> Had twenty pupils today. I am well pleased in some particulars with my school. The scholars are sociable and kind. I have one that appears to be a hard case. Some have cultivated a shockingly careless disposition in everything they go at. They have all been shamefully neglected in their writing. Their reading has been neglected also. They have been taught in arithmetic but they have little grammar.

The following Sunday, John hitched Duck to the wagon and took his family to Daniel Goods to spend the day while he and Daniel went on to Weavers Church for the morning service. It was almost time for the service to begin when they arrived, and he noticed with great uneasiness that, so far, no other minister or deacon was present. Anxiously he watched the people arriving, becoming more and more disturbed at the possibility of being left alone in the pulpit. With his mind in a whirl he walked to the little grove at the back of the church, mentally groping for a text and suitable opening passage. For a time he was too worried to think clearly. He had never been left entirely alone with a service and since he was totally unprepared he felt frightened and was suddenly seized with a dreadful nausea.

In desperation he fell to his knees and began to pray, pleading for wisdom and guidance and for someone to assist him. Then rising from his knees his mind cleared as he felt assured of God's help. Almost immediately a suitable topic came to mind and he was surprised at the ease with which an outline took shape as he slowly made his way back to the church.

He smiled with relief as he spied Preacher David Landis hanging up his hat as he came in the door. Surely, he thought, God had heard and had sent help even before he asked it. Landis opened the meeting that morning and John preached from the text, "Render unto Caesar."

The experience troubled John in spite of his renewed faith in prayer.

"You know, Bettie, sometimes I wonder whether I really am cut out for a preacher," he confided that night as they prepared for bed. "Sometimes I feel so—so unfit."

"Why, John, what makes you say that?" Bettie asked in surprise. "Most folks think you're adoin' all right."

He told her then of his morning's experience.

"Well," she comforted, "I reckon any young preacher'd feel uneasy left alone like that, 'specially if he didn't know what he was agoin' to preach about. You should always be ready, that's all."

"Yes, I know," John replied, "and I should be ashamed to let myself be caught like that. It's the second time lately, and it isn't right that I should let my other work come ahead of the Lord's work." John paced the floor as he talked, a picture of remorse.

"But you can't let it worry you," Bettie insisted. "You aren't the only one. Why, hardly any of our preachers plan their sermons, and you know it. They just get up and talk and that's all there's to it. Of course it sounds like it sometimes."

"I know," John returned, "but that doesn't excuse me. And that's what makes me feel too that I'm not much of a preacher. They can get up at a moment's notice and carry on for an hour or more. But I can't. The words just won't come."

"Well, you don't have to," consoled Bettie; "so quit worryin'. The Lord helped you today, and He'll help you get your sermons ready earlier too, if you ask Him."

* * *

Samuel Fred had the croup. In fact, the whole family had colds. But it was such an unusually warm day for February that Mother had let them play outside. Now, after supper, Sammy's cough suddenly turned to croup and he lay on the couch beside the stove fighting for his breath. The usual remedies weren't helping much, Bettie noted anxiously as she sat watching him.

"Why don't you rub his chest with linseed oil?" suggested Grandmother Heatwole, who sat rocking fretful little Fannie. "That's the best thing for croup." Grandmother had been at the Coffmans for a week now, ever since Fannie was a few days old.

"I've already rubbed him with camphor," Bettie said. "I don't know if we have any linseed in the house. I do wish John'd hurry and get back."

"If he was one of mine, I'd give him some lye and molasses. It works faster 'n anything I've ever tried, and we've had lots of croup." This from Aunt Lydia, Uncle Gabe Heatwole's wife. She and Gabe and their three children had come for a visit that afternoon, since Lydia was anxious to see Bettie and the new baby. They were all staying for the night.

"Y—you mean real lye?" stammered Bettie. "The kind we use to make soap?"

"Sure, real lye, just a little of course, boiled in with the molasses. And you'd better do it quick, the way that youngun's breathin'."

"Oh, I wish John'd come," groaned Bettie, as another fit of coughing seized the lad. "I don't like tryin' anything new like that without him here."

And just then John came in the door. He and Gabriel had been over visiting neighbor Switzer, who was ill. John was alarmed when he saw how sick Samuel was and quickly agreed to try the molasses-lye prescription. He also located some linseed oil which he carefully warmed and rubbed on the little chest.

While the children played noisily in the next room, the grown-ups sat anxiously watching the effect of the new treatment. Almost immediately, whether because of the radical concoction or in spite of it, the congested tubes began to clear and breathing became easier.

"Well, he does seem to be easier, don't he?" said Uncle Gabe, finally breaking a long silence.

"Yes, thank God," said John with a sigh of relief as he stroked the hot little forehead. "Croup is such a frightening thing."

"I know how you feel," said Gabe. "Several of ours get it bad every once in a while. This time of year is always dangerous."

"Yes, the weather's too warm to be healthy," agreed John. "I seem to hear coughs all day long, both at school and at home."

"I don't wonder Sammy has a cold with his hair cut short like that," chided Uncle Gabe. "I'm surprised you'd clip it this time of the year. That's a summer haircut."

"I know," John replied, glancing at the lad to see if he was sleeping. "I hated to do it right now, but I had to. We're having such a time trying to break him of the habit of sucking his fingers and pulling his hair. See the big bald spot here. He pulls out a couple of hairs at a time, then sits and tickles his nose with them while he sucks two fingers of his left hand. We simply can't find a way of making him quit."

"Have you tried spanking?" asked Lydia.

"We've warned him and spanked him so often that it doesn't have the least effect," sighed John. "I'm even beginning to think it makes him worse. So I thought I'd see if it won't help to keep his hair short for a while. So short he won't be able to pull it."

That night was a miserable one for John. Haggard and weary he got up at his usual hour next morning, but by the time he had finished his chores, helped look after the sick youngsters, and visited briefly with the guests at breakfast, it was quite late when he finally started off for school. His diary states:

> I had to run a great part of the way to school this morning. Uncle Gabe's were here, the children were sick, and all went slow. Had an examination, much the hardest I ever held. I still think they work very well. This evening I came by Dayton and bought a package of Simmons liver regulator, 50¢, and an ounce of camphor, 10¢. I got Switzer's mare to haul a load of wood this evening, as I am out of wood. The coupling pole split and the wagon came apart. I threw off the wood, fixed the wagon and put the wood on again, but the wagon came apart again. I only got a few sticks home. Mother went home today.

When Uncle Gabe Heatwole asked John to accompany him on a visit to Pendleton and Randolph counties in West Virginia that spring, John agreed enthusiastically. The Hardy County trip remained fresh in his memory and he couldn't shake from his mind the deep need and spiritual hunger that he saw in the faces of so many of those "attentive" listeners. Surely more effort should be made to help these people. An occasional preaching service during the spring and summer when the mountain trails were passable was far from adequate to meet the need.

"Don't you feel someone should go oftener or stay longer or do something to help those folks more?" John said, discussing the matter with Uncle Gabe. "Our ministers started this work, and they have a big responsibility toward them."

"Well, then, how about you and me making a longer stay this time? Mebbe a week or more? I reckon we could have a meetin' some place about every day."

"Maybe," said John, "but it seems to me, just being with them, talking and visiting, is just about as important as a meeting. Do you know enough places where we'd be welcome to stay?"

"Oh, there's plenty of homes," Heatwole replied, "if only we'd have some excuse to invite ourselves."

Both men sat quietly thinking for a few moments. "I have it," Heatwole said, his face lighting up in a broad smile. "Let's make it a grafting as well as a preaching trip. I promised a couple of men some grafts from a few of my good apple trees. And I reckon right smart more'd be glad of some good grafts. Let's try it."

Their saddlebags packed with tiny apple scions and grafting equipment the two men set out on Monday morning, May 14, on the trip which was to last for three weeks. Their first job was for Andrew Coffman on the South Fork of the Potomac, who had thirty-five grafts made in his little orchard. From there they worked their way down the ridge to Hammer's sawmill on Buffalo Run and over to Samuel Miller's on the North Fork.

Although they held no services until Saturday afternoon, they made arrangements to preach at a number of places on their return. At the Rhodeman home on the Seneca they were requested to hold a funeral service for Mrs. Rhodeman, who had died the previous fall. Neighbors from miles around gathered for this service. Uncle Gabe preached from a text chosen by the deceased before her death.

Every day as they traveled through Pendleton and Randolph counties they were able to pick up a job or two of grafting. Sometimes the orders were small, but many were for one hundred or more. The biggest job was for Kenny Hedrick near the cave in Harmon Hills, who ordered 148 grafts. Samuel Judy, a neighbor, had 127 grafts put on and Benjamin Day, near the Mouth of the Seneca, 126.

Crossing the border into Tucker County they secured an order for one hundred grafts from Perry Rains. Part of the time Uncle Gabe had to work alone on this job, for John took sick. However, some ginger tea Mrs. Rains made for him assisted in a speedy recovery. "Mrs. Rains is a very kind woman," his diary states, "just like a mother." There was a service that afternoon at Flannigan Hills school, and at Whitehead school next afternoon after a ride up Gandy Creek. The next day the two men went fishing and brought home some trout for Mrs. Martin Harper to fry for dinner. "Kate Harper knows how to fix things," was the comment in his diary that day. There was another meeting that day at Gandy's school.

Other preaching appointments on the trip were at Roaring school, Brushy Run Church, Farises (or Phares) school, Sites school, Hedrick's school, Cave schoolhouse in the Harmon Hills, Hammer's school, Pleasant Grove, Dickenson's school, and Davises school.

Concerning the service at Davises school on Sunday, June 3, John wrote in his diary:

> This was the largest congregation we had on this trip. Had good singing and interesting meeting. Text—Rom. 8:28, "And we know that all things work together for good to them that love God.
>
> June 4—At Davises on the Fork last night. Crossed the mountain and got dinner at Jos. Heltsels. Got home at five. All well, thank God. Uncle Gabe paid me $7.50 for helping to graft. Expenses on the trip 25¢ for cordial, 10¢ for peppermint, 25¢ for horse feed, 15¢ for sugar.

An interesting bit of news that John heard when he arrived

home was that John F. Funk of Elkhart, Indiana, would be arriving in a few weeks to visit the Virginia churches. Funk was the editor of the *Herald of Truth,* the leading Mennonite periodical of that time. John was delighted at the prospect of meeting this man whom he considered probably the most influential leader in the church. Through his articles and editorials as well as through personal correspondence he had come to appreciate the qualities and the earnest zeal of this editor-publisher who was blazing the trail toward more aggressive church work.

John occasionally contributed an article to the *Herald.* He well remembered the day he sent in his first manuscript. It was an essay on teaching and represented many hours of writing, revising, and recopying. Funk had not only accepted it, but asked for more. And now he was to meet the editor face to face.

John was not disappointed in the man whom he welcomed into his home that June afternoon. Although Funk was not tall, John suddenly felt small in his presence. His square, stocky frame seemed to emanate physical strength, while his high, broad forehead and sharp brown eyes revealed the vigor of mind and spirit which John had come to respect. As he studied his visitor, John noticed, too, a determined chin and jaw line which a short dark beard and side whiskers failed to hide.

Funk was accompanied by his wife and two little daughters, Martha and Phoebe. While the women visited and the children shyly got acquainted, the two men talked business. Funk wanted more articles for the *Herald of Truth* and to encourage more effort he offered John some remuneration. It was arranged that for each article he wrote John would be allowed to secure one new subscriber for the paper and keep the payment for a year's subscription. This would benefit both the writer and the publisher.

Later that afternoon John hitched Duck to the wagon to take his guests and Bettie to the home of Aunt Peggy Rhodes for supper. Annie was left alone with the boys.

"Come on, boys. Let's climb up in the ash hopper and see how long we can see the wagon," said William, starting the climb as the wagon with Father and Mother and the visitors started down the road. Samuel Fred and Jacob were soon up beside him, with little Ansel right behind.

But the ash hopper was also the place where Father stored the scythe to keep it out of reach of little hands and feet. And very soon the inevitable happened. Ansel stepped on the sharp blade and cut his foot.

Seeing how badly it was cut, Annie sent William to Switzer's for help. Chewing tobacco was the remedy Mr. Switzer recommended to stop the bleeding, and a good quantity was found under the bandages when John and Bettie dressed the wound that night.

Accident-prone Ansel gave his parents plenty of opportunity to try out their stock of home cures. Several months before this he inadvertently took a drink of lye that Bettie had left standing in a cup while stirring up a batch of soap. He was badly nauseated and his mouth was burned, but he obtained prompt relief in the form of a big piece of nice fat bacon.

Another time when he burned himself by backing too close to the stove on a chilly morning while getting dressed, his mother applied coal oil and covered the burned area with a plaster of bread dough snatched quickly from the pan of dough placed near the stove to rise. A nasty jagged cut on his cheek dealt by William's new little hatchet might have healed without a scar. But Father's skill with court plaster was severely tested when the job had to be redone several days later after the lad ran into a corner of the table.

* * *

Crops were poor that summer, 1877. John's hopes had been high in the spring. He had worked hard in his young orchard, describing his work in his diary:

> This morning I grafted four cherry trees, two with Napoleon Bigareaux, one a dark red, very early, one light red, also early. Grafted the apple tree in the hollow south west of the barn with Grimes Golden below, Nickajack higher up, White Horse on top. Put braces in the forks of two young apple trees with the intent they should grow fast at each end and form a living brace. Grafted four apple trees and four grapevines for Switzer. . . . Made a diagram of the orchard on map paper. I took pains to get it correct with all the names of the trees in their proper places. There are 180 trees in the orchard. There are three sets of trees; John Bell had planted 65 eight or nine years ago. Forty are left and some of them scrubby. Last November, two years ago, I got 103 trees of Jones from the Richmond nursery, 20¢ a piece. Ninety-six are growing. This spring I am filling the orchard with trees from Abram Wenger's nursery, 12¢ a tree.

Then it was time to plant potatoes. He tried two varieties, Peach Bloes and Early Rose. In spite of fertilizers that he tried, he sadly reported in July, "The yield is very poor."

With his corn too, he tried different varieties of fertilizers, sprinkling ashes on some hills and using hen manure on other sections. Reporting on his corn in July he wrote:

> I know that I will get no large crop. If I get some I will be glad for it. If I get but little I will be thankful for it. And if I get none I will try to be satisfied.

The wheat crop was also light. "The poorest I have yet raised since I live here." And out of the little he harvested he had to pay back quite a bit to his neighbors and to his father, for he had been forced to borrow early in the spring to keep his family in food.

Even the grapes were poor that year. As a result, John made a decision which he had been contemplating for some time:

> Oct. 2, 1877—This morning I took the plowshare to the shop and got it sharpened, borrowed a horse of Fishback and plowed in the grape patch. I am plowing out the grape vines and intend sowing it in wheat. The grapes did not do well this year. I plow them out for two reasons—1st, they are ill arranged in the order of planting. Every second row are Isabella. They are worthless. 2nd, the patch is too far from the house and very many are taken for which I get no thanks. Noah Grabill [a cousin from Illinois] helped all day.

One bright spot in the discouraging summer was a visit from a school official in nearby Dayton who called to offer him a position as teacher for the intermediate grades. His salary would be $36 per month. The offer was tempting, but John could not accept it since it would require too much time traveling to and from school each day. But at the school meeting at Bowman's several weeks later John told of the offer he had received and promised to remain at Bowman's for the same salary. Telling about the meeting in his diary later, he wrote:

> All the patrons agreed to pay it except three. One of them did not send last year, one did not pay last year and the other did not want me to teach anyway. I went away with the understanding that I am employed. It was a tight meeting. Some sharp remarks.

Harvesting was about finished by the time school commenced. Annie helped, and even the three older boys, aged four, five, and six, were furnished with corn choppers and manfully worked a day or two helping to cut corn. To hire an extra hand that season was quite out of the question.

That year at Bowman's was to be John's last in the teaching profession. He found he could neither keep up the pace nor do justice to either teaching, preaching, or farming. During the winter he was troubled considerably with nagging pains which he described as cramp cholic. In January he wrote in his diary:

> I was unwell and the pupils said I was cross and out of humor all day. I think I am better this evening. I have staid up late correcting examination papers.

In trying to get at the root of his trouble John finally analyzed the situation as follows:

> Feb. 4, 1878—I was sick all day. I think I am dispeptic. I am low spirited and my digestion is sadly deranged. I think a number of causes combine to make me as I am. Probably I have been careless in my diet by eating too much at improper times, and too hastily dispatching my meals to go to work or study. And I may have been exercising too violently at times and too soon after eating. And I think teaching school is very unhealthy

for me as it gives me too much to do in connection with my other work. I have my family to see after, my affairs about home, my singing class, my school, all in connection with my ministerial labors. The result is overwork, no rest, disturbed sleep and hasty eating. Enough, I think, to make anyone sick. I feel it is high time to make arrangements that will suit me better.

That summer he made the decision to give up teaching in favor of better farming and more time for his work as a minister. His diary records his decision:

Sept. 5—I am taking particular pains this fall to put out my wheat crop well, more than I have since I live here. Heretofore I have been teaching every winter to the neglect of the farm. I see that it does not pay, so I am going to do my best to make farming pay. I cannot be much worse off not to teach than I am so.

More and more that winter John found himself becoming involved in the work of the church. Usually it was John who was asked to fill the appointments at one of the more distant churches. And as time went on, he was more frequently "pressed" into "taking the text," when several ministers were present. Regularly he made the rounds of the congregations in the valley, preaching at the Bank, Weavers, Pike, Timber Ridge, Mount Pleasant, Franklin, Stonewall school, Sangersville, Brock's Gap, Hildebrand's, Singers Glen, Mount Clinton, Brenneman's, St. Johns, Wilbourn school, Mount Carmel school, Trissels, and Fairview school.

He also maintained his interest in good church music and conducted a successful singing school at the Pike Church during the winter of 1877 and '78:

Dec. 22—Started to the Pike to meet my appointment for singing at one o'clock. Took my blackboard along and gave a lesson on it. We had a nice singing but only a few boys were there. The consequence was a poor bass. Got my supper at the widow Shoemakers. Then the young folks and I went to the Pike again for the night session. Had an excellent singing, about the best I ever had.

His interest in music resulted in another job that winter, helping to select English hymns to replace the German section in the hymnbook, *Psalms and Hymns*. This was the hymnbook used in most Mennonite communities at that time. The last edition contained 402 English hymns and an appendix of 37 in the German language. A new edition was proposed with only English hymns in the appendix. John met with a committee on New Year's Day to help with the job of selecting suitable hymns:

Jan. 1, 1878—This morning Samuel and Michael Shank and myself went to John Geils according to appointment, to arrange and select hymns to put in the place of the former German hymns in our hymn book. We were appointed a committee for this purpose. All the brethren and sisters who desired were requested to send in their selections which the committee was to examine and select from. We got to the work about 9 o'clock and continued busily until dark. We have not yet selected hymns enough though we worked together harmoniously and kept on busily. There was some sharp arguing and pleasant conversing.

But along with increased responsibility in church affairs came spiritual growth and development which continued all through life. Like the John of old he was conscious of his total dependence on God and early in his ministry began to learn the value of prayer. On Jan. 28 he confided in his diary:

Of late I have been much encouraged in my devotion, especially in prayer. I feel sure that God has answered my prayers on several occasions. I still pray that my faith in prayer may be increased.

*While at church today my soul became heavy with sorrow for the poor wayward sinners, especially for some special ones, and with this sorrow came a determination to continue in fervent prayer in their behalf.*—Diary.

# 10

"All right, boys, all hands on the job," called Father, coming from the barn with a bucket of corn and a big handful of horsehair. Quickly the children scrambled to their places around the kitchen table, ready for the mysterious job Father had promised.

"Now here's what I want you to do," he said, taking a darning needle from Mother and threading it with a horsehair; "you just push it through the corn—it's been soaked, so it's nice and soft—and then you tie a knot in the hair and cut it off about a foot below the knot. Now see how many you can fix like that before bedtime."

"But why? What's it for?" William asked as he threaded his needle. "It won't make the corn grow any better, will it?"

"No," replied Father, "this corn isn't going to be planted. We're going to feed it to the crows so they won't bother pulling up what we've planted."

"But what's the hair for?" Samuel Fred asked wonderingly.

"Well, you see, they won't be able to swallow it; so it will be left hanging out of their beaks. Switzer says it'll bother them so much they won't want any more for a while."

"What about that mess you fixed for 'em the other day?" asked Mother. "Didn't it do no good?"

"No, I'm afraid not," sighed John. "They seemed to like pepper with their corn. Reckon I'll have to find something stronger if these hairs don't discourage them."

Apparently the horsehair was not as effective as John had hoped. Four days later he wrote in his diary:

> June 1, 1878—Plowed corn all day. William replanted while I was plowing where the crows have pulled up the corn. I am much discouraged with my corn. The crows have pulled up much the greater part of it and are still vigorously pulling. They pulled up a large quantity while I was gone to supper. This evening I dug some may apple root, boiled it and soaked corn in the decoction. They say it makes the crows sick when they eat corn thus prepared.

In desperation he went for Fishback's gun one day, and eventually succeeded in getting a bird to hang from the homemade rope he stretched across the field. With great satisfaction he reported:

> June 5, 1878—Today is the first time that the crows appear scary and seem inclined to leave the corn alone.

The following winter John discovered the base camp of these marauders, a woods on a bluff of Dry River; "The crows came by in myriads," he wrote in his diary. "I can't think there were less than 100,000 in the woods this evening." (Feb. 25, 1879.) Against such odds he realized his defensive tactics had been feeble, indeed. Surely God had a hand in helping to save his little crop.

Almost as bad as the crows were neighbor Haney's hogs:

> June 12, 1878—Went early to look if the hogs were in the wheat again. They had been in yesterday and got in again today. They did thresh it down shameful. Five large hogs of Haneys have been getting in for four or five days. I went to see if they would not pen them up for a while. They said they would. I hope to have no more trouble with them.

In spite of these adversities he managed to harvest sixty-four bushels of wheat that year, as well as a fair crop of corn. The potatoes, however, again turned out "poorly."

Since he had decided to put all his efforts into making farming pay, he commenced experimenting that fall with commercial fertilizers, ordering a half ton of a ready-mixed variety, "Pleasant Valley," from Earman and a half ton of chemicals from Wallace Minnich which he mixed himself and named "Dale Enterprise." On a third test plot he applied "British mixture." "It remains to see which will do best," he wrote after sowing eight acres of wheat and one of rye.

Ever since Noah Grabill's visit the previous fall, 1877, John found himself frequently thinking of his conversation with the young man from Illinois. Noah and John were second cousins.

"Why don't you quit trying to farm this stone pile?" he said as he helped to plow out the grapes. "You could sell this farm and buy a hundred acres of good land in Illinois for what you'd get out of it."

"You really think I could?" John looked interested.

"I know you could," Noah replied. "And it's wonderful land, I'm tellin' you. But you better do it soon. Land's being took up fast out there. We've got several families from Virginia out there and they're doin' real good."

"I know," John replied. "Cousin Susan Heckleman was back this spring and tried to persuade me to move out. But there's more than farming to think of. I've a big responsibility here as a minister, and the Lord's work comes first, you know."

"Right," Noah agreed. "And that's exactly why you should come to Illinois. We need a minister bad. We could have a real good congregation back home, if we had a preacher. Here you've got lots, sometimes three and four at one meeting. It'd only be right, I think, to share with some of us."

John hardly knew how to answer this. Unquestionably there was a real need in Illinois, and a field of service for someone. Possibly he could accomplish more for Christ and the church by going out there. Although he did not consider the proposition too seriously at the time, the idea took root and was the subject of much prayerful thought.

As he grubbed away in his stony fields, he frequently envisioned a hundred acres of rich, fertile land, and a glint came in his eye as he pictured the golden wheat fields and acres of tall corn. Surely it wasn't wrong to dream of a farm like that if at the same time he envisioned the opportunity for greater Christian service.

Grabill had seen the glint in his eyes, and he sensed an interest in his proposal. And so on his return to Illinois he tried to maintain this interest through a persistent correspondence. One letter reached John about a month after his departure, dated December 19, 1877.

"Well, what does he say?" Bettie asked as John finished reading the letter.

"He says the folks are all well and that they're having some real winter weather out there."

"Is that all?"

"No—o," John replied cautiously. "He still thinks we should move out there. In fact, he practically insists it's my Christian duty to come, and if I can't sell the farm he suggests we come anyway for a year and see how we like it."

"Well!" exclaimed Bettie. "Well!" Then drawing a deep breath, "Who does he think he is, anyway, tellin' you what you should do? You ain't athinkin' about it, are you? I thought you'd given it up."

"To tell the truth, Dear, I'm afraid it has been on my mind. Just a little, of course."

"But—but it's so far away," Bettie sputtered. "A way out in the sticks. It don't seem right to go so far with the children and all, and no tellin' what might happen. This is your home. You've got your church and your farm here, and this is where you belong."

With a sigh John tried to put the matter out of his mind. Bettie didn't usually make such long speeches, and he could feel that she was strongly opposed to the idea of going west. That night he wrote in his diary:

> Got a letter from Noah Grabill. He insisted that I must move out for a year anyhow. I would go if Bettie would consent to go with me.

In spite of the discouraging tone of John's replies, Grabill kept up the correspondence all through the following spring and summer. He tried hard to impress John with their need for a minister, finally urging him to at least visit the country. In one letter he enthusiastically invited him to make the trip at the expense of the Livingston County brethren. The offer was very generous and John, who had been longing to see the West and visit other churches outside the valley, resolved to make use of the unusual opportunity. Happily he made plans to start out as soon as the fall work was finished.

But a few weeks later came another letter from Grabill stating that he had been a bit hasty in his offer of full expense. He was sure, however, that the people would be liberal and would no doubt meet most of his expenses. John's heart sank as he read this letter. He had been looking forward to this trip so eagerly. Maybe he should have faith enough to go anyway. But where would he get enough money for a ticket?

This was one time he didn't get the usual comfort and encouragement from Bettie.

"I know you want to go bad," she said, "but we ain't got enough even to buy a ticket to Pennsylvania, say nothin' of the West. And we need so many things right now. Every last one of us need shoes. And with three boys in school this winter, I just don't see how we're agoin' to keep 'em in clothes."

"If they'd only give me my school money for last year!" moaned John. "I still have nearly $80 coming to me. That would be a big help. Surely I'll get it sometime this fall."

"Mebbe, but you can't be sure," Bettie warned. "And our butter and egg money don't go far with butter at eight cents a pound. Even bacon's only five and six cents. I don't know what's goin' to happen to the farmers."

"Maybe the price of corn and wheat will stay up," John suggested hopefully. "A dollar a bushel is pretty good for wheat and they say corn is 65¢. I only wish I had more of it to sell. But I suppose I'd better forget the trip. In a way it will be a relief not to go."

Instead of buying a ticket to Illinois, John rode up to Dale Enterprise next day and bought shoes—shoes for himself, for Bettie, the four boys, and his baby daughter. There was great excitement that evening when he arrived home with his big parcel and the boys discovered the new boots. Soon a parade formed, with William taking the lead and little Fannie toddling in the rear. Mother in her new calfskins and Father in his heavy high-tops reviewed the parade as it marched into the living room and circled back around the table in the kitchen. They watched closely for the least sign of discomfort.

"Are you sure yours feel all right, Jake? They don't pinch anywhere?" asked Father.

"Oh, no, they're just right," replied Jake.

"And yours, Sammy? You're sure they're not a bit short?"

"No, my toes have lots of room. They don't hurt a bit."

"William, yours look just a bit large. Don't they feel too loose?"

"N—no, Father. I—I don't think so," hedged William. "But of course they're bigger 'n my old ones."

"Come here and let me look at them."

Reluctantly William submitted to the inspection.

"I'm afraid they're a whole size too large," Father said firmly. But seeing the disappointed look he quickly added, "If you take them off right away, I'll let you ride Duck over to the store tomorrow to get another pair yourself."

His entry in the diary for that day reads:

> Oct. 7, 1878—Got a pair of calf skin shoes of Father for Bettie, $2.50. Went to Dale Enterprise and bought boots for myself, $4.50; a pair for William, $2.50; a pair for Samuel and Jacob each $1.75; and shoes for Ansel and Fannie, $1.00. So the family is shod new and it cost $15. There was great rejoicing among the boys over their new boots. A time long to be remembered.

Clad in their second-best suits and the new shoes which had been well greased the night before, William, Samuel Fred, and Jacob were seated under a big umbrella on the floor of the wagon a few weeks later, on the way to school. It was a new experience for six-year-old Samuel F. and five-year-old Jacob. But William at the age of seven was a veteran. He already had three years of schooling behind him. In spite of his assertions that there was nothing to be afraid of, the two younger boys were apprehensive. Samuel picked away at the side of his head trying hard to find a hair to pull, but Father had again clipped his hair close to his head, leaving him only the consolation of sucking his fingers. Jacob, who was of less nervous temperament, sat stolidly in his corner of the wagon watching the rain splash in the mud holes and saying very little.

"Do you think the teacher will be cross?" Samuel F. queried as Father turned Duck into the school lane.

"Humph! what if he is," said William, scrambling to his feet. And away he went over the side of the wagon to join his pals crowded in the doorway.

But Father had heard the anxious question, and remembering his first experience at school he replied gently, "If you're good and do what he tells you, he won't need to be cross with you, Samuel. And, Jacob, speak right up when he asks you a question."

John remained at school for a little while to learn what he could about the man who was to instruct his children.

> Glick has 30 pupils this week. . . . He has a variety of methods to conduct his exercises which I like very much. He don't know just how in some cases as an experienced teacher would. . . . Went for the boys again tonight. Jacob has not yet recited. Lewis Heatwole and Mary came on a visit this evening. Mary brought each of the boys a calico shirt.

In a few days Samuel Fred's greatest fears were realized. The new teacher relied strongly on his birch switch, and it was a sorry-looking Samuel who came home one evening with a tale of a flogging.

"He was sticking pages together in his reader," explained William.

"With paste?" Father asked, astonished.

"No, I—I just stuck 'em together with little pieces of paper that I wet on my tongue. They didn't really stick," sobbed the future bookbinder.

* * *

Interest in the trip west was renewed later that fall when John learned of an excursion to Ohio that Peter Hartman was trying to arrange with the railway company. If he got cheap rates to Ohio, he figured, no doubt he could manage somehow to get to Illinois. And then one day when he received the promise of a $35 loan for the trip, he finally made up his mind he would go, and wrote to his friends accordingly.

He waited hopefully for excursion plans to materialize, but when they were still indefinite by the first of November he decided to wait no longer. In town one day he bought a ticket to Peoria, Illinois, emigrant fare for $13.95. He decided to leave on Thursday morning, November 7.

Meantime there was much to be done—butchering, husking corn, chopping wood, and fixing up the barn for cold weather. He couldn't leave without making sure that his family would have enough to eat and enough wood to keep them warm while he was away. Neighbors Switzer and John Hill promised to look after his chores.

It was noon on Thursday when John boarded the train at Harrisonburg. As the engine puffed away from the depot, he thought again of that other time he had left home by train—a wagon train. Then he had been forced by circumstances to leave. This time he was leaving by choice. Or was he? Was there not, after all, some compelling force drawing him toward an unknown destiny? With a flash of insight he suddenly knew that this journey was to be more than a sight-seeing trip or a friendly visit to old friends, that somehow his future depended on it. As the train gathered speed and familiar scenery rushed past his window, his heart was deeply stirred. "I will lift up mine eyes unto the hills, from whence cometh my help," he quoted softly to himself, raising his eyes toward the towering peaks and breathing a prayer for this help and divine guidance.

Two nights and a day on the train brought him to Ipava, Illinois, where there was a little colony of Mennonites:

> Got to Cincinnati after dark. Regret very much that I cannot see the city on account of the dark, nor Indianapolis for the same reason. Slept till nearly day. Looked up at times and could see by the light of the moon that the country was beautiful and level. Got to Ipava at 3 o'clock. Walked to Boyers, where I was kindly received by sister Boyer and the whole family as they came in.

Here, as in Livingston County, where Noah Grabill lived, he learned, there were enough Mennonite families to establish a congregation if they had a minister. On Sunday morning Mr. Boyer took John to Summium to the home of an influential member, John Shank. Then in the afternoon they met at the Reformed Church for a service. It was a rainy day and the congregation was small, but John preached with a great deal of feeling on the all-important subject of conversion. He remained with them several days, holding services in the Washington school near Boyers.

At Canton, Illinois, where he arrived after dark on Wednesday evening, John looked around for Emmanuel Hartman. But Hartman had failed to receive his note and no one was at the depot to meet him. On inquiring about Mennonites he was directed to the home of Peter Stuckey. This meant a mile walk down a dark, lonely country road, but he received a warm welcome from Stuckey, a minister in a branch of the Amish Church known as the Stuckey Amish. Next morning the good brother took him out to the Hartmans and arrangements were soon made for a meeting at the church that evening.

John had no fears of being stranded when he stepped from the train at Chatsworth, Illinois, next day. This was Noah Grabill's community. Noah would be there.

> Nov. 15, 1878—Got to Chatsworth at 11:45 where I met Noah Grabill. He backed against the depot so I should not see him, but I knew him so soon as I saw him though he has a heavy beard but was shaved when I saw him last. Came to Isaac Harshbergers.

Driving out over the rough country road to the Harshbergers, John tried to feel enthusiastic about this wonderful new country. Grabill was in a jovial mood, pointing out to his guest everything that could possibly be of interest. But it was November, and under the thick blanket of threatening, gray clouds the wide stretches of fertile fields were bleak and forbidding. No friendly little hillock or protective mountain appeared on the horizon to relieve the awesome expanse. Suddenly Bettie and the children seemed very, very far away.

"Well, what do you think of our country?" Grabill asked as they approached the Harshberger homestead.

"It's pretty hard to judge at this time of the year," John answered. "But there seems to be an awful lot of elbow room out here. I reckon I miss our mountains just a little."

For the next few days the gloomy weather continued, dull, rainy, and cool. On Sunday evening he confided in his diary:

> Nov. 17—Cool and damp. Did not see the sun since Friday evening. The weather is so gloomy that I cannot take a good impression of the country.

In spite of the weather, John enjoyed his visit in this community. The people were friendly and took a keen interest in the services he held each evening in the schoolhouses of the district, Hartman's, Hack's, and Longmyer's. A deep evangelistic theme ran through the entire series of talks, for he sensed the great spiritual need of this leaderless group. "The Wages of Sin," "Excuses," "Conversion," "Only One Way," some of the topics selected.

> Nov. 19—I was well treated by all that met me in Livingston. All the brethren and sisters seemed interested and helped me liberally. They made many requests that I should move out here and made excellent offers. I never met more attentive congregations. Many outsiders seemed interested. I feel sad to part with the friends I became acquainted with. The country has many advantages and disadvantages.

John made himself fairly comfortable on the car seats that night as the train sped eastward toward Indiana. But it was hard to get to sleep. His body was tired, but his mind kept working, weighing over and over again the advantages and disadvantages of Livingston County, Illinois. It was a good country, he had to admit it. The families settled there were prospering and felt there was a future for the Illinois farmer. But he was not so much interested in the land as in the people. As a minister their need weighed heavily on his conscience and somehow he felt a sense of responsibility toward them. Could it be that God was calling him to Illinois? Although he wasn't sure, he did realize that he had come to a place of decision, and that he could never again be quite satisfied with his limited sphere of service in the Shenandoah Valley. Compared with this country, the people there were well supplied with ministers. He must somehow make Bettie conscious of these greater needs. Before falling asleep he again laid the problem before his Master, asking for definite guidance and a clear manifestation of God's will.

On his arrival at New Paris, Indiana, next morning, John walked five miles to the home of his cousins, Mary Ann and Amos Blosser, near Nappanee. In this community he enjoyed a visit with a number of relatives and former Virginia friends, but the high light of the trip to Indiana was his visit to John F. Funk's publishing house at Elkhart.

> Nov. 21, 1878—Stopped at the book store of John F. Funk. He soon brought us around to his home where I wrote a while.

Wrote a letter home. This evening I had a pleasant time with the brethren and sisters at Brother Funk's. We had a little service at his house. Quite a number gathered in. Bro. Funk was all life and was in the highest humor for talk. Staid till after midnight.

The next morning Funk took John on a tour of his printing establishment. It was interesting to watch the typesetters at work and to see the printed sheets of the *Herald of Truth* coming off the press. The book-binding department was equally fascinating, also the mailing department where stacks of *Family Almanacs* were being wrapped for shipping and copies of the *Words of Cheer* were being sent out. It was all most impressive.

"You know, I had no idea of the amount of work you did here," John said as he followed Funk into his office to settle the accounts of a number of Virginia friends. "This is a wonderful thing for the church."

"Well," said Funk, "we do what we can. But I feel this is only the beginning of something that's bound to grow. More and more of our people are beginning to see the need of good literature, I think. Anyway our subscription lists are getting longer and we seem to be getting busier every day."

"Good," John replied. "Just keep it up, brother. I want you to know that a lot of us really appreciate what you're doing."

"But there's one thing about it," Funk said. "It's getting hard to find the kind of help we need. Right now I could use someone to help with the *Herald*. He'd have to have some literary ability of course, as well as Bible knowledge and interest in church work. You wouldn't have anyone to suggest?"

"Why, no, not off hand," John replied thoughtfully. "But I'll keep it in mind. Maybe I'll think of someone."

"What about yourself?"

John gasped. Uttered in Funk's deep throaty voice and with his eyes searching his very soul, the question had a startling effect on John. He could feel the color rushing to his face and without realizing what he was doing he rose from his chair and started pacing the floor.

"I—I must admit I had never thought about it," he stammered. "It would be interesting work, but—but—"

"Well, think about it," Funk ordered curtly. "No need to make up your mind right now, but think it over and let me know. You wouldn't make a fortune here, but at least we wouldn't let you starve."

Although he was surprised and no doubt slightly elated that Funk should consider him capable of being an editorial assistant, John lightly dismissed the suggestion after a little thought. He went to bed early that night out in the country at cousin John H. Christophels, and he thought it all out before he went to sleep. No, he had neither the training nor the experience for that type of work.

The job wasn't for him. True, he had written a little, but each article of his in the *Herald of Truth* represented hours of hard work. No, he was a farmer or a teacher, but first of all a minister. And if he made a change, surely first consideration should be given to that pastorless congregation in Illinois. But he would discuss the matter with Bettie and let her help to decide. Maybe she wouldn't mind quite so much coming as far west as Indiana with so many relatives and Virginia friends here. But this was God's work, he decided, and the decision should be His.

On Sunday, John preached three times, at Holdeman's in the morning, Yellow Creek in the afternoon, and at Elkhart in the evening.

John's next stop was in Ohio. Arriving at the home of C. B. Brenneman in Elida, he was surprised to find another guest, Samuel Shank, his fellow traveler of the first West Virginia expedition. Shank had arrived a few days earlier to visit the churches and families that had moved there from Virginia. The two remained in Allen County for a week, and conducted services each evening at Sherrick's and Good's meetinghouses.

Stopping briefly at Orrville the following Monday, the two ministers went on to Pittsburgh, where they boarded the steamer, the *John Snowden,* for the next leg of their journey:

> Dec. 4—We had a good time on the boat. Sat up till 9 o'clock. Then we retired to our bunks and slept by spells till 5 o'clock when we were wakened to get ready for landing. We were let off into the dark. A man that got off showed us the way, partly, to Masontown. Got to Bro. Nicholas Johnsons where we put up for the night. This is a rolling country with plenty of lumber and immense quantities of coal.

Five days were spent at Masontown, with a preaching service at the church each evening. The congregation here, John decided, was a bit different from any he had found so far in his travels. There were two ministers, John Durr, whom he described as a "fine young man, 25 years old," and "a bishop in the church for several years already." The other was Christian Deffenbaugh, "a nice young man, but he is rather stylish and seems rather discouraged in his work."

Commenting on the services and the congregation John wrote:

> Dec. 5—There was a fair congregation, mostly young folks. They sing well but too fast for church and the tunes are rather lively for church use.
>
> Dec. 8, Sunday—The brethren and sisters in Fayette county are kind and sociable but they are not well conformed in general to the forms of the church. Their ways and manners of dress are not as we would like to see them. We hope it may still improve in this respect. In parting from them many of them expressed their thanks for our visit and their regret at parting

> and their satisfaction with our work. I feel interested for the church here.

An hour's ride on the train brought the pair to another Mennonite settlement of Southwestern Pennsylvania, Scottdale.

> Found Bro. Loucks directly. He lives on the edge of town. He is well fixed. We went to Bro. Abraham Overholts and from there to the widow of Bishop John D. Overholt. Went to an appointment at Scottdale in town. A nice congregation.

Arriving at the home of Christian Livengood in Meyersdale next day they learned that once more a notice of their arrival had not reached its destination. Consequently no service was at this place.

Continuing their tour of Pennsylvania they spent several days at Thompsontown, holding services at the "Crossroads," at the "Brick" Church, and at a schoolhouse near Richfield, and on Sunday evening at the Delaware Church near Salem.

In Cumberland County, where they spent three days, John was happy to meet so many of his old friends of the Civil War days. It was almost like a home-coming. But there were changes here, too, in the fourteen years that had elapsed, especially in the Zimmerman household where he had lived. Preacher Samuel Zimmerman no longer filled his accustomed place, and the farm was now operated by Samuel, Jr. Little Sarah was now a young lady, and Leah had married Edward Shope. John visited them in their home.

After a service at the Slate Hill Church on Tuesday morning, John wrote in his diary:

> Samuel took me to church. There were a number of folks there that I had been acquainted with when I was there before. I can tell no one how I felt on meeting them. There was no large congregation there. Took my text, Luke 14:16, Excuses. Samuel Shank followed and closed.

The final visit of the trip was in the vicinity of Maugansville, Maryland. Here John was again in a well-known community and his mind went back to the other time when he had arrived there, a shy, homesick lad of sixteen. He visited the Peter Eschleman's where Peter Hartman had worked, and also his friends, Samuel Horsts.

> On Saturday morning there was a service at Whitmer's Church: The weather being so inclement there were not so many people there. I felt much embarrassed at that place because I knew that we were watched. The congregation was attentive.
>
> Sunday, Dec. 22—This morning the snow is four inches deep with a crust of ice over it. Br. Daniel Roth hitched into a trotting buggy for Samuel and me. We went to the appointment at Clearspring church. There were not many there on account of the cold weather. . . . Afternoon we went to an appointment at Pinesburg school. . . . We think our visit is now finished.

*The triumphs of a Christian faith are to overcome doubts; to believe and realize that God does really answer prayers and that we have faith now to pray, believing for what we had not sufficient faith in time past. The Christian may enter new fields continually, and tread into a sacred nearness to God by faith where his weakness and doubts once would not permit him to stand.*—Diary.

# 11

The drive from Dale Enterprise to Gravelly Hill seemed unusually long that evening, but it was made in record time as John urged Duck into a brisk trot. Annie and William had met him at Dale after his tramp through the snow from Harrisonburg. As the graying skies deepened into the purplish gray of night, William began to count the stars. But to John the friendly lights shining through uncurtained windows had a much stronger appeal than stars. Soon he would see the twinkling lights of his own little house. Soon he would be home. Home, after six long weeks!

His welcome was tumultuous, with the whole family crowding into the doorway to get the first kiss, and everyone talking at the same time. A good hot supper was on the table in a twinkling, and only then, with order restored, was John able to get the gist of the news the children had been trying to convey to him.

The four youngest had had chicken pox, they said; Samuel F. another spell of croup; Ansel a convulsion; Peter Paul had drowned in Dry River; William Lewis and his black mare had drowned in the Shenandoah; sister Anna's little daughter Fannie had died of croup; Emmanuel Heatwole's had a new daughter, and Hugh Brunk's a son.

But John, too, had much to tell that evening and for a long time they sat around the table listening intently to the account of the places he visited and the people he had met.

"Did you see many cowboys?" asked William.

"Well, I saw a lot of boys looking after cattle."

"Were they riding horses and swinging lassos?"

"Yes, some of them were galloping around on horses."

"Oh—oh! Just wait till we get out there," exclaimed William, prancing around the table. "I'll ride Duck and round up hundreds and hundreds of cows."

"Now, William," chided Mother sharply, "who said we're agoin' west, anyways? Here, take this crust and sop up your plate. There's enough gravy there to make someone a good meal."

To change the subject John suddenly left the table and, depositing his heavy valise on his chair, began rummaging through its contents.

"Here," John said, placing a dainty china dish on the table in front of Bettie, "how do you like this?"

"Oh, John, is it for me? Where'd you get it?" exclaimed the excited Bettie, her good humor again restored.

"It's a present from Aunt Becky Good, in Ohio," John said, "and here are two more from Fannie Shenk. I'm certainly glad to get them off my hands. I was so afraid they'd get broken."

While Bettie and the children admiringly examined the dishes, John hauled several lengths of cloth from his bag. "Some calico for a dress from Mrs. C. B. Brenneman in Ohio, and stuff for an apron from Susanna," he explained handing the material to Bettie.

"Now wasn't that right nice of 'em," she exclaimed, her face beaming. "It almost looks as if it'd be enough for a dress for me and Fannie both."

"Oh, yes, and here's a couple of handkerchiefs from Mrs. Grabill in Illinois," he said, still rummaging in the bag. "She sent a little money for you too, and so did Lizzie Shantz, and Mrs. Brenneman and Annie. Reckon I'll be borrowing from you one of these days."

"My, oh, my!" sighed Bettie, happily. "All these things for me! Why, it's just like Christmas."

"Well, it is Christmas, just about anyway," said William.

"That's right," said Father, gently removing several pairs of prying little fingers before slowly closing his bag. "I have a few more things in here, but day after tomorrow is Christmas Day; so if you're up in time for breakfast that morning, you'll each find something on your plate."

"What's that black stuff you've got there?" asked Bettie, looking intently at another piece of cloth John had removed from the bag.

"That's my present," he replied. "Some stuff for a pair of pants Susan Heckleman gave me. I'll get my pattern and cut them out and have Lizzie sew them. She did a good job on the last pair."

Next day another letter arrived from Noah Grabill. Bettie turned a little pale when she saw the postmark, but said nothing. John read the letter in silence, glancing anxiously at Bettie as he returned it to the envelope. There was something about the set of her mouth and the vicious way she was wielding her darning needle that troubled him. The silence became quite foreboding. But sometime they had to talk this matter out.

"Bettie," he began softly, "I think I know how you feel about going west. You told me once. I don't suppose you've changed your mind?"

Dropping the mending into her lap, Bettie sat staring out the window for a minute or two, watching the children playing in the snow. Gradually the lines in her face relaxed, but her eyes were filled with distress and her lips trembled as she looked up at John.

"I—I'm tryin' to change my mind," she quavered. "But I just can't change my feelin's. If you want to, of course I'll go. But something in me keeps apullin' back, even though I try hard not to feel like that."

"I know," John said, drawing up a little stool beside her, "it wouldn't be easy for either of us to leave our home and our families and friends."

"But do you have to? Surely there's aplenty to do right around here," Bettie pleaded.

"Of course there's plenty," John replied calmly. "Everywhere you might look there's plenty to do for the Master and not enough folks to do it. But think, Bettie. Think of all those dear people in Illinois, no church, no preacher. About a dozen families, I reckon. Unless someone goes, and that right soon, I fear many of them will be lost to the church."

"But can't they get somebody else? Or can't they ordain one of their own men?"

"Maybe they could. But right now no one seems suited for the ministry. They're mostly just farmers."

Bettie was silent a moment. "Well, I reckon they should have a preacher," she replied, "but I still think it should be someone a little nearer. Let them send one from Indiana or Ohio. They've like as not got plenty there."

"Yes, they have quite a few in some places," John replied quietly, "but maybe they want to stay home too. The thing is, Bettie, I feel a responsibility toward these people. Somehow, I felt that I belonged there. If you'd been with me, you'd have felt it too, I'm sure. And they all wanted me to come so badly. In this letter Grabill says they keep asking him how soon we are coming. I just don't know what to tell them."

Bettie was darning again, and rocking—rocking hard, her brows puckered in deep thought.

"You don't have to answer right away, do you?"

"No, I couldn't. Something like this takes a lot of thought, and prayer. Much prayer. But, Bettie, if we feel God is calling us to Illinois, that it is His will, you'll be willing to go, won't you?"

"Yes, John," she said, and he was relieved to see that now her eyes were calm. "If it is God calling you, and not just Noah Grabill, I will go."

* * *

John looked happy when he came home from town several days later.

"Oh," said Bettie, looking up from her sewing and seeing the smile on his face, "you got it."

"At last," John smiled happily. "Seventy-eight whole dollars, Now I'm all paid up for my teaching except for a few parents that I reckon never will pay."

"And how much of it's left?" Bettie asked shrewdly. "I reckon you settled up a few things on your way home."

"Well, I did pay some bills, and I have a lot more to pay tomorrow. By the time I'm finished I reckon there won't be much left. I saw Jacob Shank and paid back the money he loaned me for the trip. It was $35, but he kindly gave me back ten."

"That was good of him. I see you bought a few things too."

"Yes, a diary and a new hymnbook, *Gospel Hymns, No. 2*. I've been wanting one for a long time. And I got a couple of readers for Samuel and Jacob, and some wooden pegs to mend our boots. I still have about $50 left."

"And how much of that do we owe, I wonder?"

"I'm going to figure that out right now," John replied, sitting down to the table and pulling a piece of paper out of his pocket.

"Now, let's see. I've been owing John Bradburn over $8.00 for the last two years; Joseph Byrd, $1.00; Daniel Garber, $1.75 for fodder; Abram Wenger, $10.00 for nursery stock, and of course Wallace Minnich for groceries. I'll have to get that bill from him."

"And how did you make out on the trip?" Bettie asked. "You said you got around $64. Did that cover it?"

"Yes, just about right," John replied. "The fare was $62.34, but I'm expecting a six-dollar refund on the ticket I didn't use when we took the boat. So that's taken care of, thank God. He does look after us, you know, if we trust Him."

* * *

One January day John returned from the post office with two letters. Bettie had become wary of John's letters, but felt easier when she recognized John Funk's handwriting on one of the envelopes. The other was postmarked Kansas.

"I wonder who that's from?" she remarked as John took his knife from his pocket and slit the envelope.

"We'll soon see," he replied, unfolding the letter. "It's signed Bare, B. W. Bare. I don't think I know the man. Maybe he saw my name in the *Herald of Truth*."

"Well, what does he want? Hurry up and read it," urged Bettie.

"Hm—m! How would you like to move to Kansas?" John looked

teasingly at Bettie as he quickly glanced over the second page.

"Now, John, just what does he want? This ain't no jokin' matter."

"Well, that's what he wants. He says there are quite a few families out there now, and they need someone who can preach in English. Shall we go?"

"Humph!" exclaimed Bettie. "You know what I think about that. Why, it's even further than Illinois, ain't it?"

"Quite a bit further," John replied, opening Funk's letter.

"All I can say is, I hope they can find someone," Bettie sighed. "And what's Funk got to say?"

"How strange, two in one day!" John remarked as he finished reading the second letter. "A call from Kansas and one from Indiana. Funk wants to know about my trip and whether I've been thinking of his proposal to come and help him at Elkhart."

"I reckon you ain't been thinkin' much about that," said Bettie.

"Oh, it's been on my mind, but somehow I don't think I'm the man for the job. Or would you—maybe—think it might be better than Illinois?"

"I can't say, John, I just don't know," Bettie shrugged, looking helplessly at her husband. "There we'd be in town, I reckon, and that wouldn't be so good for the children."

"No, we're country folks. I don't like town either," John agreed. "But, Bettie, I really do feel God has another job for me, somewhere, and we must pray that He will show us plainly where He wants us to be."

Working around the farm that winter, or helping with odd jobs around the house, John's thoughts constantly wandered westward. All kinds of plans began taking shape for the farm and the church in Illinois. But sometimes his imagination took him to a desk at the publishing house in Elkhart. It would be such interesting work if only—

Some days there wasn't much time for thinking. Most of February, it seemed, was spent helping Bettie look after sick children. And when Bettie took sick, he was left entirely alone, for Annie was helping at neighbor Fishbacks for a month or so. Calling at the doctor's office to pick up some medicine for several of the children who seemed to have developed pneumonia, John learned that "there was scarcely a well person in town." In his diary he wrote:

> The children all appear better today. But this is the worst case of colds that we have had for a long time. It seems as though it is contagious.

And then word came from Fishbacks that Annie was alarmingly ill. After she had lapsed into unconsciousness several times, they decided to send for a doctor. For two weeks she hovered between life and death. But as soon as she was able to be moved she begged John to bring her home.

For months Annie's health caused great concern. Her continued weakness together with a hard dry cough was a symptom seen too frequently in the valley and one which everyone feared.

By mid-March John decided to try an old family remedy when he saw that the doctor's pills didn't seem to be doing much for Annie. Taking Fishback with him he went to the woods one day and carefully selected good specimens of a plant known as golden thread or Aronprice, some ground ivy, and a few stems of black cohosh or rattleweed. Bettie made tea of the mixture which Annie drank at regular intervals. A few days later John noted in his diary:

> March 12, 1879—Annie is much better today, better than she has been at any time since she is sick.

Fortunately the boys were well enough to go to the infare at Grandfather's home when brother Joseph was married. The event was a bright spot after their long siege of illness.

> March 7, 1879—This morning we got all the boys ready and took them in the spring wagon to Father's to see Joe bring home his wife (Sarah Heatwole). They were married yesterday at Joseph Heatwole's. They got to Father's at 12 o'clock. There were two couples of attendants, Daniel Coffman and Fannie Heatwole, and Eli Brunk and Lizzie Heatwole. All the children and grandchildren were there except Wallace Minnich and Bettie and Fannie who were here at home with Annie who is still not well. Mother sent them a bucket full of cake and other victuals. Many thanks.

It was a bright, sunny morning early in March. Just right for a walk, John decided, as he got ready for church. The service was at Franklin school that day, a walk of several miles which gave him a little extra time to be alone to think.

Illinois or Indiana? Would he ever be able to decide, he wondered, as his thoughts immediately followed the old familiar pattern. He had practically made up his mind that it would be Illinois until a letter from Funk opened up a new line of thought. Would he really be doing more for the church as an assistant editor of the *Herald of Truth* than by preaching for that little congregation in Illinois? Of course it would be a position of influence and responsibility, but was he capable and ready for such a responsibility? Funk said he had definite talent, and certainly he wanted to let God use his talents, but was this the answer?

After church John went to his old home for dinner, so that he could discuss his problem with his father and mother. Although he could see advantages and disadvantages to both propositions, Father Coffman favored the country for John and his family.

"If you got a farm," he advised, "there'll always be something for the children to eat. And they'll be healthier, too, I reckon."

Mother didn't say much, but she sat with her eyes closed part of the time, and John knew she was praying. "But the *Herald of Truth* is tolerable important," she reminded the men. "Though I dare say a farm would be better for you all."

"Of course the *Herald's* important," Father replied, "but there ain't nothin' to hinder sendin' in an article every once in a while. That way you could help Funk and farm too."

That evening John told Bettie of his father's advice.

"I reckon he's right," she sighed; "so if we gotta move, it might as well be Illinois."

"But, Bettie, don't you feel that it is right? That we should go?"

Bettie shook her head sadly. "No, I just ain't sure. Somehow it seems Indiana'd be better. But mebbe we'd best just forget it all and go to Augusta County like Jake Hildebrand wanted you to, if that farm's still for sale."

"No, Bettie, that's out. If I stay in Virginia, it'll be right here. But haven't you been thinking of that letter you got from cousin Lizzie last week? Just think, you'd have a new house, the prettiest in the neighborhood, she said; and forty acres of land to farm free for five years; and Sue Heckleman says we can live in part of her house till the new one is built. Doesn't that sound good?"

"Yes, it sounds good," said Bettie, tonelessly, "but I'd sooner have my old house in Virginia than a new one 'way out there. But if Lizzie'd go to the ends of the earth with her husband if he was a preacher, like she says, I reckon I can too."

"No," said John, "not if you feel like that. We'll have to think about it some more, and pray more."

Frankly, John was troubled. He had intended to write to Grabill next evening setting an approximate date for their arrival in Illinois. But all day Monday his mind was on Elkhart. If Bettie felt so strongly about the matter, maybe it should be given more consideration. Once more he reread Funk's letter, and as he gave serious thought to his proposition he began to see new advantages. As a publishing house employee, no doubt he would have more time for Bible study. His work would require it, and it certainly would be more interesting and more suited to his nature than farming. As to the children, there was more to consider than merely food and clothing. What of their future? Maybe he should write to Funk and state his problem clearly. He might be able to advise him a little better when he had all the facts.

John wrote to Funk that evening, instead of to Noah Grabill:

> Dear brother—I received your letters of Feb. 25 and 27, a week ago. The letters were not unexpected, but much of the substance which they contained was altogether unexpected. I was unprepared to answer your earnest entreaty and am yet in a great measure. But I must confess that your letter had the effect to put me to unusual hard thinking. But all my thinking has brought

me to no definite conclusion. I will try to make some plain, candid statements from which you may learn my circumstances and feelings.

With respect to my inclinations, if I understand myself, it is my will to serve my Master in the best way and place that I can do the most good and be of the greatest service in promoting His glory. From childhood it has been my inclination to read and write and gain information and improve myself in a literary way. The work you would have at Elkhart would exactly suit my natural inclinations. But I much regret that my attainments in that direction are so limited. But I could learn faster now than at any previous period if circumstances permitted.

I sometimes reason like this. The church needs other members than farmers alone, and if I could get my boys as they grow up to unite with the church and become interested in her publishing interests I would be glad to see them engage in so important a work. I would be glad to engage in it myself. But some of my friends discourage such an idea all they can. But I am not willing to be governed by friends in all cases against my own judgment. My wife would go to Elkhart rather than to Illinois. My mind is not settled at all on the subject, but since I thought over your letter I am inclined to favor going to Elkhart if I can make arrangements in my unfavorable circumstances that will do at all.

Please write to me and let me know what my chances would be to get a place to live out of town in my circumstances. And what would be the chance you could favor me with at the work. How about ague, fever and chills, etc., in the section I would necessarily have to locate in? . . .

March 10, 1879.

During the next few days John found his thoughts turning more and more toward the larger sphere of service at the publishing house. Was it God speaking to him, or was self-interest influencing him? Day and night he was in an agony of indecision. For two days the struggle continued.

"Bettie, I can't stand this any longer," he finally said on Tuesday night. "We must settle this question one way or another right now. Let's pray about it once more."

Together they knelt at their bedside while John poured out his heart in an urgent appeal for direction in the important decision. When he rose from his knees, there was a smile on his face.

"Bettie," he whispered, taking her in his arms and looking deep into her eyes, "do you feel, too, that it's Elkhart?"

"Yes, John," she smiled. "I feel right about it now. Surely that must be the place for us. I—I reckon I never did feel right about Illinois."

The next morning John hurriedly wrote another letter to John Funk:

> Dear brother—I wrote you a letter a few days ago in which I wrote something of going to Elkhart. Since I wrote, it has been on my mind continually. The more I consider it the more I think it expedient to go. Now I want to give you a little more satisfaction. There are several reasons why I want to make the change. Not that I think there is nothing to do for me here in the ministerial work, but I am not *particularly* needed here. They can ordain a minister here any time. They have the material. I hope and pray that I am not moved by any vain aspirations, but I do aspire to more usefulness than to merely gain what information and improvement I can at night after a hard day's work at manual labor and go around only in my own neighborhood and preach on Sundays on subjects the people take but little interest in and have heard till they are tired of them. We need in the church preachers that excite interest and command attention. This is not saying that I can or could under favorable circumstances do this, but when I see the necessity as I claim some do not, I will be more apt to work in that direction at least. The work you would have for me, I think, would be abundant opportunity to improve myself and then I would have the satisfaction of working for the interests of the church generally. This is the principal reason why I have considered your claims on me, as you term it.
>
> One other reason why I want to make a change is that I have not such a home here, and such business as will enable me to keep my family together. I would be obliged to put my children out among strangers to earn something, and I cannot bear the idea of letting the raising or bringing up of my children into other hands as long as I live. . . . I think if you could give me wages something like those you spoke of when I was there and probably help me a little to a place to live as you wrote at first, I could do much better than I am doing here. . . .
>
> Since I wrote it came to my mind that I gave you no satisfaction as to the time I could get ready. I would like to move this spring, about the last of May or the first of June. . . .
>
> Yours in haste,
> March 13, 1879

Putting William on Duck he sent him off to the post office to mail the letter. In an hour William was back and he was in tears. He had lost the letter and the money for the stamp. A big hole in his coat pocket solved the mystery.

For a minute the thought struck him that this might be providential. Perhaps Funk wasn't supposed to get the letter. But he soon dismissed the thought. It was purely accidental. The decision was right. Going to the house he immediately wrote another letter which he had neighbor Switzer mail for him in Dayton that afternoon.

A reply from Funk was not long in coming. He was delighted with John's decision and made him an offer of $500 a year. He also promised to find a suitable house and have it ready for their arrival.

Five hundred a year sounded pretty good at first. But when they realized that it was not quite $42 per month, John and Bettie sat down to do some figuring. There would be no wheat and corn to provide flour and corn meal; no hogs to fatten for meat; no cows for milk and butter; no big garden, not that year anyway; no orchard or vineyard to keep them in fruit. Their store bills would be much higher than the bills for incidentals they had been accustomed to. Besides, there would be rent.

"Do you think we can do it?" Bettie asked anxiously, quite awed by the prospect of having to shop for all their food as well as clothing. "The boys are growin' so, and it'll cost more all the time."

"Well," John replied calmly, "we can at least try it. Likely we'll have a little garden, and maybe we can even keep a cow and a few chickens. We'll see. Anyway, Funk said they won't let us starve."

Bettie was certain they couldn't possibly be ready to move by the middle of June. But John promised Funk they would leave as soon as the spring term of school was finished. The boys had lost so much time at school that winter that John decided they should have the benefit of the extra spring term.

Spring crops were put out as usual. Finding no immediate buyer for the farm, John bargained with John Hill to harvest the crops on a share basis. However, within a few weeks he agreed to sell to Emmanuel Heatwole:

> May 17, 1879—He is to pay $50 before I go away; $250 Apr. 1, 1880; and $175 Apr. 1, '81, '82, '83, '84, making $1,000 with interest from Apr. 1, '80, which will make $105, in all including interest $1,105. I paid $1,149.42 in $677.42 down and four annual payments of $118.

Besides all this extra business, John had to spend a great deal of time that spring working on the new road being opened up past his farm. He had worked hard to get permission for the road which would give a number of farms access to a main thoroughfare. Some farmers had bitterly opposed giving land for the purpose, but now at last they were all persuaded and they had been given till May court day to get the road in shape. Besides clearing the roadway of stumps and filling in holes to even the surface, it meant building a fence along both sides. Fences required rails. For several months John spent hours in the woods splitting rails:

"I have made over 1,600 this winter for Fishback and myself."

For Bettie the days were filled with sewing and cutting carpet rags. Her home in town should have new carpet throughout, she decided. Ann Frank wove the carpeting for her, twenty-one yards, for $1.50.

Also, if they were to live in town, she decided, they would all need a lot of new clothes. They couldn't go looking like tramps. Then, too, there was extra sewing for a new arrival in the family, young Daniel, who was born late in April. Realizing Bettie's problem the women of the Heatwole and Coffman families came to her assistance and spent days at Gravelly Hill, visiting and sewing. Sister Lizzie made a white linen suit for each of the older boys.

"What would you like to do now that we're moving?" John asked Annie Sauers one evening, shortly after they had decided to move to Elkhart. "Would you like to find another place around here or would you rather go home to your mother until you're strong again?"

"Neither," Annie replied quickly. "I want to go with you. Can't I?"

"Yes, I reckon you can if you want to," John said. "We'll be glad to take you along. But don't you think you should ask your mother about it before you decide?"

"Well," said Annie, with a determined lift of her chin, "you can ask her if you like, but I'm agoin' with you. This is my home now."

John was a trifle worried about Annie's determination, especially when a letter from Rachel Sauers begged Annie not to go so far away. But her mind was made up. "You can say what you like," said Annie to her sister Sarah, who also tried to dissuade her. "My mind is made up."

On the tenth of June, John and Bettie sold their little stock of furniture, tools, etc., at an auction sale. It seemed advisable to take only clothing and bedding with them to their new home. On the day before the sale Mother Coffman and some of the neighbors came in to help them:

> They scoured and brushed up the furniture, stove etc. and made the property look very well to sell better.
>
> June 10—Today I had my sale. There were a good many persons present, men and women. Some of my property sold low but some of it was not worth much. Some sold tolerable well. In the main it was a moderate sale. This evening Father brought all our things and all of us except the three oldest boys over to his house. The boys staid at Fishbacks. The sale amounted to $215, a little more than I expected. Today Bettie and I signed away our right to the property on the hill.

On Sunday there was a final service at the Bank Church:

> There were many folks present, more than usual. The brethren insisted on me to take the text as it is my last Sunday before I go to Indiana. I was in poor plight for speaking as I have had my mind overcharged with business.

Long after the service was dismissed John and Bettie stood at the door saying good-by to their friends. The boys were with them that day and they, too, shook hands with the folks crowding around.

"Here, Frederick," said old Deacon Frederick Rhodes as he said farewell to his namesake, Samuel F., "here is something to remember me by." Reaching into his pocket he pulled out a big red bandanna handkerchief and a shiny quarter. Samuel F. was delighted. Now he had a quarter to twirl as well as Jacob, who had received his in reluctant exchange for one pet hen.

There was a big dinner at the Samuel Coffman home that day with both Coffman and Heatwole relatives present.

"This is almost like an infare," John suggested to Bettie as they drove up to the house and saw the yard filling up with horses and wagons.

"It seems like ours was a long time ago," Bettie said, hugging baby Daniel close and surveying the rest of the family seated around her in the wagon.

"Yes, I reckon we're not exactly young any more," John observed, "and sometimes I feel as if I'm getting old, with half a dozen children to provide for."

> There were many folks here at Father's for dinner . . . 46 persons in all. We spent some of the time this evening in singing. I bid many of the friends goodbye at the church and here as they left.
>
> Tuesday—This morning we got ready hurriedly to start to town. Father and Dan hauled us in. I rode to C. Goods and walked to Dale Enterprise. William and Samuel staid at C. Goods last night. Mother H. and Anne Good brought them to town. We went to Samuel Brunks and got our dinner. There were a good many persons there to see us start. It was hard for us to bid our friends goodbye. It seems hard, but it is really more imaginary than otherwise. I did pretty well till it came to leaving my mother. That almost broke me down. This evening we are in the depot at Harper's Ferry waiting for the train. They all stood the trip well. Paid G. Grove Heatwole $4; Fred Brunk $1 and 90 cents at Wallaces for Annie. Paid 25 cents toll for wagons to town.

*It is not the easiest matter for a father to know just where to allow his children to go, and when to say positively no. I am trying to use wisdom in this, but may make a mistake. My prayer is continually, Guide me, O Lord.*—Diary.

# 12

It was two o'clock in the morning when the train from the east pulled in at Milford Junction, Indiana. Carrying a heavy suitcase as well as a tiny daughter asleep on his arm, John walked down the platform, herding three sleepy little boys in front of him. Recalling former experiences John was relieved to discover that this time someone was at the depot to meet him. Joseph and Susanna Blosser were waiting for them with a team and a big wagon. David Burkholder was also there with his team.

"We're a dirty-lookin' bunch," apologized Bettie, following her husband with baby Daniel in her arms. "It's been so hot, and all that soot and smoke acomin' in the windows—I reckon the boys' white suits will never be white again."

"Well, never mind. We know what trains are like," consoled Mrs. Blosser, bustling around. "Here, let's get them boys in the wagon so they can get back to sleep." Seeing Annie bringing up the rear half pulling and half carrying little Ansel, she picked up the lad and deposited him on the soft straw and blankets spread out on the wagon floor. The other boys were soon stretched out beside him and slept peacefully during the two-hour trip to the Blosser farm.

Next day the Blossers took the family and all their luggage to Elkhart. As they neared the city, Bettie and the children were filled with excitement, wondering what their new home would be like. They were not disappointed. Built on Eden Street, the modest two-story frame house resembled many others around it. But after the dilapidated Gravelly Hill house it looked like a palace to Bettie.

"And just see, Dear, we have a garden," John gloated, leading Bettie to the kitchen door after a quick inspection of the house. "It's a nice big one and someone has already planted part of it for us."

"Yes, there's an extra lot here," Funk explained, joining them on their tour. "Mr. Parker has agreed to let you have the house and the two lots for $7.00 a month."

"Fair enough," said John. "And I see there's a little stable back there; so I could keep a cow or a horse if I like."

Deacon Henry Brenneman and wife kindly took the family in for a few days while John looked around the town for bargains in furniture. By Saturday evening he had secured a good secondhand cook stove, beds, chairs, a table, and a bureau. He had also spent a good half day chopping straw and filling straw ticks and bolsters for the beds. Friends in town as well as relatives in the country donated many smaller pieces of furniture and a good supply of food. By Monday they were ready to move into the new house.

Sunday was the day the boys had been looking forward to ever since they knew they were coming to Elkhart. At last they could go to Sunday school. Eagerly they accompanied their father the short distance to church and joined the group of children assembling for Sunday school. William, Samuel F., and Jacob enrolled in the ABC class while Ansel joined the beginners. In the boys' class, part of the time was spent in learning the German language so that the children would eventually be able to participate in the German services held every two weeks.

John was slightly disappointed that so much of the precious Sunday-school hour should be used in mere language study. He also noticed that the school was noisy and the classes poorly arranged. Someday, maybe, he would have an opportunity to make a few suggestions for improvement.

Bettie arrived for the church service after Sunday school and heard John preach his first sermon as one of the Elkhart ministers. Funk had gone off to the Holdeman Church for a baptismal service and asked John to preach at Elkhart. After the sermon, Deacon Henry Brenneman gave a short talk in German for the benefit of a few members who understood little English.

"Well, what do you think of the Elkhart church?" John asked, as he and Bettie walked back to the Brenneman home for dinner. "Do you think you can feel at home here?"

"Mebbe sometime, but it—it's tolerable different," she replied. "I thought there'd be more people, but there was only thirty or forty, I reckon, countin' the children."

"Yes, this church is small. You see, most of our people live out in the country and go to the country churches," John explained. "Here they're mostly folks working for the Publishing Company and a number of German families living in town."

"And did you see that the women left their bonnets on? Most of them anyway. It looked as if they had their coverings on underneath; so why wouldn't they take 'em off?"

"I suppose it's just their custom. Perhaps they think a city church has to be different—that they have to be like other churches. But more than likely they just don't understand the meaning of a special covering for the head during prayer," John replied thoughtfully.

"Do they always have part of the service in German?" Bettie continued her questioning.

"I think so," John answered. "Every other week they say the sermon will be in German."

"I reckon that won't be so good," sighed Bettie.

"Why, didn't you understand Brenneman this morning?"

"Oh, tolerable, but I'm athinkin' of the boys. Do you think they could sit through a German sermon?"

John shrugged. "They can understand a bit, and with a little more German in Sunday school they'll pick up more right along. At least it won't hurt them."

John walked slowly toward the office that first morning. It was a big responsibility that he was taking on, and he felt so incompetent. At family prayers that morning he made a special plea for wisdom and strength for the new task. But his employer, he found, was very considerate. Funk greeted him cordially and spent several hours acquainting him with the general work of the company. Then showing him his desk, he gave him his first assignment—the selection of a few short articles suitable for the *Family Almanac*. On the desk was a pile of religious publications from which he was to make the selections. The second morning his job was proofreading and writing letters to solicit advertisements for the *Almanac*.

The next week found John seriously at work as assistant editor of the *Herald of Truth*.

"Here you are," said Funk, shoving a small pile of manuscripts in front of him, "some articles sent in for the *Herald*. See what you can do with them. This one from Hershey has some good ideas, but it will take a lot of rewriting."

All morning John worked at the article, trying to retain as much of the author's style as possible and yet present his ideas in readable form. This, he decided after an hour or two, was really hard work. Looking over a few more of the manuscripts, some quite impossible, the prospect of writing articles of his own no longer seemed so awesome.

"I think it would be a lot easier to sit down and write something original than to try to make these over," he told Funk when he dropped by to see how he was getting on.

"Well, go ahead. Write as much as you want to," Funk replied.

"But, of course, we'll have to use as many of these articles as we can."

A few days later John began an article on the subject dearest to his heart, "Come to Jesus." But the job, he found, was after all not as easy as he thought it would be. Writing was much more difficult than preaching, he decided, shoving it aside to be finished some other day. On his third attempt he finally finished it. That night he wrote in his diary:

> July 1, 1879—This morning I went to the office and finished and copied my article under the caption, "Come to Jesus." I did a hard day's work and am not well satisfied with the article.

But it wasn't long before his thoughts began flowing more smoothly as he endeavored to set them down on paper. Reading through the exchanges which came to the office from other denominational publishing concerns, and thinking of the problems and needs of the church, he was amazed at the number of ideas that came popping into his head, clamoring for expression. "A Greater Than John Is Here"; "Dress in Church"; "Military Toys and Pictures for Children"; "The Lord's Day"; "Conscience"; "Prosperity of the Church"—these were among the topics discussed in the columns of the *Herald of Truth* during the fall of 1879, signed with a small "c."

One of the biggest problems of city life, John and Bettie found, was keeping four lively boys suitably occupied. The boys, of course, found plenty of interest, with the help of the Firestone boys across the street. But to keep them in their own back yard was pretty difficult. "They have not elbow room enough," John recorded in his diary.

During the raspberry season William and Samuel F. spent several days at Burton's, about a mile and a half out in the country, helping to pick berries. William came home proudly with his 14¢ the first day, but Samuel F. was in tears. He had lost half of his day's wages and had only one nickel left.

John was glad when Funk suggested that William, aged eight and a half, might be old enough to help with a few odd jobs around the publishing house. At least one boy would be off the street. William felt quite important that first day as he trudged to the office with his father and Annie, who was now working part time in the binding department. He was accustomed to work and was not afraid of a new job. Compared with a day's hoeing or husking corn, a job at the publishing house, he decided, would be sheer play.

William watched carefully while the foreman showed him how to assemble *Almanacs*. All he had to do was take one section from each pile and lay them together in the right order. He was to be paid two cents for each hundred that he gathered.

At first it was fun. But soon the room felt hot and stuffy and time was beginning to drag when suddenly in walked his mother and brothers. They had come to make a tour of the establishment and stood watching the new employee who immediately perked up and worked manfully. He worked only till noon that first day and earned a total of seven cents by gathering 350 books. Annie, who stitched signatures, proudly announced that she had done 950 signatures that day at five cents a hundred.

To celebrate the change in the family's fortune John stopped at a confectionery on his way home that evening and bought a pint of ice cream. This was something the children had been hearing about since their arrival, but had never tasted. At 20¢ a pint few people could afford such a luxury. Divided among eight people the portions were small, but everyone ate slowly savoring to the full each tiny spoonful of the delicious, cool sweetness.

"Well, that was good," said Bettie, smacking her lips as she finished her tiny portion. "But there goes our meat for tomorrow, I fear."

"I reckon it was worth it," said John, watching the happy children vigorously scraping their dishes for the very last speck of the cream. "Surely there was a bit left from today's roast that will make soup or something."

"A very little," Bettie sighed. "Thirty cents' worth don't go far around here, and we can't go abuyin' meat every day at seven and eight cents a pound. When I think of all them hams and bacons we used to have a plenty back home. . . ."

"Well, don't worry," comforted John. "I know we had meat and lots of milk and eggs too, but the folks have been good to us. We haven't gone hungry yet."

"I know," Bettie nodded. "But I reckon we would of it it wasn't for the stuff you keep bringin' home every time you go out to the country."

"I'll have to get more potatoes somewhere next time I go out," John said. "I hope I can get them cheap. There's not much left of this month's pay. I had to pay a whole dollar to get my boots half-soled. It's outrageous what they charge for that out here."

Bettie turned pale. "And there's a lot more shoes aneedin' soles. Mebbe you'd best get a last and start doin' it yourself."

One day John Yoder came to the house with an unusual gift. The boys watched expectantly as he lifted a big box from the back of the wagon. But grunts and squeals soon gave away the secret. They were delighted to have a little pig to care for. John made a pen in a corner of the garden and looked forward to the day when they would again have hams and shoulders to cure.

A few weeks later John Funk brought over a cow which he suggested they try for a few weeks. If they decided they'd like to keep her, he would give them a good price. John was happy with the arrangement. How good it was to have all the milk and butter they could use, plus a few quarts to sell! The deal was closed several months later when he gave Funk a note for $25.

In September the boys enrolled for their first term in the city schools. John recorded the event:

> Sept. 15, 1879—Samuel likes his teacher especially well. I got them Readers, slates, and an arithmetic. William is to go through another examination tomorrow. It may be that he will get into the A grade.

With the boys in school, life settled down into a routine, with the entire household busily and happily employed. In a letter to his mother that fall John describes the busy scene:

> Bettie says, write that we all told her she would not have much to do here in town, but she has been trying to make herself a dress for two weeks and has not finished it yet. She has considerable sewing now. They are making winter clothes for the boys. Annie works in the office nearly all the time but sews in the evening till bed time. . . . Bettie says Fannie is more hearty than she was. She is getting fleshy and stout. The people say Bettie looks well. . . . A few days ago I put up a stove in the room. Bro. Summers gave us a large ten-plate stove. It is a very good and nice one, only it is large. But I know I can save wood. He said we might have it if it was good enough. . . . You all seem to wonder about our living in town. It seemed a little strange at first, but it did not take long to get used to it. I seldom think about it that I am in town. In going back and forth to the office the rows of houses, stores, saloons, taverns, groceries, etc., attract my attention little more than a fence row. The boys are in company with other children but little, except one family that lives just across the alley. . . . The brethren and sisters are very clever [generous] here and give us many things. Susan Blosser and Sister Henry Brenneman are both like a mother to us. . . . I hope Father has a nice time in Pennsylvania. He must send us an account of his trip when he gets home. Our love to you. Know that we appreciate your love and kindness as parents more and more as time moves on.

To help Bettie with her sewing problem John decided she should have one of those new inventions called sewing machines. At first when a salesman called they were somewhat wary. Bettie was amazed to see a long seam being stitched evenly and neatly within a few seconds. It was uncanny! Although they were both intrigued, they decided not to be too hasty in making a decision. They couldn't possibly spare that much money for something that might not be too satisfactory.

It took Henry A. Mumaw to eventually sell them a machine. An aggressive young man from Ohio, Mumaw had recently arrived in town to help at the publishing house. Through him John ordered a machine for $25, thereby lightening one of Bettie's most burdensome tasks.

Sundays in Indiana were much the same for John as Sundays in Virginia. Occasionally he preached at the Elkhart church and enjoyed a restful day. But usually the day was spent with one of the congregations in the country, where services were alternated in the various districts. Regularly he made the rounds of the Yellow Creek, Holdeman, and Shaum's [Olive] congregations. There were also appointments at Jones' school, Paulus' school, Kulp's school and visits to other nearby churches—Clinton, the church "at the lake," or Shore, and the Amish congregation at the Haw Patch, near Topeka. Besides this, there were several small congregations in Michigan which the Indiana ministers frequently visited.

John's first visit to the church near Burr Oak, in Branch County, Michigan, took place in October, 1879. Joseph Summers and his wife accompanied him and generously paid his train fare. It was a beautiful time of year, sunny and warm for October. The gorgeous autumn scenery as well as the warm friendliness of the people made the trip most enjoyable.

> Oct. 4, 1879, Saturday—They made an appointment at the church at candle-light. An interesting congregation, full attention. Text—Heb. 4:16.
>
> Sunday—Last night I went home with David Garbers from the meeting. They are clever folks. They brought me to the regular appointment at 10. There were a good many out. They told me that nearly all of Krupp's [Mennonite Brethren in Christ] members were there. Text—Heb. 4:14. Got along more easily than sometimes. Took dinner at Bro. Daniel Beery's (deacon). Had a talk with John O. Smith. He is dissatisfied but seems to think he ought to come back to the church. Had meeting again at night, a full congregation. Acts 3:14, "conversion." Went home with Bro. Harvey Friesner (minister). He is a kind, nice brother and does the best he can.

This visit to a small congregation which had so recently suffered a serious split set John thinking. They were rebellious thoughts, following the pattern set a year ago when he had visited little churches in Illinois, Ohio, and Pennsylvania as well as small groups in West Virginia. "These people need help," he almost shouted the words as he sat in Funk's office, reporting on the visit. "But how can they be helped? Who is to help them?"

Funk shook his head thoughtfully but said nothing, waiting for John to continue.

"What they need is more straight Gospel preaching, yes, and a lot more good Bible teaching. Far too many of our people get only diluted milk when they badly need meat. As things are, what can we expect but weak congregations and divisions?" The words fairly burst from John's lips, and his fist came down hard on the desk.

"Well, so what do you propose?" asked Funk in a matter-of-fact tone. "You know very well that most of our ministers haven't had much teaching themselves; so what can they do?"

"Can't we at least wake them up? Get them to see their responsibility—that souls of men are at stake? They must make more effort and not just depend on some formal practices to keep a church alive."

"Certainly," replied Funk in his deep voice. "I quite agree. We've been trying for years to do some waking up through the *Herald*. But we can only go so far, you know. Our people don't take kindly to new ideas, and are very slow to break with old customs. Things have to be done just like their fathers used to do. It will take a long time and a lot of patience to make any changes."

John had risen from his chair while Funk was speaking and slowly paced the floor, lost in thought. "But it's now that we must get help to these people. It will be too late for many of them if we go too slow or have too much patience. There must be some way. If we could only get a good minister in to preach for them oftener, or maybe stay with them a few days or a week or two and really work."

For a moment neither spoke. John stood staring unseeingly at the brick wall of the building next door, the only view which the office window afforded. Finally Funk spoke.

"You see that brick wall there? That's what we're up against. The minds of most of our people are made up. They're adamant. Put together they make a solid brick wall. Whatever you do, don't mention continued meetings in this part of the country or Michigan. They've had enough. You'll only be bruising yourself, battering against a brick wall."

"I suppose you're referring to Daniel Brenneman's work. But he had a good idea, you know. He meant only good."

"Certainly, his intentions were good. He was like you. He wanted to help the church and went about it the best way he knew, staying with the congregations and holding protracted meetings, getting folks stirred up. But his big trouble was that he was in too much of a hurry, and took things in his own hands instead of working patiently with church leaders. It was bound to cause trouble."

"And it did, in a good many places, I understand," remarked John.

"A movement like that must be cautious and carry the whole church with it, not just half the church," Funk continued. "Ever since Brenneman's last visit there's been trouble up there in Burr Oak. He tried to stir them up and succeeded only too well. There's been a serious split and dissatisfaction in practically every district he's visited."

John listened patiently, still facing the brick wall. Now he turned to face Funk, and there was a look of determination in the piercing gray-blue eyes. "But it wouldn't be impossible, you know, to break down that wall across the alley," he said slowly. "It could be done, even by hand, brick by brick. There's no real reason why a few nights or a few weeks of good straight preaching should offend anyone, least of all a minister. It should heal troubles rather than stir up more, and it could do so much good."

"You're right, of course," replied Funk, thoughtfully. "Evangelists are building up churches in other denominations, yes, even getting quite a few of our people. But the way things are in our church, about all we can do right now is pray."

In October, John attended his first session of the Indiana church conference. It was held at Yellow Creek. John Funk borrowed a three-seated buggy for the day and took a load from Elkhart out to the conference. To John's surprise, Preacher Jacob Hildebrand had arrived from Virginia for the conference. John and Bettie were both pleased to have a visitor from their old home. Then when he arrived at Yellow Creek, he had another surprise—two more visitors from Virginia: Bettie's sister Anna and her husband, Christian Good.

John was a little disappointed in the conference. It was different from the sessions he had been accustomed to in Virginia:

> Oct. 10, 1879—They have not much order in their proceedings, and do but little business. There is much room for improvement which I hope the brethren will see soon and be willing to put to practice.

But if there was little business, there was much exhortation. Twenty-two bishops, ministers, and deacons were present, including three visiting bishops—Hildebrand from Virginia, George Brenneman from Allen County, Ohio, and John Speicher from Kent County, Michigan. From the bishops and ministers came sermons on the doctrines and practices of the church, nonresistance, separation from the world, nurture and admonition of children, inconsistency of uniting with secret societies, and self-denial. After a discussion on the impropriety of brethren going into saloons to drink, conference came to the decision recorded in the minutes: "It is not a proper place for professors [of Christianity] to be found. It shows a bad example and has led many a man to sin and to a drunkard's grave."

Bettie was overjoyed when she saw the visitors John brought home that night. For the next week the family routine was pleasantly disrupted while she took time to visit relatives in the country with her sister. Annie Sauers went with them for a few days, leaving John to take care of the boys.

> Oct. 15, 1879—I had to do my own housekeeping, prepare my own meals, etc. It came rather unhandy for me, but I did pretty well. The boys were all at school but Ansel, and him I took along to the office. Matilda Brenneman asked me whether I liked to stay alone. I told her "God saw that it was not good for man to be alone." She said she thinks it does very well for the

men to be left alone so they may see how the women have it. Bought 1 lb. cheese, 11 cents; 1 lb. halibut, smoked, 10 cents.

One morning in November, John sat down at his desk, sharpened his pencil, and taking a clean sheet of paper began to write. He wrote rapidly at first, for it was a subject that had been on his mind constantly since his talk with Funk—the need for greater and more direct effort by Mennonite ministers to bring men to Christ.

> The time has come when there is urgent necessity to work for the prosperity of the church. As there has been neglect in this respect, it is the more important that a special effort be made at once. . . . There are many of our brethren who do not see the necessity of this work as many others do, and some would even oppose evangelizing. But if some of our brethren who are settled down with a prosperous, growing church should go to visit and preach for the weak, scattered churches . . . they would see the necessity of special work as they never saw it before. . . .

This is pretty plain speaking, John thought, as he read the paragraph over. But it was true. He didn't particularly intend it for publication, but at least it was good to be writing exactly what he thought.

> Thousands of souls are hungering and thirsting for the preaching of the Word, and there is none that will serve them. Many of our ministers remain at home, surrounded by plenty, living in comfort (possibly luxury), while souls are perishing on every hand. . . . Is the matter of too small importance? Are so few willing to sacrifice comfort, time, and means for the salvation of souls? Is not the church willing to help her ministers to the means to labor for the conversion of those for whom Christ died? . . .

How he wished he could get this message across to his ministering brothers! He began to wish that Funk would use the article. If it would only stir up a few—save even one lost soul. . . .

> There are at the present time influences at work against us that must be met or we must suffer. In many places where we have organized churches other societies are holding their meetings right among our members, preaching their doctrine with power and effect. . . . These efforts would be for us rather than against us if we were only as active as others. . . . How often do we hear persons say, "I would have united with the Mennonite church if they would have had preaching here. . . ." Some might argue that when we hold pure principles and teach only Gospel truth that God will prosper us in upholding that doctrine without special effort on our part. But it is a noteworthy fact that no doctrine, however pure, has ever spread to any great extent unless it was zealously advocated and valiantly defended. . . .

If this were printed, he realized, as he filled page after page, he could expect criticism, some most severe. But in a cause like this, criticism could be tolerated, yes, even welcomed.

> Paul did not settle calmly down in Jerusalem and wait for anxious souls to come and hear his preaching, neither did he try to convert all the people of one place before he went to another. . . . Menno Simon did not remain quiet in his native Witmarsum. He did not confine his labors to Friesland, nor even to the Netherlands, but from the German Ocean to the Gulf of Finland was the broad theatre of his apostolic life and labors. . . . He was persecuted and pursued for his life, yet he did not hide away in some secluded spot where he might enjoy peace and safety. . . . We should make known the leading Bible principles upon which the church is grounded outside of our immediate surroundings. Sometimes there are flattering things said, and truthfully said, by members of other societies concerning the history and faith of the Mennonite church, while our own actions indicate that they are worth but little. . . .

Finally he came to the last paragraph. For a long time he sat staring at the ceiling, completely lost in thought, his lips moving in silent communion with his Master. Then, taking up his pencil he wrote again, rapidly finishing the article:

> Who will dare say that he or she, as an individual, is doing all in his power? Who will dare say that the church is doing all she can for the upbuilding of the Kingdom of God and the salvation of souls? Will we admit that we are not doing our whole duty and then take the position that we are justified in not working more directly because some who are workers in other societies do not work according to plans which we could approve? This is no argument, because we have our own plans, and not those of others to conduct our regular work, and we can have our own approved plans for our special work. . . .

Shoving the sheaf of papers into a drawer, he walked quickly out of the building. He would leave the article for a few days, then come back to it with a fresh mind. Perhaps Funk would refuse to use it since it was so contrary to the thinking of most Mennonite ministers. But it was the truth, and it might help some to see the light. Maybe if it was neatly written and carefully punctuated, Funk might be tempted to use it.

The article appeared in the December issue of the *Herald of Truth.*

In December, John was called on to fill a new role in church affairs. Along with Deacon Henry Brenneman he was delegated to try to bring about a peaceful settlement to a serious difficulty in the Holdeman congregation. Originally the trouble involved only Preacher James Culbertson and Deacon Joseph Holdeman, but gradually it spread through the congregation and the entire district as ministers and bishops endeavored to bring about a reconciliation. Not only did Culbertson and Holdeman withdraw from membership, but the whole congregation announced that they were withdrawing from "all the bishops and ministers until they recall what they have done in the case of Joseph Holdeman. . . ." As a newcomer John Coffman was not involved in the trouble and for this reason was chosen to make the new attempt. In a letter to his father on Christmas Day, he briefly explained the situation:

> Last Tuesday there was another meeting and the bishops confessed their faults and submitted to the counsel, while Holdeman and Culbertson did not. Brenneman and I again took the counsel and asked each one, 1st, whether he thought enough was done to satisfy the dissatisfied parties; 2nd, whether they had anything to ask of anyone that submitted to the church; 3rd, whether they desired that Culbertson come with the church again. Nearly all came in and all answered satisfied and wished C. back again if he wished. So C. and H. are both out with an invitation to come in as soon as they are willing to let the church say what they must do. . . . I know that the move did good. . . . Many that were not satisfied with the bishops are now satisfied and a good part of C.'s party will hold with the church. . . . I believe H. will be ready to come back, but I have serious doubts whether C. will ever come. . . . I stayed with him two nights and talked a great deal. I spent over a week in visiting among them up here. I could hardly afford it but if as much good results from our labor as I hope, I am well paid.
>
> There are some very excellent brethren and sisters there full of charity and forbearance, but there are some that are determined to rule or ruin. There are about fifty here who want to run the *machine* church, each one to his own fancy, and seem presumptuous enough to take the authority to say to their brethren, "you must" do so and so and withdraw their recognition of brotherhood before a brother is charged by the church. I believe many are beginning to see better. I believe this present difficulty taught some good lessons.
>
> We are well. I was at Shaums at meeting today. Funks with Lydia Rhodes were all here for dinner after meeting. We got some Christmas presents from the brethren and sisters, a new hat and handkerchief for me; bonnet, cap, and handkerchief for Bettie; comfort and handkerchief for Annie; a nice little wagon, candy, cards, etc., for the boys. So we had a Merry Christmas. Every once in a while some of the good people bring us something to eat from the country. Have seen the sun but little for two weeks, ground frozen hard all the time. A little snow and a cake of ice. Good sleighing. Mercury down to eight. Our love to you as ever. John and Bettie.

*Today I have been thinking much about the necessity of the church making a more active effort to make converts. When we see what others are doing and see the success which follows their efforts we are sorely grieved at the apathy of our own members on the subject of evangelizing. I sometimes feel like cutting loose and going all the time.*—Diary.

# 13

It was wonderful to be living in such an interesting age! And city life did have its advantages, John decided, as he hurried home to tell Bettie and the children what he had seen up town that day. Certainly if he had been living out on a farm somewhere, his chances would have been pretty slim for hearing that queer little talking machine. Quite a way to advertise a patent medicine, he thought. In a very short time a big crowd had collected around the thing.

Bettie was incredulous. "Must have been some kind of a trick," she remarked. "There couldn't of been just a voice acomin' from a box."

But William had heard the big boys discussing the machines. Someday, he declared, people might even have them in their homes.

"Well, I just don't know what we're acomin' to," said Bettie, "all these newfangled things, sewin' machines and talkin' machines, and what was that big heatin' thing Funk put in the cellar at the Publishing Company?"

"Oh, you mean his furnace," John supplied.

"Yes, that's it. Does it work good?"

"Fine," John replied. "It has pipes going to every room and he heats the whole building."

Bettie shook her head. "What next, I wonder?"

"Well, there's telephones," suggested Samuel Fred.

John nodded. "Yes, I reckon it won't be long before we'll be using them. Funk's been talking about getting one in the office. Several of the men downtown are getting them in."

"I just can't see how they can work," said Bettie, shaking her head dubiously, "talkin' to someone a mile or more away!"

"Well, just wait. It won't be long now," prophesied John, "before you'll be talking on one yourself."

"And what about magic lanterns?" asked William. "Will Mr. Funk get one of them too?"

"I don't know," Father replied. "Maybe someday he will."

"I'd like to see one. They say they can make pictures come on a wall so big that everybody in the room can see them," William exclaimed enthusiastically.

"Likely somebody will be bringing one to town one of these days," John said.

True to his prediction, the magic lantern was soon being used in Elkhart. John got his introduction at a scientific lecture when pictures were used to illustrate varying conditions of the sun. Later Henry Mumaw bought a lantern and was soon furnishing a new type of entertainment for his friends.

John took advantage of educational lectures and programs that were frequently presented in town, and over the years heard many interesting speakers on a wide variety of topics. He became deeply interested in the subject of phrenology as presented by Dr. Palmer one winter. Seeing in it possibilities of guidance through assessing natural traits and abilities, he had charts made of the heads of his three eldest. William and Samuel F. were found to be mechanically inclined, while Jacob was termed a "literarian."

One morning in April, Funk appeared in John's office with a bundle of proof sheets in his hands.

"Here," he said, handing them over to John, "here are the proof sheets for the primary Sunday-school book we're printing for Lancaster County. What do you think of it?"

"Why, not bad," answered John, glancing over the first few pages of questions and answers. "The questions are simple and the answers quite clear. They seem to touch the high points of the lessons pretty well, I think."

"Yes," said Funk, "I think it's a wise step they're taking. We need our own lesson materials, and with this book and the one they're getting up for the intermediate grades, it'll be a pretty fair system."

"They cover the same lessons, I suppose?" asked John.

"Yes, sixty-one lessons in each, on the life of Christ. There are about ten lessons on the Sermon on the Mount. That's where nonresistance comes in that the bishops are so concerned about. Have you looked at the Foreword yet?"

"I'm just glancing at it now," replied John. "Why?"

"Well, look at the last paragraph," Funk ordered.

"Hm—m," mused John. "So they are planning to have two more books in the series, one for very young children, and one for an adult Bible class. That's good. We need something like that. This material will reach a lot more schools than the Sunday-school page we started lately in the *Words of Cheer*."

"Yes, these will likely reach a lot more schools, but the *Words of Cheer* page will help out where they use the International lessons. But this book for very young children," Funk continued, "they've asked me to suggest someone to do the writing."

"Why, I thought they appointed their own committees to do the job."

"They did for the first two books, but apparently they want help for the others. It's a little hard to find someone to write simply enough for little children. But I think I know the man for the job. Will you try it?"

"Why—why, I reckon I could try," stammered John, once more surprised by Funk.

"Well, see what you can do," replied Funk, considering the matter settled. "You've done good work on the *Words of Cheer* page for older children; now see what you can do for the beginners."

The Sunday-school book was soon finished, and John was able to give more time then to the *Herald of Truth,* which was his chief concern. In July he recorded in his diary:

> July 21, 1880—I have just now determined to use all my efforts to make the *Herald of Truth* more interesting than it was the last year. I am especially interested in the editorial department. We intend to be more pointed on doctrinal subjects. We have a number of criticisms on some articles in exchanges.

John's work at the office was, however, not always of an editorial nature. He was frequently called on to fill in when help was needed in other departments. One of the hardest jobs he occasionally had to do was mailing. This process he described in a letter to his brother-in-law, L. J. Heatwole, March 3, 1881:

> We use a mailing machine that must be seen to be appreciated and must be used in order to realize the pangs of the overworked muscles of the left arm on which it hangs while in use. I have mailed the last four numbers, and begin to think I am getting tolerable proficient in the use of the machine. I finished in less than eight hours yesterday. Nearly so much has been mailed by Samuel Frick in five hours, but that took some years' practice.

During March, John made several trips to Michigan. The second time he went farther north to visit two small churches in Kent County, the Bowne and Caledonia congregations. He remained with them several days, holding two services at both places.

Writing up his diary the following evening, John sat at the kitchen table for a long time, lost in deep thought. The children were in bed and Bettie, too, had retired. He was alone. As he thought back over the week's experiences, jotting down the names of the people he had visited and events that took place, he felt suddenly overwhelmed with the needs of these people and his responsibility toward them. He heard again the earnest voices speaking in confidence, telling of trials, difficulties, differences of opinion which led to disastrous divisions in small congregations. He heard, too, voices of entreaty begging him to come back soon and help the struggling church in Caledonia. There would be hope, the people said, if only someone would help. He thought again of the handful of members he had visited at Vicksburg on the way to Kent County, of the little church at Burr Oak, and, yes, of the persistent requests coming to him from Illinois. He had promised to visit them, but so far it had been impossible. Finally, glancing at the clock, he picked up his pen to finish the entry in the diary:

> April 7, 1880—Today I have been studying the necessity of laboring for the interests of the church. I begin to see it as I never saw it before. I see plainly that if it were so that my family was supported, I would have work at preaching all the time.

For weeks the problem of the care of these churches weighed heavily on his mind. How to give more of his time—how to assist them personally, troubled him. But gradually he came to see the matter as a problem for the whole church, rather than an individual concern. Could not conference make some arrangement to provide more help for weak congregations? It had never been done in the Mennonite Church. It would be a new idea, but surely it would do no harm to make some suggestions.

Intrigued with the thought, he immediately hunted up Funk to discuss the idea with him. Together the two men talked of the possibilities and drew up a tentative plan for organized assistance to small, weak, or unorganized congregations, a kind of home mission effort under the jurisdiction of the church conference.

John smiled as he pushed back his chair to return to his own desk. His heart was full of hope. At last he had something concrete to think about, a definite goal in view.

"Don't set your hopes too high, though," Funk warned in his deep, gruff voice as John turned toward the door. "Don't go thinking that this matter is all settled, that the Indiana Conference is going to adopt this idea at the next session."

"Well, no. I don't suppose it will be as easy as that," replied John thoughtfully. "I reckon it will take a little time for the idea to get through."

"A good long time, I'm afraid," added Funk. "But if we work slowly, talk about it now and then, hint at it occasionally in the *Herald,* well—maybe in a few years we may see some action."

> June 23, 1880—Today I have been thinking much of the necessity of missionary work in the church. What we need is

home mission work. Conferences should make arrangements to send ministers into certain places where there is a prospect that the church could be built. A mission board should be created and evangelists should be under the care of the board.

* * *

Wednesday, August 25, was a day that had been marked on the calendar for some time and the Coffman boys were quite excited at the prospect of going to church that evening. Noah Troyer, the "sleeping preacher," had arrived in town and would preach for them.

"What is a trance, anyway?" William asked as they discussed the event at the supper table.

"It's hard to explain," Father replied. "It's almost like being asleep, and yet the man can move around a bit, with help. And he stands alone behind the pulpit and preaches for several hours, they say. The strange part is that when he wakes up, he doesn't know a thing about it."

"But what makes him get like that?" Samuel F. wanted to know.

"Nobody knows," Father replied. "It's a real mystery. It comes on him, they say, every evening, and even the doctors can't understand it."

"Does he preach every night?" asked Jake.

"Yes, I think he does. Maybe not always at a church. Sometimes it's just to a group of people that come to his house. It's strange, almost weird, but folks come to hear him that wouldn't listen to an ordinary sermon. They say he's helped a lot of folks."

Noah Troyer had gone to Joseph Summers' home that afternoon, and as evening approached, he lay on a couch in the living room and fell into a deep, trancelike sleep. When it was time for the service to begin, four men carried the couch with the sleeping preacher over to the church.

The four boys sat with their father, their eyes glued to the motionless figure on the couch. They joined only halfheartedly in the hymns which Funk announced, and then suddenly there was a slight stir on the couch. Quickly two attendants were at the side of the sleeping man as he tried to rise. Supporting him on both sides, they led him to the pulpit.

Although his eyes remained shut during the entire service, Troyer preached with vigor and earnestness, part of the time in the German language and the rest of the time in English. For two hours he held his audience, boldly exhorting them to righteous ways of living, to turn from evil and follow the example of the godly men of old. After speaking for a half hour or more he suddenly paused in his remarks, uttering the strange word "hullamatrullum." To his attendants this meant "water," and immediately a glass of water was held to his lips. Several times during the service he called for hullamatrullum.

And then he was finished. After announcing a hymn, he turned from the pulpit and was led back to the couch, where he again lay motionless. The four couch-bearers once more took up their burden, carrying him back to his room, where the deep sleep continued until morning. Awaking refreshed next morning he was entirely unaware of the proceedings of the evening before.

Strangely, a number of cases of trance preaching occurred in various parts of the country at this time. From Goshen came the report that J. D. Kauffman, a member of the Amish Mennonite congregation at the Townline Church, east of Goshen, had for some time been falling into a trance regularly each Wednesday evening. Like Troyer, he, too, spoke in both German and English, his sermons usually lasting two hours.

Then from Holmes County, Ohio, came a report to the *Herald of Truth* regarding John Opliger, a young man who for three months was seized with a spasm each evening around six o'clock. About an hour later he would commence a service by announcing a hymn. Then he began to preach. The following report appeared in the *Herald of Truth,* January 15, 1882:

> He preached very earnestly. He took no text but spoke chiefly on swearing, drunkenness, gambling, quarreling and fighting, and warned people, exhorting them to repent and be baptized. . . . Large numbers came to the house each evening. They came early, even before his eyes closed. As soon as his eyes closed he would lie down. He could tell who was present without seeing them, could tell how many were outside when they could not all get into the house, and many other singular things manifested themselves.

In spite of his heavy schedule of work at the office and at home besides numerous preaching engagements, John somehow found time to write letters to many friends and his family back home. As his work for the church increased, his correspondence increased along with it. His brother Joseph and his brother-in-law, L. J. Heatwole, sister Mary's husband, were among his most faithful correspondents. Soon after he left the valley for Indiana, John heard that Joseph and his wife were among a group received into church membership. The news called for an immediate letter of encouragement:

> Nov. 18, 1879—Joseph, you do not know how much I have been cheered by hearing that so many of you were willing to confess the Lord as Saviour. If only Jacob could find it in his heart to determine to do so. . . . I hope and believe you have been much engaged in religious meditation, reading, and prayer. I hope you keep up a form as well as a spirit of devotion. I must confess that when I was first married, which is one week over 10 years, I found it difficult to get the consent of my mind to start in a visible form of prayer at my meals and bedside. . . . I

> regret very much that so few of our Mennonite brethren practice audible family prayers.

A letter to L. J. Heatwole, January 4, 1881, reveals the extra-heavy load he had taken on that winter by attempting to teach three singing schools in widely separated districts.

> As an excuse (for not writing) I must put in my old plea, too busy! Ah, what a busy world! By way of explanation I will state that I have now three singing classes that I meet usually once a week. One four miles southwest of Elkhart, another four miles east of Goshen (Goshen is 10 miles from Elkhart and I usually go there on the train at 4 P.M.), and the third eight miles east of Goshen near the new Clinton church. I sing altogether in the evening, as it is impossible to have a singing school in this country in day time. I use *Temple Star*. I get $2 a lesson. We also have a Bible class in town which meets in the homes of the brethren once a week and on Sunday evening we have a meeting at the church. So you can imagine how much I am with my family. I feel glad every time I step into the house because I meet a warm welcome from half a dozen jabbering, seemingly delighted children and a smiling, contented wife.
>
> Last night Bro. Henry Eyman of Caledonia township, Kent county, Mich. (100 miles north), was at my house. I have been at their place several times. They have a small congregation there that has been at a standstill for some time, or retrograding, partly because of no English preaching and partly because of this Indiana division in the church. They are building a new meeting house there and both members and outsiders are unusually interested in the prosperity of the church. Bro. H. gave me a flattering invitation to meet them at regular appointments the coming year. He said I should lose nothing in railway fare or time. Since they are so really in earnest I promised to visit them and fill five appointments in two weeks from next Saturday.

John kept the appointment with the congregation at Caledonia. Arriving on Saturday afternoon, January 22, he met a good crowd at the schoolhouse that evening. On Sunday morning he preached again at the school, but after the service went home with some friends from the Bowne congregation for a service in their little log building that evening.

Although he had promised to stay for two more services on Monday, John was restless on Sunday evening after the service. He was spending the night with Mr. and Mrs. Joseph Yoder.

"I have a feeling something is wrong at home," he finally told his hosts. "I think I should leave for home on the morning train."

"Maybe it's just your cold that makes you feel a little low-spirited," suggested Mrs. Yoder. "You'll likely feel better after a good night's sleep."

"No, it's not that," John answered emphatically. "My cold is quite a lot better. It's a different kind of feeling entirely. I'm certain someone is sick or something seriously wrong."

"It could be a touch of homesickness," commented Mr. Yoder. "I've felt something like that when I've been away. But if you really want to catch the early train, I'll see that you get to the depot."

Alone in his room, John fell on his knees and for several hours struggled in prayer. He prayed for his dear ones at home, committing them entirely to God, and he prayed also for the welfare of the people at Bowne and Caledonia, for whom he felt a personal concern. Eventually, around two o'clock, a feeling of deep peace stole over him. His prayer had been heard. He knew God had answered. With the assurance that all was now well at home he went to bed and slept peacefully until morning.

"You won't have to take me to the depot this morning," he smilingly informed the Yoders when he came down to breakfast. "I prayed about it, and I have the assurance everything is all right now."

When he arrived home on Tuesday, John carefully scanned the faces of his little family. All of them appeared to be in their usual health, although Fannie looked a little pale.

"Wasn't someone sick on Sunday evening?" he asked Bettie when the desired information didn't seem to be forthcoming.

"Why, yes," Bettie replied. "How did you know?"

"I just knew," John answered gravely. "I had a strange feeling something was wrong, and had almost decided to come home. But around two o'clock I felt that a crisis was past, and all was well. Who was sick, Fannie?"

Bettie nodded. Tears were in her eyes and her throat felt so tight she could barely answer. "It was croup again. I—I was so afraid, and wished so you'd be here. We had to get the doctor and he worked hard. It was just about that time when he said she'd be all right."

It was with a pressing invitation to return soon that John left his new friends in Michigan. And then within the next few weeks came a number of urgent appeals for help. A letter from Cullom, Illinois, begged for a visit. Another from Mancelona and one from Bertrand, Michigan, made him feel that he must go to them soon. Certainly it was time for the church to take some action, or should he, perhaps, have enough faith, enough trust in the providence of God to take it upon himself to go and preach for these people? He thought of the series of meetings then in progress at the Evangelical Church with Miss Savillah Kring as evangelist. Miss Kring was back for the second time within a year. Hundreds came to hear her preach and many were added to the church. "Why can't we make a similar effort?" his mind kept repeating over and over as he sat reading and meditating late one evening. Reaching for his diary he recorded his thoughts:

> Feb. 6, 1881—Today I have been thinking much about the necessity of the church making a more active effort to make converts. When we see what others are doing and see the success which follows their efforts we are sorely grieved at the apathy of our own members on the subject of evangelizing. I sometimes feel like cutting loose and going all the time.

John hated to leave Bettie alone so frequently that winter while he went off to the singing schools so far out in the country. To return by train from Goshen after the evening singing meant getting home about 3:00 a.m. Sometimes he slept until three and then made the long trip to the depot at Goshen, getting home about six o'clock. Occasionally he stayed over in the community after the singing at Brown's school for the singing at Paulus school the next evening. But he was always glad when the sleighing was good and he could catch the night train from Goshen.

One Friday evening in March, John just didn't know what to do. He was tired. He had been to Brown's the night before, arriving home at the usual time of 3:00 A.M. And he didn't want to leave Bettie again. The week before Henry Brenneman had taken the classes for him. Brenneman was a good stand-by. He had helped John with a school at Elkhart the previous winter, and willingly helped out with his country appointments.

"Maybe I could get him to take it for me again tonight," he suggested to Bettie.

"No, John, not again," Bettie vetoed the suggestion. "He's a lot older'n you, and it's such a long, cold trip. Anyway, you needn't worry about me. I'll be all right. You just get back right soon."

John managed to get to the depot after the singing in plenty of time for the night train, only to learn that it was several hours late. There was nothing to do but sit and snooze on the uncomfortable bench in the cold, smoky little building until the train pulled in around three o'clock.

When he arrived home at 4:30, he was met at the door by Mrs. Firestone, who sleepily congratulated him on the arrival of a new daughter, Anna Barbara. The entry in his diary for March 12, 1881, states:

> Last night our little daughter, our seventh child, was born at 1:30. I was not back from Goshen. Now we are blessed with five boys and two girls. God will assist us in taking care of them if we trust Him.

There was a further addition to the family a day or so later when Daniel arrived from Virginia, to join the workers at the Publishing Company. John was glad to see his brother and get a firsthand account concerning his father and sisters, Sarah and Rebecca, who had been seriously ill for months with typhoid fever.

* * *

When several cases of smallpox broke out in town that spring, John decided to take precautions with his family. The doctors strongly advised vaccination, and since the procedure was fairly simple he determined to do the job himself and save expense. Armed with a small bottle of vaccine that the doctor provided and a sterilized needle, the operation got under way after supper one evening. Starting with William he went down the line, finishing with young Daniel. One after the other the boys bared their arms, submitting bravely to the vertical and horizontal scratching, after which the vaccine was carefully rubbed in. For a week he watched the arms carefully, but the expected swelling and soreness failed to appear.

> May 6, 1881—The vaccinating I did on the boys did not get sore, not one in six. The virus must have been worthless.

A few days later the process was repeated with some fresh vaccine, and this time it did take.

* * *

That spring John S. Coffman began a practice which undoubtedly had a marked effect on his spiritual growth and power. His diaries tell the story:

> Feb. 23, 1881—Today I took into my head not to eat anything. I am not more hungry this evening than I was before noon.

> Feb. 28—Today I fasted again. Did not taste any food since yesterday evening and do not expect to eat till tomorrow morning if my life is spared. A determined will prevents extreme hunger. I think it is good for me physically and spiritually. I am enjoying a season of much spiritual grace.

> April 13—Today I did not eat any food. I fast for 36 hours at a time every two or three weeks. I think it a help to my digestion and my health and I think it an advantage to my spiritual life. The mind is clearer and the soul is less fettered with sensuality and can soar higher into spirituality and dwell nearer to the divine nature of the Supreme.

This experience proved to be a prelude to the larger sphere of service, the more definite work, which John had been contemplating for some time.

"So you're aimin' to stay a whole month this time?" Bettie asked, as she helped John pack his valise. It was Friday evening, June 3, 1881.

"No, not quite a month, my dear, but I'm afraid it will be at least three weeks this time."

"Oh, that's so—o long!" groaned Bettie. "Where all are you goin' besides Bowne on Sunday?"

"I may be at Bowne a little longer than that," John replied slowly. "It depends on how things are. In fact, I may be there and at Caledonia about ten days."

Bettie caught her breath sharply. "You—you ain't thinkin' of protracted meetin's, are you? Will they let you do that?"

"A week for two churches wouldn't be very protracted, would it?" John smiled. "But seriously, I am hoping to stay with them a little longer, and maybe do a little more definite work. Some of the brethren have been urging special meetings, but I'll just have to wait and see if the Lord leads that way."

"And then?" prompted Bettie.

"Well, from there I go to Mancelona and on up to some little places in northern Michigan where we have a few families. The ministers here think I should visit as many of them as I can on this trip."

"Well, I just hope you don't get any more chills again. Be sure and take the powders the doctor gave you. You really shouldn't be agoin' the way you been complainin' lately."

"Never mind. I'll be all right. I only hope you and Fannie won't get any worse. This ague really gives one the miseries. It's the one bad thing about this Indiana climate."

John arrived in Bowne in time for a Saturday afternoon service. It was preparation for a baptism and communion service next day, when two members were received. Bishop John P. Speicher officiated, but John preached the sermon, both morning and evening.

Monday was Whitsuntide, and two services were announced for that day, one at 10:00 A.M. and the other in the evening.

John felt strangely moved as he faced the congregation that evening. The house was full—old folks, young folks, children, men and women in the prime of life. He knew these people pretty well by now and he realized keenly that a great many of them had never made any profession of Christianity. He had spent much time in prayer before this meeting, and as he arose and took his place behind the pulpit, his heart was raised again in silent entreaty for wisdom and power.

The sermon that night was based on Christ's parable of the rich man who made a feast and the invited guests who made excuses for not coming. With great eloquence he presented the gracious invitation offered by Christ to the world, pleading earnestly, "Come, for all things are now ready." And then came the other side, the excuses, the foolish, inane excuses of those turning down the invitation—the offer of eternal life. The power of the message struck home in many hearts. The people sat spellbound, listening to the old Gospel story presented in such a new and compelling manner. "The attention was profound," John wrote later, the most profound he had ever experienced. The people were thinking deeply. Some might make a decision, he felt, if they had a chance. Realizing that he must give them the opportunity, for the first time in his experience, he gave an invitation publicly: anyone desiring to accept Christ's gracious invitation could make it known by coming forward to the front of the church.

There was an immediate stir in the audience and one man left his seat, solemnly marching up the aisle where John met him with an outstretched hand. Soon a second, then a third responded. Finally, after a few moments of hesitation, a fourth walked up to the front, joining the little group on the front bench. By this time tears were glistening in many eyes. But there were also several countenances which registered plain disapproval.

Some hasty consultation took place next day among a few members who called on Preacher Keim and Bishop Speicher. All agreed that the sermon had been fine; that it was a good thing to encourage folks to accept Christ; that it was wonderful to see these people taking their stand on the Lord's side. It would certainly add new life to the church. But wasn't there danger in this method of evangelizing? Did not the church in general oppose it? Would it not lead to establishing the mourners' bench with all the emotionalism and excitement seen in some other churches? Was not John Coffman plainly following the path of Daniel Brenneman, and was there not real danger that like Brenneman he, too, might break with the church and cause serious disruptions?

Speaking quietly but firmly, John tried to reassure the brethren on these matters. Evangelizing was not new in the church, he pointed out. Years before, the beloved old Bishop John M. Brenneman had held meetings and given invitations as he had done last night. And so had John F. Funk, and a number of others, and with good results. It wasn't at all necessary to conduct an evangelistic meeting just like others. There was no need for the mourners' bench or an emotional after-meeting. "We must establish a pattern of our own," he said, "in keeping with our doctrines and practices."

The church was filled to capacity the next two nights with an eager, expectant crowd. Two decisions were made on Tuesday evening and the next night there was one more.

On Thursday morning John held a meeting for the instruction of the new converts. He was pleased to see that several more had made the important decision and joined the group that was to be baptized that afternoon.

There was great rejoicing among the members of the little congregation as they witnessed the baptism of nine converts at the stream near the church.

The next three days were spent in the Caledonia district. "Had only a tolerable congregation . . . preaching went hard with me this evening," John wrote after the Friday evening service. Although their new building was not quite finished, they decided to use it on Sunday for the communion service. Quite a few folks from the Bowne Church came over for the service that morning.

Henry Brenneman, of Elkhart, accompanied John on the ten-day trip into northern Michigan. Mancelona was their first stop. Here they found several Mennonite families, and after visiting them again on their return trip, John wrote: "We have great hope that a church will soon be established at this place."

A number of families were located in Petoskey, and also on farms in the surrounding districts. Crossing Little Traverse Bay they visited several groups, one five miles south of Cross Village and another ten miles east. Everywhere they received a warm welcome as well as a most pressing invitation to return. "This is only the second sermon I've heard in five years," one man informed John.

While John paid his return visit to Mancelona, Henry Brenneman returned to Bowne, where he helped organize a Sunday school the next Sunday.

> He reports an unusually pleasant time, and says he never saw a school started with better prospects for faithful labor or more earnestness among teachers and pupils.

This was the closing paragraph in the report of the Michigan trip which John wrote for the August number of the *Herald of Truth*.

*I see plainly that wherever our people make direct efforts in continued meetings they build up, but where they do not in the new places, they build very slowly or retrograde.*—Diary.

# 14

Once more it was October and time for the Indiana annual church conference. John had high hopes for this conference. On the way to Yellow Creek he and Funk discussed the plan they had devised for providing ministerial help in needy areas. They were going to present it if there was an opportunity.

The morning session, as usual, was given over to the bishops. Three of them gave talks that morning—J. A. Beutler, J. M. Christophel, and a visitor, George Brenneman from Allen County, Ohio.

Another Ohio visitor, whose coming John considered providential, was John Shenk, who had just returned from a trip with Brenneman through Kansas, Missouri, and parts of Illinois. The trip had opened his eyes to a great need in the church. In many isolated communities they had found small groups of Mennonites trying to establish themselves in newly opened districts, and in great need of spiritual help. John listened hopefully as Shenk made a strong plea for help for such groups. Certainly his talk would add weight to the matter he and Funk planned to present.

There was no time that afternoon to bring up the subject, but they went home hopeful of a hearing at Monday's sessions. John reported in his diary that evening:

> Oct. 14, 1881—This afternoon the conference went into business better and more systematically than they ever did here in Indiana since I was here. All seem to be pleased and to feel good this evening.

John was greatly disappointed when he received word that he

was to conduct a funeral service on Monday morning instead of attending conference. He did want to be there to help push the plan. But Funk promised to do all he possibly could, and so hopefully and prayerfully John started out at 5:00 A.M. with a borrowed horse on the nineteen-mile ride to Clinton Township.

As soon as the service ended at noon, John again mounted his horse and by fast riding reached Yellow Creek shortly after three. The all-important subject was being discussed when he arrived and he was in time to express his convictions and to cast his vote in favor of the following resolution:

> In regard to the work of visiting scattered members and small churches not supplied with ministers, be it resolved that we will try as far as possible to see that all the scattered and small churches in the conference district shall be visited during the present conference year—the ministers in the district to arrange the visitation as may be most convenient.
>
> To supply funds that may be needed by ministers who are not able to defray the expenses of their visits, this conference suggests that each church take a collection every three months or as often as may be deemed necessary.

"Well, it's not exactly a mission board," John smiled as he shook hands with Funk after the meeting, "but at least it's a start."

"Yes, it's a good start," Funk agreed heartily, "and somehow I have a feeling that it's going to grow into something bigger. I hope and pray that it will."

An urgent invitation came to John that fall from the church at Masontown, Pennsylvania. They had heard of the recent meetings at Bowne and wanted him to spend at least a week with them.

"What do you think I should do?" John asked Funk, showing him the letter.

"Well," Funk advised, "you got plenty of criticism for your work at Bowne. But it was a big lift to the church. As I see it, it's for you to decide which outweighs the other."

"That, my dear brother, has already been decided," John replied quickly. "It's not a question of risking criticism, but whether I should take time off again so soon. And whether I should go to Masontown when there have been calls from other places too."

"Well, as far as work's concerned," Funk replied briskly, "there's always plenty to do here, but nothing so pressing right now that it can't be left for more important work, if you feel you can afford to give more time. I'm sorry we can't keep up your pay while you're off on preaching trips, but we're not big enough yet for that."

"I understand," John nodded, "and don't expect anything like that. But with seven children depending on me I hardly know what to do sometimes. But God hasn't failed us, and if He wants me to do this work, I know He'll take care of us."

"Have you kept track of the time you've lost lately?"

"Yes, counting all the days off for meetings here and there and half days for singing schools and funerals or work at home I've lost about sixty days so far this year. That's about two months' pay. If it was only a matter of finance, I couldn't afford to go. But since it's the Lord's work, I can't afford not to. And now what do you think? Should it be Masontown?"

Funk leaned back in his chair, looking thoughtfully through the window at the brick wall across the alley.

"Well," he replied slowly, "if you're determined to pit your strength against the brick wall, I guess maybe Masontown would be as good a place as any to dislodge a few bricks. I have a soft spot in my heart for Masontown. I guess I've told you that I helped with meetings there myself, about ten years ago. I was with Daniel Brenneman that time. It was before all the trouble started. We had a wonderful time. Real soul-stirring meetings, and something like fifty converts."

"I know," John said. "They told me about it when I was there before. You and Daniel did a lot for the congregation. If only as much could be said of Daniel's last trip to the community. I guess that's why they want me right now, to help a few folks get their thinking straightened out. Some of them were pretty badly unsettled."

"It would be a good thing if you could go," suggested Funk.

"Yes, I think I should," John said. "Maybe about the middle of December."

It was two days before Christmas when John arrived in Masontown. Muddy roads were a big hindrance to attendance the first two evenings, but on Sunday, Christmas Day, there was a full house. John sensed a feeling of exceptional interest that evening as he explained the meaning of the new birth.

As he gained an insight into the deep spiritual needs of so many of these people, John became acutely conscious of his great responsibility. It was his job to present Christ in a way that would fill this deep need, that those who did not know Him could open their hearts to Him. For this he needed divine wisdom and power. Alone in his room at night, he fell on his knees, spending hours in prayer.

> Dec. 23, 1881—Last night I staid with Bro. Justus Bare and had a long interesting talk. I waked up early and could not go to sleep again. My mind was disturbed, and the weight of the labors before us for the salvation of sinners lay heavy on my soul.

Toward the end of the week he began to give invitations at the close of his sermon. There was no response until Saturday evening, when five young people made the decision. The following nights there were more, both here and at Huston's school where he preached several evenings. An instruction meeting was held the next Saturday and on Sunday twelve new members were received.

Leaving Masontown, John set out for Scottdale and a brief visit to a number of congregations in southwestern Pennsylvania. He spent two days at Stonerville, and then headed southeast into Somerset and Garrett County, Maryland. Services were held at the Elk Lick Church, Blough's school, the Folk's Church, and the "Lower" Church. He was again impressed with the great need for more definite evangelistic effort:

> Of late years the church has rapidly increased. The work here seems but fairly begun. There is a wide field here and there are calls from many places around this church that the brethren (Bishop David Keim and H. H. Blough) cannot fill. Nearly half of the church members here are young unmarried persons. . . . Here I was much impressed with the necessity of sending evangelists to labor among those who are crying for the gospel and are denied simply because the laborers are few and because conferences and churches that could, do not make arrangements to have the Word preached to those who are so situated as to be deprived of the privilege of attending our meetings.

* * *

On arriving home John heard of a small farm for sale about one and a half miles outside of town. He had been thinking for some time of moving to the country, where they could cut costs by growing their own food. This twenty-acre farm at Bunker Hill seemed to be just what he wanted.

Bettie's heart sank when she first saw the place. Another old, dilapidated house! Not quite as dilapidated, perhaps, as the Gravelly Hill abode, but bad enough. She agreed, however, that they would be better off on a farm, and the prospect of again having plenty food of their own appealed strongly to her thrifty soul. The deal was closed on February 11, 1882:

> Today I closed my bargain with F. P. Miller for the V. Marks property one and a half miles south of the corporation on Prairie street. I am to pay $2,150 and make myself responsible for the interest of $750 from June 26, 1881, and get into the bargain one young cow, an Oliver plow, about 20 cords of wood, some of it old wood, and an old shovel plow.

Through a letter to his brother Joseph he let the folks back in Virginia know about the deal:

> March 16, 1882—I have bought 20 acres of land about two miles from the office. It cost cash $2,025 or $2,100 in payments. I borrowed the money and will pay cash. A good part of the money I get from members here without interest. It was probably not very wise to do as I did, but I had to make different arrangements and it was the best I could do. The house is poor, but we can shift. The barn is good and there is a large, good orchard on it, some old trees and some young ones. The soil is black

prairie, mixed with sand and is rich and productive. It ought to be at the price. What makes it high is that it is near town. All say I am at no risk. If I cannot get through I can sell to advantage. Here I rent and it took all the rest I made to get eatables and things to wear, and I think I had better pay interest. I think we can to a great extent live off the land and save some of my wages to pay on the land so that I will not be living up all I make and have nothing to show for it.

You have no doubt heard that brother Dan has gone to Cullom, Illinois. He had a nice place here and will miss it, I know. But he gets better wages there. I got him the place when I was out there the first of the month.

It was late in February when John started out on his long-promised visit to Cullom. Since his first trip, three years ago, the number of families in the community had increased and they now had a minister, Benjamin F. Hamilton. Not having a meetinghouse they were still using Longmyer's and Hartman's schools for their regular Sunday services. For the meetings this week they arranged to use the Methodist Episcopal church along with the schools.

John spent much time in prayer before that first service at Longmyer's on Sunday morning. The feeling of responsibility was almost overwhelming as he stood behind the desk on the slightly raised platform at the front of the room. The building was packed. He realized that many of the folks had driven long miles that morning over roads almost impossibly heavy with mud. Some came with four-horse teams, some with mule teams, and some on horseback. They came expecting something. He prayed that they might not go home empty.

His sermon that morning was based on the parable of the laborers. Simply and yet eloquently he spoke of the need for laborers in the Master's vineyard today, and of the justice of His pay. So enthused did he become in his desire to make the message personal that as he spoke he kept moving closer toward the edge of the platform. Finally stepping down, he continued his appeal as he moved among them. The message reached their hearts. Each one present felt that it was directed to him, personally.

Most folks were back again for the service that evening in the Methodist church, and many town people joined them. Again John noted that the interest and attention were intense.

It was a happy week, this week with his friends in Cullom. He had many serious talks as he visited them in their homes, and together they enjoyed rich spiritual fellowship in the evening services, in spite of rain and mud. Everyone rejoiced when they learned that fifteen new converts were asking for baptism. Since there was not enough time for instruction that week, arrangements were made for a return visit and baptism service in the spring.

Before he returned home John had a talk with Preacher Hamilton and several of the men. The meetings had greatly encouraged them and the prospect of so many new members made them conscious that the time had come to give serious thought to erecting a church building. He encouraged them in this, knowing that a proper meeting place would add immeasurably to the spirit of worship, and that the congregation would be united a little more closely by working together to build it.

* * *

It was the first day of spring, and moving day for the Coffman family. John and Bettie awoke early to the sound of howling wind. Winter was having one last fling.

"Just listen to that wind," cried Bettie, rushing to the window, where she saw gusts of snow swirling across the street. "Oh, dear, we just can't move on a day like this."

"We have to," John replied calmly. "Everything's packed and George Hug's coming in with his team in a few hours. Maybe it'll clear up by then. Anyway, it's only a couple of miles out. I reckon we'll make it all right."

By midmorning two wagons were loaded and on their way down Prairie Street. Hug's load went first with John following close behind driving Funk's team. Bettie insisted on riding on the wagon with him to help look after the load.

"My, I wish you'd atied those ticks down better," remarked Bettie, pulling her shawls more tightly around her. "The storm's agettin' worse, ain't it?"

"No, I don't think so," replied John. "It's just that we feel it more out here on the open road. The ticks should be all right. They're pretty heavy and George said he'd keep an eye on them. Is everything all right back there?"

"Oh, yes, I reckon so. But don't get in them ruts. It won't take much to jiggle some of these things off. Oh, oh—this wind!"

Just then an extra strong gust seemed to rock the whole load. Bettie closed her eyes and hung on tightly. But she opened them quickly when she heard John's shout, and was just in time to see the third tick sailing from the top of Hug's load and landing in the ditch.

"Oh, John, the ticks, the ticks! Stop quick!" she shouted.

But John had already stopped. Hearing the shouts Hug had also stopped his team and in a few minutes the straw ticks were reloaded and arranged more securely.

"I—I reckon they're pretty dirty?" Bettie asked fearfully as John climbed back on the wagon.

"No, my dear, they're not. I don't know why, with all this mud around. But they're all right and we can put them right back on the beds when we get there."

By evening the family was settled in their new quarters.

"I reckon Father Coffman will be glad to know that we're back on a farm," yawned John as he finished winding the clocks that night.

"Yes, it looks as if you're both agettin' what you wanted," Bettie commented sleepily. "You're on a farm, and workin' for Funk too. But I reckon you won't be able to keep on with quite so much preachin', will you?"

"Certainly, if God wants me to," John replied quickly. "That's my first duty, you know. Nothing else is quite so important. And since we're out here on a farm, raising our own food, I'll feel freer to go off on those trips, for I'll know my family has something to eat even if I don't earn so much. The boys are old enough to help on the farm now, and we'll manage."

"Mebbe," sighed Bettie, "but ten and eleven isn't very old for all there's to do on a farm. If only Annie was a little stronger. I don't like it that she's sick so much. But—so it is. Are you still aimin' to be at the Shore Church next week?"

"Yes, I promised them I'd come for a few days. Maybe a week."

"But I thought conference was against protracted meetings."

"So it is, and I'm very sorry about it. But I've talked with some of the ministers and with Funk, and we think we can do the work in a way that won't cause trouble."

"And how's that?" asked Bettie.

"Well, since we're not to have services for more than one or two nights at any one place, we'll keep moving to the churches and schools close by. That way we'll have practically the same audience but in different places."

John sensed a feeling of apathy in the group that assembled at the Shore Church on Saturday evening. Unconcern was written plainly on many faces. He knew the task before him would be difficult. On Sunday evening he wrote in his diary:

> March 26, 1882—The people here are a little dull and somewhat hard to rouse to a real spiritual concern. Had a large congregation this morning. Text—Matt. 15, "The Sower."

By way of contrast, he was able to write several months later:

> June 18,1882—Went to the Shore to the regular services. There was an unusual crowd out. The house was crowded and many were outside. . . . The congregation was of such a character as to make it a blessed meeting.

During this week the services were held first at a school, then at the Shore Church, the Dunkard church in Forest Grove, Greiner's Church, Clinton Church, and the "Eight-square" schoolhouse.

As a result of these meetings sixteen were in the class received by baptism into the church early in July.

In a letter to his brother-in-law, L. J. Heatwole, John wrote:

> The remembrance of that week's work and the interest and the zeal of several of the converts gives me courage for renewed

effort to bring sinners to Jesus.

In June, Lewis Heatwole came to Indiana for a visit. John had been looking forward to this visit for several weeks. There were so many things he wanted to show him, to talk over with him. They shared many thoughts in their letters, but it would be so good to talk with him.

It was noon on Friday when Lewis and his cousin, Grove Heatwole, arrived. John met them at the train and after a dinner out at the farm he brought them back to town for a tour of the publishing house. He himself was so busy that it was quite late in the evening before he had time to settle down for his talk with Lewis.

They were sitting on the porch steps enjoying the coolness of the evening listening to a frog chorus coming from a corner of the little farm.

"It sounds to me as if one of your main crops here might be frog legs," Lewis teased. "Does this keep up all summer?"

John laughed. "I don't know. We haven't been here all summer. But I reckon a few frogs will disappear when the low spot down there dries up."

"Well, it looks as if you might have a pretty good place here. Everything looks good," Lewis commented.

"Yes, the grain is fine, and the garden, too, but that hard frost about ten days ago froze all the fruit, I'm afraid, except maybe a few plums. But tell me now about Virginia," John begged. "I'm anxious to hear all about the old home."

"Well, now, let's see," Lewis began. "I've already told you about the folks and the crops and the weather. As to church, I don't think there's much new, except maybe one thing that will make you happy."

"And what's that?" John asked eagerly.

"Sunday schools. At last we have a school going again at the Bank and Weavers."

"Ah, yes. I heard about it. We got a notice for the *Herald,* and I must say it did me a lot of good to arrange that column for the typesetters. I've been praying for this a long time. How's it going?"

"Fine, I think," Lewis said. "Of course there are some still opposed, but I think the worst is over."

"And the singing schools? Are they as popular as ever?"

"Yes, we had a number of schools last winter," Lewis replied. "How are they here? Did you teach your usual half dozen?"

"No, not last winter. I've been away so much that I had to give up my classes. The only one I have now is at Burr Oak."

"That's the church in Michigan, isn't it?"

"Yes, about fifty miles from here. I didn't get there too regularly this spring, but I promised to go and preach for them as often as I could, and I've been working in two singings each time I go. That's where I'm going tomorrow. I'm sorry it has to be this weekend while you're here, but I promised them; so I'll have to go. We'll have a singing tomorrow night and another on Sunday afternoon, and I rather think that this will be the last singing school I'll ever conduct."

"Why do you say that?" Lewis asked.

"Well, other work is pressing more and more. It looks as if I'll have to be away from home even more than I was last year."

For several minutes the two men sat in silence. Finally Lewis voiced the thought uppermost in the mind of each.

"So you plan, then, to continue this—this evangelizing work?"

"I do," replied John firmly. "I plan to continue preaching the Gospel to the unsaved as long as God gives me strength."

"But aren't you—uh—just a little afraid of stirring up trouble in the church?"

"Does preaching the Word stir up trouble?"

"Well, of course it shouldn't, but there are different viewpoints, you know."

"So you have been hearing some criticism?"

"Plenty, brother, and so have you. It's quite a problem in some places, you know. Where I come from they simply don't allow protracted meetings."

John sighed deeply. "That's where I came from too, and it troubles me. But Virginia isn't the only place. Right here in Indiana the situation is about the same. But you, Lewis, what do you think about it, personally?"

Lewis met John's searching gaze, and smiled at the troubled look in his eyes.

"I reckon you know my opinion," he replied slowly. "You and I always did agree on most things. And in this I am personally behind you. I know that you have already done a great deal to help one church."

"Which one do you mean?" John asked in surprise.

"Masontown. I've been getting letters from Justus Bare lately and he said some nice things about you and your meetings there. Said that you were the ablest speaker he had ever heard in all his life, and that the meetings there did them a lot of good. There's more unity and harmony among the members now than there had been for over twenty-five years."

"God grant that it may be true," John spoke softly, his eyes searching the sky where a few stars were beginning to appear. "And may the unity and harmony last a good long time."

"But I would say this, brother," Lewis continued, "be careful. Don't go too fast. It takes a lot of our people a long time to give up the old ways in favor of something new. But we did get our Sunday school, you know."

"Ah, yes, the old ways! The ways of our fathers! I'm going to write an editorial on that one of these days. What are the old ways, anyway? How far back are we to go for our fatherly examples?"

"Grandfather, I suppose, for most folks," Lewis replied.

"That's just the trouble," John said heatedly. "And so as a minister I should be an exact replica of some of our ministers of a generation or two ago who never stepped outside their own community or their own church. I should be content to settle down peacefully on my hundred acres, farm all week and preach every other Sunday or so, and consider I've done my full duty to God and man."

"There seem to be plenty around who think so."

"Altogether too many," exclaimed John, jumping up and beginning to pace back and forth in front of the porch. "Certainly, I say, go back to the old ways, but go back a little further. Let's get back to the days when the church was working vigorously, reaching out in every direction to neighboring towns and villages. Back to the days of Peter Waldo, John Huss, and yes, Menno Simons. They didn't sit at home waiting for sinners to come to them. They went and preached even though they knew it might cost them their lives. I have every respect for my grandfathers, but as a pattern for my life I must go straight back to the New Testament, to the apostles, to John the Baptist, to Paul."

* * *

After a visit to Cullom, Illinois, in September to attend the opening service in their new church building, John took great satisfaction in writing the report for the *Herald:*

> Oct. 15, 1882—The brethren in Livingston Co., Illinois, have completed their new meeting house which they have had under way during the latter part of the summer. The house is a fair-size frame building painted outside and inside. . . . The house is paid for, although there was some money borrowed to complete the payment of the debt. The entire cost was over thirteen hundred dollars. The members wish to acknowledge through the *Herald* the receipt of some money used in building the house from Canada, Pennsylvania, Whiteside Co., Illinois, and some other places, and to return their sincere thanks for the same.
>
> The first meeting was held in the new house on Sunday, Sept. 24. The brethren Emmanuel Hartman, H. L. Shelley, and J. S. Coffman were present with Bro. Hamilton, the resident minister. . . . Bro. Coffman stayed until over the next Sunday and attended a number of appointments in the vicinity. The meetings were all well attended and much interest was manifested by members and outsiders. . . . There are at present seven applicants for baptism and others were almost persuaded. . . .

* * *

At the Indiana Conference that fall there was again a visiting bishop from Virginia. This time it was Samuel Coffman, John's father. It took John back to his boyhood days to hear his father preach again. He gave the main talk the first morning and John was pleased with the vigor with which he upheld the doctrines of the church and pointed out the obligation resting on each to maintain them.

An interesting item of business that day centered around a plan by which members could assist each other in case of loss by fire. The problem had been under consideration for some time, but at this session there was a report from several Canadian visitors who told of the system of mutual aid which had been in operation there for twenty years. They presented details of the system used in Ontario and conference decided to adopt a similar system for the Indiana churches.

The next few days John spent most of his time with his father. They attended a number of midweek communion services in neighboring churches, and as a bishop Samuel was always asked to assist. On Sunday the whole family went to the service at Shaums, and then hurried back to Elkhart to be ready to receive a few guests whom they expected.

> Oct. 15, 1882—This evening before night there stopped at our home the brethren Bowman and Stauffer from Canada; Coffman and Showalter from Virginia; Friesner, Beery, and Keller from Burr Oak; [Stover] from DeKalb county: Keim from Kent, Mich.; Shaum and Miller of this county; Chris Shantz and wife of Illinois; and John Shenk of Ohio. This evening we had an excellent meeting at Elkhart. Keim, Shenk, Coffman, Bowman, I and Stauffer talked.

But the pleasant week of Grandfather's visit was not without a touch of sadness. On Tuesday morning the family said good-by to Annie Sauers. Her health had been a great source of worry to John and Bettie ever since their arrival in Indiana. Although at times she appeared quite normal, the old trouble kept reappearing and lately seemed to be much worse. Pain in her chest and a persistent cough alarmed John and Bettie. Annie's mother was worried, too. John kept her informed of Annie's condition and when she wrote begging her to come home, they felt they couldn't ignore her wishes. But Annie didn't want to go. This is my home now, she kept saying. Eventually, however, they were able to persuade her that she would improve much faster in the fresh mountain air of her Hampshire County home.

John and Bettie tried to be cheerful as they said good-by, but their hearts sank. They had said final farewells to too many friends with a cough like Annie's. By the look in her eyes, Annie, too, seemed to realize the seriousness of her illness, and she sobbed uncontrollably when John drove up with Funk's horse and buggy to take her to the depot.

After a visit to a few churches in Illinois, Father Coffman accompanied John to Burr Oak, Michigan, for a weekend. On Sunday morning John again had the privilege of listening to his father preach and in the evening Father Coffman listened to his son.

During his father's visit John had had many serious talks with him and occasionally the conversation turned to the subject of evangelization. As a bishop from Virginia, where evangelistic services were regarded with disfavor, however, Samuel shrewdly kept his counsel, seemingly taking a neutral stand on the issue. But that night as he listened to his son speaking so simply and yet so forcefully to this little congregation, his heart was touched. He knew that the Spirit of God was upon him. He knew that he was now witnessing the fulfillment of that revelation which he and Frances had cherished in their hearts all these years. Surely this was the special service to which his son was being called. Like John the Baptist he was calling men to repentance.

Early next morning father and son parted at the depot, Samuel to return to Virginia, John to board a train for a visit to Ontario, Canada.

"God bless you, John," Samuel said, clasping him a little closer than usual as he said good-by. "I reckon you remember what we told you, your mother and I—about the revelation that God had some special service for you? Well, I—I feel you've found that service. Keep on, son; remember you're another John called to serve the Master. But be patient, and go slow. If you're careful, you'll avoid a lot of trouble for yourself and others."

John's heart was singing as he set out for a new country and more churches that badly needed spiritual assistance. He knew now that his father approved of his work, and he knew he had his blessing. How much more was this true of his heavenly Father!

*It is infinite satisfaction to me to be settled down at home for a few days with my family. I praise God for His goodness in giving the weary toiler a place he can call home—a place where glad ones meet him and sad ones speak good-byes. Sometime this meeting and parting will end. May that be one happy glorious meeting.*—Diary.

# 15

In the gray dawn of a bleak November morning J. S. Coffman caught his first glimpse of Waterloo County, Ontario. He had been looking forward to this visit to Canada for a long time, and gazed about him with interest as he stepped from the train at Berlin (now Kitchener) at 4:00 A.M. With him were two young women from Indiana, Hannah Nusbaum and Sarah Weaver, who planned to visit relatives here and also in Pennsylvania.

"You're in a foreign country now," John remarked as he led the way into the depot. "We'll be living under a queen for the next few weeks, you know."

"It doesn't feel or look any different as far as I can see," said Hannah, looking around the dimly lit depot. "Do you think we'll notice much difference?"

"No, I don't think so. A lot of the people around here originally came from Lancaster County, Pennsylvania; so quite likely we'll get a little sample of what to expect in Pennsylvania."

Noah Stauffer met the visitors, and after leaving the girls at the home of Preacher Moses Erb in Berlin, he took John out to his home near Strasburg.

"So this is the Waterloo I've been hearing about," said John as they turned down the road toward Doon. "I can't see much yet in this half light, but it looks as if there might be pretty good land around here. Are many of these farms owned by Mennonites?"

"Yes, most of them, I'd say. You see, this was the biggest Mennonite settlement in the province, and back, say seventy-five or eighty years ago, our people bought up about 60,000 acres. Then a few years later they got another big piece in Woolwich Township, most of the township, I guess. We don't own it all now, of course, but most of the farmland still belongs to our people."

"And how many churches do you have?"

"Oh, let's see, about eighteen or twenty, I'd say, besides the Amish and the New Mennonites."

"And how often do you have services?"

"Most churches have every two weeks. Some once a month."

"And what about Sunday schools?" John continued.

"Well, we have a couple, not many. There's one at Centerville for the Berlin children that's been goin' for quite a few years now. At Wanner's they've had one about fifteen years, and there's a good one at Cressman's in Breslau started about ten years ago. But it's not clear sailing at any of these places. There's plenty of opposition. Most of the churches can't have them because the ministers are so set against them."

"Too bad," sighed John. "We had the same trouble back in Virginia. If only they realized how much they can help the church. But how are things in general here? Is the church growing? Are you reaching the young people?"

Stauffer slackened his hold on the reins and drove on in silence for a moment or two.

"Without Sunday schools, with no evening meetings, and services only once or twice a month," Stauffer spoke slowly, studying his words carefully, "and with other churches around us holding protracted meetings and getting our young people interested, what do you think would happen?"

"I understand," replied John. "I have seen the answer in far too many of our churches. We must wake up soon or it will be too late."

"I wish you could stay and help us a while," said Stauffer, "but Waterloo County is like Elkhart. Protracted meetings mustn't even be mentioned."

"It's the Brenneman movement here too, I suppose," ventured John. "Let's see, how long ago was it you had that split?"

"Just seven years. Brenneman was here earlier than that, but it was his influence. Solomon Eby held the meetings that caused the final break. A lot of our people went with him."

"And have you ever figured out why, and just what did cause the break?"

"Well, looking back on it," Stauffer began thoughtfully, "I'd say there wasn't really so much difference in beliefs. It wasn't Sunday school, for we did have a few. They said they wanted prayer meetings, but conference wasn't against them! And it wasn't against revival meetings either then, though they didn't approve of continuing them too long. As I see it, the big trouble was that the church was going at these things too slow, for Eby, and our people didn't like some of the methods Eby and his men were using."

"I can understand them partly," John remarked. "I feel myself we're far too slow sometimes, but we do have to be patient, for we must above all avoid more division. The same thing happened down at the 'Twenty,' I suppose."

"Yes, but there they had more trouble—two bad breaks, one at the same time as ours up here, and one back in '49 when Daniel Hoch went off. They've had a real bad time."

"And yet folks can't see that we need some kind of special effort not only to keep the church alive but to keep it growing."

"No, they can't. They're afraid of special meetings now—afraid they'll cause more trouble, more divisions. Our young people, even the young married folks, are standing outside looking on, not knowing which way to go. You can't blame them for not wanting to join a church where there's splits and bad feeling and bickering. There's nothing to make them want to come in."

"Exactly," exclaimed John. "That's what I've been trying to tell our people. What we need more than anything else is some plain Bible teaching. We have a strong foundation, and we can talk about our faith, the faith of our fathers, but it won't mean much to the young people unless it's understood. But I have noticed that when it is made plain it means as much to our young people today as it did to those first Anabaptists who even gave their lives for it."

John had a visit with Preacher Samuel S. Bowman that morning and in the afternoon Stauffer took him to Breslau for a service at two. His audience was not large, but there were a number of ministers present and all of them listened intently as John poured out his heart on a favorite theme, "Zeal for salvation of others."

The next day, Canadian Thanksgiving Day, was fittingly celebrated with a service at the Christian Eby Church in Berlin. John was pleased to see the church nearly filled for the service. But he noticed, sadly, that very few young people were present.

During the next four days John preached twice each day, and each time at a different church: Snyder's, the Methodist church in Waterloo, Shantz Church, Latschar, Blenheim, Detweiler's, Strasburg, and at the Detweiler home in Doon.

On Monday he left for the "Twenty" in Lincoln County, the Indiana girls still with him. Preacher Abraham K. Hunsberger met them at the depot and walked with them to the home of a fellow minister, Daniel Honsberger, where they had dinner. That afternoon there was a meeting at the Moyer Church on the main road, about one mile west of Jordan. This was the first organized congregation of Mennonites in Canada, he learned. But his heart was heavy as he looked over the small group assembled: only a few middle-aged and elderly people. The same was true of the service held the next day at the church on the "mountain" near Campden.

Hunsberger was glad for the opportunity of discussing church problems with John. Although suffering already from two aggressive movements, the church seemed heading for another division. This time a group was pulling in the opposite direction. Quite a number were frowning on the Sunday-school work which the church had been carrying on for years. They also disapproved of Hunsberger's occasional sermon in English. Like Stauffer and several Waterloo County ministers, Hunsberger would have welcomed assistance from Coffman. But with conference opposed, he agreed they had better wait a little longer.

It didn't take John long to discover that:

> The feeling in the church here is not harmonious and the young people are not uniting with the church as [they] should be.—Nov. 15, 1882.

Hunsberger accompanied John and his traveling companions to Dunnville to spend a few days with the churches at South Cayuga and in Rainham Township on Lake Erie. The trip took them along the banks of the Welland Canal between Merriton and Port Colborne. John was keenly interested in the marvelous engineering project which permitted ocean vessels to navigate between Lake Erie and Lake Ontario.

They spent five days in the area, holding services at Cayuga and at the little church at the lake, near Selkirk. On Saturday and Sunday evening the meeting was held in the Disciples church in Selkirk. The building was filled on Sunday night and the congregation listened with great interest to the sermon on Christian growth. In his diary John commented: "There is some interest here, but the people need waking up."

Although Preacher Leonard Hoover preached in English quite frequently, some members wanted more English in the services, while others clung to the old regime, fearful of straying from the ways of the fathers.

At Sherkston, the next stop, John also found a great need. Here there were only a few members left of a once flourishing congregation. Much effort would be needed if the church was to survive.

On the way to Clarence Center, New York, next day the group stopped to see the famous falls at Niagara. John described the event in his diary:

> Nov. 23, 1882—I am well satisfied and my curiosity is gratified by our visit to the falls. We had an excellent view from the Canadian side, but the spray rained on us so fast that we were soon wet. We saw the falls, the suspension bridge, and the whirlpool, and the expense for all was, including hack drives, 70 cents.

The Mennonite church at Clarence Center, New York, which

John visited over the weekend was affiliated with the Ontario Conference. Here, too, there had been serious divisions and the church was in a weakened state. John had a long talk with the minister, Jacob Hahn, and also consulted with a former minister, Jacob Krehbiel, who had withdrawn from the church and was now affiliated with the more liberal Mennonite faction, the General Conference group. At Good's Church, where he preached several times, the attendance was not large, but he found the interest good.

Tuesday, November 28, found John and his traveling companions on the train bound for Mount Joy in Lancaster County, Pennsylvania. John had looked forward to this visit for a long time. This was the largest Mennonite community on the continent, and since the church here differed considerably in customs and practices, John was anxious to meet the ministers and bishops and to see for himself how the church prospered. He also wanted to learn of their needs and problems in order to make the *Herald of Truth* of more benefit to them.

A Thanksgiving service at the Kraybill Church the day after his arrival reminded him of the service in Berlin a few weeks earlier. Here, too, the congregation was composed largely of older people. At Habecker's next day the congregation was swelled by the arrival of children from a nearby school. Amos Lehman was their teacher. Knowing that Coffman had once been a teacher, he felt he might be able to interest his young charges. And he was not disappointed. John directed the first part of his talk to them.

During his week in the county John was invited to speak in many of the churches and met a great many church leaders and a number of *Herald* correspondents. He was especially glad for a good talk with Jacob N. Brubacher, one of the leading bishops in the county. He had been one of the first promoters of Sunday schools in Pennsylvania and was particularly interested in singing. John soon discovered that in other respects he was quite conservative and also sensed that his influence was far-reaching. At Millersville on the last evening of his visit John was surprised to find two other visitors present. Bettie's uncle, Gabriel Heatwole, and Joseph Driver from Virginia. The three shared the pulpit that evening.

From Lancaster County, John went to Masontown, Pennsylvania, for another week of meetings. The 46-day trip ended with a brief visit to old Mrs. Freed, widow of Preacher Joseph Freed, at Richland, Ohio. His heart ached when she told him she was the only member left of a once prosperous congregation, and that the old church building was now being used by a Methodist group.

In writing about his visit to Canada and Pennsylvania, John summed up his observations for readers of the *Herald of Truth:*

Jan. 1, 1883—Were I to write a description in detail of all that I saw and felt, refer to the work that is being done and the work

> that is needed . . . it would make my article too long. . . . It gave me a clearer insight to the workings and wants of the church; and as one that is connected with the work of publishing our church paper, better prepared me for my duties and at the same time threw around me a caution to keep a jealous eye upon the literature given out as the teachings of the church lest it educate the readers away from the doctrines of the Bible which our people have maintained with the apostles for centuries in the past.

* * *

"Hello, everybody," called John, stamping the snow from his boots as he stepped into the kitchen one cold January evening.

"Oh, Papa, Papa," shouted Dannie and little Barbara, who came running to greet him.

"Why, I believe she knows me this time," said John, picking up his tiny daughter, while Dannie started rummaging through his pockets in search of some interesting trifle. "Last time she seemed to think I was a stranger."

"Well, it's been only three and a half days this time," said Bettie stepping into the welcoming line. "After that last long stay—I wonder any of 'em knew you."

"It's not as bad as that," laughed John. "Anyway, I'm home now. Everybody all right?"

"Oh, tolerable," said Bettie. "The rest are all out skating. Is there any mail?"

"A letter and another copy of the old *Commonwealth* from Virginia. And here's a nice little parcel from home. Open it, Dannie, and show Mother the nice present sister Lizzie sent me."

"Oh, another batch of collars. Now ain't that nice of Lizzie, keepin' you in collars like that," said Mother, carefully examining the box of snowy white, stiffly starched collars. "She makes 'em real good."

"Yes, I feel I'm fortunate, having a sister like that. So many folks are good to me."

"Even folks you don't know," commented Bettie. "That five-dollar bill comin' in a letter last week, I just can't get over it. I reckon the good Lord is alookin' after us all right. Who's the letter from now?"

"Annie Sauers."

"Oh, how is she, poor soul? Have you read it?"

"Yes, I read it. She seems pretty homesick."

"Give it to me quick. I want to read it."

"But isn't supper ready? I thought you'd want supper first."

"No, I want to read this," said Bettie, sitting down to the table and drawing the lamp closer. "Call the children a while so's they can be gettin' ready for supper."

Bettie was wiping tears from her eyes when John returned to the kitchen after calling the children. He stood looking over her shoulder.

"My, that poor girl!" sighed Bettie. "She must have terrible homesick, crying like that every night. I—I could almost cry myself."

"Yes, it's too bad," John agreed, pulling a handkerchief from his pocket and applying it to his own eyes. "But I'm afraid there's nothing we can do about it."

"Why, John Coffman, there is too," scolded Bettie. "She wants to come back; so I reckon we can at least send her a ticket so she can come."

"But, Bettie, the girl is sick. We sent her home because she was sick; so why should we bring her back again?"

"Because she has homesick and wants to come, that's why. And she does say she's better; so—"

"Well, she might think so," John warned, "but you know how it was before, better one day and worse the next, and sometimes you'd have to nurse her for weeks. You just can't do that again."

"But, John, she needs us. And she's just like one of our own. I just can't bear it." Bettie's voice broke and tears started streaming down her cheeks.

This was too much for John. "Well, I suppose I'd better see about getting her a ticket," he replied huskily. "I know she's like a daughter, and—I reckon she won't get better very fast grieving like that."

"You got enough to buy a ticket?" Bettie asked, regaining her composure.

"Maybe, with the money I got last week from the folks out at Christophel's, some they gave me to help buy a horse, and the five in the letter and the bit that came from Canada, I guess I'll be able to make it. I'll stop at the depot tomorrow and see about it."

"Did you have good meetings at Christophel's?" Bettie asked, rushing around once more, as the children came trooping in.

"We didn't have services, after all. There was some mistake," John replied. "I guess the Yoders didn't understand I said I'd come Friday."

"Too bad, and after them comin' all this way to see if you would come."

"Yes, it was disappointing, for they're pretty anxious to have some meetings out there. But I had a good visit."

"Didn't you preach at Christophel's on Sunday?"

"No, it was Yellow Creek. I only wish I could stay with them for a week or so. But I'm afraid that won't be for a while yet. I almost went too far for some of them on Sunday evening."

"Why, what did you do?" Bettie asked, getting the youngest seated at the table.

"Well, I gave an invitation after the sermon. A few folks were under such conviction that I just had to. It sort of took them by surprise, I guess. So this morning old Daniel Hoover came over to Christophel's to see me. I guess some of them got together to talk about it last night."

"Did they think you done wrong?"

"Well, not exactly wrong. They're just afraid I'll go like Daniel Brenneman, that's all. But I had a good talk with Hoover and he seemed to be fairly satisfied when he left."

About the middle of January, John set out on a long-promised visit to Morgan County, Missouri. The trip started out badly. The train due at 4:40 A.M. was an hour late, which meant that he missed his train in Chicago and had a twelve-hour wait. At St. Louis the next morning the experience was repeated, but he didn't consider the day wasted:

> Jan. 20, 1883—Spent the day first, by taking a walk in the city out to the river to see the bridge and business houses. The bridge is fine and the river majestic. Then I wrote a number of letters to my correspondents. Toward evening I met a lady who appears to be a true Christian. Had a good talk. She gave our supper and presented me with $2.00. (Mrs. Samuel Yoder accompanied him on this trip to visit friends in Missouri.)

About a month later John was surprised to receive another gift from this lady whom he chanced to meet in the depot in St. Louis—a set of commentaries on the first five books of the Bible.

John arrived at his destination on Sunday morning just in time for a quick cup of coffee before going to church. He attended service at Bethel, which he referred to as the "Sweitzer" church, since most of the congregation was composed of Swiss families coming from Holmes County, Ohio, in the sixty's. He was invited to give a talk after the sermon by P. P. Lehman, their minister.

That afternoon John learned a little about the history of the church in Morgan County from Lewis Shank. The first Mennonite settlers were the Swiss from Ohio, but they were followed a few years later by settlers from a number of other states, each with his own particular ideas regarding customs and practices of the church. In spite of diversity of opinions the people came together for Sunday worship, at first in their homes and schools, until a building was erected in 1869. There were about thirty-five families in the community by then, and for some time they respected and tolerated each other's opinions. In order to keep peace a formal resolution was adopted, granting each member liberty to serve God according to his own customs or conscience. "In the essentials, unity; in the non-essentials, liberty; in all, charity," became the church motto.

Two years later, however, a serious disagreement arose over the practice of the ordinance of foot washing. For a time the peace of the church was threatened until negotiations culminated in a peaceful division into two congregations. Fifty-one members remained with the Swiss group at Bethel and P. P. Lehman was elected minister of the congregation. The other group worshiped in a schoolhouse for several years before building the church which they named Mount Zion. D. D. Kauffman was ordained to take charge of this group in 1875. Daniel Driver was now his associate. It was because so many of their young people had apparently no interest in the church or spiritual affairs that they decided to invite Coffman to work with them for a while.

John remained for two weeks, holding services in schools, churches, and halls throughout the district. An interesting report of the visit and his personal observations appeared in the February 15 issue of the *Herald:*

> I was much pleased to see how much harmony and good feeling prevails between these factions (Bethel and Mount Zion) and thought, so little as appears to stand between them it might be an easy and at the same time a blessed thing for each one to give up a few preferences for the good of his brother, uniting all their strength and working together in perfect harmony. . . . The appointments were nearly all well attended and the interest seemed to grow to the last. . . . Six young persons expressed their willingness to begin the new life in Christ.
>
> On the 2nd of Feb. I left Tipton en route for Elkhart but stopped over Sunday at Varna, Marshall county, Illinois, where two meetings were held at a place where the people, with a few exceptions, had never heard a discourse by one of our ministers. It seems to me that if some of the brethren were to go into such places and see with what interest the people hear the Word as we teach it, and hear the expressions of approval of the doctrine, they might receive courage to make greater efforts where we have only a few members or none at all.

* * *

On arriving home in February, John found a letter from his brother Daniel, telling of his marriage to Sarah Guyer in Virginia. He had left his job in Illinois and since Sarah didn't want to leave Virginia he was planning to settle down there.

Then in March came news of another wedding. This time it was his friend, Noah Grabill. Noah had come to Indiana for his bride. Once he had made a special trip to seek the hand of Annie Sauers. But when that dream was shattered, he had found the love and companionship he desired in the person of a young widow, Emmaline Hernley.

With the close of the country school at the end of March, William, now twelve, and Samuel F., ten, commenced work as regular hands at the Mennonite Publishing Company for the summer. In a letter to L. J. Heatwole, John told about the work they were doing:

Aug. 17, 1883—William works at the case, setting type, taking proofs, etc., and has become one of the substantial hands in the composing room. He likes it quite well now and has quite a good opinion of his abilities as a printer for one of his years. Yet he seems to have a preference for outdoor work and considers it a treat to be out a day at hard work. Samuel works in the bindery, folding papers, pasting tablets, sewing books, etc. He likes his work very well and carefully watches all the processes of book binding and has already acquired considerable knowledge and skill. He can earn from twenty to forty cents per day. Unlike William he would slip away from work at home and work in the bindery any time.

One of John's jobs at the office that spring was reading proof for a new songbook, *Bible School Hymns,* edited by his friend, C. H. Brunk, which Funk was publishing. One of the selections Brunk wanted to include in his book was a song John had written for use in evangelistic services. Brunk also requested him to compose the music for it.

"There, that sounds better. It should be all right now," John said, making a few last-minute revisions on the composition. "You men can go back to work again. Thanks for helping," he said, dismissing the quartet he had hastily assembled to try out the harmony.

"Yes, it sounds pretty good," said Funk. "Have you chosen a name for it yet?"

"I've been thinking about it," John replied. "I think I'll call it 'Barr.' "

"Barr?" Funk exclaimed in surprise. "After Mattie Barr?"

"Yes, why not? She's been working hard setting type for the book and deserves a little recognition. All the hymn writers and composers as well as the editor and publisher will be recognized, but the folks that do a lot of the hard work are never mentioned. So if Mattie doesn't mind, I think I'll just name my little tune in her honor."

Alone at his desk John once more took out his tuning fork and hummed the air softly to himself. And then, just to assure himself that the melody was right and really suited the words he sang through the three stanzas of the hymn destined to move many hearts during the next few decades:

O weary wanderer, come home,
    Thy Saviour bids thee come,
Thou long in sin didst love to roam,
    Yet still He calls thee, come.

Think of thy Father's house today,
    So blest with plenteous store;

Think of thy sinful, wandering way,
Then come, and roam no more.

Poor prodigal, come home and rest,
Come and be reconciled;
Here lean upon thy Father's breast,
He loves His wandering child.

*Refrain:*
Help me, dear Saviour, Thee to own,
And ever faithful be;
And when Thou sittest on Thy throne,
O Lord, remember me.

John was quite unaware that the whole office staff was listening, and that a number hastily wiped a few tears as the beautiful solo ended.

That spring Bettie began to make preparations for a trip back home to Virginia. She was longing to see her old home and her relatives and friends in the valley. Annie was back with them, her health greatly improved. She would be able to look after things while Mother was away.

Taking the two youngest with her, Bettie left early in June. Martha Funk accompanied her to help look after the children, while Barbara Maust came in from Bristol to help Annie with the work at home.

John was surprised when Bettie wrote saying that she wouldn't be home until about the first of August. Originally she had planned on six weeks. And then came another letter saying she would like to stay until the middle of August. This was a great disappointment, for home just wasn't the same with Bettie away. He missed her even more than when he was off on his long trips. Was this how she felt when he was gone? With a pang he suddenly realized what his work for the church cost his wife. Surely her sacrifice was as great as his own. In a very literal sense she was a colaborer. Certainly she deserved this holiday, and even though he continued to miss her, he was suddenly glad she could have this visit. In his next letter he told her to stay until her visit was really finished.

But John was not prepared for the shock which came in the form of a letter from his brother Joseph one day. Some of Bettie's relatives, Joe reported, were showing considerable sympathy for her in her hard lot as the wife of a preacher who left her and the family alone so much of the time.

He felt himself grow warm as he read the letter. Tossing it on the desk he walked over to the window and stood staring blindly at the brick wall.

"Sympathy!" he mused. "They're pitying her for marrying me. I'm a heartless man with no thought for my wife and family. And of course I don't suffer having to leave Bettie and the children so much of the time! O God, please help them to understand," he prayed. And then came the thought that he wasn't the first John to be misunderstood or criticized. What must people have said about the Baptist, leaving home, living like a wild man in the wilderness, not even attempting to settle down to make a living? But he was obedient to the call of God. It was what God required of him.

This was one letter which demanded an immediate answer, he decided. Returning to his desk he started to pour out his heart to his brother on a subject which had been on his mind a long time.

Joseph and Sallie Coffman,

Dear brother and sister:

> Your letter has just been received and read, and it gave me much pleasure, and made several impressions on my mind that were of more than ordinary character. One especially, which I will notice at once. It was this: that some of Bettie's relatives sympathize so much with her sad lot of having to be alone with the family so much of the time. The sympathy is all right, and shows their affection and concern for her, but how they manifest it I do not know; whether they pour into her ears a stream of complaining sorrow-laden words, enough to make any one miserable, or whether they are trying to show up the bright side of this question, which they really do not know much about, I do not know. I am not a heartless wretch that leaves my wife and family unprovided for and miserable while I travel around having a good time, and I don't believe any one thinks so. I married my wife because I loved her, and I have the satisfaction that by the blessing of God that youthful, impulsive, passionate love has been and is yet ripening into a broader, deeper, purer love as my years of toil pass on.
>
> . . . I have every reason to believe now that the Lord did shape the circumstances of my life, and gave me such a companion that, while she is not an intellectual helper in my God service, is yet just what I needed, a faithful wife, a fruitful mother, and a kind parent and in no ways a hindrance to the work that the Lord has called me to do and brought so plainly before me and so easily within my reach. I have rejoiced that Bettie does appear to enjoy life, and that she likes it here where our lot is cast. There are too many people in the world that profess to follow Jesus who do not love God and the souls of ruined sinners enough to make any earthly sacrifice of comfort, money, or social pleasure. . . . I believe, but I do not know it, that I make a greater sacrifice than Bettie does. I do not make these visits for pleasure. It is hard for me to go, and my greatest

concern is for my family and the extra care it puts upon the mother. But in addition to this, how often this weary body and the mind, burdened with thoughts, concern for souls and prayers, until rest and sleep fly away, scarcely to be wooed back, would fain be at home and rest, enjoying the sacred intimacy of own loved ones instead of stranger friends. . . . There are two sides to this picture, and one of them is beautiful. The joy that I have found in these labors as the Lord came with spiritual blessing, and prospering His work, I would not give for all the riches of the world, and I am glad to believe that Bettie mingles her joys with mine, and that this life of toil in which she is willing to do her part brings her pleasure that enables her gladly to spend her lonely hours working at what God has given her to do. . . . Now does this letter murmur in your ears a sad refrain? If so, you take it wrong. We are living happily, and I have often thought that as for myself, I have so much pleasure in life that at some time I may have to pass through deep sorrows, but it will all be for the best, come what may. I think Bettie is happy, and we are all happy and contented. It has been somewhat lonely since she is gone, but I am happy to think that she is enjoying herself with her friends of long ago. We like the country and the people, and I, as much as I love the friends in Virginia, especially my parents, brothers and sisters, have not the least desire to live there again; because the Lord has shown me that my field of labor is elsewhere. . . .

This letter is of such a general character that if you wish you may let some others read it, Nas Heatwole and Mother Heatwole, Christian Good and Father if you have the opportunity.

August 11, 1883.

It was Thursday evening, August 23, when John met Bettie and the children at the depot. Home-comings were always happy, but this one was special, for suddenly everyone realized how much they had missed Mother and the little ones. The three travelers were also overjoyed as they were welcomed back by the delighted family.

That night, instead of Father, it was Mother who dipped into the satchel and handed out presents.

"And here are a few things for you, John," Bettie said after each of the children had received his portion from the mysterious bag. "Sister Lizzie sent you this tie. These suspenders are from Lewis, and this shirt from Margaret Heatwole. And here's a nice handkerchief from your mother, and some more from Sarah Sharpes and Catharine Heatwole. And I have a little money for you too, from a few friends."

"Are you really happy to be home again?" John asked later that evening as they sat talking in the kitchen after the children were in bed. John had been unusually quiet all evening and he watched

Bettie thoughtfully and listened for possible tones of regret as she recalled events of her visit.

Bettie didn't use words to reply, but John needed no further assurance of her complete happiness. Apparently the undue sympathy from well-meaning relatives had left no ill effects.

* * *

Several weeks later John was back in Missouri, setting out from Morgan County on an unusual trip to Jasper County.

Nine people made the trip across country with horses and two wagons. Besides John there were Mr. and Mrs. Daniel Driver, Mr. and Mrs. Jonas Wenger, John C. Driver, Jonas Detweiler, Lewis and Jacob Shank. Picnicking along the way, and finding lodging in country homes at night, the group spent an enjoyable four days on the road.

On Thursday evening they reached their destination, the home of John's uncle, Joseph Weaver, who lived near the little town of Oronogo. Weaver had come to Missouri from Virginia about fourteen years earlier, and had been ordained as the minister of the little group of Mennonites settling in this district. They had no church building but held services regularly in White Hall schoolhouse. They also participated in a union Sunday school organized in the community in the early seventies.

It was threshing season, a busy time for these Missouri farmers, but they weren't too busy to attend a few meetings over the weekend, nor to enjoy this visit from friends. The *Herald* reported:

> Nov. 1, 1883—It was clear to be seen how much encouragement such visits give to these little scattered flocks, how much a little help is appreciated, and how much might be done to build them up by faithful, earnest teaching in a number of meetings held in the fear of the Lord. This was a season of refreshing for visitors and those visited.

After spending another week in Morgan County, holding meetings and attending their annual church conference, John returned home by way of Crawford and Edgar counties, Illinois, and also stopped in Clay and Owen counties, Indiana, to visit a few families. These visits were made at the request of the Evangelizing Committee, and he had been given a little cash from their fund to help with expenses.

In each of these communities John visited the few families and held services in schools or churches of other denominations. Regarding the church in Clay County he wrote:

> Nov. 15, 1883—What members are here are not especially blessed with this world's goods, and they have been at the additional disadvantage of having their church house destroyed by one of the last summer cyclones. They have the new house well under way . . . a little assistance would be very much appreciated.

The members here are much less in number than they were some years ago, and it is plain to be seen that unless greater efforts are made to interest the young people and gain them into membership the church will rapidly decline and ere long become extinct. While Bro. Daniel Royer and some of the ministers in the past have been doing their duty as well as they could under the circumstances it is certain that this congregation has not received the encouragement due it from other parts of the brotherhood. Some of the members told me that I was the second minister that visited them in 15 years. I found souls here that are under deep conviction and seem almost persuaded to begin a new life. . . .

*These gratuitous contributions I consider as sent from God in answer to trust and prayer that He shall provide and supply my needs and the needs of my family, while I go to preach His Gospel.*—Diary.

# 16

"Wake up, boys, there's a surprise outside," John called from the foot of the stairs one cold December morning. The first snow of the season had fallen during the night, covering the earth with a shimmering white blanket.

"Oh—oh, look here!" cried Ansel, sitting straight up in bed and rubbing his eyes. "William, Sammy, look quick, look at our bed."

Crawling carefully from under the covers, Ansel rushed to the door to call Father and Mother.

"Come here quick," he cried. "We've got a surprise here, too."

John laughed with the boys when he saw the dainty little snow-drift that had formed at the foot of Jake and Ansel's bed.

"Well," he said, "you must have been warm with that extra blanket over your feet. That's what snow is for, you know, to keep things warm."

But in his heart John wasn't laughing, and the look he exchanged with Bettie was quite serious. What kind of provider was he, that his family had to live in a house where snow drifts formed on their beds?

The thought troubled him greatly. Was it right that he should leave his family in such a run-down, dilapidated house? Sometimes he wondered whether it would stand up in a heavy wind. He had tried to patch the roof and fill in the worst cracks that made the place so drafty. But it was impossible to mend all of them. Bettie wasn't a complaining type, but lately she had mentioned several times that the house was hard to heat. She was afraid of overheating the stoves in such an old building.

In spite of all his thinking, John could see no solution to his problem. Even if he stayed home and worked steadily, it would be years before he could afford to build a better house, for he was already heavily in debt for the farm. But for Bettie's sake there was one thing he could do, he decided. At least he could stay a little nearer home that winter and not leave her alone so much of the time.

Because of this decision John was able to give a little help to some of the nearby congregations that winter. The Yellow Creek and Christophel churches were visited several times. There were now a number of converts in this area and a stirring of new life. Mr. and Mrs. Samuel Yoder were staunch supporters of the evangelistic effort. John spent several days with them just before Christmas. When he arrived home, he was greatly surprised to discover that the envelope Yoder handed him as a Christmas gift contained fifty dollars.

That winter a call came to him from the Amish Mennonite church near Ligonier, in Lagrange County, Indiana, commonly known as the Hawpatch Church. John weighed the matter carefully and consulted with a number of his fellow ministers before accepting the invitation.

Bettie was plainly upset when John told her of his intended visit to the Hawpatch. She was sitting on a stool at the kitchen table peeling a pan of apples. John saw the tears come into her eyes and watched anxiously as she finished peeling an apple in silence.

"But I thought you was agoin' to stay home this winter and just be away over Sundays now and then," she quavered, brushing a sleeve across her eyes.

"We—e—ell, it will just be two weekends and the five days in between," John hedged, picking up a knife to help. "That won't be very long, and it isn't far away, just an hour or so by train. You can easily reach me if you need me."

"I know, but—but it's not even one of our own churches," she sputtered. "How come you're astartin' to preach for the Amish? Ain't they got enough preachers of their own? Like as not six or seven in that very church."

John sighed. He realized Bettie was simply voicing a keen disappointment. Patiently he began to explain his recent decision.

"Yes, my dear, they do have ministers, a bishop and three ministers, to be exact, two quite old and two younger ones. But you know how it is in some of our churches. It isn't the number that counts; it's the kind. I don't know much about the men at the Hawpatch. Young Hartzler, I understand, is a teacher and should be better qualified. But they have asked me to come, and who am I that I should turn down a call to help someone find Christ? The Amish have souls, you know, the same as anyone else."

"Of course," replied Bettie tartly, viciously quartering an apple. "But I'm just sayin' they might do more to help themselves."

"Yes, and so could a lot of our own people." John tried to keep his voice calm. "But I am hoping that we can help them to help themselves better. I feel strongly that I should go, for the Amish are after all not so different from us. A few generations ago we were one church. Our doctrines are practically the same, and who knows, perhaps with a little co-operation and a little more understanding we might once more become one church."

Bettie was silent for a minute or two, but made one more gibe before giving up the argument. "Are you sure they'll want you there? The young preachers might think you're all right, but what about the older ones? You won't dare polish your shoes or slick up too much or you'll be too proud for 'em."

"Well," said John, looking down at his dusty working clothes, "they wouldn't think me proud right now. But I intend to be tidy no matter what folks think. And I aim to hold up Christ so plainly that they won't notice me."

This was John's first experience in an Amish congregation and it proved to be a pleasant one, paving the way for entrance into many more Amish communities. The situation in these churches he found to be the same as in most Mennonite congregations, an overemphasis on formalities and customs handed down from older generations, and a general lack of knowledge regarding the Scriptural basis for their faith. This lack of teaching was strongly evident in the attitude of the young people who had begun to resent the harsh discipline of the church and its practices which they could not understand.

A Sunday school had been established, but lack of training was as evident among the teachers as among the preachers. The young gained little from the Sunday services and were rapidly being drawn away. Some found satisfaction in other denominations, while many were being absorbed into an irreligious society.

In spite of his invitation to hold meetings here, John found he had to proceed with the same caution as in other places where this work was new. On Sunday the senior minister, David Morrel, preached first, a long tedious sermon in German. John followed in a half-hour talk in English on the same theme, "Rest." On Tuesday morning Morrel spoke again at great length before giving over the pulpit to John. That morning John spoke simply and plainly on the fallacy of observing forms of worship without the spirit.

Interest increased in the evening services and on Sunday evening the house was packed. Again John used a favorite topic, "Excuses," and once more hearts were touched and the indifferent made to think. When an invitation was given, eight responded. On Monday evening there were seven more. By this time most of the opposition had ceased and John had gained many new lifelong friends.

With the coming of spring John was off again on preaching tours. He had mixed feelings about the trip planned for May. This time he was going back to Virginia. Certainly it would be a pleasure to see his family and old friends again. But he realized that this visit could not be for pleasure alone. He was under obligation to his Lord and Master to preach the Gospel. But in light of his recent activities in this line, would he be welcome in the Virginia churches? He knew he would be watched and criticized. He knew he would be barred from direct evangelistic effort, but he hoped by some means to be able to reach the hearts of some of his old neighbors and relatives for whom he had long been praying.

John arrived in the valley in time for the annual spring conference. He found he was cordially received and invited to take part in the discussions. Since a communion service was scheduled for Weavers on Sunday, a preparatory service was held on Saturday evening after the conference sessions. John was invited to speak at this service, and also to preach for the communion service next day. He was surprised at the size of the crowd that assembled for the service.

> May 11, 1884 —There was an immense crowd of people there, over 1,000, I suppose. Driver introduced. I spoke on the subject of communion; Hildebrand and Shank officiated.

The week was filled with visiting and preaching each evening not at Weavers only, but also at other churches, one service at a time. One day John and his three brothers went to town to have a photograph taken. The ladies of the family insisted on this. They had been photographed a short time before and wanted a companion picture of the men.

One of his final appointments that week was at his old school in Montezuma. The building was filled for the meeting, and once more a feeling of responsibility almost overwhelmed him. Many of these people, he knew, didn't hear Gospel sermons very often. Probably most of them came just to hear their former teacher. They went away with a message that made them think deeply.

After a visit to Annie Sauers' home, John set out for Somerset County, Pennsylvania. He had visited churches in this area and across the border in Maryland on his trip two years before and had received a pressing invitation to return. Besides holding services in a number of schools he spent nearly a week with the congregation at the Folk's Church, now known as the Springs congregation. One of the final meetings here was an instruction service for a class of nine converts.

In this community he found a large group of Amish Mennonites, many of whom attended the services. He visited Amish homes as well as Mennonite, and received a warm welcome. He became especially interested in the John Bender family. Here was a family of bright young boys who seemed to take an exceptional interest in the meetings. He was surprised to find the whole family, parents as well as children, using the English language constantly. But he soon learned that the mother could not speak German and was not a member of the Amish Church. Mrs. Bender was glad for the opportunity of talking with John. He found her keenly interested in spiritual matters and in sympathy with the teachings of the church when he made them plain to her in a language she could understand.

Back in Masontown for the spring communion service on Sunday, John noted that the church was so crowded that quite a number were unable to get in. Jacob Johnson's barn at Middle Run was used for a service that afternoon. It was encouraging to see a little interest, but John was conscious that there was still a deep need which must be met if the congregation was to grow.

* * *

It was a hot July evening. John, along with a few other Elkhart men, was waiting at the depot in Rome City. They had come out on an excursion train from Elkhart that morning to spend the day at the popular island assembly and hear some of the top-ranking religious speakers of the day. Lyman Abbott was one of the speakers, and that afternoon they had listened to Talmage's popular lecture on Ingersolism.

"What did you think of Talmage?" John asked, turning to his companions, A. K. Funk and A. E. Summers.

"I thought he was very good," replied Funk. "He's a forceful speaker. What's your opinion?"

"He is forceful and convincing," John answered thoughtfully. "I must say I enjoyed it, but somehow—well, maybe I was expecting too much. I'm afraid I was just a little disappointed. Maybe it was the subject or the heat or the crowds. But of course you can't judge a man by just one talk. The pictures tonight were good, though."

"Oh, very good," said Summers. "I could almost imagine myself in one of those boats going up the Nile. The camera and the magic lantern are two remarkable inventions."

"I suppose it's trite to say it again, but certainly we are living in a wonderful age," remarked John, gazing at the lights that illuminated the depot as well as the outside platform. "Just look at those brilliant lights. I still can't get over the miracle of electricity. What a difference it has made in our office, and in our street lighting!"

"And what an improvement it will be when they get that new water system working!" added Funk. "I for one will be happy when the wife can just turn a tap for her water."

"Speaking of improvements," observed John, checking his watch with the station clock, "I think one of the greatest is the new time system. It's wonderful to know just what time it will be when you get to a certain place. Before this meridian system you could only half guess at it, but now with definite time zones, it's wonderful."

"Well, I wish I knew what time it'll be when we get back to Elkhart," Funk said. "That train certainly is late tonight. So you're going on to Ohio instead of back to town," he added, turning to John.

"Yes. I got a telegram this afternoon. They want me for David Shank's funeral tomorrow; so I figured I could make better time this way. That's another good old friend gone. There have been so many lately. It seems I get a call to preach at some funeral nearly every week."

* * *

One Sunday that fall the Coffmans were all invited to the Joseph Summers home for dinner. While Bettie helped Mrs. Summers with the dishes, John and his host settled themselves in the parlor for a good talk.

"Well, how are things going this fall?" Summers began. "Are you booked up for a lot of meetings, or are you planning to spend more time at home like you did last winter?"

John sighed. "I hardly know what to do. I've promised to spend ten days at Cullom soon, and a week at DeKalb, and there are a lot of other calls. I'll feel guilty if I turn them all down, and I'll also feel guilty if I go and leave Bettie with things as they are. That old house! It's beginning to worry me."

"Yes, I imagine it would," Summers said. "It's been an old house for a long, long time. Get's pretty drafty, I suppose."

"Regular little blizzards, sometimes," John said, "and so cold that the covers sometimes are frozen fast to the beds. I just have to manage to rebuild or fix up the place somehow. We can't go on like this. But I don't see how it can be done. Sometimes I think it would be wiser to sell the farm and rent a place in town again. I've been praying about it, and I feel certain God will have a plan for me soon."

The two men sat in silence for a moment or two. "But there's one thing about it," John continued. "If I stay home more, maybe I can do a little more for the young people here. We can't have special meetings, but we might be able to put a little more effort into the meetings we do have. I'm concerned about our church here. We must work harder. I'm glad for the interest in the children's meetings we've been having lately, but we must somehow get something going for the older ones."

"Yes, I think you're right," Summers replied. "And there's no doubt you could do a lot to help the young folks if you were around a little more. But, you know, some of us have been thinking about your problem lately, and we don't think that a man who can do as much good for the church as you should be hindered because of a little money. You need cash, of course, and for a lot of things besides a house. And you need your farm to support your family."

"Yes, but—but—" John began.

"Now, now, don't stop me; just let me finish," Summers said, clearing his throat as he continued. "Now, we look at it this way. Why shouldn't we help to pay for a new house so that you can keep on with the work you're doing for the churches? So you can go off for a month or so, knowing that your family is comfortable in a good warm house? That way we could feel we were having a share in the good work too."

John's eyes widened in surprise, and color rushed into his cheeks as Summers made his speech. Then rising slowly from his chair he walked over to the window. Summers heard him blow his nose, but said nothing. Finally he turned from the window and tried to speak, but the words wouldn't come.

"Of course I haven't got any cash to hand over just yet," Summers said, pretending not to notice John's difficulty. "But as soon as you decide to go ahead and replace that ramshackle building I promise you I'll have a little contribution. Go find a carpenter and see what it will cost. I'm sure you'll find a lot of folks just waiting to help."

His faith strengthened by this talk with Summers, John decided that the time had definitely come to make plans for a new home. And so next morning he took Bettie out into the yard to decide where the new house should be located.

"Now, John, do you really think we should be atalkin' about a new house?" Bettie asked, reluctantly leaving a washtub to make a tour of the yard with him. "Don't you think we might better just fix up this old one a bit? Where will you ever get enough money for a brand-new one?"

"I don't know yet where the money will all come from," John replied firmly. "But God knows. And He knows we need a house. That's all that matters. Now where do you think we should put it?"

"Why, it don't matter much. It will have to be a little ways away from the old one, for we can't tear this one down till the other's ready to move in."

"You know what I think? Right over there's the spot." John pointed toward a clump of tall pines. We can build so that there will be two pine trees in front of the house and two on the south. It's nice to have trees close to a house. They look nice, and they give shade, and besides, you'll always have birds around."

"But wouldn't that bring it up pretty close to the old one?"

John walked over to the clump and started stepping off the measurements. "Yes, I'm afraid it will run right into a corner of the old living room. We'll have to tear down a little piece before we can start to build."

Bettie laughed. "If that ain't just like you. Seems to me it'd be more sense to cut down a few trees and move the house over a few feet."

John shook his head as he looked at the beautiful lines of the old pines. "No, Dear. I'd hate to cut down those old trees. We can manage for a few months without that part of the house. Very soon we'll forget about the inconvenience. But those trees! We'd miss them a long time. It takes years to grow a tree. We'll wait till it's warm enough to tear down that part of the house, but we'll start now to make our plans and get the materials together so that we'll be ready to build as soon as the weather is right."

The family spent many enjoyable evenings over the plans for the new house. John called in a carpenter to estimate the materials required and in order to keep down the expenses he took advantage of the lower winter prices and ordered in advance as much of the stone, brick, lumber, and hardware as possible.

Word of the venture soon reached John's friends in a number of communities he had visited, and all through the spring and summer of 1885 contributions for the new house came trickling it. Donations were handed to him by his friends at Elkhart. Dollar bills and money orders for five or ten dollars arrived in letters. From Noah Grabill came $23, collected from a few friends in Cullom. This was the first of three contributions from Cullom. From Caledonia came $41; from the church in Columbiana, Ohio, $51; and the church at the Hawpatch, $61. And so the fund grew. By the end of the year John was able to estimate in round figures how amply his faith had been rewarded. Well over $500 had been contributed by friends for the building, while the itemized expenses as recorded in the back of his diary amounted to about $600. Besides, there had been gifts of labor and of materials. John gave fervent thanks to the Father above as well as to the kind donors as each gift arrived.

Knowing that he would be very busy at home that spring, John decided to take a trip to Ohio in February. He had promised to hold evangelistic services at Menno Chapel in New Stark, and decided at the same time to go farther east into Medina, Wayne, and Holmes counties, and to visit a few small congregations in Fairfield and Perry counties. He knew the Ohio conference, like Indiana, was opposed to continued meetings. But he also realized that a start must be made in breaking down opposition. With a stout heart and prayer for divine help and guidance he set out on his mission.

On Saturday evening and Sunday he preached at the two churches in the vicinity of Elida—Sherrick's, now Salem, and Good's, now known as the Pike. In his diary John wrote, "The members seem very much in earnest here to learn the truth still further."

A high light of his long weekend here was Monday's visit with the old bishop, John M. Brenneman. From him he again received inspiration as well as some excellent advice. Brenneman was well acquainted with all the Ohio churches and their leaders. He knew their problems and the difficulties standing in the way of progress. He also knew the grim story of dissension from lack of Christian charity and understanding.

"Our people need help," Brenneman told him, "no doubt about it. And if something isn't done soon, some of the small churches will die. Maybe as an outsider you will be able to do more for them than I could. But be wise and try to keep the good will of the brethren. If you don't, we'll only have more trouble."

Mr. and Mrs. John Blosser were at the meeting at Sherrick's on Monday evening. They had come with a horse and wagon all the way from New Stark so that they could take John back with them for the services at Menno Chapel. Although the thermometer registered ten below zero next morning, blankets and hot bricks kept the travelers fairly comfortable during the thirty-mile return trip.

New Stark was quite a young congregation, made up of families originally worshiping at Riley Creek, near Bluffton. The building was erected in 1878, and even before a minister had been ordained a group of zealous young men organized a Sunday school, which from the first was a union school attended by children of all denominations.

Although the church was filled night after night, it was crowded several times when John announced he would explain the distinctive teachings and doctrines of the Mennonite Church. There were fourteen decisions that week, including several at the church at Riley Creek which he visited one day.

The young minister at New Stark, Jacob Horning, accompanied John on his visit to the eastern counties. Mr. and Mrs. Adam Brenneman furnished transportation for the trip to Medina County, and in spite of sub-zero weather the sleigh ride across the snowy countryside was an enjoyable experience.

Here John found a discouraged little group of Mennonites. For the *Herald of Truth* he wrote:

> April 1, 1885—The church in Medina county has gone through many sad experiences that have a tendency to discourage both members and outsiders, but I have much reason to believe from the interest which was manifested that the Lord has here an abundant harvest that might be gathered. . . . There is one applicant for baptism and a number more that seem almost persuaded. Seldom have I been in a church for whom I had to feel so much sympathy as those dear disciples in Medina.

From the minister, Martin Leatherman, John heard the old, old story of what happens when two strong personalities disagree.

"Yes, we once had a large congregation," he said. The three sat talking together after the evening service at Kopp's school.

"So I suppose most of them went off with the Wisler group," John said. "Let's see, about thirteen years ago?"

Leatherman nodded. "Yes, it took most of them. In some other places the groups were pretty well divided, but not here. Only a handful left."

"Why do you think it went that way?" John inquired.

"Strong leadership. Old Bishop Abraham Rohrer was a powerful man, and even though he was in the seventies when the trouble began, he vigorously denounced anything new—Sunday schools, English preaching, evening services, and all. So when Wisler severed his connections with the church in Indiana, Rohrer did the same in Ohio. Practically the whole church stayed with him. If it hadn't been for John F. Funk, I don't know whether we'd have any members left. He made quite a few trips down here and encouraged a few families to stay with the conference. That's when they began calling us the Funks."

"You can still use the church, I suppose?" John asked.

"Yes, we get it every other Sunday. But they make us feel they're doing us a great favor in letting us use it."

"Do you have a Sunday School?"

Leatherman shook his head. "No, there are hardly enough of us to run one. But some of our children go to a union school."

"It would be a good thing if you could have one of your own," John advised. "It would be good for the older ones as well as the children, for they need some responsibility. Sunday schools are filling a very important place in our churches."

Schoolhouses and several different churches were used that week for the services. The Guilford Church used by both groups was filled with a large and interested audience several times. John's sermons were largely evangelistic, although he spent several evenings explaining the doctrines of the church for the benefit of the Mennonite families as well as the many non-Mennonites who attended each evening.

Before leaving the community John had some heart-to-heart talks with a number of young married couples who were standing outside, not wanting to join the ultraconservative Wisler group and not willing to throw in their lot with the struggling minority. He knew that their problem went deeper, that it was a spiritual problem and not just a matter of church affiliation. And so as he visited them in their homes, the Kreiders and the Linds and a few others, he always had Bible study and prayer with them.

In Fairfield County, John held three services at Pleasant Hill Church. Although a fair crowd attended the services, there were only five members left of the once thriving congregation—A. Beery, his wife, and three daughters. This was the home church of the influential Brenneman family, where the bishops, John and George, the evangelist, Daniel, and Coffman's good friend, Henry Brenneman, grew to manhood. The church here had the first Sunday school in Ohio, Beery told him. It was organized by the Brennemans. But when Father Brenneman died and his sons moved away, the church suffered a loss from which it never did recover.

A few miles away, in Perry County, John found another congregation, Turkey Run, also in a weakened state. But it wasn't hopeless, he decided. With a little effort it could be built up.

At home John once again did a little bookkeeping. On adding up a few figures from his notebook he discovered he had received $65.80 in gifts to help defray his expenses on this trip. He had also received a commission of $6.75 from the Publishing Company for subscriptions and books sold for the company. The figures looked good until he realized that the time lost from the office was worth $58, while his traveling expenses came to $19, and Horning's fare which he paid amounted to $6.40.

"I guess no one can accuse me of going off on these trips for the money that's in it," John remarked ruefully as he showed Bettie the figures.

Bettie sighed but said nothing.

"I know I'm a few dollars out, but it's worth it. Even if I hadn't received a cent, it would still be worth it just to save one soul or encourage one believer. And somehow, I feel we were able to encourage quite a few."

Seeing the rapt, faraway look in her husband's shining gray eyes as he sat staring unseeingly at the figures on the paper, Bettie checked the words that were on the tip of her tongue and tucked the grocery bill back in the cupboard drawer. "He can see it in the morning," she decided.

A warm spell early in May meant that at last building operations could get under way at the Coffman home. John spent several days at home helping to tear down part of the old house. Then came the day when he staked off the site for the new, and commenced digging for the foundation. Jacob was his right-hand man at home, and with his help and that of the Burton boys they were soon ready for the stone masons. Fortunately a sand pit was discovered on a corner of the farm, which saved considerable expense.

John managed to secure good masons and a good carpenter for the job, but he was enough of a builder to take more than a passing interest in the work going on at home. Whenever he could spare a little time from the office he came out to work with the gang, helping to cut down a little on labor cost.

September 23 was a red-letter day for the family. Although some painting and a few odd jobs remained to be finished, John decided that moving time had arrived. Several of the boys stayed home to help with the moving, and John smiled as he watched them hurrying back and forth with their loads. That was one day he had no trouble keeping them at their jobs. Supper in the new house that evening seemed a festive occasion to children and adults alike.

"How do you like it, Bettie?" John asked as they made a final inspection after the children were in bed. "Do you think it will be all right after we get the painting and graining finished?"

"All right?" echoed Bettie. "Why, I think it's wonderful. Almost too grand for me. After the houses we've been alivin' in, this is a—

a palace. I almost feel like a queen or something."

"Well, you won't feel quite so grand once you get washing a sinkful of dirty dishes. And all these cupboards you've got, you'll need them. I reckon it's just as cheap to build them as buy them. It's right that you should have things handy with me gone so much of the time."

> Sept. 23, 1885—Did not go to town today. We moved out of our old house into the new. We have been thankful for the shelter of the old house, but now feel especially thankful that we have a convenient, comfortable house which we very much needed. We feel that it is our Heavenly Father that provides for us, and to Him we give our thanks and render our praise.

*I have of late been much exercised in mind concerning my work for Christ in the church. The way has sometimes looked dark to me on account of my weakness and spiritual poverty, but the Lord has graciously kept me and made me feel fully willing to give up all my preferences and do His will.*—Diary.

# 17

By the middle of October John was able to record with great satisfaction, "Our house is now completed." One week later, knowing that his family would be comfortable in their new abode, he again took to the road, this time for a six-week stay in western Pennsylvania.

The little church in the village of Stonerville, now known as Alverton, on the border of Fayette and Westmoreland counties, had been without a minister for nearly seven years. Looking after the congregation was John Durr of Masontown, some thirty miles southwest, and Herman Snyder of Blair County, between forty and fifty miles northeast. These ministers took turns in conducting a Sunday service once a month. Durr was with John that first Sunday, having arrived for the spring communion service. John noticed that most of the members in the small congregation were middle-aged or older.

Jacob Loucks, a son of a former minister, Martin Loucks, was one of the most influential members here. John visited him in his fine home on the outskirts of a growing little community known as Scottdale. The entire area had once been the Loucks farm, but the new coal industry which gave rise to many other industries had changed the economy of this community.

John listened with interest to Loucks's story of the settlement in this valley. The first Mennonites had come from eastern Pennsylvania at the turn of the century. By 1850 there were about two hundred members in the district.

"And where are they now, the children of those two hundred? It's hard to believe that a congregation that size could dwindle to thirty or forty in such a short time," John said.

"Well, a lot of them moved farther west—to Ohio, Indiana, Illinois, and Missouri. There's always been a lot of shifting around here—right from the start. But we have to admit that quite a few have gone to other churches."

"Why?" John asked. "Was it the fault of the ministers? You had plenty of them years ago."

Loucks sat stroking his chin thoughtfully. "Yes, we had plenty at first. Maybe too many. Not enough responsibility. But with none at all, right now, we can't expect to hold our young people. A service once a month just isn't enough. Look at my own boys, several of them married and with families, and not one in the church. But what can we do?"

John's eyes reflected Loucks's deep concern. "It is a pity," he sighed.

"But one thing is plain. If there is to be a church here twenty years from now, there will have to be a real effort made soon. What do you think started the decline, say thirty or forty years ago?"

"Well, one thing, as I see it, was German preaching. They hung on too long here."

"But you did have one English preacher. Jonas Blauch preached in English, didn't he?"

"Yes, he was a good hand at it. But he came too late. A lot of the folks had already gone over to other churches by then. But there were other things too. We might as well face it. Making money became a bit too important to most folks. They just weren't interested enough in church matters."

John nodded. "That's about it. The almighty dollar is one of Satan's sharpest weapons."

During the week which he spent in this area John was able to arouse considerable interest. Besides preaching at the church in Stonerville he also held several services in the United Brethren church in Scottdale.

Two of Jacob Loucks's sons lived in the Masontown area, and John had several good talks with them while he was holding meetings there the next week:

> Nov. 4, 1885—We went to David Loucks's over dinner and had a talk with David and Abraham. I feel very much interested in Bro. Loucks's boys and their wives. I am much attached to them and believe they will yet make workers in the church.

After another week in Somerset County and northern Maryland, John's next stop was in Bedford County. This was new territory to him. The church was in charge of Herman Snyder and his brother Jacob. Although there were a number of members around Manns Choice, there was no church building and the services on Sunday and Monday were held in school buildings.

As he rode across the mountains next day with Herman Snyder

on his way to his home in Morrison's Cove, John realized the hardship and personal sacrifice made by the Snyder brothers in serving the widely scattered congregations in their district. In all kinds of weather they made long trips, sometimes by train but more often on horseback. This time Snyder came with a horse and buggy and John was thrilled with the delightful mountain scenery as they made their way over hills and through valleys.

John stayed with the Snyders for nearly a week, visiting their members and preaching once or twice each day at the Martinsburg Church and one at the Dunkard church near Woodbury. Describing this visit in the *Herald of Truth* John wrote:

> Dec. 15, 1885—There are a good many members here, but they are considerably scattered and the ministering brethren have such a large field that their appointments are not frequent enough to keep up the interest as it should be. I was sorry indeed to see the young people not belonging to the church. It seemed to me an extra effort to get them saved and into the church would be well-pleasing to the Lord. I am fully convinced that they are taught the pure truths of the Gospel, but likely they hear too much of another character between these teachings. I was rejoiced in my heart to see the interest that was here manifested. The church here is in charge of Jacob Snyder, a dear aged brother who has labored long with them as their bishop.

Johnstown was next on the itinerary. Here he was pleased to find several large churches in an apparently prosperous condition. This church, he learned, was established a little earlier than the settlement around Stonerville. But unlike the latter it had continued to grow and many young people were members of the congregation. John held services in the Blauch Church and the Stahl Church during his visit here.

* * *

John didn't spend much time at home that winter. In February he headed west, stopping first at the little town of Cherry Box in Shelby County, Missouri. He received a warm welcome from the members of the small Mennonite church located about a mile and a half south of the town. Again he found a discouraged group feeling keenly the loss of a number of influential members. Some, he learned, had moved away, while others had withdrawn membership. It was the Lapp family that they missed the most. They were among the first to settle in the community around 1850, and had supplied three of the ministers of the congregation—Martin, Benjamin, and Abraham. But some trouble arose over the sharing of the meetinghouse with the Dunkards. Eventually this led to the silencing of Martin, who soon left the district. A short time later his brothers, Christian and Abraham, withdrew and joined the Dunkard church.

After the first few meetings that week the crowds grew so big that a number had to be turned away. It was then decided to use a larger building and permission was granted to hold the services in the Methodist church. By the end of the week three converts had made application for membership in the congregation.

In Cass County, where John went after a rainy, muddy week in Versailles, John found himself in an Amish community divided into two factions. One group in charge of Preacher Jacob Kenagy had built a new church in 1882, while the other group worshiped in the old church with Moses Yoder as their minister. Here John also found several Mennonite families who could not worship sympathetically with either congregation, although they attended the Yoder Church. They realized the great spiritual need in the community and begged John to return soon to hold a series of meetings for them.

After a week with his Uncle Joseph Weaver's congregation in Jasper County, John set out on his first extended tour of Kansas, where quite a few Mennonite and Amish families had recently settled in small colonies. The visits were brief but gave him a good insight into the condition of the settlers, both physical and spiritual.

At Newton he found quite a large group of settlers from Pennsylvania. They had organized a congregation and David Weaver had been ordained the previous fall to serve as their minister. Prospects were good for a flourishing church, John recorded.

There were two settlements in McPherson County, the largest near West Liberty. Mathias Cooprider and Samuel Miller were in charge of the church here. Bishop Daniel Brundage and Jacob Holdeman looked after the small congregation at Spring Valley. "I can see no reason why, with earnest effort, there should not be a large prosperous church here, also, in a few years," John wrote.

In Marion County he found a prosperous congregation in charge of Daniel Wismer and B. F. Hamilton. He attended a baptismal service in a schoolhouse near Peabody in the morning when six members were received. In the evening there was a service at Good's Church.

"A good many members, some comfortably settled," was John's comment regarding the church at Columbus in Cherokee County. Samuel Mishler was the minister. In Harper County there were only a few members, but they had a service in a school building. In Cowley and Butler counties he also found only a few members, but he remained in Butler several days, and held services in the town of Butler which were greatly appreciated.

In May, John returned to Cass County, Missouri, for the meetings he had promised earlier in the year. After attending Sunday school at the Yoder Church he went over to the Kenagy Church for the regular morning service. Kenagy invited him to speak. "The house was crowded," his diary records, "and the interest was intense. Text—'Born of water and the Spirit.' "

On Sunday evening and for the remainder of the week the meetings were held in the Yoder Church. Each evening the crowds grew larger as members from both churches as well as people from other denominations flocked to hear the Mennonite evangelist. Realizing the undue emphasis which had been placed on forms in both churches, John spent several evenings endeavoring to explain the spiritual truth underlying the practices observed by the church. They needed a reason for their faith, he concluded. Other sermons were more evangelistic, appealing particularly to the young people who had seldom given much thought to religious matters. Five young people made the good decision one evening after listening to a stirring message on "the cost of a soul."

> May 31, 1886—I had the greatest interest in Cass county that I ever had anywhere in a week's meetings. Members and outsiders were alike concerned. Both factions seemed deeply interested as well as our own members direct. Eighteen converts came forward and others almost persuaded.

Before the week ended, several men spoke to John about organizing a Mennonite congregation in the area.

"Yes, I suppose it will come to that," John replied thoughtfully as he met the small delegation at Norman Shepp's home one morning. "I've been thinking of that possibility, although it does seem too bad that there should be three churches so nearly alike in one community."

"But you can see how it is," Shepp argued. "We aren't at home in either church. And we have our children to think about. Some of them have just made a start in these meetings and we can't ask them to be baptized in either of the other churches."

"No, I can see that," John agreed, "but I want you brethren to have a little patience and not press the matter. For the good of all concerned I think we should move slowly. We don't want to antagonize anyone. If either Bro. Yoder or Kenagy feel we've come in here just to get members away from them, I'm afraid our meetings will do more harm than good. We want to help them as much as possible as well as our own folks."

"But some of their folks aren't satisfied either and want to join us if we start a church here," Shepp remarked.

"I know," John replied. "A few of them spoke to me about it. But likely most of the converts will join their home churches. We must be careful and try to keep the good will of the ministers if at all possible. But I suppose there will be some hard feelings if we organize."

When John returned to Cass County for his third visit that fall, he was accompanied by Bishop D. D. Kauffman and Preacher Driver from Morgan County. After discussing the matter they agreed that some action should be taken soon for the sake of the young people desiring to unite with the Mennonite Church.

Being greatly concerned for this new congregation which as yet had no pastor, John returned for another visit in March of the following year. This time he was accompanied by an Amish minister, Daniel J. Johns of the Clinton Amish Mennonite Church near Goshen. No doubt this was in deference to his Amish friends in Cass County, and an attempt to show them that it was possible for Amish and Mennonites to work together in harmony.

For about ten days Johns and Coffman shared the pulpit in both churches, but John was conscious of a growing resentment on the part of the ministers. Many of their members attended the services each evening with great interest. This time there were again eighteen converts.

With hopes of an increasing membership the little group commenced talking that spring of erecting a church of their own. John encouraged them to go ahead, with the result that by November the building was completed and John was invited to be present for the first service:

> Nov. 25, 1887—C. Kauffman came along and took me to the church the brethren are building. The house is 38 by 52, the ceiling 14 feet. It is three miles from Garden City and 2½ miles from the other meeting houses. It will cost about $1,500.

That Sunday morning John expected to visit his Amish friends in the Kenagy Church, but to his astonishment found the doors closed and the people leaving to go to the Yoder Church. Although he was assured by some of the members that the meeting was called off in order that they might hear a visiting Dunkard minister, Chris Holdeman, at the Yoder Church, John read a deeper meaning in the action. He knew Kenagy was not in the habit of calling off his services in favor of other appointments, and realized with a pang that it was a deliberate act of closing the door of the church to him. However, even though he could no longer go to the Amish at Sycamore Grove, they continued to flock to his meetings at Bethel. Many were present that night at the first service in the new building.

This time John stayed with them for two weeks, preaching evangelistic sermons and holding instruction meetings for the applicants for baptism. The final service took place on Sunday, December 5:

> Meeting at 9:30. A good attendance. Two persons were received by letter, members from Indiana; two that had been of the Wisler church in Ohio; three by letter that had been in the Amish church in Iowa; five that had belonged to the Yoder church and five that had been members in the Kenagy church. Seventeen in all. Eleven converts were baptized, making an addition to the church of twenty-eight. After returning from the pool where they kneeled in the water and were baptized by

pouring, we held communion service. Fifty-five members communed. Bro. D. D. Kauffman officiated at the baptism and communion.

When John returned home from a meeting in Ada, Ohio, in February of that year, 1887, he found his family quarantined for scarlet fever. Fannie was in bed but was apparently well on the way to recovery. The rest of the family, Bettie said, had all had symptoms which the doctor considered to be a mild form of the disease. John was almost unnerved by the suddenness of the news. Bettie was plainly worn out and sobbed as she told him of the days and nights of worry and constant nursing. The fact that the letter informing him of the illness had not reached him also troubled him. Scarlet fever was serious. He didn't allow himself to dwell on what might have happened, but rather thanked God for taking care of his loved ones. For the next few days he relieved Bettie as much as possible in the sickroom. Fannie was delighted with the new nurse. Father was a good storyteller.

In spite of work which had piled up in the office, and spring work on the farm, John decided to spend a week with the church in Medina County, Ohio, in April. They were begging him for the kind of help he had been giving in a number of other places.

Even though the Ohio Conference did not sanction this type of help, he was able to meet their requirements by alternating the meetings at Kopp's school, Baker's school, Guilford Church, and the Honsberger Church. There were a number of converts, and the whole congregation was greatly encouraged.

* * *

"Father, I—I've got something I want to ask you," stammered William on the way home from work one evening.

"All right, son, what is it?" John asked.

"Why, I—I just wondered if—well, it's like this. I'd like to go to Canada for a little visit."

"To Canada?" The quick, anxious look from William made John realize his voice had betrayed his surprise. "But why Canada?" he asked a little more calmly. "That's a long ways away."

"Well, there's a bunch going from here," William explained. "A. B. Kolb and the Funk girls, and some others, and they asked me to go along. It'd be kind of nice to see a new place and do something different for a change."

"Yes, William, it would be nice," John agreed. "And I think you'd like Canada and the folks up there. But you know how much it would cost just for train fare."

"I know it's a lot." William kicked at a stone and sent it rolling down the road. "But A. B. thought maybe we could get excursion fares. Anyway, we never do get a holiday and—and never spend money for things like a lot of fellows."

John felt himself grow warm. He knew it was the truth. He knew his boys worked harder than most boys of their age, and had for years spent all their spare time in the shop. But were they beginning to resent it? The tone of William's voice troubled him. And Samuel F. and Jacob were right at his heels, taking in every word.

"Yes, boys, I know only too well that you don't get holidays like some boys. We need every bit you earn to help keep us in food and clothing. I'm sorry I can't earn enough myself to keep all of you. But I hoped you might understand how it is. I have a more important work than just my job at the office. And when you boys work and bring home your pay during the holidays, you're helping in this more important work too."

"We know that," said William with a slight touch of impatience. "But I did think that maybe just once—"

"It would be wonderful, I know," John replied patiently, "but it's a big thing you're asking. When do they want to go?"

"The first week in July."

"And how long are they staying?"

William kicked at a few more stones before answering. "Why, I think they're planning to stay a month."

John heaved a sigh. "That would mean just about your whole summer's wages, wouldn't it? And where would you get money for your books and clothes for school next year? Remember, boys," and here he glanced back over his shoulder at Samuel F. and Jacob, "I consider your education very important. Most folks think you should all be working steadily instead of going to high school. But I want every one of you, if at all possible, to finish high school. That's one reason we can't have holidays and all the other things some boys have."

Seeing William's downcast face and knowing how much it meant to him, John added, "But I won't give you a final answer now, William. I want to think it over."

Discussing the matter with Bettie and considering it from all angles, they finally decided it would be wise to let William go on the trip. Instead of a month his visit was shortened to two weeks.

That summer (1887) John and Bettie took a trip to Virginia together. It was for the sake of Uncle Henry Heatwole and his wife that they went at this time. The Heatwoles were anxious to get back to their old home and see the folks again, and since they were getting older, they didn't want to venture going alone and so made arrangements with John and Bettie to go along.

Probably the high light of the visit was a family reunion at Father Coffman's home on Sunday, August 14. John recorded the event in his diary:

This morning C. Good took us again to the meeting at the Pike. A full house. Text—Gal. 5:6, the law in contrast with the

Gospel. Here I entered the work with a heavy heart, but the Lord helped me. Jos. Coffman took Bettie, and John Swartz took me, in the buggies and we went to Father's where all the family had gathered. We had a pleasant afternoon together and likely this will never again occur that all the children will meet with Father and Mother at the old homestead at once. We had a season of pleasant devotions. Two of the family are ministers, myself and L. J. Heatwole. All the children except Jacob belong to the Mennonite church. John T. Heatwole, Sarah's husband, belongs to the Disciples or Christians. John W. Minnich and John Swartz do not belong to any church. None of the grandchildren have professed religion. The four boys and six girls are all married except the two youngest, Fannie and Rebecca. Father, Mother, 10 children, 8 sons and daughters-in-law, John's 7 children, Jacob's 2, Lizzie's 3, Annie's 6, Mary's 5, Joseph's 2, Daniel's 3, Sarah's 2, number just 50 souls. All were present except John's 7. Only three grandchildren have died, one for Jacob, one for Annie Swartz, and one for Mary Heatwole.

* * *

On the train coming home from Pretty Prairie in northern Indiana early in January, 1888, John's thoughts kept returning to the one topic which had for years lain heavily on his heart, the need of special evangelistic work in his own church at Elkhart. He recalled with pleasure the few days he had just spent with the small Amish congregation at Pretty Prairie, and the special interest shown by the young people. There were many young people at Elkhart now. How he longed to see them aroused to an active interest in spiritual matters. He recalled also his recent visit in Branch County, Michigan, with Bishop Shaum. He shivered as he remembered the New Year's Day baptismal service. Shaum had sent him to Sayer's Creek to baptize the four applicants. It was cold wading into the water, and it must have been cold kneeling in it. But they had all chosen to be baptized in the stream, and the happy look on their faces as he welcomed them into church fellowship had warmed his heart. If only they could have even a few meetings at Elkhart to bring help like that to his own loved ones!

But bound by customs and traditions it had so far seemed unwise to the heads of the Indiana churches to grant permission for a series of meetings in any one church. In an agony of spirit John called on God to open the way, and to give wisdom and direction in the work at Elkhart.

During the next few weeks he discussed the matter a number of times with Funk and several other ministers. All agreed that it would be a good thing, but—

"But what?" challenged John, his eyes smoldering.

"Well, what about some of the bishops?"

"And what about our children, my sons and daughters—your sons and daughters? It's high time we thought of them first. Brethren, let us at least pray about it. We've made a start at a few places in Indiana, and we must go ahead, not backward."

As a result of prayer and much prayerful thinking, the Elkhart ministers finally decided to hold a short series of services during the last week of January.

John spent hours in prayer and study before commencing the series. So much was at stake. Not only the spiritual welfare of the Elkhart young people, his own sons included, but the welfare of the church at large. He couldn't hope for acceptance by the conference, but would there be at least tolerance? Certainly he would receive personal criticism, but would there be serious consequences?

> Jan. 20, 1888—My mind is much taken up with the evangelizing work and especially have I been considering how we can get our young people at Elkhart to make a start in the Christian life. Over this I have wept and prayed, and I look to God for direction in this matter.
>
> Jan. 21, Saturday—This evening after working hours I spent the time in my office alone, reading and in prayer that the Lord would lead and bless the effort we have seen best to make in a few meetings here at Elkhart. We had meeting with only a fair attendance. I took the third chapter of John for a foundation of my remarks and a series of discourses. May God direct to His glory.

John noticed that his talk on repentance had made a strong impression on some of his listeners on Sunday evening. He could plainly see that a number of the young people were thinking deep thoughts. They were aware of sin and a need of repentance. His own boys were unusually quiet as they trudged home over the snowy roads. He longed to speak to them and help them somehow. But he noticed that William walked swiftly on ahead and that Samuel F. seemed to be loitering purposely some distance behind. It was a decision each had to make for himself, he realized, and so left them to themselves while he communed with his divine Master as he walked home alone.

The next evening he again noticed the marked attention and rapt expression on many faces as he spoke on the spiritual significance of baptism. At the close of the sermon when an invitation was given he could see that the matter was being weighed seriously, but no one seemed willing to make the start. Finally Phoebe Funk, John F.'s daughter, rose to her feet and made her way down the aisle. Phoebe's tears were not the only ones in evidence. All over the church there was a flutter of handkerchiefs.

Continuing the study of church ordinances with their Scriptural background and meaning, John used Hebrews 9:1 as his text on Tuesday evening. In setting a pattern for worship, he explained, God prescribed even minute details. No doubt the people in those early days had difficulty in understanding why all those forms were necessary. But now, he said, we can see how beautifully they symbolized the things which were to come, the things fulfilled in Christ. Just so these commands which have been given to us to keep in this age are also symbolic. They represent the unseen things of the realm of the Spirit, and are given to us to help us remember what Christ has accomplished for us.

As he continued his explanation and unfolded the beautiful meaning of a number of the ordinances, John noticed the intense concentration of young Samuel F. His blue eyes shone and he seemed oblivious to his surroundings as the new line of thought opened up before him. When he gave the invitation that evening, John saw a glad response in the eyes of the lad. They had barely begun to sing the invitation hymn when Samuel F. rose to his feet and started toward the front. John's heart sang with joy as he stepped down from the platform to welcome his son into the new and richer life.

After the service that night John noticed that Samuel F. once more fell behind as they started on the long walk home. This time he slackened his pace. He wanted a talk with the lad.

"It's a fine night for a walk," John began.

Samuel took a deep breath of the cold, invigorating air. "Yes," he replied quietly, "it's a *wonderful* night."

For a time the two walked on in silence, listening to the squeak of the snow underfoot and observing the long shadows cast by the moonlight on the snowy countryside.

"It's a wonderful feeling of relief when you finally make the decision, isn't it?" John ventured. In a way it was rather difficult to talk to his 15-year-old son. He seemed almost a stranger.

"It—it's hard to describe the feeling," Samuel continued thoughtfully. "It's like a load being lifted."

"I know. I went through it too," John said. "It was a long time ago, but I remember that it was the most wonderful feeling I've ever experienced."

Samuel F. nodded mutely. "I felt awful last night and the night before. In fact, I haven't felt right for a long time. But tonight everything is changed. As if a big weight is gone."

"That's just what happened, son. The load of sin you were carrying was completely taken away when you acknowledged your sin and asked God's forgiveness. Now you are free. Christ paid your debt."

"Things seem so clear when you explain them," Samuel observed, making a little trench in the snow with the toe of a boot. "I—I never understood before what all those practices of the church meant. Some folks—well, sort of make fun of them. But they do seem important the way you explained them."

"I could see you were interested, Samuel. And let me tell you this. The Bible is full of interesting things, and it's all important—all of it! And the more we study it, the more interesting it becomes."

"And so all those rules and regulations and sacrifices and things in the Old Testament had a meaning?" he remarked wonderingly.

"That's what Bible scholars tell us. I haven't studied it too carefully myself, but I'm convinced God had some purpose in every single detail."

The walk home didn't seem half as long as usual that night to Samuel F. as he got his first glimpse into the wonderful new world of the Spirit from the lips of his father. As for John, he marveled at the interest and insight shown by the boy. He hadn't realized it was in him. Now if it had been William, he wouldn't have been so surprised. But Samuel F. was always a bit hard to talk to. Maybe he didn't know him as well as he thought he did. Maybe he didn't know the rest of the family too well, either. Perhaps he should stay home more and get acquainted!

*God has helped us and we have been richly blessed—far above that we are worthy. God chose changes for us against our choosing, which were for our prosperity and happiness. God knows best. Let His will be done. Continue, O Father, to lead the way.*—Diary.

# 18

The children greeted John with their usual exuberance when he arrived home that February evening. But Bettie, somehow, seemed a little distant. The hasty peck of a kiss as she rushed to look after a roast in the oven seemed to lack the usual warmth. He had expected a little more after another ten days' absence, this time in the Clinton area. As she bent to examine the roast, John couldn't help noticing her lips quiver. And her eyes! Usually they were bright and smiling. But not tonight. They were red and troubled-looking, rimmed with dark circles as if she hadn't been sleeping. Maybe crying instead, John decided with a pang.

"Is something wrong, Bettie? Something happen while I was away?" he whispered, bending over to look at the roast with her.

Bettie shook her head and struggled to keep back the tears. "No, nothin's wrong. Just go and get ready for supper."

"But you—you—"

"Never mind. I reckon I'm tired. Just go and see that Dannie and Barbara are washed."

With Mother and Father both so quiet, supper wasn't the usual gay home-coming event. John carefully scanned the faces around the table and asked probing questions, but apparently nothing unusual had occurred.

Eventually the hour arrived when the children were asleep and the big boys sent off upstairs.

"Now, Bettie, please tell me what's wrong," John commanded, seating himself on the sofa and drawing her down beside him. "You've been fighting tears all evening. Cry if you want to, but please tell me why."

Feeling her husband's strong arms around her, Bettie burst into tears, her whole body shaking with sobs. John let her cry quietly for several minutes.

"Now can you tell me?" he begged, as she became a little calmer.

"I don't know, John. I just don't know," she sobbed. "It's—it's just me. But—but I just don't see how we can go on like this."

"Like what?" John asked in alarm.

"Oh, with you away so much—and—and—" Bettie swallowed hard and dabbed at her eyes with a corner of her apron.

"You mean you're just lonely?" John asked, lifting her chin so that he could look into her eyes.

"Yes, John, so—o—o lonely! Seems as if you're not home at all any more. Do you have to go so much?"

"Oh, my dear, my dear," cried John, drawing her close and mingling his tears with hers. "You don't know how much I miss you too, and the children. The long, lonely hours when I wish so I could be home. It's hard leaving you so often, but I must."

"But why do you have to?" The old fire was returning to Bettie's eyes as she again wiped her tears and sat facing him. "Ain't you done enough now? Surely you can be home for a little while. There's not another preacher in the whole church that's away as much as you. Why should you have to?"

John turned pale at this question. He wished Bettie weren't so upset. They needed clear minds to consider a question like that. They had discussed it before, and the answer was always the same, even though their hearts weren't always willing to accept it.

"You know why, Bettie. Even though it hurts, you really do know." Patience and love shone out of John's blue-gray eyes and burned deep into Bettie's soul. But she also saw the fire of zeal and devotion to duty, and into her own came a look of rebellion.

"Listen, John, I've thought and thought about it, and I don't think God meant for a man to leave his wife and children so much. The Bible says he should leave his father and mother, but he should 'cleave' unto his wife. It says 'cleave,' John, not 'leave.' "

John winced. A pained look crossed his face, but he answered as tenderly as possible. "Yes, Bettie, I know the verse, and I've used it quite often. But there's another that I think about too. 'He that loveth father or mother more than me is not worthy of me: and he that loveth son or daughter more than me is not worthy of me.' "

"But it don't say wife," exulted Bettie.

John shook his head sadly. "No, but it means wife, just the same," he replied softly, reaching for her hand. "Bettie, you know I love you. Love you as much as anyone could possibly love another being. But—but you wouldn't have my love for you come between me and my Lord! Shall I disobey the voice of the Spirit, the command to go and preach, just because I love you so much?"

Once more Bettie was weeping, burying her face in her big, blue apron.

"Listen, Dear," John said comfortingly, "I know how you feel, for I feel just the same. And I do feel badly that I have to leave the responsibility of the children to you so much of the time. Have they been more of a problem this time, or why do you feel so much worse tonight?"

Bettie shook her head. "I don't know. I reckon I'm just athinkin' of myself too much, that's all. It always hurts more when you're so close and yet we can't see you. The children are tolerable good, but boys do need a father to look after them. Sometimes I just don't know what to do."

"Well, the little ones you can spank, but the big ones—"

"No, my spankings don't do no good. I tried spanking Dannie the other day and it was almost like—like the time I tried spanking the whole lot. Remember? When I got through, they were all alaughin' and I had to do it all over again." Bettie sighed deeply.

"It's a problem, I know," John said, "but one which we must leave to God. If He calls me to His work, He will help us in some special way to look after our children. Why don't we pray about it right now?"

Together on their knees beside the sofa they poured out their hearts to God, asking for greater wisdom, more strength, and complete surrender to His divine will.

Several days later John sat down to unburden his heart in an intimate letter to his dearest friend, Lewis J. Heatwole:

> We have much reason to be thankful for good health this winter. I have never had a better year. For a few days I felt a slight twinge of rheumatism or neuralgia. Elizabeth has had very good health and works hard to take care of the family while I am away. But this winter the trial of our patience (mine as well as hers) has been almost too much, for in this that I have yielded to the demands to "Go teach" to such an extent that I have been at home very little since the first of September. We have wept together over the matter when no one knew it but ourselves and God, and tried to speak words of encouragement to each other. . . . When I returned on Monday I found Elizabeth feeling sadder over my continued absence than ever before. But probably it was because I have promised to start on Saturday to Illinois to stay till about the seventh of March. . . .
>
> The children are all going to school, the three eldest to town. William is in the A High school grade and will graduate in June if all goes well. Samuel is in the C High school, second

year of the four-year course. Jacob is in the A Grammar. The rest go to Bunker Hill. Ansel is the greatest lover of books of all the children, and one of the finest singers for his age in these United States. This is saying a good deal, but I say it without boasting, because I know it is true.

You state that your work in the ministry has not come up to your ideal. I am glad you have set your ideal higher than I think your present work could possibly be. When men attain to their ideal of perfection in any calling, there is but little prospect for further improvement. . . . You say you have lately felt great concern for the unconverted part of your community. This is one of the grandest parts of your qualifications for the work of winning souls. Then be willing to work! . . . You ask, are the ministers to blame, or the people, or both that there are so many not Christians? I think both. The ministry and the church are certainly not doing what they might do if they were fully consecrated to God's service. Our ministers are looking first to money and means, and a living, and they are then willing to do a little for Christ, outside of earthly considerations. "As they can," they say. . . . Other denominations have their preachers in the same difficulty, only worse, because they are looking first every one to his quarter, besides being hampered by the consciousness that they will have to preach to please their people in order to get their money. . . . Your remarks in this line of thought have aroused me and I can scarcely keep my pen from spinning out thoughts. . . .

Feb. 15, 1888.

But it was with a heavy heart that John set out for Cullom, Illinois, after being home for only five days. Not only was he concerned about leaving Bettie with all the responsibilities, but there was a note falling due in a few weeks, a note for $75. His honest soul dreaded the thought of not being able to meet a payment.

Ever since his talk with Bettie, John had been doing some hard thinking as well as praying. Was he doing the right thing, after all, in leaving his family so much of the time? Was it right to permit debts to accumulate while he gave so much time to church work? He had gone over the accounts with Bettie and settled as many bills as possible. Bettie looked grim, but said nothing when they figured out that he had worked only ninety-eight days in 1887. The year before it had been 110 days. Perhaps 1888 would mean even less income. Was this right? He continued to pray about the note and to seek guidance as he journeyed toward Cullom.

This worry was to be removed sooner than he had expected. God had been preparing the answer to this prayer even before he asked.

After church on Sunday morning John went home with Samuel

Shearer. Peter Unzicker and his wife were also there for dinner. As they sat around the table talking, suddenly Unzicker reached into his pocket and pulled out a small leather purse which he laid beside John's plate along with a note.

"Here's something I've been asked to give you," he said.

John's face turned red and then pale as he read the note from the congregation, and then discovered the five twenty-dollar bills in the purse. Sweat stood out on his forehead, and for a minute he couldn't speak.

"Brethren, you can't realize what this means to me," he remarked huskily. "It's a direct answer to prayer. Certainly God is taking care of me and my family while I work for Him. I—well, I might as well tell you that I had an urgent debt to pay and didn't know where the money was coming from. But here it is, and more besides. I thank you, and I thank the good Lord for taking care of the matter."

With his mind freed of the financial worry and with his faith renewed, John preached with power that week, and five more young people were led to confess their faith in Christ.

On arriving back in Elkhart, John called at his brother Dan's house before going home. After months of indecision Daniel had finally decided to take John's advice and move his family from Virginia to Elkhart.

"So you decided to come after all," John remarked as he greeted Daniel and his family.

"Didn't you expect me to, after that letter you wrote Joe?"

"Oh, so he gave it to you to read!"

"Did he!" grinned Dan. "He's lettin' everybody read it. But he says it ain't gettin' him out here. The folks there are thinkin' you ain't got much love for the old home state any more."

"Why, I—I didn't think I said anything like that. I just meant that the West offers more opportunity to a young fellow. More room for growth in new territory."

"Well, it didn't sound quite like that, even if that's what you meant."

"Why, what did I say? I don't recall exactly."

"Just that if you had money to buy a farm and intended to live by farming, you wouldn't do it in Virginia; if you was goin' to live by day labor, you wouldn't do it in Virginia; and if you intended to preach and build up the church, you wouldn't locate in Virginia."

John's face turned a deep pink. "I'm afraid I didn't realize it was quite so strong, but that's the way I still feel about it. There is better farming land and more opportunity out here, and certainly a greater need for ministers than in the valley, where they have two to five preachers sitting behind the pulpit almost every Sunday. Anyway, I'm glad I came, and that you did too, Dan and Sarah."

It was a beautiful Sunday morning in early June, in Somerset County, Pennsylvania. A welcome shower of rain had refreshed the countryside, and John's nature-loving soul drank in the beauty of the green fields and trees as he walked to church with his young friend, Daniel H. Bender.

But it was a silent walk. Daniel tried to start a conversation, but for some reason it was difficult. He had spent the night at Daniel Miller's with Coffman and they had talked for hours about spiritual matters and church affairs. John had taken a real fatherly interest in young Bender and was pleased with his spiritual progress. He was one of John Bender's sons, and a convert at the meetings John had held in Somerset several years earlier. The whole Bender family was now in the church except the two youngest boys. John was especially happy over Daniel's decision. He was about to unite with another denomination and was thinking seriously of the ministry when John's meetings in Somerset gave him a new insight into the faith of his forefathers. It was with a deep sense of appreciation that he accepted this faith. A short time later he was ordained as a minister in the Mennonite Church and was proving to be a valuable assistant in the churches of the district.

Bender couldn't quite figure out why John should be so quiet that morning. In fact, he seemed almost depressed. It was so unlike him. All week he had been full of life, preaching powerful sermons. On Saturday he had given such a good talk to the class of nineteen converts, and his sermon at the baptismal service was one long to be remembered. Strange he should be so dejected now, the morning of the spring communion service!

As they came to the church and turned into the yard, John sighed deeply.

"See that long line of horses and wagons, Daniel, and all those people going into the church?" he said.

"Why, yes, I see them. Looks like a good crowd this morning."

John sighed again. "My heart is heavy this morning. When I see all those people and realize my responsibility toward them, it's almost crushing. Almost more than I can bear. What if I fail them?"

With these words John turned and walked rapidly away. Daniel watched him hurry through the crowd to the back of the church, where he slid under a fence and disappeared in an orchard.

"He's going back there to pray," Daniel remarked to a bystander.

Daniel waited outside the church until he saw John returning. A feeling of awe thrilled him as he noticed the change that had taken place. Now he knew that he had indeed been praying, that he had spent a few quiet moments in the very presence of the Father. No longer was his step slow and uncertain, but brisk and confident. His shoulders were erect and his head held high. About his face there was a glow that reminded him of Moses. As John drew nearer, Daniel saw the gray-blue eyes shining with a light that he had never seen there before. His lips flashed into a smile as he motioned to Daniel, and the two entered the church together.

During the summer and fall of 1888 John saw with great satisfaction the outward evidence of growth in his beloved church. Four times he was invited to the dedication of a new meeting house. For him this also symbolized the new outreach of the church.

The dedication at Freeport, Illinois, took place on July 28:

> This morning Bro. J. S. Lehman brought me to the meeting at the new church. It is a neatly arranged house, but not very large. Bro. Snavely introduced after Solomon's prayer at the dedication had been read by Bro. P. Nice of Sterling. I spoke from Haggai 2:9, a contrast between the law and the Gospel.

In August the new Howard-Miami Church at North Grove in Miami County, Indiana, was ready for use:

> Aug. 3, Saturday—There was a large attendance as we met for the first time in their new house. It is 36 by 50 with small anterooms in front on each side of the central aisle. It is a neatly arranged house.
>
> Sunday—Today the house was crowded. The services were made to correspond in a measure to the occasion. . . . The attention was excellent. A crowded house this evening and many outside.

On Sunday, September 30, the official dedication service was held for the new Bethel Church in Cass County, Missouri, following the annual Missouri Conference held here for the first time. The church had been in use since the previous winter.

A fourth dedication at which John assisted was that of the Shaum Church in Indiana, now known as the Olive Church. This took place on Christmas Day. John returned from a trip to Virginia and Pennsylvania just in time to attend this service.

> This morning I arrived at Elkhart on the train at 3 A.M. I walked out home and carried my packages. Took a sound nap yet. At 10 Elizabeth and Daniel and I attended the meeting at Shaums. It was both a Christmas and a dedicatory service. The brethren insisted on me to speak the principal discourse. Text—Haggai 2:9. The contrast between the two temples of the Jews, the two covenants, and the use we shall make of this house under this new covenant.

* * *

On the train on his way to Virginia about the middle of November, John had plenty of time to meditate on the work before him on this trip. The main purpose was to serve on a committee to compile a new English hymnbook. The church in Virginia wanted a new book to use in regular church services. John had been chosen to represent the western conferences on the committee to make the selections.

He felt keenly the responsibility of this work. But he also had another mission this time. A number of the Virginia ministers had intimated that the time seemed to be propitious for a beginning in evangelistic work, and they were urging him to hold a few evening meetings at Weavers or the Bank. It was also arranged that he should spend a week or so visiting congregations in other districts.

John felt his pulse quicken as he contemplated the possibilities before him. For years he had been praying for the opportunity and he had frequently discussed the situation with Lewis Heatwole. Several years earlier he had revealed to Lewis his great concern in a letter:

> Jan. 1, 1885—Since I was in Virginia I have been more pressed than ever to preach to the dear people there. The first few months after I left I did not think much about it, but within the last two months I have several times been seized with sudden impulses to go to dear old Virginia, not for the pleasure I would have in being there, so that I felt almost compelled to go. The Lord has shown me that the true doctrine of the Scriptures needs to be aggressively pushed before the people there. Now, you might think I consider the teachers there too weak or unfaithful, or that I think I could do better than they. God forbid. I think they are faithfully preaching the Gospel and are stronger than I in many ways, but could not the Lord use me as a helper to them? . . . The greatest discouragement I feel is the fact that should I go to Virginia and attempt to help the work along in a number of discourses, some of the dear brethren would see my weaknesses and feel that I wished only to claim and show out abilities that I have not. . . . I do not feel satisfied not to go, as it seems to me the Lord wants me to go. Yet I fear to go lest some dear brethren will not understand my motives. . . .

There was one minister, not in the middle district, who he felt sure would misunderstand his motives. He recalled several letters he had received with personal criticisms and general criticisms of the work as carried on by the evangelizing committee:

> Feb. 22, April 22, 1887—According to your language it requires a different capacity and talent for an evangelist than for a minister, and you say you labor more in that capacity than many others. Who gave you the authority to evangelize? When you were ordained you was ordained just like the rest of us. Were you authorized to evangelize since you left here? Please answer these questions. . . . Dear brother, I am not wounded because you evangelize, but I do think it would be better for you not to call yourself by that name. . . . It does wound me to see that you like to make it known so well what you are doing in this work. . . . I am in favor of evangelizing but not according to the plan laid by the Elkhart conference. . . .

And now at last he was on his way to fulfill this great desire of his heart—to minister as an evangelist among his own dear people. He knew he would need the utmost tact—need to be prepared to face opposition and personal criticism, and even to yield in case serious objections threatened the welfare of the church. Earnestly he prayed for divine guidance, and the power of the Spirit in the effort.

The hymnbook work came first. In his diary John wrote a day-to-day account of the work:

> Nov. 21, 1888—There were five of us, Henry Rupp of Shiremanstown, Pa.; and the Virginia brethren who started the move for the new book appointed Samuel Shank, Emmanuel Suter, and Christ Brunk.
>
> Nov. 22—Yesterday we went to work on the selection of hymns. We first took our Mennonite hymn book and made selections of hymns that passed the critical examination to which each one was put. They were read and every word and line that did not meet approbation was criticized. . . . Then we took the *Manual of Praise* . . . and the Brethren hymn book. So we propose getting hymns from all the books we have at command. . . .
>
> 23—There are selections sent in from all parts of the brotherhood and all are examined. . . . When there is a difference of opinion it is left to vote as there are five of us and it is easily decided by majority. But when any member raises a positive objection to any hymn it is rejected.
>
> 27—All the tunes which are not well known are sung and their merits considered. . . .
>
> 28—The purpose of this book is to use sufficient variety that both young and old will approve of it and yet not have a superfluity of hymns and tunes that will seldom or never be used. The object is to bring the young and the aged together and have them sing together. The young will learn to love the good, fine, slow tunes that the old have learned and the old will help the young to sing the more modern music and in this way the young people will be with us, and it is with them that the church must be built up. Our prayer is, "The Lord use this book for His glory and for a blessing to mankind."

Evening meetings were not too common in Virginia at this time, but the weather was good, the roads in fair condition, and so there was a fair crowd at Weavers for the Monday evening meeting. Realizing that some of the folks were saying that it was all right for him to preach—just so he didn't stir up a revival, John was careful in his choice of a subject the first few evenings. They were topics which would lay the groundwork for the soul-stirring message of Wednesday evening, "Regeneration." That evening the interest was intense. He could see conviction written deeply on many of the faces before him.

"Repent," he pleaded, like the John of old, "turn from sin, and accept the forgiveness and the new life you may have in Christ."

It was one of the happiest moments of his life when all over the church he saw one after another rise in response to his invitation. After a hasty consultation with a few ministers, a service was announced for the next evening. Again there was a good response. A few folks were still fearful, but the good that was being done was too evident—the meetings must continue for the remainder of the week. John saw with joy that the converts included the sons and daughters of many of his own relatives and friends. And he gave thanks to God that also among them were the children of some of his severest critics.

By the end of the week much of the opposition had broken down as each evening saw more and more young people respond. Forty-five new members were added to the district churches that spring as a result of this short series of meetings.

John's father joined in the rejoicing. It was like the dawning of a new day. But he didn't say much to John. Somehow, they could understand each other without too many words. John noticed that his mother missed several of the meetings, and he knew why.

"Thank you, Mother, for your prayers," he whispered as he said good-by. "Keep on praying for the work."

"I will, John, I always will," she promised. And into her dark eyes came the same burning zeal which she so often saw in his.

* * *

It was New Year's Day, 1889. Alone at his desk that night John opened his new diary to make his first entry for the year. Thinking over his schedule for the next few months and the trend of the last few years, he suddenly realized that he could scarcely be considered a regular employee of the Mennonite Publishing Company. First of all he was an evangelist, and in his spare time an assistant to the editor of the *Herald of Truth*. Dipping his pen in the ink he wrote:

> I began the year at work in the office of the M.P.Co. It is my purpose, if spared, to work at intervals when I am at home on the editorial work of the *Herald,* but to spend the greater part of the time traveling and holding meetings. This, however, gives me a wide field of correspondence which I must principally attend to at home and leaves me but little time for actual work on the *Herald*. Today I wrote many letters. This morning it was a pleasure to be with my family and wish each a happy New Year and hear a greeting of the same kind from each.

A little group of Amish in Ohio came first on his schedule that year. Known locally as the "Miller" people, the group was composed of some of the more progressive members from the large Amish congregation—South Union and Walnut Grove in Logan and Champaign counties. Because of their desire for more freedom in the conduct of their church and Sunday school as well as in personal affairs, they had severed connections with the older churches several years before and were affiliated with the Indiana Amish Mennonite Conference. Bishop Eli Miller of the Clinton Amish Mennonite Church east of Goshen had helped them organize and ordained their first minister Samuel Detweiler. This was the reason for the name "Miller."

Realizing that the situation again called for a great deal of tact, John once more called for the assistance of his Amish colaborer, Daniel J. Johns. Although the ministers of the older congregations were not free to invite an English-speaking minister to preach, the new group was free to do so. Since the two groups used the same buildings, large crowds of both factions attended both morning and evening services held by the two Indiana men that week. At their request John spent one evening explaining the ordinances of the church. For an hour and a half they listened, almost spellbound, hearing for the first time the meaning of some of their formal practices.

By coincidence, David Yoder, a minister of the Amish Church in Wayne County, Ohio, was also in the community that week. He joined the Indiana men in visiting the ministers and influential members of the two groups as they tried to find some way to solve differences and restore unity in the church. John, however, saw more complications ahead when a number of young people came to him asking for help in getting an English class started in their Sunday school. Since many of them knew only a little German, they insisted on their right to have some English instruction. But there the Amish leaders drew the line. The German language must be maintained. John could do nothing. "Then let us organize a Mennonite church," they urged.

Returning from another visit to Logan and Allen counties that summer, when Bettie was with him, John found several letters from Ohio waiting for him. One was from David Amstutz of Wayne County, inviting him to come into his district to hold some meetings, and one from another Amish minister begging him to come and help settle the difficulties of the Wayne County Amish. John readily accepted the first invitation, but did considerable thinking and praying before taking on the second task.

The October meetings in Wayne County drew large crowds and resulted in a number of conversions. Here John once more used the method of alternating the services in several neighboring churches. He also preached a number of times in the nearby communities in Holmes and Medina counties.

Before he returned home a meeting was held in the Amish church where a committee met with the congregation to endeavor to settle their trouble. Members of the committee included Joseph Schlegel of Nebraska, D. J. Johns and Jonathan Kurtz of Indiana, David Amstutz of Wayne County, and J. S. Coffman.

The committee worked several days hearing complaints and preparing a report. After presenting the report with charges against a number of members and some who had withdrawn, John wrote:

> Oct. 8, 1888—They all confessed the faults with which they were charged and asked forbearance from the church. It took some time before they all agreed to do so. But we see that there are heavy hearts and that the wounds are too deep to heal immediately.

John had a long talk with David Hostetler next day. He sympathized with him in his desire for progress and more activity, but strongly advised him to be patient in order to avoid a possible schism in the church. Hostetler did try, but the tide of progress was too strong, his position too difficult. A short time later he with a number of members withdrew to form the Salem Mennonite congregation.

In February and March of 1889, John made another tour of the settlements in Kansas, in an effort to help build up the young churches. He spent a week at West Liberty in McPherson County and on Monday morning, February 18, there was a baptismal service:

> This morning the six converts were baptized. The brethren here put the work on me in the absence of a bishop. I had rather not do it, but they thought it best and I consented. George Brunk was baptized in the house and with the rest we went to the river. A clear, sandy bottom—a nice place. I spoke on the subject of baptism, its meaning and use. . . . A cold day after the blizzard though it is milder this evening. Mercury was 7 below zero this morning.

Late in the fall he again traveled westward, this time covering a wide area in Nebraska, Kansas, Illinois, and Iowa, visiting many isolated communities where only a few Mennonite families were located. Tiskilwa, Illinois, was the first stop, then Wayland, Iowa, where he visited the Henry County congregation. It was corn-husking time, a very busy season for the Iowa farmers, but many of them found time to attend a few services. The next stop was Kalona, where he found several large Amish congregations:

> Nov. 8, 1889—After dinner we went to Jacob Boller, four miles from Kalona. He lives near the meeting house in which Christian Werri preaches. This is the only Mennonite meeting house in this country, although there are about five large congregations here. The old brethren which compose nearly all the church here do not think it right to build church houses and worship in them. It is sad that all the Mennonites cannot see alike.
>
> Nov. 9—Went to the funeral of Noah Detweiler, a young brother in the old Amish church who died of consumption. This was the first time I was in a place of worship with this class of brethren. Their ways and their preaching were of the oldest forms. Their preaching was not very able or logical or instructive, but they told much truth. Some wrong shades of thought were brought

out for want of better enlightenment or information.

At South English he visited two former Virginia families and held several services in the Locust Grove school. At Milford, Nebraska, he also found a number of former acquaintances. Services here were held in Eicher's school. There was a large Amish congregation in this community which, he said, "is in excellent order. The spiritual life is above average. They have good teachers or preachers."

Five days were spent with the congregation at Roseland, Nebraska:

> Nov. 26—This evening there was a full house and the interest has increased at each meeting. The meetings should have continued.

In eastern Kansas he visited an Amish community near Oberlin. The minister here was Joseph Burcky. There were about twenty families in the congregation, he learned, with half of them Burckys.

> Nov. 29—The brethren here have a very nice church house west of Shibboleth which they built this year out of lumber. The people about all live in sod houses but they appear contented and happy. The church here is rather of the rigid type of Amish. They wear the hooks, observe the ban, and use the prayer book instead of extemporaneous prayer.

From here John went to Goodland and on to Topland for services. He was quite intrigued with a mirage he saw next morning just after sunrise:

> I saw Goodland 16 miles away and it seemed not more than three miles distant. At one time there were two sets of houses, one set above the others, the upper ones reversed. Meeting this evening with a good attendance for this place. The meeting was in the sod store room where the post office is located.

He remained several days in this community, holding services on Sunday and for several evenings. Among the converts were four people from the town, not of Mennonite background, also some Amish from P. Rulet's church in Davis County, Iowa:

> Dec. 5—Just here I will note about our meetings at Topland. We had the meeting in a low, sod house in which they had the post office. There was no floor in it except the natural earth. The stove was an old rusty one with the pipe barely reaching through the sod roof. The fires were made with what the people here call government wood or buffalo chips which are really the droppings of the cattle which eat the prairie buffalo grass. Of other feed they would not make fuel. They use this to warm their houses and cook their meals.

The long tour ended with a week of meetings in McPherson County, Kansas. Most of the services were held at West Liberty, where there were nine converts. At the Spring Valley Church one evening eight decisions were made.

*I am thinking much of the communion we can have with God in the Spirit. So long as we are holding in our attention only the material life and dealing with material things we know little of God. We may know something about God, but we do not know God till we deal with the immaterial world which is as real as the material.*—Diary.

# 19

The muffled tooting of an amateur brass band woke John from a Sunday afternoon nap.

"My, this feels good," he yawned, with a luxurious stretch. "A quiet Sunday afternoon at home for a change."

"It's a change, all right," agreed Bettie, who had been dozing in a rocker beside the couch, "but if this is quiet—"

John laughed. "Yes, I hear the boys have company. Must have been those horns that woke me. But it sounds good to me."

"I tried to keep 'em quiet a little longer," said Bettie, "but I reckon they just couldn't wait."

"They seem to be having a good time," John remarked. "Are both the Kolb boys here? I can't quite see who all's in the room from here."

"Yes, they're both here, and Martha and Phoebe Funk. Their singing is almost drowned out by the horns."

"I'm surprised how well the boys are doing on the horns," observed John. "Young Kolb must be a good teacher. I think William's going to be quite a cornet player, don't you?"

"Mebbe, but I can hardly think at all in all this noise. What's Samuel playin'?"

"The alto horn. He's getting it pretty good too. And Jake's catching on to the bass better than I thought he would."

Bettie shook her head resignedly. "I can't make much out of it. What are they playin' anyway? I can't even make that out."

"Why, it's one of the pieces from the new *Hymns and Tunes,"* laughed John. "They brought home a few proof sheets so they could learn some of the new pieces."

"Oh, so that's it. Will the book be done soon?"

"In a few more weeks, maybe, if Samuel keeps coming in after school to help with the proofreading. He wants to bind a copy all by himself so we'll have the first book off the press."

"Well, I'll be sorry when it's finished. Like as not you'll be off on another one of your long trips then."

John detected the edge in Bettie's voice. "Yes, I suppose so," he replied quietly. "But let's not spoil the afternoon by crossing bridges. Just look at our sons in there, Bettie," he said, changing the subject. "Don't they look manly today? Are they really grown up or is it just the new suits?"

"Well," said Bettie, "I reckon when you paid $50 for four suits you found out that a couple of 'em were man-size. It's awful what their clothes cost lately."

"I know," said John patiently. "But I saved quite a bit getting the four at once. That's only a little over $12 each. And they're good quality and certainly look good. But I just can't get over how grown up they seem today. Let's see, William is nineteen now; so Samuel will be eighteen in June; and Jacob, is it sixteen? And Ansel, now when was he born?"

"He'll be fifteen in April," Bettie supplied, "and if you're agoin' down the line, Fannie was thirteen just last week."

"All in their teens except the two little ones," exclaimed John, looking almost surprised as he reached for Bettie's hand. "You know, Dear, we are getting older." He paused and a faraway look came into his eyes as he continued thoughtfully. "It makes us think. And it should make us think about the future. Who knows, the time may not be far off when some of us are called to the other side. If only we could be sure that we'll all be together over there! I'm so happy that two of the children have made a start in the Christian life. I'm pleased with the way Samuel's developing. He's getting to be a real worker in the Sunday school and young people's meetings. And Ansel—well, he'll get his turn soon. We'll have to keep praying hard for William and Jake. They know, all right, but it's something they must decide for themselves. But why don't we go and help them sing for a while? They almost got stuck in a few spots in that last piece."

"You go," replied Bettie, jumping up and starting toward the kitchen. "I must call the children. They've been playing out in the snow long enough. And it's time to see what I can find for supper."

When the new hymnbook was finally completed, John found himself with a new editorial job on his hands. That winter Funk had decided the time had come when they must provide more adequate material for the increasing number of Sunday schools. The lesson page John had edited in *Words of Cheer* and the German *Jugendfreund* was not enough. Teachers were demanding more help and many schools were using materials being published by other denominations. Since John had experience in this type of work, it was decided that he should write the material which was to be published monthly in pamphlet form.

> Feb. 28, 1890—Worked in the office; arranged a poem and a long article for the *Herald of Truth* and wrote the rest of the 4th Sunday school lesson (for April), thus the first monthly that the Mennonite Publishing Company is getting out.

For the remainder of the year Funk continued to publish the lesson material monthly, but in 1891 the helps came out in quarterly editions.

> Nov. 21, 1890—This morning I set to work in earnest to complete the S. S. lesson for Dec. '90, which I succeeded in doing. My next work in the office will be to get out a quarterly for the first three months of '91.

This work, requiring hours of study and writing, proved to be a great help to John in his ministry. It was hard, demanding work. Sometimes it was almost impossible to meet the deadline. But from the study came inspiration and deep spiritual insight which lent a constant freshness and zest to his sermons.

Financially, too, the new job was a help. It was a job which he could take with him when he was off on his evangelistic missions, ensuring a small but steady income to supplement his diminishing wages.

In April, John returned once more to Logan County, Ohio. By this time there was quite a group of young people asking that a Mennonite church be established. John F. Funk had recently held a series of meetings there and a class of twenty-four was being instructed in preparation for baptism, the majority desiring to unite with a Mennonite church.

John sensed the feeling of tension in the community. With the three large Amish congregations, it didn't seem right that there should be another division, another church of like faith but separated in fellowship. But the enthusiastic group of sincere young Christians were strong in their demand for a church in which they could worship in a language they could understand. So deeply did they feel about this matter that some of them, although under strong conviction, had held back during Funk's meetings until it was understood they would be permitted to join the Mennonites.

Again John tried hard to bring about a reconciliation, but the language problem was the big stumbling block. Later that spring Funk visited the community and received twelve converts into the fellowship of the Mennonite Church. The group held membership in the Salem congregation in Allen County, until a Mennonite church was erected in Logan in 1895.

A little side trip to Elida before he returned home in April was purely for pleasure this time. It was a visit to his sister Fannie, who had recently married and was now living on a farm near Elida with her husband, Abram Shenk.

A trip to Kansas that spring was timed so that he could attend the annual conference held at West Liberty, May 2 and 3:

> This morning conference met. The committee that was to prepare the questions for consideration by conference had not done their work and was not all present. Bro. S. Miller was one, and Bro. E. Shellenberger and myself were chosen to help on this work. We prepared them till 1:30 and conference met again and had a pleasant session this afternoon. . . . There was a very harmonious working of all the ministers on all questions. There were ministers present from Virginia, Indiana, Illinois, Missouri, and Kansas. Two brethren were here from Nebraska. About all the churches in Kansas were represented.

On this trip John again visited many of the churches, spending part of a week with the Canton congregation before the conference, and about five days with the Pennsylvania congregation at Hesston afterward. During his stay in the area R. J. Heatwole took him in his care, furnishing transportation for his visits to members and making arrangements for his entertainment.

"Well, where do I go tonight?" John asked on Friday evening after the service.

"Why, I thought maybe you would like to go out to David Zook's, the Amish bishop, and get acquainted with him," Heatwole replied.

"What was that?" asked a young man anxiously stepping up to Heatwole. "Did I hear you say he was to go out to Father's place?"

"Why, yes. I thought it might be a good idea to get the two together, and let them get acquainted."

"Oh, no! That wouldn't do at all. You know my father. He's so set in his ways and—and—well, you must know he's been trying his best to keep folks from coming to these meetings. I'm afraid Brother Coffman wouldn't get much of a welcome."

"Well, in that case," John began, "I wouldn't want to intrude on anyone."

"No, it's all right," Heatwole contended. "I stopped by there myself this afternoon and told them you'd be coming. They said they had no objections and they'll have a bed ready for you."

"Maybe so, but I still think it's a mistake," exclaimed young Zook. "We can still change plans. Let Brother Coffman come home with me and we'll stop there on the way and tell them."

"No," said John, kindly laying his hands on the young man's shoulder. "I appreciate your offer, but I think we'd better leave the plans as they are. Your folks will be expecting me; so I'd better go.

Don't worry. I think your father and I will get along all right."

Although his host seemed a trifle aloof at first, John was given a warm, comfortable bed that night. Next morning at the breakfast table he carefully steered the conversation to religious topics. Much to his surprise Zook soon found that they agreed on most points. All morning the two talked on, parting toward noon as the best of friends.

Sunday happened to be the day when the Amish congregation under David Zook had the use of the church building for the morning service. John attended the service and was surprised when Zook invited him to preach. But John's surprise was no greater than that of the congregation when they saw him sitting with the Amish ministers on the bench behind the pulpit. The church was crowded that morning, and John could almost hear the gasp that went over the audience when he got up to preach. At Zook's request he spoke on the ordinances of the church, once more explaining to a custom-ridden people the spiritual meaning of the practices which they had held so tenaciously over the years. There were tears in Zook's eyes when he shook hands with John after the service, and thanked him for the clear and simple exposition he had given his people.

Returning east, John stopped off in Missouri for another visit to the church in Cass County. He was sorry to hear of some differences between some of the members and he once more found it necessary to play the role of peacemaker. As he preached each evening, he looked forward to the time when the congregation would have a minister of their own. Only recently he had learned that Lewis Heatwole, his brother-in-law, had decided to come west and had promised to take charge of the Cass County church. John had been suggesting the idea for some time and was pleased with the decision. Fifteen converts met for instruction on the last day of his visit. The trouble seemed to be fairly well ironed out and the future looked bright for the little group.

When John arrived home, late in May, he found arrangements being made for a special family party in honor of some very special company—his father and mother from Virginia. This was the first trip west for John's mother, and her first visit to their home since they left Virginia. She planned to stay with them for a few weeks while Father Coffman accompanied John Funk to the annual conference in Ontario.

For one member of the family this was an exceptionally exciting week. It was the final week of high school for Samuel F. Graduation was only a few days away. He was delighted that Father would be at home for the exercises, and how wonderful that Grandmother had also arrived in time for the great occasion!

Proudly Samuel F. accompanied his father downtown to be fitted for a new suit and to select the new stand-up collar and white bow tie to be worn that night.

"Sixteen and a quarter," sighed John as they left the store with their purchases. "And this is the second suit for you, young man, in the last six months."

"Thank you, Father," replied the boy, too happy to be worried about expenses. "It's really a good-looking suit, and I'll take real good care of it so it will last for years. But let's hurry. I have to be up at Goff's to have my picture taken in a few minutes."

After the graduation exercises on Friday evening, John again walked home with the boys. Samuel F. didn't seem to be in a talkative mood at first. His head was in the clouds. He had done well, and had been selected by the teachers as winner of the scholarship to Wabash College.

"Well, my boy, this is another one of those days we've been looking forward to for a long time," John began, falling in step beside him. "You've done well, and I must say I'm pleased."

Samuel smiled self-consciously. "We—ell, I—I guess I did do a little better after you let me drop Latin. It was good of them, wasn't it, to let me graduate without it?"

"Good? I'd say it was remarkable! You don't know how close you came to forfeiting a diploma because of it. It isn't every school board that would make a concession like that for just one pupil. And don't get the idea that you're going to get favors like that all your life."

"I know, I know," Samuel F. replied. "But I didn't see much sense in keeping on with Latin. I really don't need it, unless—"

"Unless what?"

"Why, I was just thinking—what if I should happen to use this scholarship? I don't suppose I will, but if—if I should just happen to. I guess maybe some courses might require Latin."

John didn't reply immediately. Finally S. F. broke the silence.

"I guess there won't be much chance of ever using it, though. I was just daydreaming a bit."

John cleared his throat. "I wish you could go to Wabash, Samuel. Wish it with all my heart. But I don't see how we could manage it. Not right now, anyway. I've done what I can for you and Will, and I want to do the same for the rest. So if they're to go on to high school, both of you will have to help me for a few years. After that—when you're of age, it's up to you. If you still want to go to college then, you'll have to make your own way."

"I realize that," S. F. replied, "and likely I'll never see college. But it's nice to dream."

"What courses would you like to take if you could go? Have you thought of that?" John asked.

"Oh, there are so many interesting things—history, science, astronomy, physiology. I'd have an awful time deciding. But sometimes I think I'd like to be a doctor."

"For that you'd certainly need more Latin," laughed John.

"I guess you're right," Samuel F. agreed ruefully. "But at least I'll have a few years to think about it."

Working at the Publishing Company that year was a scholarly young man, John Horsch, who had come from Germany a few years earlier. Horsch came into John's office one morning with a manuscript in German dealing with the origin and early history of the Mennonites, first known as Anabaptists and Swiss Brethren.

"Would you kindly give me help with the translating?" asked Horsch, his well-chosen words still carrying a typical German accent.

"Certainly," replied John, glancing over a neatly written page. "What's it for, the *Herald of Truth?*"

"Oh, no. It's for a book. A church history which a man in Columbus, Ohio, wishes to publish."

"You know, Horsch, this is very interesting," said John, quickly scanning several pages. "Now if we can manage a good translation, I think it would be of great interest to our own people. There are some things here I never knew before. Why don't we get Funk to publish it in a pamphlet so we can have it too?"

Since Funk readily agreed, John worked with the young historian translating and revising the article which became one of the first publications on Mennonite church history to be printed in America.

Another valuable and significant contribution to Mennonite literature that year was a manual for the use of ministers in special services and religious ceremonies:

> July 26, 1890—Read and corrected a part of the manual for church services, etc., that they are getting out at this office. I find it a critical work to get out a book of form for the church, as there has not been anything printed by the church in the English language.
>
> July 29—Wrote a number of letters and revised at the form book. This book of forms or minister's manual has been a long felt want in the church for many years. It is a very particular and laborious work to get it up in a way that will make it truly a blessing for the church. One danger of the book is that it may encourage ritualism. The tendency of all such books is in that direction.

Before leaving for a weekend at Sterling, Illinois, in August, John wrote this enthusiastic letter to his brother Joseph:

> Aug. 11, 1890—Next Friday I go for a few days to Sterling, Ill., where the church work seemed so very dead last winter. A dispatch was sent for me and I went at once and continued work over two Sundays. I was almost discouraged as I could not see any visible fruits of the meetings, but soon there was a great interest and the prayers and work of the members and the blessing of God wrought a great change there. The young peo-

ple came to church again, instead of going to the meetings of other denominations. They begun this spring with a vigorous S.S. in which old and young took part, and they held a teachers' meeting one evening every week to study the S.S. lesson and to discuss Scripture subjects at which meeting all who wished could take part. Soon there were some applicants and six or eight were received, and next Sunday 11 more are to be received. They have written to me to come and help them. You see, God blesses the work where there is work done. We have received nine members into our little Elkhart church this spring, and the attendance and interest is still increasing in the church and Sunday school.

John had mixed feelings about his trip to Cass County, Missouri, early in September. Lewis Heatwole was now settled there with his family and he was eager for a visit with them. But that difficulty between a few members still persisted, and he was to try once more to settle it. His gentle peace-loving disposition shrank from the task, but at the same time was one of his greatest assets in restoring harmony where trouble existed.

When he arrived at Garden City, John found Lewis Heatwole waiting at the depot. He was not waiting for him, however, but for another train to take him to Olathe, Kansas, for an appointment on Sunday. The two men had only a few minutes together before Lewis left. But John enjoyed a good visit with his sister Mary that evening.

After several satisfactory meetings with the Bethel congregation, John went on to Versailles. He had been asked to hold another series of meetings here, and also to attend the Missouri Conference at Mount Zion on Friday.

This time John spent quite a bit of time at the home of Bishop D. D. Kauffman. One morning Kauffman opened up his heart to him regarding his son, Daniel.

"I just don't know what will become of that young man," he said as they stood at the window watching Daniel mount his horse and ride off down the road toward his school.

"Why, doesn't he intend to keep on teaching?" John inquired. "I thought he was county commissioner."

"Yes, he's still commissioner, and he's doing well at teaching, they say. But right now he has greater ambitions. He's running for the job of circuit clerk and recorder of Morgan County. And from there on—who knows?"

"Hm! a political career!" mused John. "Well, he seems to have what it takes for politics—brains, ambition, and a strong personality. Would to God we could win him for the church. We need men like that."

Turning from the window Kauffman sank into a chair where he sat silent for a few minutes.

The old Weaver homestead purchased by Samuel Coffman, father of John S. Coffman, prior to the Civil War. The family lived here at the time of John's marriage.

The Heatwole family homestead, birthplace of Elizabeth Heatwole, wife of John S. Coffman.

The Coffman home on Gravelly Hill, now completely remodeled and modernized.

The Montezuma School where John S. Coffman taught for several years. Mole Hill is seen in the background.

A four-generation picture. Right to left: Frances Coffman in her eightieth year, wife of Samuel Coffman and mother of John S. Coffman; her daughter, Mrs. L. J. Heatwole; her granddaughter, Mrs. E. C. Suter; and great-granddaughter, Blanche Suter Rhodes.

Bishop Samuel Coffman (1822-94), father of John S. Coffman.

Samuel F. Coffman, son of John S. Coffman, as a member of the Elkhart High School graduating class of 1890.

John F. Funk, favorite picture of the Coffman family.

An inside view of the Elkhart Institute. Photo by A. C. Kolb.

The first and only building of the Elkhart Institute was dedicated February 22, 1896. It was located on South Prairie St., Elkhart, Ind., almost opposite the Mennonite meetinghouse.

The new house John S. Coffman erected for his family on the Bunker Hill Farm, south of Elkhart, Ind.

The John S. Coffman family. Seated, left to right: John S., Barbara (Mrs. Dillman Gingrich), Elizabeth (Mrs. John S. Coffman), Daniel. Standing, left to right: Anna Sauers, Samuel F., Jacob, Fannie (Mrs. J. C. Landis), William P., Ansel.

The Mennonite Publishing Company, Elkhart, Ind., staff of workers. In front row seated: second from left, John S. Coffman; next, Henry Brenneman; next, Joseph Summers; next, Abram Funk, brother of John F. Funk; and last in row, A. C. Kolb, editor of **Herald of Truth.** Boy in front is S. F. Coffman, son of John S. Coffman, who served as printer's errand boy.

"Somehow, somewhere, I've failed," he sighed, as if talking to himself. "I've failed my boys and I've failed my church. Not one of my boys in the church. O God, what have I done, or what have I not done?" he groaned, covering his face with his hands.

John remained at the window, staring at the rain-drenched countryside.

"You know, David, we all feel like that sometimes," he said comfortingly. "I have boys growing up too. Some are in the church, but not all. We can only give them the truth and pray that the Spirit may do His work. There's still hope, you know. Doesn't Daniel seem a little more serious, since—since his wife passed away?"

"We—ell, a little, maybe," Kauffman replied, studying the pattern of the old rag carpet. "But Daniel always has been serious. It's his nature. Maybe he's been a little more thoughtful, though. But whether it's politics or religion, I can't say."

"I think I know a little of how he feels," John remarked, seating himself quietly on a chair beside Kauffman. "I was strongly tempted by politics once myself. But, thank God, I found something much more important."

"Maybe—maybe you could talk to him sometime," suggested Kauffman hopefully. "He seems to think a lot of you. But us fathers—well, we're just fathers and quite out of date."

John nodded. "I know. Yes, I'll try to talk with Daniel. I had several good talks with him the last time I was here. He's a thinker and I enjoy talking with him."

To everyone's surprise Daniel attended the meetings faithfully that week. With his two-year-old motherless son at his side, he came to church evening after evening, even though it meant giving up precious campaign time. John noticed how intently he listened and could almost feel the mental conflict raging behind that broad forehead. Each night as he gave the invitation John raised his heart in anguished prayer that the troubled soul might yield and find peace. But there was no response.

Failing to find an opportunity for a private talk with Daniel, John called at his school one morning. Daniel welcomed him and, knowing John's interest in schools, invited him to give a talk to the children. At noon he was still there, discussing school problems. But gradually he managed to steer the conversation into more serious lines. Gently he reminded Daniel of his responsibility to himself, his pupils, and above all to his own young son. He had a right to a Christian home and Christian upbringing. Before leaving he had prayer with Daniel, praying that he might find truth and experience the joy of a new birth.

That night he kept glancing hopefully at Daniel when the invitation was given. A number of young people rose and made their way to the front, but Daniel sat with downcast eyes, holding his little sleeping son. Saturday night was the same and again Sunday night, the closing night of the meetings. While the invitation hymn was sung, Daniel sat motionless, hugging little Jimmie close. Somehow, John felt he couldn't give up. He knew Daniel was deeply moved. For a moment he stood quietly on the platform, his head bowed. A deep silence hung over the church. Then softly he began to sing the song which had moved many young hearts before:

O weary wanderer, come home,
Thy Saviour bids thee come;
Thou long in sin didst love to roam,
Yet still He calls thee, come.

Gradually, here and there other voices joined in, while behind the pulpit D. D. Kauffman sat with bowed head, tears streaming down his face. The first verse was sung—the second—the third.

In his heart Daniel felt a tremendous stirring, he told John afterward. He knew he was a sinner. All too well he knew he needed a Saviour. He wanted salvation and peace with God more than anything else in the world—fame, fortune, popularity, or wealth. "Choose you this day whom ye will serve." The words of the text kept ringing in his ears. He must choose either one way or the other. Why not choose God? He finally decided, and immediately struggled to his feet, walking with firm step down the aisle with little Jimmie still asleep in his arms.

* * *

After a few weeks at home, John was back in Missouri, this time to visit a number of small congregations, the first being in Mendon, Chariton County. He had visited the few families that lived here the previous year, but they were anxious to have him return. The Methodist Episcopal church was used for services this time and many from other denominations attended each evening. There were nine converts by the end of the week.

One of the first things John did after arriving at the home of J. L. Kreider in Mendon was to write a letter to one of the Kolb boys back home. Somehow he couldn't get Aaron off his mind. He looked so troubled and unhappy lately. He had tried several times to talk to him, but circumstances didn't seem favorable and it was hard to reach him. A letter might help, he decided.

Within a few days a reply came from Aaron, a letter in which he poured out his heart to John, and which made him both sad and happy. Sad for the frustrated, troubled state of mind it revealed, but happy that he felt he could confide in him.

> Oct. 24, 1890—Your very welcome letter reached me and was eagerly read. Please accept my sincere thanks for the same. I always love to read letters like that and I also like to speak about those things when I and the party to whom I speak are all by ourselves. Like the night I was at your house when Fred

[Samuel F.] and I talked three hours steady about these things that concern all humanity so very much. I must say that I have often wished and do sincerely wish yet that I could or rather were walking with God's people. It seems to me it would be such a great blessing. I have already been on the verge of giving myself into the hands of my Almighty Maker, but there was always something that prevented me and would turn my thoughts in another direction in spite of my struggle against it. And it is just in those times that I wish there would be someone to help me a little. . . . I tell you that I have often wished I could get out of this bondage so that I would not need to concern myself at all about this load of sin and how I might get rid of it. But as soon as I get just a certain distance in the matter I get entangled so that at last I am in such a position that I cannot move as it were. . . . That night I talked so with Fred was the best talk that I ever had on the subject, and I was indeed glad for the conversation that I had with him. I could hardly bear it when I noticed how calmly he could speak about his own soul while my thoughts were agitated all the time. . . .

On and on he wrote, a soul begging for help and for prayer. Immediately John sat down and tried to point out clearly and plainly the way to peace and happiness. This was only one of many letters he was constantly writing to friends, both new and old, who came to him for spiritual help.

Cherry Box was also visited again that fall. The converts from the spring meetings were to be baptized. It was a happy occasion for the congregation. With seven new members added to the roll they now numbered twenty-five.

A week with the little group of Mennonites living near Olathe, Kansas, proved to be a discouraging week. Services were held in the Methodist church, but the attendance was not large:

Nov. 6—This evening we had a fair turn out but not so many as last night. I cannot help feeling discouraged concerning the work here. There is so much against us as a people. . . . Almost everything was against us in the meetings this week, politics, the dark of the moon, rain, and other things.

A month later in Cullom, Illinois, his tone was quite different:

Dec. 21—A fine, beautiful day. Not cold. The roads are fine. Had the finest roads I ever had at Cullom when we had meetings, the finest moonlight, the best attendance, the greatest interest, the deepest spirituality, and the greatest number of converts (19). A full house this forenoon. Text—I Thess. 4:3, Sanctification. We believe in it, experience it, but do not seek it in the excitable way many do. . . . The church house was filled to overflowing this evening. Eleven persons came out to confess Christ. We had a pentecost of interest and blessing.

Early in January, 1891, John set out on another visit to Ontario, this time at the invitation of a number of ministers and laymen who were anxious about the future of the church. They were urging definite evangelistic effort in spite of a few who were strongly opposed. One of the men was Jacob Z. Kolb, father of Abram B. and Aaron, who were employees of the Publishing Company at Elkhart.

John had a long talk with Aaron after his return from Missouri, but Aaron still held back, unable to make the decision he knew he should make. In telling him of his plans to visit Ontario, John had said, "I'll be seeing your father and mother, Aaron. I'm glad I can tell them you're well, but I wish I could say all is well spiritually, too."

As he was boarding the train at the depot on his way to Canada, he was surprised to see Aaron suddenly rushing from the depot out to the platform. He paused a moment at the top of the steps, thinking Aaron might have a message for him, but the boy came to a sudden halt in the middle of the platform.

While he was getting settled in the car, however, he was again surprised by Aaron.

"Oh, here you are," said the boy, pushing his way down the aisle and dropping onto the seat beside him.

"Why, Aaron," John said, "what's all this? Have you decided to come with me?"

"No, not this time," Aaron replied, looking strangely serious. "I—I just came in to tell you that—that you can tell my folks it's all right now, all right with my soul too. I've just decided."

"All aboard!" called the conductor.

"Fine," replied John with a reassuring pat on his back as Aaron rose hastily and rushed from the car.

A few days later at Berlin, Ontario, John received another letter from Aaron:

> Jan. 10, 1891—May God's blessing rest on you and the work you intend to take in hand. I cannot forget how I left you in the car, and wished I could have gone a short distance with you and talked with you. You may tell my friends that I shall endeavor by the help of God to serve the Lord, and I wish they would all make the same determination. It is so wonderful how the Lord may bring about His ends. I often wished that you could tell this news at home, but even at the depot I thought you could not. When you were on the car I do not know just how it was, but I started to follow you, not knowing for certain what to say. I was walking toward the car almost before I knew it and thanks be to God I was permitted even at almost the last chance to tell you that you might say what you said you wished you could. Now I earnestly ask you to remember me in your prayers that God may give me grace and strength that I may go on, and not become weak in faith.

*I see more than ever that to win and save souls we must preach not so much good works and self effort, but Christ, a personal Saviour. Jesus is all—saving power and grace to the saved soul. It is Jesus that saves and not ourselves.*—Diary.

# 20

A Sunday morning service entirely in English was something quite unusual in the Christian Eby Church in Berlin—something that probably hadn't happened since John's previous visit nine years ago. The few young people who happened to be at church that morning were delighted and told their friends about the interesting sermon. But some of the older folk sat tight-lipped, thinking it would have looked better if he had tried a little German. At least he could have read the Scripture in German! Was he going to break with all their customs? Perhaps even hold meetings as he had been doing in Illinois and Missouri? In many hearts there was hope, in others a nameless fear.

With his usual caution John began his work in the county by holding services at different churches. On Sunday evening he preached at Breslau, on Monday evening at the Wanner Church near Preston, and on Tuesday at Hagey's, a few miles south of Wanner's. But a few folks were urging him to stay right at Berlin for a while. It was time to break with a custom or ruling so obviously man-made. Back in Berlin on Wednesday evening he found himself speaking to a crowd that filled every seat of the good-sized auditorium. Another meeting was announced for the following evening.

John noticed the smiles that lit up many faces at the announcement. But he was also quick to detect some startled looks and a few frowns. Next day as he visited various homes he heard some criticisms and felt discouraged when he learned that one of the bishops of the district was bitterly opposed, asking that the meetings be discontinued.

The situation required careful handling. John was accustomed to opposition, but it was not his policy to force the issue. After praying for guidance, he decided to throw the responsibility for the next meeting on the congregation.

"Shall we have a meeting here tomorrow night?" he asked the audience at the close of Thursday evening's meeting.

There was no need to count hands. The decision was almost unanimous.

But on Friday John heard that several bishops were displeased and a number of supporting ministers were becoming fearful.

"I think I had better pack up and go home," John announced to his host, Jacob Z. Kolb. "I don't like to intrude where I'm not wanted. Perhaps the time isn't quite ripe."

"I know it's hard on you," Kolb sympathized, "but can't you hang on just a few more nights? The meetings are stirring up a tremendous interest. The church was fuller last night than I've ever seen it."

John nodded. "I know. It's not a question of interest. A lot of your young people are beginning to see the light, and it would be a pity to have to quit now. But we must avoid trouble. Any more divisions here would be disastrous."

Kolb sat thoughtfully stroking his beard. "You know," he said, "somehow I don't think there's going to be any real trouble. As I see it, it's more a matter of jealousy than anything else. I have an idea some of those men will be out to a meeting one of these nights. Their curiosity will get the better of them. And once they come and hear the plain truth, they'll change their tune."

Kolb was right. On Friday night the long bench behind the pulpit was filled with ministers and bishops. The church was again crowded. Extra benches in the aisles were filled and many were standing in the anterooms. There was a deep hush over the congregation during the entire sermon. The ministers on the bench behind the pulpit felt they were hearing again the voice of John the Baptist as this John earnestly pleaded, "Repent—turn from your sin." From time to time John turned to face these ministers, directing remarks to them. He was encouraged with their show of interest. Singly and together heads nodded agreement and even the opposing bishops occasionally uttered a weak "Amen."

That night there were few dissenting votes when the question of another meeting was brought up. Most of the ministers sat red-faced during the voting, not daring to express themselves.

After the sermon the next evening John gave an invitation—the first for this series of meetings. The sermon had made a deep impression, making clear the need for a personal acceptance of Christ as Saviour. For a long minute or two it seemed there would be no response. John could see tears glistening in many eyes while the invitation hymn was sung, but no one ventured to make a start. And then from a seat halfway back in the church thirteen-year-old Elizabeth Gingrich got to her feet. Pushing her way to the end of the bench, she walked rapidly down the aisle.

John's heart was touched. With tears in his own eyes he stepped down from the platform to meet the girl. Then leading her up onto the platform he held her by the hand while he turned to the audience and said softly, "And a little child shall lead them. Elizabeth has made the start; now who will follow?"

Soon from all over the church others began making their way down the aisles to the front bench.

The entry in John's diary for Sunday, January 18, 1891, reads:

> I never saw such a jam of people as were crowded into that house. Not near all in. Text—Heb. 9:15, the Mediator of the New Testament. It was too warm and close. I could hardly speak. A number came out this evening.

Never had the Berlin Church seen such crowds as flocked to the church the next few nights. An hour before the service they started to come, and a half hour later every available inch of standing room was taken. Town people of all denominations came on foot and in cutters, while huge sleigh loads of young and old came from miles out in the country to hear this Mennonite preacher who preached in a way you could understand—yes, even made the Bible interesting.

"Who is that man in the middle of the bench?" asked one of the town's businessmen attending the meeting for the first time.

"Why, that's Coffman, the man that's been doing the preaching," replied his neighbor.

"He's not a Mennonite."

"Oh, yes, he is, and a good one too."

"But he looks so—so different—so neat and rather refined and intellectual. Most of your ministers are farmers, and—well—they look it!"

"He used to be a farmer, but they say he always was neat. Just wait till you hear him preach. He'll let you know he's a Mennonite."

Among the faithful attendants at the meetings that week was young Eli Hallman. Although he came from a Mennonite family, he had recently been converted and joined the Methodists. Both he and his wife were members of their choir. Eli was the sixth child of Abraham Hallman's family of twelve, none of whom were in the church. Mrs. Hallman was a daughter of George Clemens, who had worked with Kolb to bring Coffman into the community. All of his children had by this time joined other denominations.

Young Hallman was impressed by the meetings at the old church. As he listened to the sermons night after night, he gradually gained a new insight and appreciation for the principles which he had cast aside as meaningless formality.

"I just didn't know they had a preacher like that in the Mennonite Church," he remarked one day to a business friend who had accompanied him to the service.

"I didn't either. I was really surprised," replied the friend. "His messages are simple but strangely powerful and convincing. I've heard Talmage preach, but I'd say this man gets as much out of God's Word as Talmage, if not more."

"You know," Hallman continued, "I've been thinking that maybe my place is back in that church. They've been slow in getting around to this job of soul-winning, but if this is something that's going to keep on, I feel I should give it my whole support. Those doctrines are right there in the Bible. The church has real truth to stand on, and I feel that's where I belong."

When the converts met for their first instruction class, Eli Hallman and his wife joined them, and eagerly continued their study of principles and doctrines for which the church had stood during almost four centuries. John felt that the interest and enthusiasm of this young man boded well for the church in Canada.

The services at Breslau the following week repeated the pattern set at Berlin—large crowds, tremendous interest, and many confessions.

Several times that week John returned to Berlin for morning services and was surprised to find the church just as crowded as it had been for the evening meetings.

> Jan. 29, 1891—This morning I worked hard for some time to finish my outline for my discourse today. The house was crowded full of persons of all denominations about Berlin as well as the recent converts and church members. The discourse was listened to with rapt attention for one hour and forty minutes. I had to tell many severe truths but they appeared to be taken without offense.

After the stirring experiences in Waterloo County the visit to the Twenty in Lincoln County was quite a letdown to John. Here interest in religion seemed to be at a low ebb. The little frame church on the "Mountain" near Campden was only about half full that first evening. Even on Sunday morning the crowd was small, mostly elderly people. But he continued the services for a week, alternating between the Campden Church and the Moyer Church at Vineland. Regarding this visit John wrote to his brother Joseph:

> May 23, 1891—The church here is composed of old people nearly ready for their graves and their young people have grown up and are scattered to the four winds, not one in the Mennonite church. Why? Because the old people disagreed and really quarreled. What about? English preaching and Sunday school and evening meetings, while the young people looked on till they became disgusted and prejudiced and went off to other

> churches. When one wanted to work and do something the others would find fault and say, "That is not the way father and grandfather done." There was about as much ignorant prejudice here as any place I have yet met. . . . If our people at the Bank and other places were wise, they would learn a lesson from this. "How long, O Lord, how long!"

In spite of the discouraging outlook John saw that there was still a little hope for the church here. Toward the end of the week there was a noticeable increase in both interest and attendance. But he saw that a long, continued effort would be necessary, and so after a serious talk with Preacher John F. Rittenhouse and a few of the members it was decided that he should return later in the spring and remain with them for several weeks.

A few days with the congregation at Blenheim before returning to Indiana revived his sinking spirits. It wasn't simply a matter of crowds. He knew some came from sheer curiosity. But in both young and old there seemed to be a burning desire for something they did not have. This was especially evident among the young people. Perhaps the sudden death of twenty-year-old Amos Hallman a few weeks earlier had something to do in turning their thoughts into serious channels. He had been killed instantly in a fall from a sleigh. John had attended the funeral.

Shortly after his return home John summarized his winter's work in a letter to his brother Joseph:

> March 13, 1891—Since you seem anxious to know about the work I will give you a little report provided you keep it to yourself or tell it only where it is necessary. I wrote Sunday school lessons till the 10th [of January], then went to Canada and staid a month, three weeks of the time in Waterloo county. I was nearly a week at Jordan, at the Twenty. At this place there were no direct results. I was principally at three places in Waterloo county. At the three places about 110 or 115 souls made a start in the good work. And the work has been going on since, so that the last letter from there reported 135 who were receiving instruction to be baptized. At Forest Grove [Indiana] there were 10 converts, at Clinton nine. I would be at the Clinton Amish church now, were it not for the very bad roads. I will go there as soon as the roads dry up.

Although he knew hard work was ahead of him as he set out on his promised visit to the Twenty in May, John eagerly accepted the challenge and also looked forward to attending a Sunday-school workers' meeting which would be held at the Berlin Church on the eighteenth. A Sunday-school conference was an entirely new venture in the Mennonite Church and John was anxious to see how the program would be carried out. He had listened with interest when they had told him of their first meeting on Whit Monday the year before.

When the conference opened that May morning, John joined heartily in the discussions. The topics were chiefly on problems confronting teachers and Sunday-school workers. In his diary he recorded:

> The house was filled and the interest excellent. The talks on the various subjects and the discussion of themes were very interesting. All the decisions on questions were unanimous. It seems to me to have been a very interesting and profitable meeting, and the workers and teachers can go forth to their duties better prepared than before. But in the west end of the district there is some opposition to these meetings.

John arrived at Jordan on Thursday afternoon, May 21. A beautiful time of year to visit this garden spot, he decided, as his eye caught the beauty of fruit trees in bloom, shimmering grain fields, and neat garden patches. Noting the return to life all over the countryside as he walked from the station to the home of Preacher Daniel Honsberger, he suddenly felt a surge of hope. Surely the God who had accomplished the miracle in nature could perform even greater miracles in the hearts of men.

He was not discouraged by the size of the crowds the first few evenings. On Sunday morning there was a fair turnout at Campden. Then on Sunday evening at Moyer's he carefully laid the groundwork for his campaign by preaching a strong sermon on repentance. By Wednesday evening he began to see signs of an awakening. That night the service was at Campden.

> May 27, 1891—The house was crowded. Text—I Cor. 10:16, 17, Communion, our reason for not holding a free communion. The interest was almost intense.

As John recorded these words, the thought suddenly struck him that here, perhaps, was the key to the apathy and indifference which was slowly killing the church. It was the same in so many places, lack of understanding. When the people understood, they were interested. Only here the situation was aggravated by so much controversy that the young people no longer tried to understand. If only he could get them interested, he reasoned. And so instead of ignoring the doctrines of the church which had long been the subject of heated arguments and disagreements, he launched into a vigorous program of teaching what the Mennonite Church stood for, and why. Immediately the crowds began to come and people of all denominations listened with interest to his clear and forceful expositions.

On Friday the annual church conference was held at the Moyer Church and many of the visitors remained for the Sunday communion service. There was a large crowd at church on Sunday morning, and in the evening the crowd was so large that a number had to remain outside, listening to the sermon through the open windows. That night John again had the rapt attention of the audience as he explained the Bible teaching concerning the veiling of the woman's head during prayer.

For another week crowds continued to come each evening, both at Campden and at Moyer's. Not only was the interest intense, but each evening decisions were made, many of them young married people who had as yet no church affiliation. The climax came on Sunday, June 7, the last night of the meetings, when there was once more an overflow crowd at Moyer's. John was concerned when he saw so many outside not able to get in. But his voice carried well through the open windows and the congregation outside was as quiet and attentive as the one inside. He made a strong appeal that night to the unsaved, preaching from John 3:16. When he gave the invitation, eighteen young people responded. It was difficult getting through the crowds, but a number standing outside elbowed their way into the building and down the aisle to the front of the church. New life had at last come to the little congregation. There were now thirty-eight applicants for baptism.

The next morning Henry Fretz hitched a team of horses to an open buggy and set out with John across country on a forty-mile trip to South Cayuga. It was a hot, dusty drive, but they arrived in time to have supper and to freshen up before the evening service. John sensed that here, too, was need of long earnest effort since the church had suffered a serious division only a few years before. The majority of the members now belonged to the faction led by Christian Gayman. They had the use of the building on alternate Sundays and John attended their service on Sunday morning. Joseph Wismer from Jordan was present to speak to them that day. The house was crowded that afternoon and evening for the services which John conducted.

The rest of the week John spent with the congregation in Rainham Township, near Selkirk. After his first service here John wrote:

> June 15, 1891—The attendance was fair, but the house was not filled. I fear it is a hard place to get up much interest. . . . I find it difficult to preach the truth here in a way that it will be considered attentively. The letter of the Word has been preached here by the so-called Disciples till it is difficult to get them to understand spirit.

But patient, prayerful effort and personal interest bore fruit. Several times the little church was crowded, with a number of Methodists and Disciples present. Eleven young people were converted.

* * *

When John arrived home, he found his two eldest sons busy with preparations for a holiday in Canada. Now that they were both working they had saved money to purchase bicycles and they figured that by riding the bikes they could save train fare and enjoy an economical holiday. The two Kolb boys joined in the arrangements, one to ride a high wheeler like the Coffmans, and the other a new safety model.

John approved the plans since he felt that the trip as well as the contact with the people in Ontario would be good for all of them.

About five weeks later the boys returned. The last two days of the trip were oppressively hot. But tired though they were, they sat up late that night telling of their adventures. A. B. Kolb took sick on the way home and finished the trip by train.

Samuel F., too, had a short train ride. On a side trip from Waterloo to Lincoln County something went wrong with his bicycle and so he stopped at a little town for repairs while the rest rode on. An hour or so later he was again on the road riding fast in order to reach Jordan before evening. At Grimsby, about ten miles west of Jordan, it began to rain. And then it happened, the grand spill, the worst of the whole trip. Riding down a board walk just outside of town he ducked his head to avoid some low tree branches when suddenly his bicycle skidded and over the top he went, landing head-first in a gravel pile! Jumping quickly to his feet he was relieved to discover that he and the bike were both intact, but his new straw hat and one shoe were damaged beyond repair.

Happening on a Saturday afternoon this situation was serious. Unfortunately Grimsby had few shops, and it was impossible to buy either shoes or hats. Since he couldn't ride with his boot so badly torn, he decided to take the train for the ten-mile ride to Jordan.

Although he felt like a tramp arriving at Honsbergers in such a dilapidated condition, his humiliation was even greater when he discovered that new shoes were also unobtainable in Jordan. All the village shoemaker could do was offer him a pair of old farm boots that had been left in his shop some months before. Though they were several sizes too large and very clumsy, he had to accept.

Samuel F. never forgot his first undignified appearance at the Moyer Church next morning. He was certain every eye went straight from his hatless head to the oversized clogs on his feet. But he soon forgot himself in the enjoyment of the service and in the friendly fellowship. The people seemed to show the same warmth of feeling for the Coffman boys that they had given their father. S. F. was especially impressed with the enthusiasm and zeal of those who had recently been converted at his father's meetings and he enjoyed a number of spiritual talks with these new friends.

A trip east in the late fall of 1891 took John to Somerset, Pennsylvania, to the valley churches in Virginia, to a little settlement of Mennonites in Fauquier County, Virginia, and to a small congregation of Amish in Long Green, Maryland. John commented on this visit in a letter to his brother Joseph:

> Jan. 21, 1892—I had not thought of publishing an account of my late trip to Virginia and Maryland. I was somewhat depressed all the while in the valley because I saw that I was working all the while in the way that could not possibly be

followed by any marked results for good. The situation is just this—the church is dead and cold or sleepy through the entire east, and they do not know it, consequently they cannot stand to be told, and no one can think hard of them. All that can be done is to pity them and pray for them and do what little one can to help them. The time is here that we must make continued, earnest effort, looking to God for power of the Spirit and His work and blessing on all we do. The churches that are doing this are prospering, at least in gathering souls to their number. Those that do not are scarcely holding their own and many are dying out. . . . In Fauquier county I had nothing to work with save one family, and some others who were well interested, yet too far away from our doctrine to be won in so short a time. In Baltimore, Maryland, I found about 20 members struggling along, but the church is dying for want of clear teaching and earnest effort. But one could work there, and I think I could have gained some more there if I had only a little more time. Only had three meetings. They are near enough dead there that they would allow one to work directly and in continued effort. I would be very glad to go back if I had time.

The new year commenced with a series of meetings in the home church at Elkhart. Realizing that within a few weeks his eldest son would be twenty-one, John was greatly concerned about William, and prayed earnestly for him.

Three days later his prayers were answered. At the close of the service one evening William along with three other young people made the important decision, committing his life to Christ. One of the group was a young woman whom John had seen in William's company a number of times. Lydia Hug was an attractive and intelligent young woman. For several years she had taught a children's class in Sunday school and John had learned to appreciate her many fine qualities. His heart rejoiced at the brighter future which appeared to be opening up before these young people.

On January 13 he recorded in his diary:

Today is William's birthday, 21 years old. It is a matter of considerable thought and prayer to see a child go on his own responsibility out from under a father's direct care. My prayer has been answered in this that it has long been my prayer that he should not leave his father's care till he had given himself into his Heavenly Father's care. He confessed Christ on the 5th day of January. I bought him a suit of clothes with overcoat, a watch for not spending money for tobacco and intoxicants, also an umbrella. May God ever care for and bless him.

* * *

When the evangelizing committee met at the Salem Church near New Paris, Indiana, on January 20, the Elkhart delegation was ready with a plan that would expand the work to include other conference districts and some Amish conferences that had shown an interest in supporting the work.

John listened with interest to the report of the secretary, especially the figures he read. Although many churches had not sent in reports, a total of 785 accessions were reported for the previous year, with 558 coming in as a result of direct evangelistic work. The year before the numbers were 617 and 417. What would the numbers have been if no effort had been made? he asked the audience when it was his turn to speak. And what will the figures be when more men get on the field to do the work the church has been called to do?

The treasurer's report showed that $432 had been paid out in 1891 to help defray expenses of evangelists and ministers who had visited scattered members or churches without a regular minister. Receipts amounted to $560. In 1890 receipts had been higher, $718, and disbursements $559. But there had been a steady growth in the work since the organization was effected ten years earlier, when receipts and expenditures hovered around $100. This was a healthy growth, John pointed out, but it also called for greater activity and an enlarged organization. The Amish conference at Seward, Nebraska, he reported, had requested to join them in maintaining an evangelizing fund, and had appointed a committee to serve with them. No doubt others would welcome the opportunity to participate.

And so it was that a new organization was formed that day to be known as the Mennonite Evangelizing Board of America. The purpose of the board as outlined in the bylaws was to collect funds and maintain a treasury for the purpose of carrying on general missionary work; to send men to labor wherever there was a need or where a field was open, either among Mennonites or other classes of people, but especially among scattered members or unsupplied churches.

The board was to be composed of not less than seven members and at least one from each conference district. Members elected were: Herman Yoder, Goshen; C. Z. Yoder, Weilersville, Ohio; Joseph Summers, Elkhart; Noah Hoover, Goshen; Fred Brunk, Elkhart; A. B. Kolb, Lewis Kulp, Elkhart; Daniel Shenk, Elida, Ohio; Christ Albrecht, Tiskilwa, Illinois; Levi Yoder, East Lynne, Missouri; J. C. Driver, Excelsior, Missouri; R. J. Heatwole, Newton, Kansas; J. M. T. Miller, Milford, Nebraska.

A resolution was passed inviting all conferences in harmony with the preamble and constitution to co-operate and elect one man from conference as a member of the board. Each member was asked to report quarterly regarding places under his observation needing work, also to influence persons to contribute to the fund. In May, P. S. Hartman was named to the board representing the Virginia Conference, and S. T. Miller representing Iowa. Receipts that year increased to a total of $972.

When J. S. Coffman returned to Ontario in February for his second series of meetings in Waterloo County, he was met at the depot by Bishop Daniel Wismer and spent most of the day in conference with the bishops Wismer, Amos Cressman, and Elias Weber. Deacon Jacob Z. Kolb was also present to take part in the discussion of church conditions and methods of evangelizing.

John was glad for the opportunity of a frank talk with these church leaders, even though they did not all share in his views of the subject. He could see that the results of the meetings last year had made a decided impression and there was no sharp, harsh criticism. As bishops, however, they felt it their duty to warn John to be cautious, and not to do anything which might jeopardize the harmony of the church. Conference had not sanctioned protracted meetings. But it was not only criticism from their own conference members they feared. Close ties existed with the mother conference of eastern Pennsylvania, and they did not want to strain these relations.

Typical of the attitude of some of the young people of the county toward these meetings was that of young Jacob Schmidt (later better known as J. B. Smith) of the Latschar district, who was working that winter for Allan Erb near Waterloo. On the way to the wood lot to chop wood one morning young Schmidt happened to meet his friend, Moses Honsberger.

"I hear there's big doin's at the Eby Church again this week," remarked Jacob after chatting a while with Honsberger.

"Ah, yes, they say they're bein' converted by the dozens." Honsberger clasped his hands and rolled his eyes heavenward in mock piety.

"I suppose you'll be the next, then, to hit the sawdust trail."

"Who knows?" Honsberger replied, gravely wagging his head. "And what about yourself? When are you going to take the walk?"

Shocked by the sudden direct question, even though it was asked in jest, Jacob felt his face redden. "Just count me out, brother," he replied heatedly. "You won't get me up there."

But all morning the question kept bothering him as he chopped away at a pile of wood. He had heard Coffman preach several times, and had been waging an inner battle ever since. "When—when are you going to take the walk? When?" How was he going to answer that? Sometime or other he had to face the question.

Then suddenly he was overwhelmed with conviction. The truth dawned. He was a lost man, a sinner separated by a deep gulf from a righteous God. That was what the preacher had said, he remembered. And Christ was God extending a hand to bridge that gulf. All he needed to do was grasp that hand.

"No, no—I can't—I can't," he groaned, chopping harder and faster while the sweat rolled down his face.

With a great effort he tried to shut off all thought, swinging his ax rhythmically, counting the strokes and watching the chips fly in all directions. Pausing briefly to wipe the sweat from his forehead he was surprised to hear someone calling him.

"Jacob," the voice seemed quite near.

"Yes, here I am," he called, looking around to see who was coming.

But there was no answer and no one was in sight.

"Here, I'm over here," he called again while his heart pounded hard against his ribs. "Who is it?"

How eerie his voice sounded in the great empty woods.

And then the awful truth dawned. It was the voice of God he had heard. God was calling him. Falling on his knees in the snow, great choking sobs racked his body as he acknowledged his sin and implored forgiveness.

"And, Father," he prayed, "if I find some way of going to that meeting at Eby's tonight, I'll take that walk. I'll confess you before all men."

The opportunity did come to go to the meeting. Neighbor Gishler invited him to go with him in his cutter. For a while it almost seemed as if they might not get there. A strong wind had come up and the roads were drifting badly. Three times the cutter upset.

"Perhaps we'd better just go back," suggested Jacob who was beginning to repent of his rash promise to God. He just couldn't do it. Just couldn't walk all the way up that aisle with a crowd of people watching.

"No," Gishler said, "we won't go back now. We've come so far and we'll go the rest of the way."

It was late when they arrived at the church and the building was packed. The only standing room they could find was in the women's lobby. Sheepishly they went in, joining the group lining the back wall.

But as soon as Coffman began to speak, Jacob forgot himself, lost completely in the stirring words from the pulpit. Once more he was overwhelmed with conviction. Once again he heard the voice in the woods calling to him. He must respond. When the invitation came, he had only one thought—to go forward as quickly as possible and grasp that hand extended so invitingly to sinners like himself.

He had to push his way through the crowd in the lobby and pick his way carefully up the aisle. In trying to get around the old box stove standing in the middle of the room he caught his foot and went sprawling into the lap of a woman seated in the aisle. Ordinarily he would have been painfully embarrassed, but not tonight. It was merely another obstacle encountered on his way to victory. Seeing the earnest look on the lad's face, John shook his hand warmly.

Later, as Jacob looked around at the group gathered at the front, he was not surprised to see his friend, Moses Honsberger. Nor was he surprised to find that Gishler had followed him up the aisle. The boys smiled at each other. But the smiles were quite different from those they had exchanged that morning.

Sixty decisions were made that week in Berlin. The next week there were twenty-six more at Blenheim, making a total of ninety-nine during this visit to Waterloo County:

> February 19, 1892—Five more came to confess Christ at the meeting tonight. We simply speak with them after they come out and instruct them how to go on in prayer and looking to God for peace and forgiveness.

After another week at the Twenty, where there were seven more converts, John made his first visit to the York County district where a number of Mennonite churches had been established. It was with some foreboding that he entered this district, for he knew that here, too, there were strong opponents of any departure from the old ways. A few folks from the Twenty came with him to visit friends and attend the meetings. Preacher Noah Stauffer from Waterloo also came to be with him that first week. After talking with Stauffer he recorded in his diary:

> March 14, 1892—Brother Stauffer of Waterloo was here and says the conditions of the church here are not flattering.

Most of the services were held at the Wideman Church, although he also preached at Almira, Altona, and Cedar Grove. Although small at first, the attendance continued to increase each evening and by the end of the week Wideman's was well filled. John was encouraged by the progress made here. It was evident not only in the numbers, but in the warm handclasps of the folks as they said good-by, and in the pressing invitations to return soon.

* * *

Stepping from the train at Chicago one morning in May, John peered anxiously over the crowd on the platform and soon spotted William rushing to meet him. William had been working in Chicago for some time now, and John usually managed to see him when he passed through. Since this was Decoration Day and William had a holiday, they planned to spend a few hours together.

"Well, how was the trip west? and the conference? And how are the folks at home? Tell me everything," William began as they sauntered down the street toward a park.

John laughed. "Not so fast there, boy. One thing at a time. The trip west? Well, it was good. I had about ten days at the Pennsylvania Church in Kansas, a week at Peabody, and another at Spring Valley."

"Many converts?"

"None at Peabody this time, but there were ten at the Pennsylvania Church and fourteen at Spring Valley."

"Did you see Uncle Lewis and Aunt Molly?"

"I saw Molly. I was there several days before conference, but Lewis wasn't home. We had a good meeting there one evening. Eight confessions."

"A good conference at Freeport?"

"Yes, very good, but nothing outstanding."

"And how's everybody at home?"

"That, my boy, you know about as well as I do," John replied as they turned into the park. "You were home at Easter, and it was just a week later that I left."

"I guess you're right. But it seems ages since I was home."

"Time may go slow for you, but not for me. Let's go and sit on that bench over there while you tell me about yourself. Are things going all right?"

"Yes, I guess so," William replied, but his voice lacked the usual enthusiasm.

"Are you still satisfied with your job?" John inquired.

William toyed with the top button of his coat while he studied this question. "I—I don't know," he replied slowly. "In some ways I like it, but—but it isn't exactly satisfying."

"Maybe you're just a little bit homesick."

"N—n—o—o, I don't think so. It would be nice to be home, of course. But it's the work. I'm not as satisfied as I thought I'd be. It's hard, and the days are long and much more monotonous than at the Publishing Company."

"But you still like printing?"

"Yes, in a way. But I'm not sure I want it for a career. Isn't there something else, maybe, that I might like better and might do more people more good?"

"I'm glad you are thinking that way, William. That's the way a Christian should think. Life should be a service, both to God and to our fellow man. But God first. Have you thought of something you would rather do?"

"Well," William began slowly, still toying with the button. "I was thinking a bit about music. I love music and it seems to me it might be a kind of service to the church to go around holding singing schools."

Seeing the surprised expression cross his father's face, William added quickly, "Or don't you think it's such a good idea?"

Rising from the bench John started pacing slowly back and forth in front of it. This matter took some thought.

"Yes, William, I think it would be a great service—a very important service to the church. And you have talent as well as ability in that line. You did well with the classes back home. If you could only be sure of steady work, it might be a very good idea."

"Well, there are a lot of churches without even going too far away: Indiana, Illinois, Ohio, Michigan—even Missouri isn't too far. Why couldn't I go from one place to another? Maybe stay at one place three or four months?"

"It would certainly do a lot to improve our church music if we could convince the churches of the need. But I'm afraid it would mean quite a sacrifice on your part."

"Sacrifice?" William asked quickly.

"Yes, a real financial sacrifice. You would get a fee, of course. But you couldn't hope to earn what you are getting now."

"I know. I had thought of that. But maybe I could get other odd jobs helping farmers or something like that."

"Well, you might try it. You can always go back to printing," John advised.

"I think I should have a little more training, though," William suggested. "They say they have a good musical normal school at LaFayette, a four-week course. If you think it's advisable at all, perhaps I should get my application in."

"It won't hurt to send it in, but maybe we should think about it and pray a little more before you plan too much," John said. "And I'll start making some inquiries about singing schools for you."

After his talk with William, John began to wonder whether he shouldn't have a similar talk with Jacob. He was a good-natured boy, quick-witted, and a good worker. But it bothered John that he didn't seem to have any particular aim or ambition. He had been working at odd jobs at the Publishing Company during holidays, but he had little interest in the work. Although he did his share on the farm, he definitely wasn't a farmer.

He broached the subject of a career while they were walking home from work one evening, and he was surprised to learn that Jacob had been thinking about teaching.

This pleased John, and even though it meant added financial strain he decided to send him to summer school at Valparaiso.

When Jacob left for school early in June, he was accompanied by Andrew Mumaw, son of Dr. H. A. Mumaw, who was now back in Elkhart after studying medicine for a few years at Hahnemann Medical College in Chicago.

John couldn't go to the depot with Jacob that morning, for he was leaving early to go to Yellow Creek. A bishop was to be ordained that day and John was among those who had received votes for the office. One of the candidates was to be selected by lot.

Realizing the seriousness of the decision to be made and the great responsibility which would rest on the one chosen, John wanted to spend the hours before the meeting alone. That was why he decided to walk to Yellow Creek. He didn't shrink from the possible responsibility, but he knew that if he were chosen it would curtail some of his evangelistic work. He realized, too, that a good bishop was badly needed in the district. The Indiana Conference needed a man with keen judgment and foresight. A man like Funk, he decided, could do much toward getting them out of the rut of formalism which was such a hindrance to the growth of the church. Surely Funk was the man. But was he God's choice? John had fasted and prayed much the last few days, and he continued to commune with his God on that early morning walk, pleading that His will might be done.

One by one all the ministers who had received votes were closeted for a short time with the bishops whose task it was to determine their fitness and qualifications. Out of the number, five were selected to be in the lot, among them Coffman and Funk.

Sitting on the front bench with the rest of the nominees John felt himself grow tense as the moment arrived for the choice to be made. Somehow he had again expected a sign, but this time there was none. With a prayer in his heart he stepped up in turn to select a book which might or might not conceal the portentous slip of paper.

This slip was found in Funk's book. And so it was John F. Funk who was ordained that morning to be the new bishop in the Indiana Conference. It was with a definite sense of relief that John wrote in his diary that night:

> June 1, 1892—I started early and walked nearly all the way to Yellow Creek church. The congregation gathered at 10 for the purpose of ordaining a bishop. After examination of those who had received votes five of us were taken to cast lots between us, John Funk, David Burkholder, Amos Mumaw, Joseph Lehman, and myself. Bro. Funk was chosen and ordained. It is a trying time to be placed in a position where so grave a responsibility may fall on you.

*At present the Lord is very gracious to me in giving me an understanding of the Scriptures. There are many passages that I can read with more interest than ever before. By His help I will try to read the Bible more than ever before. May the Lord be my helper.*—Diary.

# 21

It seemed strange at home that summer with both William and Jacob away in school. Samuel F., now twenty, remained at his post in the Mennonite Publishing Company. He had recently been promoted to the position of boss bookbinder. Ansel assisted part time in the bindery department that summer, leaving thirteen-year-old Daniel to be head man on the farm.

John was at home most of the summer, spending a great deal of time writing Sunday-school lesson copy. The necessary study was enriching and refreshing, preparing him for the strenuous days ahead when he would again be sharing these vital truths:

> July 25, 1892—This morning I went to town and wrote out lesson no. 10. The work among the Gentiles of Asia Minor gives us many excellent suggestions as to the present evangelizing and missionary work. My soul is stirred to do more work in this line. Possibly I am doing about what I have strength for, but there are other workers who could do more. There are many more needed among our people. We need Spirit-baptized men who will go forth in the strength of the Almighty. May God come to our aid right early. Lord, help us.
>
> July 27, 1892—I learned as much from this quarter, I think, as I ever learned from any quarter I wrote up. It is grand to look at the development of the church as first planted. The zeal and boldness of those first workers is astonishing. What a mighty work might now be done both in Christendom and heathendom if those who claim to be called to the preaching of the Gospel

> would be possessed with such a zeal and such a love for the cause and be so entirely separated from the love of the world.
>
> July 30, 1892—It was quite a relief to finish these lessons. But in studying and writing them an impression has been made on my mind that all time can not efface. No money could buy the little I learned in studying and writing the lessons of 1892. May God help me to use the knowledge for His glory and the salvation of souls as long as I live.

John's good friend, Joseph Summers, known to *Words of Cheer* readers as "Dear Uncle Joseph," died in August. Along with other members of the Elkhart congregation John had taken his turn in helping to care for him during his illness. A few hours after his funeral he set out again for Ontario.

This time he worked with a number of small congregations—the Twenty, Markham, Rainham, Sherkston in Welland County, and a small group in Mosa Township, Elgin County, in the western part of the province. The church here was made up of a number of families who had settled there around 1870, coming from other Ontario settlements. Even though the church was isolated by distance, it did not escape the discord which had disrupted other congregations. Help was needed very badly. In his diary John wrote:

> Aug. 27, 1892—There are about 17 members here, scattered over considerable territory. The meetings have interested them, but they need much more stirring up. There is a possibility of building up the church here, but it will take earnest and direct work. It looks pitiful in places like this.

From Sherkston John wrote to M. S. Steiner, who had recently come from Ohio to work in the publishing house. He was one of the converts in the Riley Creek district in whom John was particularly interested. He was a talented lad, now deeply interested in the church of his fathers and eager to work for it in any way he could:

> Sept. 6, 1892—The meetings at Rainham were well attended and the interest was good. Five, one boy and four girls, came out. One of the girls, over 30, is a fashionable dress maker. She is fully convinced but I don't know how she will be in practice, but she wants to be baptized into our church. . . . I came here [to Bertie Township] on Monday and stay till Thursday. Life is low here. I have again learned a great lesson of the manner in which many of our old Mennonites have sacrificed their children to Moloch. I suppose I will say hard things yet before I leave. I expect to be at Jordan till the 18th or later. Pray for me, brother. I have heavy work and sore trials. . . .
>
> I have been wondering very much how the Sunday school conference prospects are. You no doubt heard from a number who are on the program. I hope they are all favorably impressed with their subjects. No doubt there are many fears expressed by

the naturally fearful, but I pray God that He may give grace that the teaching and exercises will convince the most fault-finding that we must give our young members work, and that they will work for the principles of our doctrine with all the energy of the older members. . . . I did not finish my letter yesterday. I had a sad night thinking and praying over the condition of things here in Bertie.

* * *

From the enthusiasm of the people who attended, the conference John wrote about in his letter to Steiner was a real success. The committee had worked hard to prepare an interesting program for this first meeting, and when John saw the crowds filling up the Clinton Frame Church, his heart rejoiced at the interest being shown. And it continued to rejoice as he listened to the talks of young men and women who only a year or two before were quite disinterested in religion. His own son, Samuel F., was on the program, discussing the topic, "The Evergreen Sunday School." He couldn't help feeling a fatherly anxiety as S. F. faced this large audience. But the talk had been well prepared, and he did a good job of arguing in favor of year-round Sunday schools. With a little more practice, John decided, S. F. could develop into a fairly good speaker.

Oct. 6, 1892—This morning at 9 we began the services, M. S. Steiner in the chair; J. S. Hartzler, J. S. Coffman, and Jonathan Zook secretaries; C. Z. Yoder and A. B. Kolb choristers; C. P. Yoder treasurer. The program was readily carried out all day and the proceedings were very interesting and displayed talent among our young people that was a surprise to many. The good part was that it was practical teaching that will enable every observant Sunday school worker to go to his work better prepared. All were fed on the ground by a lunch brought by the neighbors.

Between sessions of the conference John met with several members of the Book and Tract Society to discuss ways of making their work more effective. The society had been formed about three years earlier, with J. S. Coffman, president; David Burkholder, vice-president; M. S. Steiner, secretary; and George L. Bender, treasurer. Their object had been to make Christian literature available to ministers and other worthy individuals at cost, and from donations to issue free literature and tracts. But little had been accomplished during those three years and John felt it was time to get busy. Tract work was definitely evangelistic work and should be expanded. Mennonite publications as well as Mennonite preaching reached only a fringe outside the church, but through tracts they could reach more.

In discussing this phase of the work at a meeting of the society held on Monday after the Sunday-school conference, a decision was made which gave John a new responsibility. Since one of their big problems was scarcity of tracts that were both interesting and orthodox in teaching, they decided to publish some of their own. John was appointed tract editor.

When Bettie tried to persuade her husband to call off his promised visit to Ohio late in November, it wasn't simply because she'd be lonely. She was plainly worried about his health.

"I'm tellin' you one thing, John Coffman," she said, rubbing hot liniment on his chest, "you're not agoin' off to Ohio next week. It's time you started thinkin' about yourself a little. There's no sense wearin' yourself out."

"I am taking care of myself, my dear," John replied, relaxing in his chair while Bettie rubbed. "This isn't anything to worry about. Just a touch of rheumatism or neuralgia. I'll be over it in a few days."

"Maybe so, but this is the worst spell you've had in years." Bettie noticed with alarm the pale cheeks and the dark circles under his eyes and rubbed extra hard. "It's just plain, common overwork. You sit right down and get a letter off tellin' 'em you're not comin'."

"But if I don't go now, Bettie, I don't know when I'll get there. I'm promised up till 'way next summer. And I can't disappoint them. They've been asking me for so long."

Bettie sighed. It was no use. All she could do was doctor him up and pray and hope for the best.

Writing in his diary that night, John showed a little more concern regarding his health:

> Nov. 18, 1892—Last night I had a rather hard time. I could not rest and sleep on account of neuralgia or rheumatism in the stomach and breast. I had not been bothered with this for a long time. I have been overworked with the Sunday-school lessons in the day and meetings in the evening. I shall try to have a little more rest. It is God's will, no doubt, that we are to work and work hard, but it cannot be right to overwork. May I be kept from sin in this as in other things.

But it was with his usual zest that John commenced the meetings in Medina County. He was happy to be with this little group, and was challenged by their great need. Since his first visit a few years earlier they had organized a Sunday school which reached the children of a few families still remaining aloof from church.

Most of the services were held in Baker's school, but on Sunday it was their turn to use the Guilford Church. That evening there was one convert, Katie Lind, the young daughter of Jacob Lind who had recently moved into the community. After that there were a few confessions nearly every evening. John was happy to see Jonas Kreider coming forward one evening. The next evening his wife was among the group that responded. Several other young married couples made decisions that week, and the little congregation was greatly encouraged when ten of the eleven converts asked to be baptized.

John's parting advice to the church here was to strengthen their teaching program by starting a midweek Bible study class for adults. He also suggested that they consider building a church of their own since the present arrangement of sharing a meetinghouse with the Wisler group was far from satisfactory.

From Medina John went to Mahoning County at the invitation of an active young church worker, Abram Metzler. This work in Ohio was described in a letter to M. S. Steiner, written from Canton:

> Dec. 14, 1892—Seven days meetings in Mahoning county, nearly twice every day, scattered to three places resulted in 14 converts, for which we thank the Lord and give to Him the praise. Most of the meetings, however, were held at the Central point, Oberholzers. We could not proceed just as I thought the best way to work, but probably the best under the circumstances. We could not give an invitation to come out publicly for fear of offending some, but came as near it as possible. There are many more convicted souls there, and the work is only begun, but it may be that a good many will yet come out with those who have started. The boys just got started at the last meeting. Four middle-aged men came out. The others are mostly young folks. The success of this work settled about all objections.

* * *

Sunday, December 25, 1892, was one of those special days for the Coffman family. The younger children were up early, not just because it was Christmas Day, but because they were anxious to see their father, who had come in on a late train the night before. The big boys were up early, for they didn't want to miss family devotions that morning, with everyone home once more. William had arrived the day before from Illinois, where he had spent the fall months conducting singing schools. Fannie was up early because she couldn't sleep. This was a very special day for her personally, for it was the day she was to be baptized and received into the church. Family worship that morning was a happy experience. John's heart was full as he truly gave thanks to God for all His good gifts, including home and family.

But the Coffmans weren't the only happy folks entering the church that morning. Everybody seemed happy, for today they were able to use the new addition to the church for the first time. They were glad to have it finished in time for the Christmas service. Six young people were in the class that received baptism during the service. All were converts at the meetings John had held before going to Ohio that fall. Altogether it was a memorable service.

An important wedding took place at Elkhart early in the new year. One morning A. B. Kolb slipped quietly up to John's desk, asking him whether he could come to J. F. Funk's home that evening to conduct a marriage ceremony for him. The bride was Phoebe

Funk, J. F.'s younger daughter. John willingly complied, going home early that afternoon to get ready for the wedding at seven o'clock. It was a simple ceremony with only a few friends present.

Another ceremony of particular interest to John that spring was the ordination of young Menno Steiner. Knowing that the voice of the congregation was to be taken to select a new minister and deacon to assist at Elkhart and other churches in the area, John again fasted and prayed that the will of God might be clearly shown. Steiner received the unanimous vote of the congregation and was ordained by Funk at a Thursday evening service. Four names were in the lot for the office of deacon, and the lot fell to John's brother, Daniel Coffman.

When his brother-in-law, Lewis Heatwole, wrote to him that spring telling him that he was planning to return to Virginia because of his health, John was greatly concerned. But as usual he saw the hand of God in the situation and was able to write an encouraging letter to Lewis:

> March 17, 1893—I cannot help feeling somewhat grieved that you cannot remain in your Missouri field of labor where you are so very much needed, and where your labors were so much appreciated. But you can be useful wherever you may be if life is spared; and it is not impossible for you to be even more useful in Virginia than in Missouri. It is not so great a matter of regret to find you moving from one field of operations to another, but I have my sincere regrets that your health has given way to the extent you seem to think. As to any advice concerning the work in Missouri or the filling of the vacant place, I cannot say much. It would be very unfortunate for the church to have the charge you leave given to an incompetent or unsuitable one. Better to leave the place vacant a while. I can simply say nothing. The brethren in the Missouri conference will no doubt act wisely.

Continued meetings in the home state took much of John's time that spring. First he was at the Shore Church, then Shipshewana, followed by Waterloo and Kokomo. He was pleased with the results at Kokomo, where twenty-four decisions were made. He was also pleased with the interest shown in the meetings by his son William, who was conducting singing schools in the community. During his meetings at Waterloo a group of young people from Elkhart came out to spend the weekend and attend the meetings. Samuel F. was in the group. Was he only imagining it, or did S. F.'s eyes travel frequently in the direction of one particularly attractive young lady with snappy brown eyes and dark curly hair? Occasionally he caught Ella Mann returning the look. Samuel gave a good talk to the Sunday school on Sunday morning at the request of the superintendent. Fourteen decisions were made here during the series.

Late in August, John set out on another visit to Ohio. His first stop was in Medina County where on Sunday morning, the twenty-seventh, he preached the first sermon in the new church the congregation had built for themselves near Wadsworth:

> This is the first meeting in the new house on the hill west of Wadsworth. The old Mennonite Brethren have their house nearby but refused to let our people worship in it, so they could do nothing less than build a house. The house is nicely arranged frame, heating from a furnace in the basement . . . slat seats from an eastern factory. The house was densely crowded, not all in.

Plans for the remainder of the trip were explained in a letter to his brother Joseph, September 5, 1893:

> I came to David Amstutz church on Saturday. They are Swiss and a part of their church has gone with the Sprunger element already, and it will take hard work to keep their young people from going the same way. Should they oppose night meetings and continued efforts their plain church would soon be a thing of the past. . . . I will go to Salem one day near Smithville. This is a new house and near Bro. Hostetler. The congregation was mostly Amish but is now in the Mennonite conference. Then I go to Holmes county, Winesburg, where there is a poor broken down congregation. They want and need a continued effort very much, but it is in Bro. Horst's charge, and I will not go against his will. . . . I have promised to go to Masontown, Pennsylvania, and help if possible to get Bro. Durr's church into church order. He says he will stand their worldly conformity no longer. Then I expect to be at Scottdale when they open their new house. I expect to be at Nappanee also when their new house is opened in October.

* * *

In November of 1893 John began to see the fulfillment of a long-cherished dream. Young Steiner stepped into his office one morning. He had just returned from Ohio, where he had taken part in a Sunday-school conference at the Zion Church near Bluffton.

"Are you busy, or can you spare a few minutes?" Steiner asked as John looked up from his work.

"Never too busy to talk to you," John replied, smiling, as he laid aside his pen and leaned back in his chair. "Sit down and tell me what's on your mind."

"I got a letter from Ebersole this morning," Steiner said.

"Dr. Ebersole in Chicago?"

Steiner nodded. "He thinks we should get busy right away. It's going to be a hard winter for a lot of folks in Chicago. A good many will need help, and he thinks we would get a good start in mission work if we started now and operated a kind of dispensary along with a mission."

"Fine, if you can find a suitable place, and, of course, someone to look after the work."

"He says he has several places in mind that we might rent."

"I suppose he'd be willing to help. And we have a few young men going to school or working in the city who might help. But who's going to take the responsibility?" John looked keenly at Steiner.

"That's what I wanted to talk to you about," Steiner replied. He threw back his shoulders and returned John's gaze squarely, but a flood of color betrayed deep emotion.

"I've been thinking the matter over," he said thoughtfully, "and praying about it too. And the more I think and pray, the more convinced I am that I should go."

John sat studying the young man in front of him.

"I must say I'm not surprised," he said quietly. "I felt it coming in some of your stirring talks at the conference. You're sure it's not just enthusiasm? Quite a few folks were enthused with the idea of a mission. Maybe it should be one of them."

"No, I talked with some of them. Not one was ready. They either have something they must do or they don't feel qualified. I know I haven't much training either, but someone has to make a start."

"It will be hard work—lots of disappointments—plenty of criticism, and no pay," John cautioned.

"I know. I've thought about it all, but it's sort of—well—like your work. I guess the Lord can take care of me as well as you. Anyway, I'm willing to try."

"That's right, son. I'm glad to hear you say it. I know God will be with you and bless your effort. When do you plan to go?"

"I think I'll go next week and help Ebersole look around for a place. Quite a few folks are interested, and once we get something started, I'm sure they'll back us up."

"Have you talked to Funk about this?"

"Yes, I've seen him and have his blessing," Steiner replied.

When the mission formally opened on 119th Street, Chicago, in December of 1893, John was in Pennsylvania holding meetings. The fact that young converts like Steiner, Daniel Kauffman, and Daniel Bender were now actively engaged in evangelism made a deep impression on John. How many others might soon be at work in Virginia and Eastern Pennsylvania if only some effort were made to reach them? The thought stirred him deeply and inspired several letters to brother Joe and to Lewis Heatwole that fall:

To L. J. H., Nov. 9, 1893:

> I am truly rejoiced that at least some of our dear people see that they should be at work in the great harvest for souls. No person on earth knows the grief of heart I have had concerning our young people who are lost to the faith of the Bible as God

has shown it to the holy martyrs who were willing to seal it with their blood. . . . God will break up this lethargy if He has to break down the church and set up one that will work and maintain His truth. . . . It seems to take as much to wake up our people in places as it did to awaken the Philippian jailor. I am glad for the souls the Lord has given you. May God bless your meetings at Weavers. Yes, have occasional meetings like that if you dare not have more. Work as God opens the way. But the tide is rising and our people will work differently from what they did. The necessity demands it, and you might as well try to stop the Mississippi as to stop our people from holding more meetings and doing more work. They may keep it back a while in Virginia and lose much by it, but it is coming even there. Two years will see a great change in Pennsylvania. Some were afraid I would make trouble there, but I see that the work is taking fire without me. All the dear brethren had better help to work and direct it in the right channel so it does not carry us to ruin. If God lets me live a while I expect to have to work harder to keep this work in the right channel than I ever worked to help get it started. When people get started even in a good work they get blinded to truth, and go wrong if not rightly directed. I expect to have a hard place to work in Pennsylvania as the church at two places where I go, Masontown and Scottdale, are very much out of order. Pray for me that God may use me to His will in this work.

To Joseph Coffman, Dec. 6, 1893:

I was glad to hear of the activity and earnestness of the church in Virginia. I am sure the church will be driven to greater action. If our own preachers cannot do it the United Brethren or Dunkards will. . . . I could truly rejoice because of your recent ingathering. Gathering in the young is indeed the way to work. The young people should all be gathered in not later than sixteen years old—truly converted at that age, then there would not be so much to lead them away when they are started and we would not have these old, hardened sinners to deal with. . . . I do not take the position that my way of work is the only way to work, but work we must, and if the Linville's Creek brethren or any others have a way to work that will win, different from my way, I am right with them without a word against them.

To L. J. H., Dec. 12, 1893:

I rejoice for our Bro. A. Shenk and his earnest work. I do hope he will have a blessed influence upon the work in general in Virginia. I know his disadvantage in being allowed only meetings enough to get people interested and not fully brought out. I have now held meetings many times in many places and sometimes where numbers have confessed Christ. I have often in such meetings begun on Saturday evening and give invitations to accept Christ now every evening. But very seldom, indeed, have I seen any make a start before Thursday evening. I have learned to my satisfaction that the limit to three evenings is just sufficient to prevent any direct results. Our dear brethren no doubt mean it well, and I do not cease to love them for their opposition to what I believe to be good and scriptural. But I think they must—with the many that were as positively against this continued work as they, see that it is after all necessary to the life of the church. You should have heard the talks from silver-haired ministers in our late Indiana conference on this subject, and seen their earnestness to encourage continued meetings. . . .

I can see very well the position that some of our brethren take as to *keeping our young people down.* But those dear brethren do not see how much mistaken they are. Keeping out of the active church work does not keep them down. They take from the young people the very thing that would keep them down. The Virginia church and conference has done much legislating to keep our people down out of the world in dress and other things, but in spite of all the *keeping down* they have done, their young men are now more conformed to the world than ours at Elkhart where we do not legislate much, but do some teaching on this point, and instead put our young people to work and have them contend for these principles. . . . They have tried too much to do by force of law what grace alone can do. What is it worth to keep people down in any sense if they submit only by constraint? We are in the dispensation of grace, and I shall never again help to legislate on outward forms as I did once in the Virginia conference when I did not know better. But I shall work harder in another way for the same principle.

That was gratifying news to me to learn that your young brother Daniel Kauffman of Missouri was already able to take up a continued work. I hope and pray that God may bless his work. . . . I am thinking that God is raising up workers so that the churches in Missouri and Kansas will soon be able to take care of themselves and do much evangelizing besides.

I confess that I have not much spirit to make any effort to obtain direct results in Virginia. . . . I have little courage to hold meetings. I am not the man for Virginia. . . . No doubt I told you in my former letter of the situation at Masontown, Pa. I am glad to believe that things are getting into a shape that the church can prosper. But it will take courageous work there yet. Believe me when I came to Westmoreland county that it was a sad sight to me to get to places like Stonerville and a place about ten miles into Fayette county where the congregations lie buried in the grave yards and the houses stand empty. There lie the people who contended in all goodness of heart for the *old ways*. That was right, but they failed to work in a way that kept the good old ways alive. Our faith is nearly lost here. Only one family, "Loucks," is left [in Scottdale] that still holds to the faith. There are several old members yet in the neighborhood of Stonerville. The Loucks family is bright and intelligent, and there is hopes that nearly all of their large family of children can be gathered into the church. Aaron, about 28 years old, is ordained to the ministry, and I have hopes that he will be an able minister. He makes a good start. Three of the children have made a start since I am here. They have a nice little church house opened for worship on the 3rd of December and expect to organize a Sunday school and to hold regular services. I have good hopes for the church here. This southwestern district of Pennsylvania is alive to the work, as you can see by the conference report, and they are getting able ministers. I expect to be here till Thursday morning, then go by Meyersdale to Tub [Springs], and to Maryland at Casselman church to be with Bro. Bender a week. . . . I have had hopes that Samuel F. would meet me at Tub, but he did not promise in his last letter.

Samuel F. did meet his father at Tub, coming from Virginia where he had spent several weeks visiting relatives. In later life it meant much to him to have had this week with his father. For four evenings during this series of meetings at Casselman's, John based his sermons on the theme of the tabernacle—"The Court of the Tabernacle," "A Royal Priesthood," "The Holy Place," "The Ark of the Covenant." Probably the most eager listener in the audience was his son who drank in every word of the beautiful interpretation, showing Christ as the fulfillment of the Old Testament symbolism.

* * *

John wondered why none of the boys waited to walk home with him one evening in January. He had worked a little later than usual and it was dark as he walked briskly along the frozen road. His pace quickened as he neared Bunker Hill and saw the lights twinkling in the Coffman home. That evening it seemed the whole house was lit up. Everybody must be home, he thought, and he wasn't surprised to hear singing and the toot of several horns as he crossed the yard.

Elizabeth was alone in the kitchen.

"Well, what's this? A brass band to welcome me home?" he asked.

Bettie gave him a quick smile and immediately turned to stir the pot of soup on the stove. Just then a new sound reached his ears. The horns were momentarily silent, but blending with the treble voices of his daughters came quavering uncertain tones, sounding much like an organ.

"What's that?" John asked, straightening up after removing an overshoe.

"Go and see," Bettie replied quietly without looking around.

In a flash John was at the parlor door, staring dumfounded at the scene before him.

It was an organ. Samuel F. was seated on the high, round stool, inexpertly picking out a melody with two fingers of his right hand, while the left sought out an occasional bass note. Standing around the instrument were the other six, the girls and Daniel singing lustily, while William, Jacob, and Ansel worked out three-part harmony on the horns.

Reaching the end of a verse the music ceased and the smiling musicians turned to face their father. John quietly scanned the group, his eyes asking the question which failed to reach his lips.

"Well?" he finally asked.

"How do you like it?" William blithely responded.

"Why, I—I can't say yet. Haven't heard it enough. But that's beside the point. Whose is it, and how did it get here?"

"Why, it's ours," replied Samuel F., rising and offering the stool to his father. "Here, sit down and try it."

"Now, boys, what kind of a trick is this?" John chided, ignoring the stool and looking very serious. "You know very well we have no money for such a luxury. Besides, what will people think?"

"Well, never mind what people think. And don't worry about the cost," William explained. "It's all paid for, and it didn't cost much, I assure you. I heard of a sale in town and went and bought it. It's a present to the family from Samuel F. and me. We had it hauled out this afternoon. Now do come and try it."

To the boys' delight John slipped off his coat and, smiling, started picking out a tune and experimenting with simple harmony.

Nevertheless John had a few qualms regarding the propriety of spending money for something as unessential as an organ. To his diary he confided:

> Jan. 5, 1894—Today William and S. F. had an organ put into the house, the first organ I ever had on my premises. I always maintained it not right for me to buy a luxury with money that I earned or that was given me for necessities. I have always had to be very economical and I am glad to be so as I am thankful that I am poor in this world's goods. God provides.

* * *

For some time John had been contemplating a trip south to Louisiana, Tennessee, and Florida. A number of Mennonite families had recently settled in these states, largely for health reasons. And from various places came urgent requests for a visit, in the hope that small congregations might be started.

But equally pressing were the appeals from so many other states.

It was hard to decide which were the most urgent. On learning that several Virginia ministers had recently made a tour of the southern communities, John decided to postpone his visit there and help out the church in Cumberland County, Pennsylvania. A letter to his brother Joseph tells of this visit:

> Jan. 22, 1894—Well, you see I did not go south. I was so severely urged by the Pennsylvania brethren and some of the ministers, Bender of Tub, Pa., and Hostetler of Wayne county, Ohio, that I could not find it in my heart to go south where I did not know of an immediate necessity. I came here on the 20th and expect to be in this county for three weeks, and then go to Lancaster county. There is little opposition from the people here. The opposition is from abroad and the folks here have concluded that it is time they use their own judgment. . . . They feel sure before many years more of the churches will be empty if no special effort is made. There is good interest at Churchtown, and I have good hopes that we will have an ingathering. Appointments have been made for the whole week for this one place. I write this letter more than anything else to ask you to pray earnestly to God to bless the work here to His glory. . . . I am here near the spot where I refugeed 29 years ago. I see children's children of those who associated with me. The church is not as strong here as it was then. You need not wonder that these people are becoming alarmed, and rise up for direct efforts. Yet there are some who are trying to keep them from doing anything more than what grandfather done. Oh, that the Lord would help us out of the ruts, but keep us in the road. I do hope that God will give me grace that I may not have my credit spoiled that I cannot go to Lancaster.

In spite of the interest and co-operation of the ministers and members at Churchtown, John found the work extremely difficult. Interest had been lagging too long. Here he was working in a district administered by the Lancaster Conference, and it troubled him that he was working without their approval. Consequences might be serious. As a rule, the opposition turned up at some of the meetings to see and hear for themselves what was going on. But not this time. The entire bishop body remained aloof in their own county, basing their judgment of the man and his work solely upon hearsay.

To L. J. Heatwole he wrote:

> Jan. 27, 1894—I have been here over a week [Churchtown]. I have found it a hard place to get anything loose. The people have been intensely interested but the confidence in the church is so low that the young people seem not disposed to join, even when they are deeply convicted. They have waited too long here, but there is still hope. One convert to the two that came out in Bro. Bender's meetings makes three for this place. . . . I expect

to be at Slate Hill about one week and at Newville about a week. That will make it near the middle of February. Then I expect to be in Lancaster some weeks.

A few more days at Churchtown saw a tremendous interest aroused among the young people, and on Sunday morning, February 18, thirteen converts were baptized. Even greater results were apparent at Slate Hill when twenty-three were received into the church on March 1.

With courage and hope he set out for Lancaster County.

*Finished moving out of the old shelving into the new desk and book case. It is strange how many curious and forgotten things are unearthed on such occasions. Probably when we come up for judgment according to the deeds done in the body, many things will come up that we cannot think of today.*—Diary.

# 22

John was rather surprised that no one was at the depot to meet him when he arrived at Lancaster. But things like that had happened before, he assured himself as he walked up the street to the home of one of the members.

When Jacob N. Brubacher called for him later in the day, John smiled as he greeted the influential bishop, but the return smile was obviously and painfully forced. The sudden chill John felt creeping down his spine wasn't caused by the weather.

On the way to his home Brubacher did most of the talking, and lost no time in informing John of the decision of the bishops in the county regarding his visit. They had met to discuss the matter and since the conference ruling forbidding protracted meetings had been completely ignored in the recent meetings in Cumberland, they had decided it would be best to make no appointments for him in the county. The dignity of conference, he pointed out, must be maintained. Once rules were ignored or disobeyed, discipline would be impossible, and there was no telling what might happen to the church.

All afternoon and evening the two talked on. John knew there was nothing to be gained by arguing, patiently he endeavored to point out the necessity of some kind of effort if the church was to survive.

Although he held no public meetings that week, John visited many members in various districts and held services in private homes. He also met a number of the ministers and a few bishops, some of whom were quite sympathetic. Regarding Amos Herr he wrote in his diary:

> Feb. 23, 1894—I had a long talk with him on the situation of the church. How I wish all could take a stand as reasonable.

It was Herr and J. K. Brubaker that finally persuaded John to preach at Rohrerstown on Sunday morning and at the Lancaster Church on Sunday afternoon:

> Feb. 25, 1894—Last night I staid at brother J. K. Brubaker's. This morning he took me to the meeting at Rohrerstown. I would have felt justified in not speaking under the circumstances, but thought I should not appear insulted or revengeful. Spoke from Rom. 5:1. Had a fairly filled house. Took dinner at Benjamin Brubaker's. We went to Lancaster to the appointment at 2 P.M. The house was crowded. Text—Matt. 14:18, the church and her foundation. There is quite a commotion among the brotherhood. May God lead them all in peace.

A few weeks after his return home John received a letter from Henry Rupp of Shiremanstown:

> March 17, 1894—I was at the conference yesterday near Lancaster. There was a very large attendance, more so than usual, and business quite brisk for a while, principally on your account in coming into our district and holding meetings.
>
> We got off better than I expected for what we had done, but our future is dark now for holding protracted meetings. You know the bishops do the business in our conference. They decided with but one dissenting voice to forbid the holding of meetings for more than once or twice in succession, days or evenings, at the same place. The bishops were sustained by fifty-seven votes against twelve for the meetings as we held them in our county. You see there was some concession by the bishops in allowing the ministers and deacons to vote. The pressure for the meetings was too strong, so the bishops did not want to carry all of the responsibility. Not one minister in Lancaster county voted for continued meetings. So the time for these meetings seems a good ways off.
>
> You or any other minister or evangelist, though, can come and they will appoint meetings for them as *they* hold meetings. Once or twice at a place. They are sending two missionaries to the west again this summer, John Erb and preacher Lehman. We would need some in Pennsylvania.

* * *

Seated at A. B. Kolb's desk at the office one day, John was trying to concentrate on a new series of Sunday-school lessons. For some reason writing didn't go well that morning. All this moving around! Why couldn't they leave his desk in the corner of the big storeroom where it had been for the last few years? Of course it took some rearranging to make space for the Tract Society, the *Young People's Paper,* and the Evangelizing Board business. But he could not help wondering where he would land. Maybe he wouldn't even have a desk to himself. He tried to feel charitable. Actually, as a part-time worker he realized he didn't rate the most consideration. But lately he had a queer feeling when he came in to work, as if, somehow, he didn't quite fit in with the present staff.

With a shrug he tightened his grip on his pencil and once more scanned the lesson title which he had written at the top of a clean sheet, "The Visit of the Wise Men." Wise men! Would to God we had a few more wise men in the church, he thought. Would he dare voice a sentiment like that in his comments, maybe say a word for training, or the value of an education? No, that was hardly a point in the lesson, and anyway the church was not ready yet for thoughts along that line. But there were a few who were thinking.

Leaning back in his chair John smiled to himself as he recalled the warm discussion regarding education at the meeting of the Evangelizing Board in Chicago a few days before. If Steiner and a few other members had their way, the church would soon have a missionary training school, operated by the Evangelizing Board. To most of the members the suggestion was too fantastic to rate serious discussion, but they agreed to give it prayerful thought and to discuss it at home so that it could be presented at a general meeting which was to be called soon to revise the constitution.

Thinking back over the work of the Evangelizing Board, John suddenly realized how far the work had come during the last few years, even to the point where incorporation was necessary. Now they were planning to merge the Evangelizing and Benevolent boards. A big step for the old church, John realized. Was it too much to hope that she might also be aroused soon to educational needs? A church school would be a great boon. Certainly the church of the future would demand trained leaders. Was it too soon to start dreaming? Perhaps something might develop out of Dr. Mumaw's idea. He planned to start a private school in town that fall and was suggesting to a few friends that it may develop into a Mennonite school.

Picking up his Bible for another look at the text, John's eyes fell on the verse he had used for his talk at the Chicago mission the week before. What an experience that was, preaching to the little crowd that came out, so different from the congregations he was accustomed to. He saw again the poor, ragged men and women, probably hoping for a little material comfort as well as spiritual; the thin, eager-faced children, delighted with a little change in the drab pattern of daily living; the few serious young men and women who listened so attentively, and the rowdy boys whose sole purpose seemed to be to create as much disturbance as possible.

A problem kept pressing on John's mind as he thought of Chicago, one he would have to face soon. Sighing, he looked hurriedly at his watch and quickly turned to the chapter on the Wise Men. He would talk to Samuel F. about Chicago that evening if possible.

S. F. was glad for the opportunity of talking to his father. The two walked home together and it was he that opened up the subject uppermost in both their minds.

"Well, what did you think of the work in Chicago?" he asked. "I haven't had much chance to talk to you since you got back. Is Steiner actually accomplishing what he had hoped?"

"Yes, I think it's going even better," John replied. "They're really stirring up interest."

"He said the people seemed to enjoy your talk last week."

John looked up quickly. "You had a letter from him, then?"

"Yes," S. F. nodded. "I've had quite a few letters from him lately."

"Well, then, I—I reckon you know what he wants?"

"I think I do," S. F. replied. "I've been wanting to talk to you about it for some time. Do you think—I—I'd fit into the program there? That I could be of some help?"

John considered the question carefully. "Well, Samuel, I've been thinking about it a lot since Steiner made the suggestion. Certainly they need more help, and I have no doubt about your ability. But you'll find the environment quite different from anything you've ever known."

"Naturally, I'd expect it to be different. But I could adjust, couldn't I?"

"Certainly, but it would take a lot of patience and a great deal of the grace of God. But if that is where the good Lord wants you, you can count on His help. I admit I hate to see you go to the city, but I can't stand in your way. How do you feel about it? Do you feel you have a call to that kind of work?"

It was now Samuel's turn to pause and consider. He gazed thoughtfully at a purplish-tinted cloud slowly changing shape on the horizon. "I don't know," he said. "How can one tell? I didn't hear a voice like the boy Samuel. I haven't had any vision or dream, but I do have a feeling that I'm needed and should go. Is that enough?"

"Yes, Samuel, that is enough. Not many of us have a miraculous or great emotional experience. God seems to appeal to us through a sense of duty. But are you sure you are ready to go into this kind of work? Have you given up college?"

"Yes, I think I have," sighed Samuel, his eyes still on the cloud. "I—I left that matter to God several years ago. There were so many interesting possibilities that I knew I could never choose; so I left it entirely to Him. I know He has a plan for me, and I told Him I'm willing to accept His plan, whatever it might be. It seems this door is opening for me now."

John's eyes were misty as he, too, studied the shifting clouds, but he said nothing as S. F. continued. "It rather looks as if this might be an opportunity for more education, though, don't you think? Steiner suggested I might be able to take a few courses at Moody's."

"That would be fine," John replied. "Working and learning go hand in hand, and as you work, you'll realize how much you have to learn. Moody's will help, but remember this, my boy, the best school is your own private study with the Holy Spirit as your teacher."

"I guess that's been your only school," commented S. F., turning to smile at his father. "If I can only be half as good as you at helping folks understand the Bible, I'll be happy."

On the ninth of May, Samuel F. said farewell to the family and set out for Chicago. There were tears in his mother's eyes as he left the house. Somehow they both felt it was a farewell to the old home. John went to the depot with him and managed a warm, encouraging smile as the train pulled out.

* * *

It was May again, and John's heart thrilled as he stepped from the train at Jordan, Ontario. Just the right time of year for a visit to the Twenty, he thought, humming softly to himself as he walked along the country road to the Daniel Honsberger home. The day was dull and cloudy, but there was the scent of apple blossoms in the air, and birds were singing merrily. His stay wouldn't be long this time, but he looked forward with pleasure to a visit with friends from many places who would be arriving for the semiannual church conference.

The first day of the conference was much like other conferences, nothing of particular importance, and no clash of opinions. But next morning the question of evangelizing was again brought up. John was surprised, for at the fall conference, only six months ago, the question had been discussed at length and once more conference had ruled against continued meetings.

That night, as he sat translating the minutes from German into the English language for use in the *Herald of Truth,* John looked up the resolution passed in the fall:

> 5th resolution—If in the course of home visits by the preachers in the various districts they be requested by the members of the church of that district to hold meetings (evangelistic) in private dwellings they shall hold such meetings according to the established rules of the church and in the same manner in which regular church meetings are held. Any preacher violating these rules will be looked upon as an offender.
>
> 6th resolution—When the appointments are supplied in districts where we have no stationary minister that not more than 3 or 4 meetings be held in succession in our meeting house.

John smiled and breathed a prayer of thanksgiving as he translated the new resolution passed that day. Surely the Spirit of God had been at work in this conference:

> 3rd resolution—That our ministers have the liberty to do

evangelistic work according to the teaching of Christ and His apostles, and the doctrine and belief of our church and with the will of the church where they labor.

4th resolution—That Bro. S. S. H. shall accept the appointment of membership on the committee of the Evangelizing Board of America.

After the conference John spent nearly three weeks with the two congregations at South Cayuga and Rainham. Although there were only three converts, he planned to continue a little longer. But suddenly his plans were changed. A telegram from Virginia informed him that his father was seriously ill. He decided to leave at once for his old home.

It was a strange home-coming; strange to have all the brothers and sisters together, and everyone so quiet. That first day it seemed to John that all he could hear was the harsh breathing and the delirious mutterings coming from the bedroom; all he could see was the ashy gray face on the pillow and the stricken, pained look in his mother's eyes as she hovered so helplessly at the bedside.

Later in the day John felt a spark of hope. For a time the breathing grew easier and occasionally a rational statement emerged from the delirium. Once or twice he even thought his father recognized him. But the doctor offered little hope.

For three weeks John remained in Virginia, helping to look after his father, who remained critically ill, and also taking care of the steady stream of visitors who called to inquire about the patient.

Occasionally he took time to visit a few friends and relatives, especially the older ones and the sick. One of these was Agnes Rhodes, who had been confined to her bed for four years.

"Do you believe in divine healing?" Agnes suddenly asked one day after John had read a chapter from the Bible.

"Certainly," John replied, turning to James 5 and reading the injunction to the sick. "Do you believe that too?"

Agnes thought a while. "I just can't be sure."

For a few minutes John talked about faith, explaining the verse to her.

"So, all I have to do is believe," she said slowly. "Yes, I think I see it now," she continued, her face brightening as the truth dawned. "Just believe. Believe in God who has power to heal. I know He has power, and I know He can heal me. Yes, and I know He will," she cried suddenly, her eyes shining like two bright stars. "I'll pray about it, and you pray too, and please come back again in a few days to pray with me again."

Several days later John did go back. His visit with Agnes that day is recorded in his diary:

July 5, 1894—This forenoon I went over to see Agnes Rhodes. She has been thinking that the Lord would heal her if she has faith. I encouraged her to believe, and we had special prayer for her healing. She has been lying in her bed for four years. After the prayer she asked me to stay a little while. Soon she raised herself on her elbow, then sat up, then put her feet to the edge of the bed and said, "I believe I can walk." I said, "Get up and walk." She walked across the room and back unassisted. She said it was the power of God by faith. Thus we can see the power of God to heal those who believe.

Day after day Father Coffman's life hung in the balance. Sometimes he seemed better, but again he grew worse. By the end of the third week, when he seemed improved, John decided to return home. His work was piling up and many matters needed attention.

"You understand, Mother," he said, as he informed her of his decision. "I hate to leave you while Father is still so sick, but I feel I must get back to my work."

"Yes, I know how it is," Mother replied, sinking tiredly into a chair. "It was good to have you here this long, and you were such a help with Father so poorly. But it's time you got back to your work. I reckon we'll make out somehow. But if—if—"

"If Father's called home?" John reached for his mother's hand as he finished the question.

Frances nodded.

"I thought of that," he said gently. "We don't know when it might happen, or where I'll be. But I feel that if I'm off holding meetings it would be better for me just to keep right on. Father would want it that way, I'm sure. I think it was much more important to have been with you now when I could be of help to—to both of you."

Frances didn't reply, but the look of love and understanding she gave her son remained with John to comfort him when word of his father's death reached him early in September.

He was holding meetings at Palmyra, Missouri, at the time, and the meeting continued as scheduled:

Sept. 3, 1894—Yesterday afternoon a card from William informed me that my dear father passed away last Tuesday, simply sinking lower and lower, dying without a struggle. He was buried at the Bank on Thursday. It is a sad hour, yet the long expectation of his death has caused the storm of grief to come slowly. In our sadness we can rejoice that he was ready and longed to go, and that he trusted solely in Christ and His work. A noble father. Would that I may be no less noble and that many more had such fathers who have not.

* * *

John was happy to have young Daniel Kauffman working with him on this visit to Missouri, and rejoiced to note the spiritual progress of the former teacher-politician. Daniel had been holding meetings at Palmyra for a week before John's arrival. Prospects for establishing a church here were not too bright at the time, since there were only two Mennonite families in the community. Realizing that a few new settlers would help the situation, John decided to give the community a little publicity through the columns of the *Herald of Truth:*

> Sept. 15, 1894—It was my pleasure to come to Palmyra, Marion county, Mo., on Saturday, Sept. 1. Here I found Daniel Kauffman of Morgan county earnestly holding forth the Word of Life. . . . There are only two families of our denomination in this county, J. L. Rohrer and J. M. Hershey, both of whom moved here from Lancaster county, Pa. There are several other families here who also came from Lancaster whose sympathies are with us, but who have not united with any church. . . . The country here is a very desirable one for our people to locate in, yet there are some objections as there are in every place. The land is of good quality and is very productive. Almost every variety of crops does well here. The seasons are not so dry as in places father west—the crops seldom fail. . . . The markets and railroad facilities are excellent. . . . The society is very good compared to many other places; yet the proximity to the Mississippi River brings an element into society that is not the most desirable. . . . It seems to me if some of our younger brethren in some of the eastern churches where they are crowded near together and the farms already divided up very small, would take advantage of a place like this they could better their financial condition and possibly their spiritual condition and could be instrumental in building up a vigorous church in some waste places without any material loss to the churches from which they remove. . . .

After a week at Cherry Box and another at Mount Zion in Morgan County, John joined a group going to Garden City for a Sunday-school conference and the annual church conference. There was considerable excitement at this conference regarding the possibility of organizing a General Conference for all the Mennonite churches of the United States and Canada. Recent articles in the *Herald of Truth* by Daniel Kauffman, and by C. Z. Yoder of Ohio, also an editorial by J. F. Funk, had started people thinking and the question was thoroughly discussed during the sessions as well as between sessions. In his editorial Funk had said:

> July 1, 1894—There are among our people at least fourteen conferences which, in a general way, hold together. Some of them draw the lines a little closer in this or that particular, yet there is withal a warm fraternal feeling existing between them all. . . . A conference is a means by which we become better acquainted with one another, by which an opportunity is offered to ex-

change opinions, to learn of different methods and means of applying our principles. . . . A general deliberation upon all matters and points of faith, ordinances, regulations, discipline and doctrine, etc., would be of great value.

Young Daniel Kauffman was an enthusiastic supporter of the conference, as was M. S. Steiner, who had arrived from Chicago. John shared their enthusiasm, realizing the great benefits of such an organization to the progress of the church. But in his travels he had felt the pulse of the church and knew that, like every forward movement, the proposal would meet stiff opposition. However, he gladly assisted the secretaries, Kauffman and Steiner, in formulating a resolution favoring a General Conference and suggesting initial steps toward its organization.

Daniel was exuberant when the resolution passed with a good majority. "That's two conferences in favor now, Illinois and Missouri," he exclaimed, rushing up to John after the afternoon session. "Only twelve more to go."

"It's a good beginning, all right," said John, "but remember, brother, these conferences are in the West. Wait till you see what happens in Indiana, to say nothing of Pennsylvania and Virginia. Changes come slowly in Mennonite circles, you know. But we can pray."

Returning to Chicago with Steiner after the conference, John had a good talk with him regarding the mission.

"And so you feel you will have to leave Chicago?" John began, looking troubled as he shifted in his seat to face the young man beside him.

"I'm afraid so," Steiner replied. "With the wife's health as it is, Chicago's hardly the place for her."

"I'm sorry," John said, "but there is work in Canton as well as Chicago, and if Clara's health is better there, no doubt that's where you're supposed to be. You've done good work in Chicago, but the question is, How will we keep it going? Who will take your place?"

Steiner turned from the window and smiled as he noticed John's troubled expression. "You're not really worried about that, are you? Why, there are several able young men at the mission, right now, and they're doing a good job. I've been away most of the time now for several months and as far as I can see they're doing all right."

"Maybe so, but in a place like that someone must be responsible, and the group there now—well—they're all school boys."

"How about the assistant manager? He'd get along fine."

"Samuel F.?" John glanced sharply at Steiner. "Why, he—he's just a boy too. Far too inexperienced for a responsibility like that."

"He may be just a boy to you, but in Chicago he's proving himself a man. And as I've told you before, he's fitting into the program very well. The folks like him. He gives wonderful talks, so logical and simple that even the children understand. And he has a knack of making things run smoothly. All the workers respect him and listen when he speaks."

John sat staring out the window while Steiner was speaking, and for a few minutes only the rumble of the train was heard. Then turning again to Steiner he said, "I'm glad to hear you say that about S. F. I only hope he'll continue to rate your high opinion. But somehow I feel he isn't exactly the type for that kind of work. He may grow into it, but I still think we should have a more experienced man. This is a new undertaking and to get the support of the church we should have someone at the head that has the confidence of the people. At least an ordained man. The mission cause would be put back for years if this effort should fail."

"You know, brother, this is the Lord's work," Steiner reminded John. "I've heard you say so many times. So surely He has a man for the job and will keep it going. Personally, I have confidence in the boys there now, and I intend to suggest S. F.'s name to the advisory committee when they meet on Monday."

John saw his son in a new light when he visited the mission on Sunday. The service was in progress when he and Steiner walked in:

> We arrived at Chicago at 11 o'clock, over an hour late. We went at once to the mission where they were holding a Sunday morning meeting. Samuel F. was talking to them. After he closed Steiner and I gave short talks. They had quite an orderly meeting. We had Sunday school at 3 o'clock and the attendance was quite large. The force of teachers was quite strong and the school went along quite well when they had about two extra workers to keep order. This evening we had first a children's meeting at 7 and a mission meeting at 8. The house was full, crowded, and the order was good while I talked on justification.
> Oct. 1, Monday—This morning the advisory committee of the Chicago mission met, A. R. Zook, D. S. Yoder, Abram Metzler (representing C. M. Brackbill), and J. S. Coffman. The brethren M. S. Steiner and S. D. Ebersole met this committee. The reports of the superintendent and secretary-treasurer were received. The committee formulated an advisory report. M. S. Steiner resigned his place at the mission to go to Canton, Ohio. S. D. Ebersole resigned his office—inconvenience and financial embarrassment. S. F. Coffman was elected manager of the Home mission and E. J. Berkey, secretary-treasurer. It is the opinion of the committee that the work of the mission shall go on and can go on successfully.

John arrived home just in time for another round of conferences: first the Sunday-school conference held at Pleasant Valley or the "Forks" Church in Lagrange County, October 3-5, then the meeting of the Evangelizing Board, October 10, followed by the Indiana Conference, October 11 and 12.

Visitors from east and west and from Ontario flocked to the Sunday school conference. It was one of the largest gatherings the Indiana church had ever experienced, and one of the most inspirational meetings ever held by the church:

> Oct. 4, 1894—Just before noon we had one of the most deeply spiritual seasons and the finest feeling of sympathy for the lost I have ever witnessed.

Many of the visitors remained in the district over Sunday in order to attend the other two meetings:

> Oct. 6, 1894—We had a party of 72 (on the train) from Middlebury to Elkhart. We took the whole party to J. F. Funks and divided them out to various places. We took Mary and Sarah Brenneman, Mary Denlinger, Peter Shantz of Wayne county, Joseph and Ida Driver of Missouri for our assignment.

Seeing in the crowd of visitors an opportunity for the promotion of his school, Dr. Mumaw announced special exercises at the Elkhart Institute on Monday morning after the Sunday-school conference, inviting visitors to attend. The school which he called the "Elkhart Institute of Science, Industry and the Arts" had opened on September 21, 1894, in the G.A.R. hall. Both academic and commercial courses were offered and, although at first only four pupils were enrolled, gradually a few more trickled in.

The program that morning was quite informal. Mumaw had asked John Coffman to open with a devotional service. There was music by the Elkhart male quartet, and short talks by a number of the visitors. Mumaw found many in the audience sympathetic toward his hopes that someday the school might develop into an institution to serve the church.

John wasn't too hopeful regarding the attitude of the Indiana Conference toward the General Conference proposition, and carefully prepared a few strong arguments in its favor. When the meeting was organized, however, he found himself placed in a position where he was unable to present his arguments:

> This afternoon the conference convened and considered some of the questions presented. To my disappointment I was chosen moderator. I wanted very much to help discuss questions. Everything passed along quietly.
>
> Oct. 12—The conference was quite harmonious, but several resolutions failed to pass. The general conference resolution failed to pass.

Writing about the matter to L. J. Heatwole after receiving word that the proposal had also been lost in Virginia, John disclosed that he was neither surprised nor too disappointed.

> Nov. 17, 1894—I was much pleased to get your report of the conference, etc. It was not much of a disappointment to me that the general conference question was so disastrously defeated.

I really believe it is best not to push that question. I believe the Lord let it be defeated in our Indiana conference. We are not really ready yet for it. I am resting more easily about the matter than I would if the work was getting into shape. . . .

Our meetings at Elkhart for nearly two weeks have been well attended in spite of the inclement weather. There were nine converts and we have hopes for more till Sunday evening. Among them are Daniel and Barbara. . . . On Monday I go to Canada to stay till Christmas.

*Much of my meditation today has been upon the condition of the world, and especially the fact that it seems so difficult to get people out of Christ to accept religion. It has been a question with me whether it is not because many churches are allowing so much of worldliness and adopt so much of the practice of the world in their life that people do not see the difference as they ought.*—Diary.

# 23

"There, at last it's done," John said to himself, hurriedly signing his name and tucking the letter in an envelope. "In a few weeks I'll be on my way south."

"I hope Lewis Shank will be satisfied," he thought, as he carefully addressed the envelope to Bowling Green, Florida. He had spent all afternoon making his plans for the trip and writing to the folks he intended to visit. By this time he had a good-sized file of letters from the South, the majority from Shank, who had moved there from Missouri.

"I can but plead with you to come! Come! Come!" he had written in July. But the plea for help from Missouri seemed even more urgent that fall. He had never been able to forget Shank's outburst of disappointment when he learned that John couldn't come:

> Aug. 19, 1894—Oh, my brother, how I was disappointed. No one but myself knows. . . . My disappointment sets hard on me because of attending circumstances. Through human weaknesses we may be easier mortified by such blasting of hopes. . . . If you could once come and see my surroundings and strike an entering wedge, then I think you would be able to know whether this was a field available for the Master's cause or not. Of course it presents a dark picture like Paul found at Athens, but he stood to the post of duty in his sphere and not in vain. . . . I don't know whether I am right or not, but it does look to me sometimes as though our ministers are a little cowardly. They do not want to go anywhere unless there are pioneers gone be-

> fore and tried a place first. And even then there is a hesitancy. I take into account also that it takes means to make a missionary tour like this would be, but think again what it must have cost the great missionary, Paul, to make his great journeys over the different countries he preached, and had to encounter the great oppositions that are told of him in the Acts of the Apostles.

John sighed as he reread the letter. How he had longed to fulfill that request and many, many more just as insistent! He had kept in touch with Shank, assuring him of his intentions to come. In October Shank wrote:

> The best time for holding meetings is now and until the first of December. January is the busiest time of the year for this country when orange gathering and shipping and preparing land for corn will be going on. The nights are generally cool and people don't like to go out nights on account of taking cold.

However, Shank willingly submitted when January was the only date John could work into his schedule.

Before leaving for the south, John had another important engagement at Elkhart. On Wednesday evening, January 9, 1895, the entire Coffman family attended a service at the church. On this particular occasion John wasn't in the pulpit but sat with his family on the front bench. As William walked down the aisle with Lydia Hug by his side, John reached over and gently squeezed Bettie's hand. It seemed only yesterday, that day when they had stood before the minister and taken those important vows. And yet, somehow, he felt like quite an old man now—almost at the end of the journey, he thought sometimes. That very afternoon he had preached the funeral sermon for a neighbor who had died suddenly. One never knew!

Preacher J. S. Lehman performed the ceremony. The church was overflowing. Practically the whole congregation was present, with many friends in from the country. A large number were invited to the wedding supper at the Hug home. In typical German style the long tables were loaded again and again from a seemingly inexhaustible store. In keeping with family tradition there was an infare at the Coffman home next evening.

* * *

The calendar said February, but to John it seemed like May. Even though he had been in Florida over a week, the warm, balmy air, the gardens and flowers were still almost unbelievable. Under a shade tree on Shank's lawn he wrote up his diary for several days:

> Jan. 31—Last night there was some rain, but the day was fine. The air is so warm that I could not stand my heavy underwear so I put on gauze and feel comfortable without my coat. Some trees are out in bloom. Some orange trees are putting out bloom buds. I can see the potatoes coming up along the rows. Vegetation is just about as it is May 1, in Northern Ind. I spent

the day writing letters. This evening we had a fair attendance but the clouds and a prayer meeting nearby kept some folks away. It does not take very much here to discourage people from coming to church. Text—Rom. 7:13, The sinfulness of sin.
Feb. 1—I was out in the rain in my shirt sleeves, did not wear my coat today. This morning Lewis and I went over Mr. Ross' orange grove and found quite a number of oranges that are fairly good, yet made unmarketable by the freeze. I ate more than ever in my life. I spent the time talking, resting, loafing. This evening Bro. Shank and I went to the school house and I borrowed the black board to put my diagram on.
Feb. 3—This morning I went with Bro. Shank to the meeting at Mount Pisgah Baptist church, three quarter mile east. Only a few present. These were standing around a stump fire in the church yard to warm. It was comfortable in the house for me without a fire. They insisted on me preaching.

Writing about his trip for the benefit of the readers of the *Herald of Truth* in a series of articles he entitled, "Notes by the Way," John described his visit to I. G. Plank's home at Macclenny and a baptism service for his two children, Katie and David; his visit with A. Hunzicker at Fairbanks, Aladma County; with John Hershberger at Merimack, Orange County; and with A. R. Housekeeper at Dover, Hillsborough County. Regarding his visit to Florida, he wrote:

March 1, 1895—The meetings at Bowling Green were continued from Jan. 30 to Feb. 10. Because of the busy season for work here only one meeting was held in the day aside from Sunday. The cold wave from the north made what was called "cold weather" here, which seriously interfered with the attendance. We had our meetings mostly in a Baptist meeting house near Bro. Shank's home. As there was no arrangement by which to warm the house the meetings had to be abandoned for several evenings. It was an unusual sight to a "northerner" to see the natives build a pine fire and stand around it to get warm before going in the meeting house. The attention to the doctrines as held and taught by us as a people was very good, and some favorable impressions have been made here. . . . On Sunday a baptismal service was held when John and Mollie Shank were received into the church by this solemn ordinance. . . .

Looking back over the work in Florida, I feel convinced that if the higher life, the fuller consecration, the more entire separation from the world, the more perfect obedience, the more holy life of our teachings were held more continually before these people whom it was my privilege to meet, some would eventually accept its truth. What the people want is teaching followed by the testimony of a few holy lives. Proper and sufficient effort of our people will build up the church in Florida.

At Roseland, Louisiana, John found a small group of members under the leadership of Philip Nice. He stayed with the Nice and J. C. Kornhaus families from February 19 to March 3, holding meetings nearly every evening in a nearby schoolhouse. The house was crowded each evening and there were a number of conversions. At a baptism service on the final Sunday four members united with the church, bringing the membership to ten.

Dickson, Tennessee, was the next stop on his journey and here, too, was a small colony of Mennonites struggling to make a living in a new location and to maintain the faith of their fathers. Here he was greeted by A. I. Yoder and several men who had arrived the week before from Illinois to study the prospects of settling in the vicinity. A Sunday school was organized during his visit and A. I. Yoder named superintendent.

John tried to encourage settlement in these southern districts, giving a detailed summary in the *Herald of Truth* of the desirable features as well as disadvantages. He concluded:

> April 1, 1895—It is, however, necessary that our people settle in the south in colonies if they settle there at all. In this way they can be of help to one another in their farming; they can mutually encourage better schools which are sadly neglected here, and they can come together to worship and build up the church with their young.

A visit to the Waldensian colony in Valdese, Tennessee, came next. Here were about thirty-six families from Italy who had settled on a 5,000-acre tract of land in 1893. John spent several days with them, getting acquainted with the leader, Pastor Soulier, and learning about the beliefs and customs of the society.

The trip ended with a visit to Knoxville, Tennessee, where he found a good-sized congregation in need of a larger church building:

> March 22, 1895—I was deeply interested to see here as settlers in this new place some of my acquaintances from Virginia, Ohio, and Michigan.
>
> April 15, 1895 *(Herald of Truth)*—I am glad to believe that there is an excellent prospect for the building up of a large congregation of our people. The country is quite good, the lands are yet rather cheap, and the climate is mild and healthful.

A formidable stack of letters as well as an immense amount of back work awaited John when he got back to the office. But it felt good to be at work again and it was a joy to be with his family once more.

Naturally there were many interruptions that first morning at work. It was midafternoon before he got around to the letters. Then came another interruption. Hearing a strange footstep in the room John looked up to see E. J. Berkey from the Chicago mission approaching his desk.

"Well, hello, Edward. I'm surprised to see you," said John, jumping up to greet the young man. Although Berkey smiled, John immediately detected the strained, worried expression in his eyes.

"Everything all right in Chicago?" he quickly asked.

"I suppose you've guessed that's what I'm here for," replied Berkey, slumping tiredly in the chair John pulled up for him. "We were hoping you'd stop in Chicago on your way home, but since you didn't, S. F. decided I'd better come up right away to talk things over with you."

"Anything special? Is S. F. all right?" John asked, trying to keep his voice casual.

"Oh, he's all right," Berkey assured him. "And the trouble isn't anything new. Just the same old thing, only more of it."

John nodded. "I think I understand. I've had quite a few letters about the mission in the mail that's been waiting here. I reckon things have been a little tough lately."

"Very tough," Berkey exclaimed. "Right now there are so many rumors floating around that folks don't know what to think. And we don't know what to do. Even some of our main supporters are holding back, wondering what's going on, and our funds—well, there simply aren't any. We've been digging into our own pockets to keep going. And now they're empty."

Both men sat silently staring into space for a few moments. John knew how things were going. He had had a number of letters hinting of the rumors and asking for the true state of affairs at Chicago. He knew too, that the treasury had been low for some time, both the regular evangelizing funds and the special mission fund.

"I'm afraid I hardly know what to advise," he finally said, drumming his finger tips on the desk. "All you can do is keep on and trust God for grace to stand up under the rumors and criticisms as well as to furnish the funds to keep going. You're not discouraged enough to quit, are you?"

"Oh, no, none of us wants to quit. And we're learning to ignore the rumors. It's just that we don't see how we can continue to operate, meet the rent, keep up the dispensary, and buy a little food now and then without some money. We've already closed the kindergarten."

Rising from his chair John began slowly pacing the floor, his hands clasped behind his back, his head bowed in thought.

"I'll tell you what I can do," he said. "I can write a little article for the *Herald* about the mission, letting folks know just how things are and what you have done. It should help to restore confidence. But we'll also have to have a meeting with some members of the evangelizing committee to decide what more can be done."

John immediately set to work on the article so that it could appear in the issue of the *Herald of Truth* about to go to press. After reviewing the history of the work and activities—Sunday school, kindergarten, dispensary, cottage meetings, as well as regular services —he stated:

> April 15, 1895—The result has been not what many might have expected or wished. Less than half a dozen of those who had been deep down in sin and degradation have been brought up into an earnest consecrated life, and are now workers right along with our members in the meetings. . . . A number of others have been greatly benefited morally, and quite a large number have professed faith in Jesus Christ as their Saviour. . . . All who have engaged in the work of rescuing the fallen souls feel that the Lord has used them in a noble work, and do not regret the time and money spent, neither the worry and labor endured, nor the unkind remarks and insinuations that have been made concerning them.
>
> The mission has passed through some experiences that were like the gloom of cloudy days. A number of different circumstances combined to bring discouragement. First, the workers were inexperienced. Then there was opposition to the mission by the very people for whose benefit it was intended, and by the Catholics of whom there were many in the vicinity. Next there was opposition by many of our own people. There were no doubt some reasons why our people did not look upon the mission with favor. The workers were all rather young in years and unmarried. It would have been preferable to have a married couple in charge. But such it appeared impossible to secure.
>
> There were many false reports circulated that spoke very disparagingly of the mission. It is difficult to understand how reports get started when they are so utterly groundless, and when they are at the same time so uncharitable as to insinuate dark, immoral conduct on the part of prayerful, consecrated workers. . . . It is sincerely to be hoped when any one hears any disparaging report concerning the Home Mission he will at least make a fair effort to find out the truth before he repeats it.
>
> I have written this article as an explanation to a number of inquiries sent to me personally. The report has gone out in places that the mission had disbanded and closed its work; in other places that it would soon close and no more money should be sent. The work of the mission has gone quietly on in the order of the church, and is under careful supervision, and will go on if the Lord will. It has, however, been running at a great disadvantage since many of its friends have ceased to remit money for its support. . . . Please send some money soon, as funds are needed now. Any inquiries . . . will be gladly answered by S. F. Coffman or E. J. Berkey, 145 West 18th St., Chicago.

After meeting with some members of the Evangelizing Board, Berkey returned to Chicago bearing the instructions to pare the expenses of the mission to the barest essentials. J. F. Funk promised to make a visit within a few weeks to see how things were going.

As a result of Funk's visit, the 22-year-old director of the mission, Samuel F. Coffman, was ordained to be the pastor of the mission congregation. Funk had taken the counsel of all the workers on Saturday evening and on Sunday afternoon, April 21, 1895, the ordination took place at the close of Sunday school.

S. F. was very self-conscious that evening when he got up to preach his first sermon as an ordained man. He had wanted Bishop Funk to preach, but Funk quickly replied, "That's what we ordained you for, young man."

John kept in close touch with the mission that spring. Some funds came in, but the work received a serious blow when three young men who were being instructed in preparation for baptism were opposed by their parents and forbidden to attend the mission. One convert was baptized, but a short time later lost interest and quit coming. John feared the effect of this setback on a situation already critical, but was not prepared for the blow which came from Funk himself a few months later.

William, who was back again with the Publishing Company, brought the *Herald* into John's office during the noon hour.

"Have you seen the new *Herald* yet?" he asked, tossing it on the desk in front of him.

"No, not yet," John replied. "Anything special?"

"Read this," William replied, pointing to an article by Funk on page two, simply headed, "A Statement."

"Oh, this is the article he said he'd write for the Evangelizing Board," said John. "He promised he'd write something to stir folks up a bit and try to get a little more in the treasury."

"It will stir folks all right," remarked William. "But it won't do Chicago any good. What's he trying to do, anyway, close the mission?"

John quickly read a few paragraphs, half aloud:

> Through the efforts of the board and the faithful work of devoted brethren in the field, hundreds of souls have been converted and gathered into the church while the membership has been encouraged. . . .

"Well, what's wrong with that?" John asked, looking up.

"Nothing. Keep on," William said.

> Since the establishment of the Chicago mission many of our most liberal contributors to the cause have directed their attention to that work, and the Evangelizing Board has suffered to such an extent that the evangelizing work is in a measure crippled.

"Oh, I see what you mean," remarked John, and then hastily read on:

> The Chicago mission has consumed about three times the amount used by the Evangelizing Board, while the results from the mission are very small indeed. . . .

"Oh, no!" gasped John. His face turned pale, and suddenly very stern as his eyes met William's.

"There's a little more yet," said William, sitting tight-lipped on the edge of his desk. John read on:

> The Chicago mission is not under the control of the Evangelizing Board. We kindly ask our people to stand by the recognized means of the church, and sustain especially the evangelizing work under the direction of the Evangelizing Board of America.

There was more, but John read no further. Laying the paper on the desk he looked up at William.

"Surely he didn't mean to make it sound as bad as that. He couldn't have meant to hurt the mission."

"I don't know what he intended," William remarked dryly. "Sometimes I can't quite understand him, but—"

John sighed. "Well, let's not lay any blame. What is written is written. I'm afraid folks will think that even Funk has turned against the mission. This may mean the end, for the time being at least. But I'll have a talk with Funk, and see if we can do something about this."

Funk was apologetic when John approached him regarding the article.

"Well, it does sound rather as if the work wasn't worth supporting," Funk agreed, thoughtfully stroking his beard. "I must say I didn't intend to leave a bad impression. Maybe I was in too much of a hurry when I wrote it."

"I would think that after all these years, you'd have learned to be pretty careful," John suggested, a little more sternly than usual.

"This statement that Chicago used three times as much as the board just isn't correct. I checked it myself. But coming from you everybody will think it's true, and—well—you know what they will think."

Funk sat with downcast eyes, his chin resting in his hands, hardly knowing what to say. "I'm sorry," he apologized again. "I—I guess it was a mistake. I really didn't mean to harm the mission. Just wanted to rouse folks to the need of the Evangelizing Board. I'll write a correction in the next issue."

"That's a good idea," John replied icily, "but I'm afraid it may be too late."

"Well, as far as that goes," Funk cleared his throat, and his voice once more rumbled with authority, "the mission is just about finished anyway, and we might as well face it."

"Hm!" exclaimed John, his eyes narrowing as he looked up at Funk.

"Now don't get me wrong, brother," Funk continued. "You know, and I know, that the church isn't ready yet for missions. The rumors have not abated in spite of your article in the *Herald,* and some of the churches are threatening to withdraw from conference unless the mission is closed."

"I'm quite aware of all that," John observed with exaggerated calm. "From much experience I know how difficult it is for our people to accept anything new. But with a little more patience and perseverance—"

"It'll take more than patience this time," the deep voice rumbled on. "As I see it, it would be better all around to close the mission for a while and maybe get a new start in a few years. Our folks don't like the big expense with the little to show for it. They don't like the idea of those young unmarried folks living in the mission building. They don't like the idea of supporting the workers, afraid they'll get lazy and it might lead to a salaried ministry." Funk ticked off each item on his fingers, while John nodded patiently.

"Now mind, I'm not saying I think these things myself," he exclaimed with unusual vehemence. "It's just what most folks are thinking and saying."

A short time later the mission home was officially closed. A number of ministers and bishops from Indiana, Illinois, and Ohio met with the evangelizing committee and the mission workers. Point by point the objections were fully discussed and it was finally decided that the work should continue but on a much smaller scale. Sunday school and regular Sunday services could be continued by a few of the workers who might volunteer to remain in the city and find jobs to support themselves. E. J. Berkey volunteered to stay, also a number of the women. The committee decided that the young minister, S. F. Coffman, should be released in order to engage in more direct evangelistic work. Calls were coming in from all parts of the country. Since several of the Ontario churches were asking for help, the committee decided young Coffman would be the man to send. With no other obligations resting on him he would be free to circulate among the churches, spending as much time as required with each.

That summer, shortly before the fateful meeting in Chicago, John had enjoyed a short holiday in Ontario, taking Bettie with him. For several years some of his Canadian friends had been begging him to come and bring his wife for a rest and visit, promising to pay the fare for both of them.

"Well, my dear, how did you like the holiday? Anxious to get home again?" John asked as the train carried them rapidly toward home.

Bettie sighed deeply. "It was wonderful, John. Everybody was so nice, and so kind. But, you know, the best part was just bein' with you so long. I wish we could have stayed another month."

John laughed. "What, and leave your garden and all that canning and everything? The house must be in a terrible state by now."

"Oh, the work will wait," Bettie replied, gazing out the coach window. "I ain't in a bit of a hurry to get back to it. Are you?"

"Yes, I'm afraid I am," John replied. "I feel I should have been back before this. My work will be piled sky high."

"Well, it will wait too, same as everybody else's," Bettie scolded. "Now don't go spoilin' the last few hours of a good holiday by startin' to worry."

"I'm not just starting," John said, "and I'm not really worrying. It's just that I've been terribly concerned about some things all the time we've been away."

"Like what?" Bettie asked, turning from the window.

"Oh, like the Chicago mission. I can't help wondering how S. F. and the others are getting along. And then there's the series of meetings in Ohio this fall. I must get working on those plans."

"Is that all?"

"No, one of the most important matters right now is the Elkhart Institute. Things are beginning to shape up, and we're to have a meeting as soon as I get back."

"Now, John, don't you go havin' a thing to do with that!" Bettie commanded, a note of alarm in her voice. "That's Mumaw's affair. You've got enough to do without apokin' your nose in that."

"I know, I know," John answered calmly. "But the school isn't just Mumaw's affair any more. It's going to be more of a school for the church, and I've got to do all I can to help get it started. They formed a stock company a few weeks ago with Mennonite shareholders, and it's to be especially for our own young people. There's to be a meeting to organize and appoint directors very soon."

"Well, I reckon I don't know much about schools or shareholders or nothin' like that," Bettie said, shaking her head bewilderedly, "but I do know one thing—you've got too much to do already. And another thing, you'd best just stay out of it. It won't go right with the kind of work you're doin'. From what I heard in some places, a lot of folks don't like the idea of a school at all. So this time you'd better just let the others go ahead."

John looked at Bettie, but she had shifted her gaze once more to the window.

"I guess you know me by now, Dear," he replied, as he, too, stared unseeingly at the changing landscape. "You know I have to work for what I believe is right, no matter what folks think. I've thought about it a lot. I know I'll be criticized. But that won't be anything new for me. It doesn't matter so much what folks think about me. It's the school that matters. We must have one if our church is to live. And with God's help I will try to do my little part, whatever it is He wants me to do."

*O Lord, do Thou hold in Thy hands the destiny of this school. Direct the management and the teachers that a deep fervent religious spirit may pervade and establish the students in the faith of our Lord Jesus Christ. May the school ever be a blessing and honor to the church that has established it.*—Diary.

# 24

John's heart thrilled when he saw the official-looking document Dr. Mumaw placed in his hands as he ushered him into his office that July day. There it was in black and white—"The Elkhart Institute Association Incorporated"—a stock company of fifteen members. Another dream about to be fulfilled—a school for his beloved church! It made his heart beat a little faster to think that he was one of the fifteen men responsible not only for its beginning, but also for its success. It must succeed!

With a happy smile John greeted the other members of the stock company as they gathered in Mumaw's office for their first meeting. The doctor was turning the school over to their management for a consideration of $1,500 in stocks. John presided at the meeting, the first business being the election of officers. Dr. Mumaw became the first president of the Board of Directors; J. S. Hartzler, vice-president; A. C. Kolb, secretary; Herman Yoder, treasurer. The other directors were D. J. Johns, Jonathan Kurtz, Fred W. Brunk, Noah Hoover, and J. S. Coffman.

Enthusiasm was high that afternoon as Mumaw painted a glowing picture of the school that was to be. Although attendance had not been high that first year, it was gradually increasing. The next few years should see the entire church aroused, with students pouring in from every direction. Financial backing, of course, was a major problem. But through the sale of stock, both in the city and throughout the Mennonite constituency, he proposed to raise $50,000 within five years for operating expenses and an endowment fund. The most urgent need, he pointed out, was for a suitable building for the school.

John found himself agreeing heartily with the need for a building. He had frequently discussed the matter with Mumaw and others. But before any building could be undertaken, they had to have some funds in sight. Where and how to obtain funds was the main item of discussion that afternoon.

Before the meeting adjourned, John had committed himself to a one-man financial campaign in distant areas of the church where he was well known. Although he had just returned from Ontario, he agreed to go back again in a few weeks to see whether he could secure financial aid for the new building. Some, he knew, were interested, for he had already persuaded a few students to enroll that first year.

But the job wouldn't be easy, he realized, as he thought over the matter on his way home that evening. Education was not a popular subject in Mennonite circles, and begging for money was likewise unpopular. He knew that in aligning himself with such a cause he would no doubt lose some warm, personal friends. Some, he felt, might even be offended and his evangelistic work would suffer. But evangelism was now well established in most areas, and with other evangelists on the field, the work would go on. It was time now to take another step ahead. Education would certainly be of vital importance to the future church.

After much searching and deliberation a lot on South Prairie Street was finally chosen as the site for the new building. It was conveniently located, not too far from the business section of town, and close to the Prairie Street Church. The lot looked pretty swampy to a few members of the board, but they were assured it was merely a problem of drainage. Building was to begin as soon as some funds could be raised.

On the train on his way to Ontario early in August, John wrote in his diary:

> Aug. 3, 1895—I am started out on a trip such as I never was before, to try to collect money for a charitable purpose, for the building of the school house for the Elkhart Institute.

Folks at Berlin were greatly surprised to see J. S. Coffman back so soon after his last trip. He didn't explain his mission when he spoke at church on Sunday morning, but announced a meeting for the next night.

> Aug. 5, 1895—This evening there was a full house at Berlin. Many persons came from quite a distance. There was quite a curiosity to know what my business is here. I preached from Psa. 139:14, man, in four aspects, physical, intellectual, moral, and spiritual. After this discourse I explained our necessity of a high school to save our young people to the church and our doctrine, and that we propose to have these people help build a house.

As he visited among the members in the county, John was pleased with the warm response from many of them. Donations and pledges in this area amounted to about $1,200.

Regarding his visit to York County he wrote:

> Aug. 19, 1895—I got some stocks and some donations, but find Markham with only a few well-to-do or rich people as compared to Waterloo. Besides this, they are not quite so well trained to give to charity.

At the Twenty he was quite successful, although his diary states:

> Aug. 23, 1895—The folks on the mountain feel considerably poorer than below, and consequently could not respond so freely. . . .But God bless them for what they did.

In the Rainham-South Cayuga area he discovered, too, that the "people felt poor." However, he felt greatly encouraged by the success of his first effort and on his return was able to report to the Association a total of $784 in cash and $1,755 in notes or pledges.

On the strength of this initial success the board decided to go ahead with building plans, provided that some assistance could be obtained from the city.

* * *

"Well, it looks as if someone's up," said John, seeing a glimmer of light in William's kitchen window that bleak November morning. "You tie up a while, Daniel, and I'll go and see if they'll let visitors in at 5:30."

John found both William and Annie in the kitchen, William looking rumpled and unshaven, but Annie Sauers, now established in William's household, looking fresh and ready for a day's work. Annie smiled broadly as John came in the door.

"Ah, I thought you'd be acomin'," she said, vigorously stirring the porridge. "Now you just set a spell till I finish this."

"I know it's an awful hour to be making a call," John apologized, "but I just couldn't leave without having a peek. Where do you keep them anyway? Could I just tiptoe—"

"No, you just set right there," Annie ordered, shoving the porridge kettle to the back of the stove. "I'll bring 'em out here to see their grampaw."

"I hear one making her presence known," said William, grinning as he followed Annie to the bedroom. "They don't seem to know that children should be seen and not heard."

Annie was soon back, carrying a tiny bundle in each arm.

"Here you are," she said, placing the two infants in his lap, both crying lustily. "Ain't they purty? I reckon I never did lay eyes on nicer lookin' babies."

John studied the wrinkled little faces of his granddaughters. Then looking up into the beaming faces of William and Annie, he could hardly tell which looked the most pleased.

"Yes," he agreed, "they are beauties. God grant them beautiful souls and a long and happy life. They were a twenty-sixth anniversary present for your mother and me. Had you thought of that, William?"

"No, I'm afraid not," William replied. "I haven't had time to do much thinking yet. It's all been rather overwhelming. Let's see, November 11, that was Grandfather Coffman's anniversary too, wasn't it? Seems to be a special day in our family."

"Have you decided on a name for these two?"

William nodded. "Yes, I think we have. Lydia likes Ethel, and we think Esther would go well with it. I suppose you're catching an early train that you're up so early?"

"Yes, the 6:20 to Chicago. I'm to be at Freeport, Illinois, tonight."

"Collecting for the school again?"

"Yes, as a side line, along with some meetings. They've been wanting me to come for some time to hold meetings."

"Aren't you afraid that begging for money, especially for education, will hurt your influence?"

"Yes, frankly I am," John replied, handing a baby to Annie while William gingerly accepted the second. "Some folks won't like it, but I'm praying that the good Lord will bless our efforts in both causes."

"You'll see Samuel F. in Chicago, I suppose. He's still there, isn't he?"

"Yes, he hasn't been able to get away yet. Berkey has been at home helping to look after his sick father. But he should be able to leave soon. S. F.'s getting pretty anxious, for he promised the folks at the Twenty he'd be there this fall."

The Illinois trip was quite successful, both spiritually and financially. John checked over the donations for the Institute before handing them over. Certainly some had been liberal, but they were still far short of their goal. Would they be able to go on? Or might he be wasting his time, after all, as many of his friends were suggesting?

He recalled the cold looks he had received in Illinois from some who had once welcomed him warmly. His heart still chilled as he remembered the rebukes of a few well-meaning individuals who couldn't understand his participation in such an unrighteous cause. Some had even stayed away from the meetings. Definitely his spiritual ministry was suffering, perhaps more than he realized. But should he give up this work for the school? Day and night his heart cried out for guidance and assurance that he was doing the will of his Father.

And then came the inspiring thought of that other John. How well he had expressed the true nature of his mission—his own insignificance in the great cause to which he was completely dedicated: "He must increase, but I must decrease." Was that not his mission too? In working to establish a school, was it not that Christ might increase? that the church might prosper in a greater way? It was Christ that was important. John S. Coffman didn't matter.

John sighed as he sat looking at the pile of letters on his desk. It was one of those blue mornings. The neuralgia in his chest was bothering him and he hadn't slept well. He had been up to see the school and should have been encouraged. It looked good on the outside, but he saw only the inside, the mere skeleton of rooms, waiting for funds so that they could be transformed into classrooms and offices.

There should be a few donations here, he told himself hopefully as he glanced quickly through the pile. Choosing a likely-looking envelope, he slit it open and smiled as he unfolded the letter and saw the money order for $25. It came from a shareholder at Berlin, Ontario.

But the next few yielded only excuses:

> Kokomo, Ind.—Dear brother, You ask me for help to finish the school house which I think I aught to do somesing for it. Bot on the account of sickness I am not able at the present.

> Morrison, Ill.—I do not feel able to give anything, and family does not want me to give any.

> Sterling, Ill.—Now as regards the money for building purposes, I understood you said men that had a family to raise and a lot of interest to pay, it wasn't asked of them to give anything. Now I think that hits me pretty well. Till I pay my interest and all my other expenses I have very little left still. I have been unfortunate the last few years I have had to pay quite a sum that was not my own debts and it came pretty hard on me so that I do not feel myself able to give any money at present. And another thing is, I can not get it clear in my mind that that is the right way to raise money for such a purpose. But let that be as it will, I hope and pray that the school may be started and run in the right way so that some good may come out of it.

"Getting some nice big checks for the school?" A. B. Kolb asked, coming into the office to return some books.

"Only one for $25 so far," replied John. "Oh, yes. Here's another for $3.90 from two friends in Markham, Ontario. Well, every little helps."

"A good crop of excuses, I suppose," Kolb suggested.

"Plenty," John replied. "But they aren't so bad when they come without those sharp little barbs."

Would he ever get accustomed to harsh criticisms? he wondered. In spite of all the hard knocks he had received over the years, he felt his face turn red as he glanced over the next letter:

> No address—We had money plenty, but we are not made of money. I was not abel to work and had to leve the farm before we was out of det. I paid the docter 200 dollars this weak and

perhaps I will have to go to Chicago yet to docter. . . . Emma said you had no business to beg at this church and John sais you had no business to preach here.

"Here, read this," John said, handing a letter to Kolb. "It's people like this that make me determined to go on and do all I can to help them in spite of themselves."

Kolb read:

Penrose, Ill.—Ditend harley know wat to write. I can tel you one thing thad I cand help you on money maters. I dont think it is write for our members to bild a high school. Our children wond to go to hirer school. We wouldn let them. The get good anough edukasion in comen school. Would it be ride to pay for others. I say no. . . . And another thing. I always thoud if anything to be don in church maters it haft to be brout before the counfrence. Why is it thad you go a hed of the counfrence. Wat is the youse to hold counfrence if we don won to live so by. Thad is my opinen, if I am rong correct me.

"Well, it does seem if a little 'hirer' edukasion' might not have hurt the brother. But that's the spirit you'll have to fight in most communities," Kolb said, folding the letter and slipping it back into the envelope.

"So we're finding out all the time," John replied. "And here's more of it. They're afraid of education. It will lead to pride and worldliness and worse—a salaried ministry. Listen."

Cullom, Ill.—I would say that I am not in favor of the school. I believe in giving our children a good common school education, and I believe they can learn enough in our common schools to do almost any kind of business that we would like to see them engaged in. We don't want to educate our boys to fill some of the worldly offices for the reason because we think it is not in our place to hold such offices. We do not want to educate our boys for preachers for the reason that if we have manufactured preachers they would soon want salery for preaching and that we can't acknowledge as right. I believe as soon as a man hiers himself out to preach for a certain amount of money he preaches more for money than to save souls.

It is very true that some of our forefathers, most noble men, were learned, educated men, but when did these men get their education? I think it was always before they were converted to God. What will become of our church when we get all our young people high school educated? There will be nothing left then but to have educated preachers also. I am sorry to say but it seems to me that our Mennonite church is drifting away into something that should not be so. And I believe that those who live a while longer will see the consequenses of it.

There were other letters, too, in the pile: the usual number of friendly letters from friends and converts desiring advice and encouragement; Macedonian appeals for help from all parts of the country; and urgent appeals from Missouri where the church, like the church at Corinth, was threatened with disruption over the question of holiness.

Daniel Kauffman wrote:

> Dec. 9, 1895—One bone of contention which at present is working havoc can, I believe, be fixed by you or anyone outside of this congregation who is well versed in Scripture, and who knows anything about diplomacy, without much trouble. I can't do it, for I ruined my reputation among holiness people by preaching a sermon on spirituality with second grace left out. . . . If you could stay here about a week, I am confident that lost souls might be brought to the light.

Early in January John made the trip to Missouri, spending ten days with the troubled congregation in Cass County. His teachings on the doctrine of sanctification helped to subside the wave of unrest which had threatened the church. There were also a number of conversions.

> Jan. 11, 1896—This evening we had a large attendance—crowded house. Text—John 17:17; I Cor. 1:30, sanctification. Much interest prevails here on this subject as many have accepted the Wesleyan theory. It is helping many even if they have taken extreme views.

Even so, the matter was far from settled. A few months later came another extremely urgent appeal from Kauffman:

> March 31, 1896—I have been thankful a thousand times that you made that visit here just after the holidays. The idea of having 29 accessions to the church within the last year seems to be bracing our members up considerably. Still there are some things that might be different. There is a man here (Coleman) from Kansas City whooping things up along second grace lines. He has his altar, and has people to worship at its shrine and receive the baptism of fire. Several have received this baptism and it makes them feel happy. He is reported to have healed quite a number. They have got so far along that they see visions, and God only knows what they will accomplish before they get through.
>
> Needless to say, our people are very much excited. They fear that this business will go on until the church is ruined. . . . I have tried to impress them with the importance of keeping cool headed in the face of danger and the certainty of fanatical religion ultimately reacting and killing itself off. . . . Still there are things here which must be straightened out. . . . Father told me that he expected to come up after the weather becomes settled, and that he would like to have some one with him. I told him

> that he could get no better person than J. S. Coffman, and he agreed. Now don't make excuses and say some one else will do as well. That won't do. We need a diplomat here.

When John returned to Cass County with D. D. Kauffman later that spring, the two took time to visit individual members and families to discuss the problem. Then came a counsel meeting:

> May 1, 1896—This afternoon we had a meeting of the members and had a talk on the usages of the church as taken from the Bible, especially on the communion and excitable meetings. Eph. 4:17-32. We had all who wished to make confession and give expression and then took counsel as to whether they wished to keep house in the church as the church has ever done. All consented, yet several held reserves to shout. Even with this the great majority counselled peace.

On the return trip from Missouri in January, John stopped in Arcadia, Indiana, to visit Andrew Kaufmann, hoping to secure a donation for the Institute. To his joy he was able to report to the board a donation of $2,000!

By this time the new building was almost finished and plans were being made for the dedication:

> Jan. 29, 1896—This afternoon at 4:30 all the teachers of Elkhart Institute and the president of the board and several of the board members met to arrange for a programme for the formal opening of the new building on the 11th and 12th. Arranged that the first evening shall be dedicatory and on the second a lecture. Decided to have a scholarly lecturer come from a distance, McKenzie from Chicago, a Congregational minister. May God direct according to His will.

Also on the first evening there was to be a lecture by one J. S. Coffman. The theme—"The Spirit of Progress."

Why did I ever consent to do this? John wondered, looking helplessly at the notes scribbled on odd bits of paper and the backs of assorted envelopes now littering his desk. He had come to the office early, determined to spend the entire day working on the topic. By noon it seemed he had barely begun.

"What's the matter, Father? You look worried," said William, coming into the room. "Aren't you going to eat your dinner?"

"I suppose so," John replied, "but I really shouldn't take time."

Slowly he gathered the notes into a neat pile and reached for his lunch basket on the floor beside the desk. "Aren't you eating with the boys downstairs today?"

"No, I thought I'd eat with you. I don't get to see my father too often any more. What is that you're working on? An article for the *Herald?*"

John shook his head. "No, it's an address for the dedication of the Institute. And why I consented to do it I'll never know. Straight sermons I enjoy. But a topic like this—progress—I'm afraid I'm biting off more than I can chew."

"Humph!" commented William. "We've never yet seen you stuck. I don't see what you're so worried about. After all, it will be mostly a sermon, I imagine."

"It's the research," John replied. "I thought I could do it in one day, but I see it's going to take days. For a lecture like this you need facts, and they have to be accurate. I see it's going to be about the biggest job I've ever undertaken."

"Well, don't worry. You have a whole week yet," comforted William. "You'll do all right."

"If I could only cut out some of the history," John muttered to himself. "But the whole thing is based on history. I must show our people that it was through education our church first came into existence. It was careful, scholarly study that brought spiritual enlightenment and stirred up the zeal that made the church flourish, even under most severe persecution. Without knowledge there can be no progress, and there is no such thing as standing still. We've been going down hill slowly but steadily for the past one hundred years or more. It's time we wake up and start making some progress, provide some educated leaders for the Mennonite Church, or we soon won't have a church."

William sat polishing an apple on his coat sleeve as he listened to his father's soliloquy. "I suppose you could say all that without digging into too much history," he offered, "but of course it will make more of an impression if you can produce the facts. You can't very well deny a fact."

> Feb. 7, 1896—Went early to the office and went earnestly to my work on the lecture. But I got on slowly as so many things have to be thought upon, and looked up in the histories. I got well on toward the end, but have to revise the whole essay. It will be impossible for me to commit it and it will be awkward work for me to read it to the audience.
>
> Feb. 8—Put in most of the day in finishing and revising my essay. . . . This evening I got my new suit from Jacob Bell, the tailor, a suit I very much needed. I stopped a while at Dr. Mumaw's office and got some medicine for my weak stomach.
>
> Feb. 10—Worked all day on letters, giving also a final revision to my lecture for Tuesday evening. Many persons are anxiously awaiting the opening exercises. The blustery weather has put a damper on some expectations. I feel more like praying over this situation than being elated. I do feel elated that we have succeeded in getting a school under the control of the church, but I feel that so great care must be exercised that it will be difficult to keep it in the line of our church work. May God be our director first, and then our Helper.

The Coffmans set out early for the program on a blustery Tuesday evening. They found the large hall was already filling up rapidly.

"The pater looks right smart tonight," William remarked to Ansel as they turned to enter the room where A. B. Kolb's choral group was assembling. "I see he got himself a new suit."

"Sh—don't let him hear you," cautioned Ansel. "He's just about ready to sit on the platform in his shirt sleeves."

"Why, what's wrong? Doesn't he like it?"

"Well, didn't you look at it? Someone saw it the other day and asked if he was turning Methodist."

William laughed. "I didn't get a very good look, but I thought it fitted him nicely. Is he going to have it changed?"

"He wanted to, but Mother put her foot down. She said it looked a lot better on him than his old style, and she wouldn't even come tonight if he wore his old one."

"Well, good for her," William applauded. "I didn't think she had it in her. How different is it?"

Ansel shrugged. "Oh, the collar's a little higher and it's a frock coat style instead of the round-cornered cutaway most ministers wear. He said he wanted it to hide his long, thin legs. I suppose he'll hear plenty about it."

"Nothing new for him," William remarked.

"I know. And he doesn't really mind for himself. It's just that he's afraid it may hurt the school before it's even properly started. Some folks are always looking for something to criticize, you know."

"Seems absurd, doesn't it," sighed William, "to think that the cut of a coat could make or break a school?"

But when John got up to speak that night the new coat was soon forgotten. For fifty-five minutes the entire roomful of people riveted their attention on the words he had so carefully prepared. Even though most of them had heard him preach countless times, this talk was different. Instinctively they felt its vital significance, not only to the school but to the church in general. It was a message recalling the glorious history of the church—a history tied up with the revival of learning and rediscovery of the Bible—a history of the triumph of faith in the very midst of untold suffering.

With simple eloquence he told the story of the Swiss Brethren or Anabaptists—Conrad Grebel, Felix Manz, George Blaurock, and others—who broke with Zwingli, the Swiss reformer and founder of the state church, claiming that the church should be composed entirely of converted persons who lived saintly lives.

> These men, so far from opposing learning and education, translated the prophetic books of the Bible from the Hebrew language into the German, and published a number of editions about five years before Luther's translation appeared. . . .

That the Mennonites in America were not averse to learning

and the publication of books is fully attested by the fact that so early as 1745, amid all the disadvantages of those times and the great expense it entailed, they undertook and accomplished in Lancaster county, Pennsylvania, the translation from the Holland language into German and its publication the large work known as *Martyrs Mirror*. . . .

Progress in education was very slow. Since the good Christopher Dock died at his desk on his knees 125 years ago, few, if any, Mennonite congregations have used their houses of worship for school. Had the church followed up the openings which were presented in educational advantages and cultivated the spirit of learning which her people originally possessed, we might be a people famed for learning and our congregations might number thousands where we now count only hundreds. . . . The spirit of progress was in the church but it was lying in great part dormant. . . . The teaching was too long continued in a language [the German] in which the younger generations had received very little education. Those who became educated in the English language were almost always lost to the church. Because of this some of our most noble-hearted people finally became opposed to education. . . .

The Elkhart Institute is but a welling up of a pent-up stream that could no longer be suppressed. Disadvantages, oppositions, fears of failure, all had to give way before the force that was driven into action by the deep consciousness of duty to God, to the church, to our young people, and to the cause of Christ in general.

Here we are at an epoch that marks a transition period in our beloved church. It is really a final crossing over of a large body of our people, the way having been gradually prepared, from the German language into the language of the country.

What will be the result of this transition? We fear and tremble as we think of what might be. Let us never say there is no danger. Only the true spirit of progress given and directed and kept by the power of God will form a pavilion round about us in which we can dwell in safety from the encroachments of popular opinion and worldly aspirations that will come dashing against us with the fury of a sweeping cyclone. Jehovah will preserve us. But on the other hand we are thrilled with pleasure as we paint in our mental vision the beautiful picture of a multitude of young men and women going out from this institution, the mind stored with knowledge, trained to make the best of all their faculties, possessed of a will to do right that will acknowledge no defeat, armed with a character that will never shrink from maintaining true principles, a trust that relies solely on the favor of God for success. . . .

"You know something," Ansel remarked to William as the two left the building together after the program, "I've just made an important decision."

"What's that?" William asked.

"I'm going to college."

"Hm! And where, may I ask, and when?"

"I don't know yet, but I'm twenty-one now, and I'll manage somehow. The spirit of progress has got me," Ansel exclaimed excitedly. "I have a feeling Father would be disappointed if none of us went on to school."

* * *

Boarding a train at Milford Junction on his way home from Ohio late in March, John was surprised to hear someone calling to him as he walked down the aisle looking for a vacant seat.

"Here's half a seat if you want it, J. S.," said the familiar voice.

John turned. "Why, Henry Mumaw. I didn't expect to find you on this train," said John, hoisting his suitcase up onto the rack and settling himself beside the doctor.

"I can't say I expected you either," replied Mumaw. "On your way home from Ohio?"

"Yes," John nodded, "I cut my visit a little short. The roads are so abominable that we couldn't go on."

"Mud or snow?"

"Both," said John. "A very bad combination. And when the snow melts, it will be more mud. So I figured I might as well come home."

"And how did you get along? Get much for the school?" asked the doctor, his voice as well as his eyes betraying his eagerness.

"Well," John replied slowly, "I'm afraid the visit wasn't too successful financially. But I do hope the spiritual returns were greater."

"Well, how much did you get?" Mumaw demanded. "Have you a list handy?"

John reached into his pocket and drew out a little notebook which he opened and handed to Mumaw. "Here we are. Doesn't come up to Illinois or Ontario, but I guess it's about all we can expect from some of these churches."

Mumaw glanced rapidly over the list. "I thought we'd do better in Logan and Medina. What's the matter anyway? Just generally opposed to education?"

"Not altogether," replied John thoughtfully. "It's like most other places. A lot of people don't see the need for more than common school. But for many more—well, they just don't trust us yet."

Mumaw looked up quickly. "What do you mean, 'Don't trust us'? Afraid we won't spend their money right? Afraid the school will fail, or what?"

"Maybe all of those things," John replied calmly. "You must

admit the idea is still very new. Education—a church school—giving money to educate other people's children—it's all new! Too new yet for most of our people. Maybe if we can win their confidence, sort of make haste slowly, we'll gradually get their support. But right now they are a bit fearful. They've heard some things that make them uneasy."

"Like what?" asked Mumaw, a slight edge to his voice, and a few wrinkles suddenly appearing on his broad, smooth forehead.

"Oh, like having mostly non-Mennonite teachers on the staff, non-Mennonite speakers at the dedication, and, of course, the dress question. They seem to have heard that some of the young women dress quite fashionably at the Elkhart Institute."

"And what, pray tell, can they expect?" exclaimed Mumaw heatedly. "Give us time. Where do they think we can get a Mennonite faculty with educated Mennonites as scarce as hen's teeth? In a few years we'll likely have a few ready to take over. But all we can do right now is use the best men we can get. We can't lower our standards just to keep the school completely Mennonite. And that goes for speakers, too. We want the best. Give our people a taste for culture. Expose them to educated trained talent. Make them want something more!"

"Oh, by the way," Mumaw continued, suddenly interrupting himself, "I've got some wonderful ideas for a few new courses next year. Just wait till I show you a couple of catalogs I picked up."

John squirmed uneasily while Mumaw fished around in his bag for the catalogs.

"Here, look at this," Mumaw said, placing a small booklet in John's hands. "We can really start expanding now that we have the new building. We'll show folks how a school should be run."

"How many colleges did you visit on this trip?" John asked, slowly leafing through the little volume.

"Oh, let's see, there were quite a few in the East. Some that a few years ago were about the size of ours. But you should see them now! If they can do it, we can."

For the next half hour, while the train rolled on toward Elkhart, Mumaw enthusiastically outlined plans for the next year or two.

"They're wonderful plans," John finally remarked, "but remember, brother, our school is simply a high school, not a college. And remember, too, that we have neither the equipment, staff, nor funds to put these new ideas into effect."

"But we will have, don't worry," Mumaw exclaimed. "We must aim high or we won't get anywhere. In five years you'll see funds rolling in, and students coming from all parts of the country. We'll have a good endowment and plenty of money from tuition to allow for expansion."

"It's a pretty big plan, though, for a start. If you had been out soliciting with me, I'm afraid you wouldn't be so optimistic."

"Well, we have to be optimistic, and we have to go forward with confidence," Mumaw declared, pounding the arm of the seat for emphasis.

Although he disagreed radically with Mumaw's policy, John could see he was in no mood to argue. All he could do was caution against any major changes which might make their burdensome debt even heavier.

*Help us, O Lord, to be entirely consecrated to Thy will; grant that we may not be unwilling to sacrifice any of our previous views or ways of action, if Thy way would lead us differently from our understanding of things in times past.*—Diary.

# 25

As the time drew near for the first annual meeting of the stockholders of the Elkhart Institute Association, John felt a tenseness in the air. Singly and in little groups members of the board came to his office to discuss school affairs, especially Mumaw's bold new plans. A few members were with him, but most saw trouble ahead.

"Maybe we should appoint someone else president," someone suggested at one of these private sessions. "Someone with a little more caution. We can't risk losing the confidence of our supporters. It would ruin us before we get properly started."

But John vetoed the idea. "I don't think that would be wise. The school was Mumaw's idea in the first place, and I think he should see it through. We can't risk a divided board, either. We'll simply have to put a damper on his big plans. Vote them down if necessary. But we must work together."

At the annual meeting on April 11, John was nominated for president along with Dr. Mumaw. Since he was so well known and respected throughout the entire church, they reasoned, his influence would be invaluable in securing the support they needed.

John hesitated about accepting the nomination. He preferred leaving the job to Mumaw, who was much more capable of handling it. But was this a time to consider his own preferences? The job would be difficult and demanding. It would require more time and energy than he could afford to give. But was this perhaps a call to a greater service, and greater sacrifice? Again he recognized the voice of his Master. He had no choice but to obey. He was elected to the office by a good majority. Dr. Mumaw was elected secretary, and J. S. Hartzler vice-president.

John's worst fears were soon realized. With the shattering of his plans and ambitions for the school, Mumaw felt he could not serve with the present board, and submitted his resignation. The blow was felt by all the members, but especially by John, torn between a sense of duty and his desire to maintain his warm relationship with Mumaw.

The new job weighed heavily on him. Since the president of the board was chief administrator, he found it necessary to spend a great deal of time at the school. Of immediate concern was the summer normal school. Courses had to be planned, teachers secured, and salaries arranged. The fall term also required careful thought and planning. And for the first time the school was to have a catalog. It was to be published as early in the summer as possible. The sudden new responsibility was very burdensome to an already overworked man.

* * *

"But, Bettie, I must get back to the office. I've had enough of this lying around to do me for a long time." Looking pale and tired, John stood at the kitchen table watching Bettie peel peaches.

"Of course," Bettie replied firmly. "But you're agoin' to have to be a lot better before you go."

"But I wasn't any worse for going to the Institute opening yesterday. In fact, I had a much better night. The first time in a long time that I didn't have some fever."

"Mebbe so, but what about that splittin' headache this morning? Malaria ain't to be fooled with. I declare men are worse than children when they're sick." Bettie finished peeling a peach, plopped it into a kettle, and started measuring out sugar for jam.

"I guess you'll need another bag of sugar soon," John observed mournfully. "And a lot of other things as well. Two whole weeks off! That's the longest I've ever been sick. I simply must get back to work!"

"Well, then, if you want to work so bad, why don't you go and write some letters? The folks back home will be wonderin' why you don't write."

"A good idea," John agreed, turning and walking slowly to his desk in the living room.

Taking a sheet of paper from a drawer he immediately started a letter to his brother Joe. His hand felt shaky at first, but soon he was writing rapidly:

> I hope to be able to work in a few days. I have yet five lessons to write for last quarter and then I am wanted in Kansas to help quiet some members who have gone to the camp meetings and got excited and got to shouting and very excitable. I may be there a week or two and then be at the Missouri conference. . . . Our

school opened yesterday with fair prospects—better than it has ever yet had. It looks as though our prospects were fair, but we will no doubt have to go through many a trial and much prayer and eternal watchfulness. Our aims are to make the school stand on the nonresistant doctrines of the Bible and equip our young people to stand up for our doctrine. . . .

Samuel expects to be at home from Canada but only on a visit in about a week. He wrote that they would not let him bring his trunk along. He would be wanted in a good many places. Barbara has started to the Institute yesterday for a four-year course. Daniel will start to the Elkhart High school in two weeks to finish his four-year course this year. Jacob and Ansel board at home and work in the office. . . . I wrote this letter partly for Mother. I hope she is well and that she keeps cheerful.

After finishing the letter, John leaned back in his chair and stared out the window. He wasn't in the least satisfied with the letter. It wasn't at all what he most wanted to say. All this small talk was small indeed, in comparison with what he longed to say to Joe and to Lewis and to many other ministers back home in Virginia. News from there was most disquieting. He feared for the future of his old home church, but he was afraid to offer any advice for fear the troublemakers might accuse him of meddling or upholding Lewis in the stand he was taking. For months he had been unable to exchange letters with Lewis. But Joe had been keeping him informed of developments since that day last fall when the congregation had met to name candidates for the new minister and deacon to be ordained for the middle district.

The trouble apparently started when Lewis preached a sermon that day on the qualifications to be considered in naming a candidate and also pointed out faults that would hinder a minister's service. As a result of this innovation very few ventured to vote and, according to Joe, "the tobacco men, the obstinate, the self-willed, and those inclined to sulk, rose up in a body against the bishop and said, 'You have grossly erred; reconcile the matter.' "

Although Lewis apologized and tried to appease the offended members, and the ordination was postponed until more nominations could be made, the dissatisfaction still continued among a small group. Joe's last letter sounded pretty serious:

June 14, 1896—A short time ago the aggrieved ones had a meeting at the Bank. I don't know whether they adopted any resolutions or not. It seems no one knows. We had our communion meetings as usual. Those advocating peace communed. The others did not. There are some grave charges brought against the church by them, viz., that we are in favor of all churches uniting. The church is being run into popery. We are in sentiment with Elkhart and the west, and so on. . . . They have come down to trying to injure others reputations and establishing their own. They declare themselves no Mennonites of the present day and say they will not be reconciled under the circumstances.

John read the letter several times. He hated to admit even to himself that there was danger of a schism, but other letters besides Joe's seemed to point to an imminent break. How he longed for a talk with Lewis! No doubt he would be powerless to prevent a break, but at least he could offer encouragement and a bit of advice if he only had a chance. Could he risk sending a bit of advice through Joe? Suddenly he felt he must write. With the future of the old church at stake, he must speak up. He wrote again:

> Aug. 29, 1896—Yesterday I wrote a letter to Samuel Brunk, but did not yet send it. In it I referred to your church troubles, and I feel like putting something on this sheet to you. But I would feel sorry to have it come out that I was advising any party in your difficulty. But this I repeat to you—if you are going on to a division I hope all will take the position that they will stand by the Bible and the conference minutes. Then there would be no division. But if any part refuses to stand by these, they are the seceders. Any committee sent from any part of the church if such committee had any kind of fairness would have to decide that the part which stands by the Bible and the conference minutes is the church. Make this your conditions, nothing more nor less. Then go on and hold all the regular appointments—hold them in spite of fate. If a seceding party comes to the regular appointments, go too, and stick to that regular appointment. If they are there give them to understand that they are with you. Go right along to the regular conference as though nothing had happened, then make another appointment on the regular time and place. Don't give an inch in this. *Hold the regular appointments and the regular conference.* If you fail in this you have lost the battle. If the minority party holds the regular appointment, stand right by them, and do not allow yourselves to be driven from the regular appointments under any circumstances.
>
> I have seen so many divisions and have seen their working. If those dear Virginia brethren could see the bitter fruits that are sure to come, they would be slow to make a decision. . . . Let the spirit of Christ in all kindness be manifested. I hope to hear good news yet from the Virginia church. I am sure God cannot prosper wrong no matter in what party it is found. Pardon me if I have said too much.

Samuel F. came home for a little visit in October, in time for the annual church conference.

"Well, what did you think of the conference?" he asked, as he rode home with his father. "Can you see much improvement?"

John smiled as he turned to look at his son. "I guess you are still pretty young in this kind of work, aren't you? I'm glad to say that there's been much improvement in many ways. There is better order in their business, but best of all they're beginning to see the task of the church. At last the church is beginning to work. Why, some of the questions they discussed today would have been unthinkable ten years ago."

"And just look what the Evangelizing Board is doing," exclaimed S. F. excitedly. "They even voted to support Chicago mission. That certainly is a big improvement."

"At least it shows that the mission spirit is growing," said John. "And with some of our young men agitating for work in India, we may yet see great things happening in our church."

"But the trouble is, all of this is in the West," S. F. remarked. "If the East would only show a little more life—"

"Give them time," John replied. "They'll wake up one of these days. They'll have to. And to tell the truth, I'm almost as fearful for some of the western churches where things are going a little too fast as I am for the East."

"Why? Any more trouble in Missouri or Kansas?"

"Not more, that I know of, but it will take a long time, I'm afraid, before there's anything like peace in some congregations. Kansas was hit pretty hard with what they call 'holiness.' I had to speak pretty plain to a few of our staunchest members that were confusing holiness with emotion."

"I know what you mean," said S. F. "I heard about the trouble when I was in Iowa."

"Let's see, you're supposed to go to Pennsylvania soon, too, aren't you?" John said. "Is it next week?"

"About Wednesday, I guess. I suppose I'll be seeing you down there some place."

"Maybe," John replied. "I've just about decided I should go. There have been so many calls that I don't feel it would be right to turn them all down. I may not be welcome everywhere, but I've been invited to some churches in Lancaster County. I think it will be a little better than last time. A. D. Wenger is down there now, and he insists we should help them as much as we can."

"Have you decided where you will go?" S. F. asked.

"Not exactly. But I had a letter from Bishop Isaac Eby of Kinzer. I'm definitely invited into his territory and he's pretty sure they'll make appointments for me in Weaverland, Groffdale, and Landis Valley, and likely in York, Adams, Juniata, and Snyder counties. I've had several invitations from some of these counties and of course from Cumberland."

"So it looks as if you might be kept busy over there."

"Yes, and they want me at their quarterly mission meeting. J. H. Mellinger wrote about that. I think I'll plan to go in time for it."

An enlightening letter from J. H. Herr, Cumberland County, Pennsylvania, told John about a recent vote taken by the Lancaster Conference regarding continued meetings. A petition requesting permission to hold meetings where the church was declining came within one vote of being passed at the fall conference:

> Nov. 1896—Don't you think it was pretty good for Lancaster county conference? The sentiment is still growing. Many who did not vote at the conference did not understand the nature of our petition but have since learned and now would vote with us. . . . I feel good over it, yet I wish the majority would have been for us. Two of us who would have voted for it were deprived by sickness. I hear that brother J. S. C. is going to visit Eastern Pa. Would be very glad especially if that would include Cumberland county.

The trip through Pennsylvania in November and December proved to be a pleasant experience for John. At Shiremanstown he met son Samuel F., and also A. D. Wenger, who reported a real awakening in Lancaster County. Over a thousand people were present at the first evening meeting held in Strasburg, they said. Young people were accepting Christ whenever an opportunity was given. Large instruction classes were being held and many young people were being received into church fellowship in a number of congregations. Never had Lancaster seen a time like this, they reported.

But this was not the case in all parts of the state. From Souderton, John wrote to M. S. Steiner:

> Nov. 17, 1896—The Lord has prospered my visit. I am not aiming at direct results of ingathering, but at unity of the brotherhood in general. I have to work carefully and prayerfully, encouraging the workers to be patient and to work so that the whole body may move in solid formation together, and trying to encourage the careful ones to have confidence and help, instead of holding back the good work. The people here and each place know their own business best, and they in each place see best for themselves how to take hold of things, yet they learn from the work of those from a distance. Work teaches most folks faster than any advice we might venture to give. I say little, think and pray much, and work as God gives grace and opens the way. I am not crowding myself or my advice. I simply let them use me as they wish. . . . I find a difference between the people here and Lancaster. There is more need of care here than there. The people here have not one mind about their affairs.
>
> Nov. 19—I am taking the rounds here among the churches of

> Bucks, Montgomery, Berks, and Chester. In one place in Bucks I was not wanted by one dear, aged brother, and I was glad not to impose my presence upon him. Appointments have been made at all the other principal places; a few of the smaller ones were passed by. I could not begin to tell you in a short letter how I find things. I am glad to find many things to commend. These people's hearts as a rule are right, their sympathies and purposes and even their inward experiences are right and in some even high. There are exceptions, however, as in all places. But the heads of many are wrong. They do not know, and they follow what they have learned wrong and think they are right. There are many noble exceptions to this. I could say the same of nearly all of us. . . . If the opposition to evening meetings could be removed, it would be different. Many things work together against the ingathering of the young people. You can hardly see the young people at all. The meeting houses are so arranged that it's almost impossible to speak a word to them at church. . . . I am saying only a little about General Conference, almost nothing about school, and the Scottdale meeting (Bible conference) has not been mentioned.

After a visit to Franconia he commented in his diary:

> Nov. 24, 1896—I see plainly that the Pennsylvania church will have to be preserved by the better educated.

Before leaving Lancaster, John again visited Bishop Jacob N. Brubacher. With a great deal of satisfaction he wrote in his diary that night:

> I had a visit with him till afternoon. My visit was pleasant to me and I think Bro. Jacob feels better of the situation than he did. We spoke very frankly together, even on points where we had some difference of views. He is, of course, holding back the element in the church that favors aggressive work, but it is to be hoped that he will not hold back too severely for the progress and peace of the church, also do we hope that the aggressive element will move considerately and submissively.

The Bible conference at Scottdale, December 28 to January 8, ended another busy year and also climaxed John's Pennsylvania tour. Daniel H. Bender and M. S. Steiner were on the program along with John, while other ministers and Sunday-school workers conducted consecration and prayer services.

John was present at two important meetings of the Scottdale congregation following the conference:

> Jan. 9, 1897—I came to the members' meeting at Jacob Loucks at 2. P.M. The voice of the church was taken by Bro. Durr for the choice of an elder or bishop. Bro. Aaron Loucks was unanimously chosen. But very kindly feelings were expressed for Bro. J. A. Ressler.

The ordination took place next day. John preached the sermon from Acts 13:2.

After the sermon Bro. Durr ordained Bro. A. Loucks. . . . Old Brother Henry Yother and I laid on hands with Bro. Durr. It was a most impressive scene to me.

Back at Elkhart, John found many matters awaiting his attention at the Institute. A small pile of stock certificates were ready for his signature. Arrangements had to be made for next term's curriculum and for the annual meeting of the board. Stacks of letters were waiting to be answered, letters from inquiring parents and prospective students, as well as applications from teachers. Most of his correspondence was now handled by the advanced students in shorthand and typing classes.

For two whole weeks he worked almost steadily at the Institute before he was free to return to his desk at the Publishing Company and his work on the Sunday-school lessons.

"And who pays you for all this?" Bettie asked rather impatiently one evening as John sat at his desk working on the new Institute catalog.

John winced at the sharpness in her voice. "This, my dear, is voluntary labor," he replied quietly without looking up. "But don't worry. I'll soon be back at the office. I've almost caught up with things at the Institute."

"Humph! Caught up mebbe for a few days. Why, you're down there at the school about as much as the teachers are. It don't seem quite right."

"I know, Bettie. It's hard, and I know too well that there are still a lot of little bills I couldn't pay today. But you know how it is. The school is just getting on its feet. There's barely enough to pay the teachers even small salaries. And a lot of folks would make a big fuss if we started paying board members. Maybe sometime we can come to that, but not for a while, I'm afraid."

Bettie bit her lips and turned away with an audible sigh.

"Please, Dear. Don't feel so badly about it. We've never really been hungry, have we?" John pleaded.

"No, not quite starvin', if that's what you mean," retorted Bettie from the kitchen doorway. "But the whole lot of us need shoes, and other things too, in this cold weather. I declare I never did see a body as could pick up so many jobs as didn't pay as you."

"I'm sorry. I know I'm not much of a provider. But somehow I just can't help it. These things have to be done, and—well, here I am. We have been going on faith all these years, you know. Surely we can hold on just a little bit longer."

But even John's faith was to suffer a big jolt on his return to the office. It seemed like a little thing, and yet it fell with the weight of a crushing blow.

With a sickening feeling in the pit of his stomach John blinked his eyes and looked again at the proof sheet lying on his desk. It was page one of the February 1 edition of the *Herald of Truth* which someone had apparently laid there for him to see. Yes, he had seen right. Up there in the left-hand corner where once there had been three names there was now only one. J. S. Coffman was no longer assistant editor of the *Herald of Truth.* After eighteen years his name along with that of J. F. Funk had been dropped. A. B. Kolb was sole editor.

For a moment the world seemed to go black, and he dropped his head dizzily onto his arms on the desk. What did this mean? Why hadn't they consulted him or informed him in a proper manner? Indignation, resentment, fear seethed in a turmoil through his troubled mind.

But not for long. The habit of trust and faith soon took over. Slipping into his coat and taking his hat from a peg on the wall he quickly made his way to the street. It was a time to be alone, he decided; a time for clear thinking and prayer.

Walking the snowy street, headed nowhere in particular, John gradually grew calmer and was able to take stock of the situation. Actually he had spent very little time at the publishing house lately, and the work he had done for the *Herald* certainly did not warrant the title of assistant editor. For several years now, his main work had been on the lesson helps.

But was this a gentle shove toward the door, a broad hint that he was being ousted in favor of steadier, more dependable employees? No doubt such a procedure would be in keeping with the company's new policy of more efficiency in business. But back in his subconscious mind was a fear—a fear he could ignore no longer. It was time now to take it out and examine it—that cold feeling he had been noticing for some time. The good old days were over. He might as well face it. No longer were the house employees one big happy family. Unquestionably, ill will, resentment, hard feelings, and jealousies were evident among some of the staff and employees. And much as it hurt his sensitive feelings, he had to admit that some of it was directed to himself, especially since his appointment as president of the Institute Board. Mumaw had many friends and sympathizers at the publishing house. Even at church, strained feelings were sometimes not too well disguised behind forced smiles or hearty handshakes.

Maybe he was imagining too much, he tried to tell himself. Maybe he was making a mountain out of a molehill, he concluded, breathing a prayer that it might be so. "Please, Father," he prayed as he trudged through the snow, "if I have wronged a brother, show me how to make it right. If I can be used to bring about peace and harmony, show me how. And please continue to care for me and my family as you have in the past, that we may not come to want."

Without realizing where his walk had taken him, John suddenly found himself nearing brother Daniel's house. He was about to go past when Dan appeared at the door.

"Hey, there! Ain't ya comin' in?" he called.

"I wasn't planning to," John replied, turning toward the house. "I should get back to the office. How are you, anyway? I haven't seen much of you since I'm back."

"Oh, I'm middlin'. I'll soon be back on the job," said Dan, ushering his visitor into the living room. "Here, come up to the stove and warm yourself."

"You'd better take it easy for a while yet," cautioned John. "Remember how sick you were last summer."

"I know, I know. But they're good to me at the tablet factory, and give me easy jobs. I'm glad I changed from the Publishing Company store. How do you get along over there lately? I hear there's a lot of changes goin' on. Some of 'em none too good."

Dan was quick to notice John's troubled expression. His head and shoulders drooped and his cheeks were unusually pale as he stood warming himself at the stove.

"Yes, Dan, there are some changes," he replied, and even his voice was colorless. "Maybe they're for the better. We can't see very far ahead, you know. But confidentially I'm afraid of what's happening over there. There's too much ill feeling and selfishness for a Christian institution like that."

Dan studied his brother's face carefully. The worried lines, the anxiety in the usually calm gray eyes meant something.

"And what have they done to you?" he asked bluntly. "Docked your pay or fired some of the boys?"

"To tell the truth, Dan, I'm not sure what they have done. No one has said anything to me, but I—I noticed my name has been left off the *Herald* that's just off the press. Maybe it means I'm being dropped as part-time worker, I don't know. I just found out about it, and that's why I've been out getting some fresh air. It helps me think."

"Well! I must say that's a pretty poor way to do business," exclaimed Dan. "But that's the way they been doin' things lately, I hear. I don't know what or who's behind it, but I reckon it's the almighty dollar they're after. Seems to me there's a few men there tryin' to run things as hadn't oughta be."

"Well, they are there, and we can't do much about it. I'm surprised that the boss lets things go on this way. I only hope he sees what's happening before it ruins the business."

"You still have the lesson helps, don't you?"

"I suppose so," John replied, seating himself in a low rocking chair beside the stove. "But I don't see that I can make a living at that alone. Maybe they'll have something else for me. I don't know. But I mean to have a good talk with Funk and find out just where I do stand."

"Well," Dan advised, "if I was you, I wouldn't count on too much, the way things are. Maybe it's time you quit working so hard anyway. With your meetings and the work at the Institute, the lesson helps may be all you should handle."

"You know," John said thoughtfully, "I was thinking of staying home more this year, and getting in more work at the office. Everything costs so much these days, and we do have to live. But maybe this is the Lord's way of showing me where my rightful place is. Sometimes He had to lead us over some pretty rough spots."

"Maybe so, maybe so," said Dan. "But to change the subject, I've been doin' some thinkin' too, lately. That little farm of yours, it ain't worth too much to you any more, is it?"

"Oh, I don't know. We grow most of our fruit and vegetables, and keep a cow and some chickens."

"But I mean actual value in dollars and cents."

"No, I can't say we have much of a cash income. Maybe we could have if someone had time to work it."

"That's just what I mean," interrupted Dan, tapping the arm of his rocker. "It ain't doing what it should be doin'. It was a fine place to live when your boys were young, but now with all of 'em workin' or goin' to school in town, it's more bother to you than it's worth. Ain't that so?"

"Well, I don't know. Maybe. What's your suggestion?" John asked wonderingly.

"This," said Dan, excitedly edging forward in his chair. "Why don't you and me trade places? You live here in town where you'll be close to school and to your work, and I'll take my family to the country where they'll be better off. I'll work the farm and give you half the crop or whatever we figure is right."

"Hm!" replied John thoughtfully, "not a bad idea. I never thought of anything like that."

"Well, think it over. I don't imagine your boys'll mind. Like as not they'll be good and glad to be rid of the farm and live in town close to their jobs."

"No, I reckon the boys won't mind. But I don't know how Elizabeth would feel. She still likes a big garden, likes to grow her own food, and likes her house pretty well, too."

"Well, if it's finances that's worryin' her, maybe you could even board a few Institute students if you lived here in town. It'd likely pay better than the farm, and we'd grow your fruit and vegetables for you."

*Life cannot all be sunshine,*
*Nor all the world a field of flowers,*
*Else where would be the useful,*
*And how should earth receive her showers?*
*Then murmur not at seeing sadness,*
*It may be mercy sent to bring you heavenly gladness.*

J. S. Coffman to a fellow employee.

# 26

Arriving at the house on Eden Street with the last load of furniture, John found Bettie and the girls busily unpacking and arranging the rooms.

"Do you think you'll be satisfied here?" he asked, joining Bettie on a tour to see how things were progressing. "These rooms look pretty good since Dan papered them."

"It'll be different livin' in town again," Bettie replied, "but I reckon I'll get used to it. Anyway, it will be lots better for you."

"There isn't much of a garden," John said, looking out the kitchen window.

"No, but there's room for a few things, and Dan's will keep us supplied. Now where do you want your desk?" she asked, surveying the living room.

"I'm not sure," John replied thoughtfully. "Maybe over there by the window."

"But I thought you said you were going to use the little bedroom for your office."

"I did. But I'm going to bring my desk from the publishing house to put in there."

"Your desk from the publishing house?" exclaimed Bettie in shocked surprise.

"Yes, I've decided to do my work right here at home," John explained quietly. "The way things are over there right now, I'll be happier and do better work right here. And likely they'll be happier without me around."

"B—but how can you," sputtered Bettie, "with all the jobs you have to do there?"

"There aren't so many jobs any more, I'm afraid," John announced calmly. "I'm done there, except for the lesson helps."

"What's that?" Bettie's voice, usually soft and gentle, became shrill in her astonishment. "John Coffman, what are you trying to tell me?" she gasped, sinking to the couch, her wide, frightened eyes searching his for some reassurance.

"Just what I said, Dear. I'm done."

"And all you have to make a living on is just those lesson helps?"

"It looks that way." John tried to keep his voice casual as he seated himself beside his wife. "But please don't worry, Dear," he begged. "Something is bound to turn up. I could have stayed on maybe a while longer doing part-time jobs. But—well, I—I just couldn't conscientiously do some of the things they asked. Some of the letters they wanted me to write—well, I'm afraid my friends would soon lose confidence in me as well as in them."

Surprise, bewilderment, exasperation, following in quick succession across Bettie's face, now gave way to grim determination. John noticed it with relief as she turned to face him.

"Well, if that's the case," she snapped, jumping up and starting to bustle around again, "I'm glad you're agettin' out." Reaching the doorway to the kitchen she turned and came slowly back again. "I'm sorry, Dear," she said, gently stroking John's graying head. "But don't go aworryin' yourself. We'll manage somehow."

When John left for Pennsylvania in April, it was on a threefold errand. Spiritual ministry always came first, and as usual there was solicitation for funds and students for the Elkhart Institute. The objective this time was money for a library and a science laboratory. The third interest was an entirely new project in Mennonite circles—raising funds to supply food for the famine sufferers in India. The terrible famine had finally touched both heart and conscience of a number of individuals, awakening in them a sense of responsibility toward their fellow men on the other side of the world. One of the moving spirits behind the project was Preacher George Lambert, who worked hard to get some organization in the effort.

On March 2 John had recorded in his diary:

> This evening there was a meeting held to organize an Indian relief committee. It was given to the Mennonite Evangelizing and Benevolent Board.
>
> March 3—A committee was appointed to write out notices and one to aid G. L. Bender in his secretarial work. Kolb and Jansen, J. S. Lehman, and J. S. Coffman were appointed to aid George Lambert in soliciting.

From time to time John kept sending back to Elkhart small

amounts he had collected for the project. Acknowledging the gifts Bender wrote to him in Lancaster:

> "We have been very successful so far and have nearly $5,000 on hand. Bro. Lambert leaves for India tomorrow, taking $5,000 with him. By investigation we found that it would cost us nearly $200 to cable the money to India. We expect to get free passage for Bro. Lambert from Liverpool or London. We have also obtained free transportation to India for corn and are busily engaged in gathering up corn in the west.

But it was hard work, this job of collecting money, especially for the school. It was a job which called for the utmost tact. Most of the soliciting was done privately, and in some places he felt it unwise even to broach the subject of school.

Right from the first he met discouragement. At Shiremanstown he recorded in his diary:

> March 24, 1897—I only mentioned school. . . . I am completely discouraged regarding help for school from Cumberland county. My spirits go down in spite of me. I must do much praying.

But he stuck to the job and was occasionally rewarded with a generous contribution or promise. Just as important, however, was his personal contact with a number of young people who expressed interest in the school.

On his return at the end of the month his report read: cash—$2,417.50; notes—$800; definite promises—$325, and hopes for considerable more.

While in Pennsylvania he was pleasantly surprised as well as challenged by a letter from A. C. Kolb of the Publishing Company.

> April 19, 1897—I must come to my subject proper. While other things seem to be making toward prosperity we must not lose sight of the fact that the ever increasing demand for our Sunday school lesson helps was never so great as at present. Last year we printed 13,000 copies for the second quarter and the result was that we ran about 500 or 600 short. This year we printed 18,000, nearly one and one half times as many, and still we will not have enough to do justice. We will in all probability be able to fill all the orders, but we cannot supply the demand for samples. You see, people want the best and they attribute this characteristic to ours. Now, the only thing that I can see that we can do is to get the next quarter out at the earliest possible moment. You will therefore please make preparation to write the lessons very soon, now, because this time we must positively have them earlier than ever before. . . . We will need at least 20,000 English helps and perhaps more to supply the demand.

In spite of pressure from the Publishing Company, John found little time for writing after his arrival home. Responsibilities at the Institute kept him exceptionally busy. His day usually started with an hour or two of dictation at the Institute, where future stenographers took his letters in shorthand for later typing. Excerpts from his diary tell the story:

> Saw Dr. Mumaw and other members of the board concerning teachers for next year—Attended chapel exercises, wrote out notices to stock holders—The committee on selecting and hiring teachers met; rose early and wrote some letters on the business of the school before breakfast—This morning at 7 the teachers Tower and Lhamon and I started for the County Teachers' Convention at Cassopolis, Mich. Had splendid bicycling to Edwardsburg, but bad roads and some sand hills from there—Tower and I looked through the laboratory of the high school—Spent most of the day getting ready for tomorrow's work at the special meeting and board meeting of the Institute—At 9 A.M. a special meeting at the Institute to increase the stock of the association. The vote stood to increase to $25,000—A board meeting ordered that $1,000 may be spent in putting in a library and laboratory—Spent time looking out plans for the laboratory. Later the committee on teachers had a meeting and we considered at some length the expenses and the work we have before us next year. We must hire teachers low—Rode to Jamestown to see Enos Hoover about teaching summer normal—Went to see about application for increase of our Institute charter, also about telephone rents—Spoke at the literary society on the value of truth—Went around to the houses of a good many of the members to find who had rooms to let to students and who would take boarders—Spent most of the time at the school, wrote some letters and arranged the school books so as to have them ready for the classes next week—Worked at the Institute, fixing up and repairing, ready for the summer term. Bought apparatus for the closets and carpet for the cellar stairs—Spent some time getting rooms for students who are coming in for the normal. Drove to the Big Four depot twice.

By the end of May the Sunday-school lesson copy was in the hands of the printers and arrangements were finally completed for the summer normal school. A last-minute change in staff became necessary when Mr. Troyer of Goshen found himself in quarantine because of diphtheria in his family. School commenced on June 8, with sixty-five enrolled.

With this matter settled, John left for Ontario for another visit with the congregation at the Twenty, also known as the Jordan-Vineland district. This was his first visit here since Samuel F. had arrived in the community to assist the aging minister, John F. Rittenhouse. The occasion was the dedication of a new church, built to replace the old structure which had been destroyed by fire the previous year. John was invited to take part on the program.

Coming in on the evening train from Buffalo, John was just in time to take part in a birthday celebration planned in honor of his son:

> June 11, 1897—After supper there was a gathering of about forty at Bro. Ezra Rittenhouse's in honor of Fred's (S. F.) birthday. They raised a collection as a present to him. They appear to appreciate his presence and his work among the people and the church here.
>
> June 13, 1897, Sunday—At 9:30 we had our first meeting at the new house at Vineland or Jordan. The house is 34 by 54 and is nicely arranged and painted inside and out. The house was densely packed with people—fully 500 were in. At 3 P.M. the house was again packed. I spoke from Matt. 16:18, "On this rock."

"Well, are you beginning to feel at home here?" John asked as he was driving home with S. F. one afternoon after having dinner with Preacher Rittenhouse. "You seem to be doing pretty well."

S. F. slackened the reins and leaned back against the buggy seat. "Yes, I like the place, and I like the people. They're all very friendly. The only thing is, I'm in rather a—shall we say peculiar situation? There are so many things I'd like to do and can't."

"We're all in that kind of a situation, more or less," consoled John.

"I suppose so," S. F. conceded, "but the way things are I hardly know where I do belong."

"They are urging you to stay, aren't they? To marry that girl back in Elkhart and settle here permanently?"

S. F. smiled self-consciously as he caught his father's eye. "So you've been hearing that too?"

"Oh, yes. In whispers, of course. But they're all talking about that beautiful girl back in Indiana and hoping that you'll marry her soon and make this your home. Might I ask whether you are making any plans along this line?"

"Nothing too definite, I'm afraid. At least not in the near future. How could I? I just don't know where I am or what I should do."

"Well, with all the young folks coming into the church here, they certainly need a younger minister."

"I know. But look at all the churches that have no minister at all. Lots of them, all over the U.S. as well as Canada."

"That's one way of looking at it," John replied. "But under the circumstances here I think you'd be justified in making this your choice. There's a lot of work to be done here."

"A lot of hard work," S. F. added. "But I'd have to have a free hand. I'd have to have a clear understanding with the whole congregation and there isn't that unity here yet. They're not ready to accept another minister even though they are using one."

"Well, just be patient, son. Things will work out."

"You know, Father, I've been doing a lot of thinking lately," S. F. said, taking the whip from its socket and trailing it in the dust. "I can stay here indefinitely, I suppose, in my present status. But while I'm still free and under no obligation, it seems to me it would be a good time to get a little more Bible training."

"You mean go back to Moody's?"

"Yes. At least it seems as if that would be the best place for me. The teaching is good. The last time I was in Chicago I didn't have much time for school. But if I went again, I'd plan on going to school and just help at the mission on Sundays."

"Well, it's something to think about and pray over," John replied. "Maybe if you're away for a while, it will help the folks here to come to a decision a little sooner."

One Saturday late in June, John set out on his bicycle along with J. S. Hartzler of the Institute staff to inspect the high-school laboratory at Goshen. They were still several miles from town when suddenly the handle bars on John's bicycle broke. Unperturbed he took a peach branch, whittled it to size, and joined the broken parts.

"Great luck," said Hartzler as they started on their way again, "two flats yesterday coming from South Bend, and now this."

"It could be worse," John replied, "but I certainly hope they can fix it for me while we're at the high school. You say the lab there is more like we'd want than the one we looked at in South Bend?"

"Yes, I think so. It's small, but it has all the essentials. I suppose we should have our order ready to present to the board at their next meeting. Let's see, is it Monday night?"

"No, that's the faculty committee. We'll be discussing salaries. Have you decided what you want next year?"

Hartzler laughed. "I guess it's hardly a matter of want. But with my big load I don't think a little raise would be out of place."

"Certainly not," John agreed quickly. "As far as work's concerned you should be getting the highest instead of the lowest salary."

"How about nine or ten a week?" Hartzler suggested. "Would that be asking too much?"

"N—no," John replied thoughtfully. "Not too much, but I can't promise it. We have some frugal men on the board who seem to think their chief duty is cutting expenses."

"I hope you can collect a bit for yourself, too," said Hartzler.

"Me? How do you think I'd get on the payroll?" John asked. "I'm only a board member."

"I know, but with all the work you're doing it simply isn't fair. Anyway, you'll be teaching next month, you know."

John smiled ruefully. "Hm! reading and history! I don't know how I let myself get talked into this, except that we couldn't afford another teacher. I'll really have to do some studying."

Early in August, John made a trip to Iowa. Although he had given up much of his evangelistic work because of responsibilities at the Institute, he could not refuse a plea from the Amish congregation near Kalona. The church was large, but suffering severely from poor leadership. Young people were growing up without faith, having no confidence in their church leaders, and very little respect. A few members were urging that a Mennonite church be established in the area.

> June 29, 1897—You are needed here. Bro. Johns has rightly said that the situation here needs the best attention from both branches of our church. I have never been any place where the prospects of building up a strong vigorous church were brighter than they are here. If only a strong vigorous ministry can be placed at the head, all will be right.

John Smith and Jonathan Kurtz accompanied John on this peace-making mission. Arriving at Kalona on Saturday the three set to work planning their campaign.

> Aug. 2, 1897—We find that we have some critical cases to deal with and the charges will be serious because they are mainly against the elder. The Word teaches us that we are to receive no charges against such without two or three witnesses.

Meeting at the church on Monday morning they methodically listed complaints and charges brought by members as they dropped in for private interviews. Then studying the situation they prepared their report:

> Aug. 4—This morning at 9 nearly the whole brotherhood had gathered. Some that were not present brought complaints. Bro. W. answered his charges and made confession of his errors. Many others confessed errors and asked forgiveness. Eventually all became willing to drop all in the past and forgive. Then we presented the plan we have made to go on in their church work. The plan is to have a minister move in and till this can be done to have some one sent here every four weeks. They all accepted the plan.

Boarding the train for Chicago at 4:30 A.M., John rested his head on the back of the seat and closed his eyes, hoping to catch a little more sleep. But his heart was too full, his mind too engrossed with anxious thoughts to permit the luxury of sleep. Those people back in Kalona, was their trouble really settled? Would the church have peace? Could a good man be found to help them, to assist in making the church the vital force Christ intended it should be?

He thought again of all those charges he had listened to. Such a long list—charges that members had brought against their elder and against each other. Some were serious, and others paltry, things that should have been forgiven and forgotten long ago. How could Christian people, he wondered, permit such hard feelings to develop?

Instead of brotherly love there was selfishness, jealousy, envy, contempt in so many hearts. It was plain to see that the great need of that congregation was basic teaching in the principles of Christian living. But what could be expected of a people led by one who himself was but a child in spiritual perception and understanding?

John thought again of that aged minister as he had looked that afternoon, sitting there in front of the congregation, his eyes glued to the floor, his cheeks burning with shame as he listened to his sins being read for all to hear. Crushed, defeated, a minister of the Gospel, and yet such a weak human being. But there was a nobility in his bearing as he got to his feet, faced the congregation, and humbly asked forgiveness as he acknowledged his guilt. Could he have been so brave? John wondered.

For some reason the Kalona affair had cut deeply. Church troubles like this always left him with a sickish feeling, but this time it was worse. He shut his eyes tight and tried to quit thinking, but little things that had been happening at Elkhart lately kept crowding into his mind. Of course there was no connection, he tried to assure himself, but what if some of those small misunderstandings should flare up into real issues! No, it couldn't happen! Never, never would he permit things to get out of hand as they had at Kalona!

But that poor old minister—over and over came the disturbing thought—had he really been guilty of all those charges, or had he simply confessed as a matter of policy, to restore order as quickly as possible? Even though the morning was warm, a chill crept down John's spine. Taking a handkerchief from his pocket he wiped the cold sweat from his forehead. "God help us," he breathed.

* * *

Seated on a plank bench just inside the tent with a group of ministers, John took an occasional sip of the lukewarm soup in his cup, and toyed with an oversized cheese sandwich. It was a good idea, he thought, serving meals like this right on the grounds. And a splendid idea having a big tent for this conference. Certainly there was no church anywhere in Ohio large enough to hold the crowd that had come to this Sunday-school conference. Fifteen to sixteen hundred, someone had estimated! The program that morning had so impressed John that it brought an ache to his heart, and the kind of satisfaction that made food seem superfluous. He couldn't eat, and he didn't want to talk just then. He looked longingly toward the wood lot beyond Stauffer's barn. If only he could slip away for a while.

Finally, just before the evening session, he did manage to wander off in the direction of the woods, his mind trying to analyze what was taking place here, right under his eyes.

Sixteen hundred folks coming out to a Sunday-school conference, most of them young people! What did it mean? Why had they come? And only a few weeks before almost as many had attended the Indiana Conference at Yellow Creek. There were so many that they had to hold the meetings outside. Surely it could mean only one thing—a spiritual awakening which demanded an outlet, some means of expressing love for Christ and a desire to do something for Him!

Service had been the keynote of this meeting. Sitting there at the moderator's table he had been quite overwhelmed that afternoon at the response to the discussion in the open session. Again the mission question was brought up—missions—foreign missions! It seemed the one important thing in the minds of these young people. So vital had the question become that the committee decided to lift an offering for some future mission project in order to permit the crowd to respond to the feeling that had been aroused. John was still surprised at the amount of the offering—sixty-eight dollars! And this from a Mennonite group and for foreign missions! Dropping to his knees he poured out his heart in thanksgiving and praise. And he asked, too, for wisdom and guidance in helping to direct this new force which was beginning to show itself among his people.

But it wasn't long before the elation of conference days began to fade. Before leaving the state John made a tour of the Ohio churches in an effort to raise more funds for the Institute. Even though the church was beginning to stir, it was discouragingly evident that the awakening was not yet general. Occasionally he received a liberal donation, but time and again he summed up the day's activities with the disheartening words:

> I have not done anything sure for the school; I have been talking school today, but apparently with poor success; I am surprised at the way these people understand giving.

* * *

The fall months passed, bringing inevitable changes to the Coffman family. Late in September, Ansel left for Chicago. He had decided on a career in music and enrolled in the music department at Northwestern University. Then Samuel F. arrived from Ontario and after a few weeks he, too, set off for Chicago to continue his studies at Moody Bible Institute. But there were no vacant rooms or empty beds at the Coffman home. Besides Harry North who had been living with the family for several years while attending the Institute, there was now a new boarder, J. W. Yoder, who had come from Pennsylvania to serve on the Institute staff. Later that fall they made room for another Pennsylvania lad, Mylin Yoder.

Early in October, John was called once more on a peacemaking mission. This time it was to the little congregation in Jasper County, Missouri. And once again an elder of the church was involved. The experience touched John deeply. How uncharitable, he thought, how un-Christlike and inconsistent were these so-called misunderstandings between Christian brethren.

"It's a terrible state of affairs," John commented to J. F. Funk and Daniel Kauffman as they sat talking in Funk's office. "I can't understand how they can let things get like that. We'd certainly not let it happen here, would we?"

Funk looked up in surprise. "Well, I should hope not," he thundered, gazing searchingly at John. "What ever made you even think of such a thing?"

"Oh, nothing in particular," John replied, returning the candid gaze. "But I see it so often, and in such unexpected places. It does make one think."

"Well, remember this," said Funk, thumping his desk with a tight fist, "it takes more than one to stir up trouble. And should it ever come here, well—"

"Well, at least two of you are against it," chimed in Kauffman. "Now let's get to work. Time is precious."

"So we're to edit this manuscript on Bible doctrines," said Funk, taking the bundle of papers from him and starting to sort out the chapters. "Did you do all this writing yourself?"

"Yes, I'm afraid it's all mine. I tried to get some help, but I guess everyone was too busy," Kauffman replied. "But since it's a matter of explaining our doctrines, I don't want the full responsibility. That's why I'm asking some of you older men to look it over and make any changes you think necessary."

"It looks like a pretty big job for one week," John said.

"I know. But A. D. Wenger will be here tomorrow and he'll help. And for you, J. S., there's a whole chapter to write. I told you some time ago I wanted you to do the chapter on sanctification, and the job is still waiting."

"Well, I guess it will have to wait a little longer," sighed John. "Maybe I can get at it next week between sessions of conference."

The following week saw the first gathering of delegates from all Mennonite conferences from east to west. This "preliminary" General Conference was held at Elida, Ohio, November 10-13. The first day was given over to the Evangelizing Board. An evangelizing sermon by J. S. Coffman was followed by their annual business meeting and a lively discussion on the subject of missions—city missions, foreign missions.

> Nov. 11, 1897—Last night I staid at Bro. John L. Brennemans where there were about 15 of us. We had a very pleasant time. Bro. L. J. Heatwole was with me. At 9 A.M. the preliminary conference opened according to appointment. Reports were given by delegates from all the conferences represented. There were persons present from all the conferences except Maryland. A number of warm speeches were made. A committee of five, Daniel Kauffman, D. J. Johns, Benjamin Gerig, Noah Stauffer, and myself, were chosen a committee to draft a call and plans for a general conference. . . .

> Nov. 12—The preliminary meeting met and after a deeply spiritual exercise the work was begun. I was asked to make a statement as chairman of the committee. The parts of the report were taken up separately and discussed. Finally the whole report was adopted unanimously. Then the matter of making a call for General Conference was taken up and discussed at length. There were some warm speeches made, but all in a kind spirit. Bro. Andrew Mack gave valuable talks showing the feeling of the Eastern Pennsylvania brethren. The call was adopted by a vote of 33 for, 3 against, several neutral.

Taking advantage of the presence of so many representatives from all parts of the church, a meeting of the Book and Tract Society was held on the last evening of the conference. As it turned out, this meeting was to have serious and immediate consequences. John wrote:

> Nov. 13—The Book and Tract society had a long meeting at the house of Simon Good. . . . They decided to handle books especially for ministers. George [Bender] is to sell to them for cost, but have 10% on other books he sells for handling them. There was quite a conflict between the society and the Mennonite Publishing Company representatives. But finally all came to an agreement. The Tract society has been doing virtually nothing the last years. We hope the work may be revived.

"Well, what's your opinion of the conference?" Sliding into the seat beside John after a group left the train at Fort Wayne, George L. Bender settled down for a good talk.

"It was a good meeting," said John. "It looks as though we'll have a General Conference now, and it should do a lot for the church."

"Only three delegates opposed," mused Bender. "It does look as if we might be able to have some kind of unity."

"It's what we've been working for all these years," John said. "But we have a long way to go yet before East meets West, I fear."

"And last night's meeting," ventured Bender, after a brief pause. "How—how did it really strike you?"

John shook his head silently as he turned toward his seatmate. "Frankly, George, I'm afraid. The Society is on the right track, but I'm afraid the action they took won't be welcomed by the Publishing Company."

"They seemed to come to an agreement with us last night," he continued thoughtfully, "but I have a feeling it's not final. Once they get home and talk things over with the rest, I have an idea we'll hear from them."

"Well, for that matter I've seen trouble brewing for some time," said Bender. "If we can keep things from boiling over for a while, maybe they'll calm down."

"No," said John, "the thing to do is to come to a definite, businesslike agreement, one that satisfies everybody, and then stick to it."

"Of course, of course," agreed Bender. "But the way business matters have been going there lately, you know as well as I that a working agreement with them will be a one-sided affair. I don't like what's been going on. I don't like the attitude that flared up at the meeting yesterday. And I don't think they'll give an inch, once the business heads get together."

"We'll just have to pray harder, George," John advised. "Our cause is good. You certainly won't be in the game for the money you get out of it. It's important that our ministers get helpful literature and most of them can't afford to pay regular prices. So we must hold on, and pray for God's help."

Try as he might, however, John found himself helpless to bridge the rift between the Tract Society and the Publishing Company caused by the action of the Society. Although he tried to keep his personal relationship with his old associates as friendly as before, strained feelings became more and more evident. It was as if the little gulf originating with the Institute affair was gradually widening. But he did not give up. Never, never would he give up the struggle to bring about peace and harmony among his brethren.

> Nov. 24, 1897—This morning I went to the office of the Mennonite Publishing company to see some of the members, but did not get them together. At 2 P.M. I went back and succeeded in getting a few together and had three hours talk with them on the situation of the relation between the Mennonite Book and Tract society and the Mennonite Publishing company. I am convinced that the late moves of both societies will engender strife if there is no radical change in their conduct. I have prayed much over the matter and simply did a hard duty. I pray God's blessing on the talk we had together.

But it was with a heavy heart that he set out for Ohio to spend several weeks preaching for a small congregation at the Little Vine Church in Ada. Soon after he arrived he looked up Blosser, the president of the Tract Society.

> Dec. 3—We think we see a plan that will satisfy about all parties and enable the work to go on in peace. There is surely a crisis on hand with regard to the book sales and publishing interests, and tract work in the church. A true, sweet, unselfish spirit in all will make all go well in spite of Satan's effort to ruin our peace.

The talk with Blosser cheered him. There was hope. The success of the meetings also brought new courage.

> Dec. 3—This evening the house was again packed. It is the house of the Bible Christians whose congregation is about broken up and the members that are left are disposed to unite with us.

> Dec. 14—I am deeply interested for the church work in Ada. The only safe way is for our people to go slowly and take in only those who are in harmony with us in doctrine. Many persons are very favorably impressed with our work, but they need much time and teaching. Few are ready to make the sacrifices we require. But they will win a congregation if they hold on faithfully.

Armed with the plan he had devised with Blosser, John lost no time in arranging a meeting with Publishing Company officials on his arrival home. David Burkholder, M. S. Steiner, G. L. Bender, and Daniel Kauffman were with him at this meeting.

> We talked all afternoon but came to no conclusions or agreement as to the work of the Tract society. What way the Lord will open I do not see at present. May His will be done.

A members' meeting called for Thursday evening, December 16, 1897, was described by him as "one of the coldest and most spiritless meetings I was ever in. The most that spoke either said or inferred that there is something wrong in the church here." It was time now, he decided, to take prompt and self-sacrificing action:

> Dec. 17, 1897—After the meeting last night I was much exercised on account of the church here, and thought and prayed much as to what could be done to restore life and prosperity. I concluded that the fault may be largely mine, and decided that I must do my part and get right myself. I went this morning to talk about it with two of the brethren. I staid till noon, and found a good many things where I was in fault which I must make right if possible. I concluded that a sweet spirit was in the brethren and I came home happy and began telling my family of the assurance I now had that all was in a good spirit with the brethren and spoke of their good qualities. When I went into prayer over the matter I was enveloped in darkness, and I was convinced of the Lord that all was not right.
>
> Dec. 18—This morning I went again to the brethren. . . . We talked till I began to hope I saw a true spirit of brotherly love and grace. I eagerly looked for it, and seized upon it with the greatest pleasure, but before I left them I found that I was entirely mistaken as to the spirit in which they are proceeding in this controversy with the B. and T. society, and with me concerning the condition of the church here. I am fearing terrible results if the spirit does not change.
>
> Dec. 19, Sunday—Text at church, Psalms 139, last two verses: "Under the eye of God," 1. search me; 2. try me; 3. know me; 4. see me; 5. lead me. Today I have experienced again the Lord's answer to prayers with almost unexpected clearness. The darkness under which I labored has cleared, and I am happy in the conscious presence of my Helper.

*Lord, give me grace to be humiliated in every particular where I am not sufficiently lowly. Grant that in my travails and humiliation I may not be grieved because my name may be cast out as evil, but only because the good I might do may be hindered. Help me to lose sight of self and to be truly Christ-like and live a holy life so that my testimony may be helpful to the unsaved.*—Diary.

# 27

John was busy at his desk when Bettie came in with a steaming cup of tea.

"Here you are," she said. "Time for more sarsaparilla."

"But it's only nine o'clock. I can't drink any more so soon."

"Well, it's two hours since breakfast and your mother said a cup every few hours, when she sent the roots. Surely you want to get better quick."

"Of course," John replied. "But I've got another plan. See here." Reaching into his pocket he pulled out a handful of neatly cut lengths of sarsaparilla root. "Instead of sousing myself with that bitter brew all day I simply put a little piece in my mouth now and then and chew on it till the flavor's gone. I think it will do me as much good as the tea."

"Well, just so you give it a good try. You do feel a little better, don't you?" she asked hopefully.

"Oh, a little, I think. This seems to be better than any medicine I've had in a long time. But that birthday dinner at William's the other day was a lesson for me. No more rich foods or pastries!"

"Now don't go talkin' like that," scolded Bettie tenderly. "If you'll just take care of yourself a while, I reckon you'll soon be over the misery. Who's the letter to, any of the folks back home?"

"Yes, ma'am," John replied, turning to address an envelope. "I've just finished a letter to Joe, and now I'm going to start one to Lewis."

"Be sure and tell 'em to thank Mother for the sarsaparilla,"

Bettie said, heading for the kitchen with the unwanted tea. "I'll be back at eleven with another cup."

After Bettie left, John turned back to his desk to commence his letter to Lewis. But instead of writing he sat for a long time staring out the window. How much better it would be to talk to him! He had written a month or so ago. Then it had been to encourage him. Now he needed encouragement of the very same kind. Why did such troubled, testing times have to come anyway? For Lewis a time of crisis was near. The church in Virginia would soon have peace. But it would come through a schism. A committee had been appointed to settle the difficulties, but a break between the contending parties seemed inevitable. Would that be the tragic ending to the Elkhart story as well?

John hated to tell Lewis about the trouble at Elkhart. He had hoped things might clear up so that he wouldn't have to say anything about it. To put things down on paper made them so much more real and formidable. But he couldn't keep the matter from Lewis any longer. News of the affair had been sifting into Virginia and it was time to give someone the facts of the case:

> Jan. 19, 1898—One reason I did not write you is that I am myself entangled in a difficulty of no small proportions right here at home. Things have not been going well here, and I have prayed and worried over the matter, losing rest and sleep till my health has been affected and I have grown quite thin in flesh. I am glad, however, that my general health is better. I do not wish to parade our troubles before the world, but I will give you just a little insight into them. For several years one of our ministers who came here not so long ago appears to have been jealous of me, and has tried to influence the people against me. I would occasionally hear something that did not just please me, but I put it away again and again, and refused to believe them. This was going on for several years. Finally the clash came at Elida, Ohio, where the Mennonite Book and Tract society held its meeting, between the B. and T. society and the Mennonite Publishing company. I went to the brethren when I learned of the steps they took to crush out entirely the Tract society and tried to get them to compromise in some way, so that the church would not become involved. But my efforts were unavailing. I fear they have taken a position that will arouse the suspicions immensely that have been slumbering for years. They say they have no fears. The Tract society is doing little in order that they may have peace. The M.P.C. has in large measure monopolized the book trade of the church, or that part of it, and that is only a little part, that our people get. I do not know how our people will take the matter; it remains to be seen.
>
> After I had done what I could to get them to take a position

toward the Tract society that would give the church confidence in them and work for peace, and failed, trouble arose right here in the church while I was away. I had nothing to do with starting it. I again went to them twice or three times after nights of prayer and sleeplessness to try to get them to take a position that would bring peace here. But they were unyielding. Their policy is to get things hushed up and smoothed over. They seem to imagine if they could get me to hush and to let them alone and just go on and call all things good, everything would be well. I would be glad to do so if that would mend things. I feel a little as if I were a John the Baptist that will lose my head for opposing sin in high places. . . . Satan is going to lie me into disrepute if possible. I see plainly that charges have been brought against me to hide some one's sins, making it appear that some are not any worse than John Coffman. There is a members' meeting appointed for Thursday evening, such as we have had every week for more than a month. These meetings have, I think, been held to smooth over and settle things without ruffling them up. I think now that I will be compelled to make some statements on Thursday evening that will be the beginning of measures to compel an investigation. There is no peace here, and there will be none till God finds us in a righteous spirit that He can bless.

When M. S. Steiner arrived in Elkhart early in February to begin a series of meetings, he was shocked at the change he saw in John. Definitely it was a sick man that met him at the train. The pale, hollow cheeks spoke plainly of physical weakness. The rapidly graying hair and dark rings around those burning, gray-blue eyes told of sleepless nights and a burden of worry and care too great for the weakened body.

"Aren't you beginning to see some prospects of a settlement?" Steiner asked as he sat talking with John in his study. "Surely there must be some way of restoring harmony between brothers in the church."

John winced. Never had Steiner seen him so dejected, almost despairing.

"I've tried," he sighed wearily. "God knows I've tried. Personally I have no hard feelings for my brethren, but I do have feelings against some things that have been going on. And I see no hope for peace as long as they continue."

"I thought you said there had been confessions some time ago. Didn't that help matters?"

"Oh, we have congregational meetings and confessions every once in a while," John replied spiritlessly. "We had another session after the service yesterday morning. Five of us confessed—four ministers and Brother Bender. Everything should be fine and good now, but—" John shook his head helplessly.

"You say you confessed?" Steiner asked wonderingly. "How could you? What have you done that you could honestly confess to, if I may ask?"

"Who of us is perfect?" replied John, meeting Steiner's surprised gaze. "Who couldn't confess to sins of negligence, misunderstandings, or mistakes of one kind or another?"

"Oh, of course, of course," Steiner replied. "If that's all, I can understand that."

"But it wasn't all." John's face reddened and he turned to look out the window as he continued. "I had to confess that I once said I wished a certain individual were in Guinea."

Steiner gulped, not sure whether to laugh or groan. "Oh, no. Surely you—you didn't say that in front of the whole congregation!"

John nodded silently, still gazing at the bleak landscape seen from his window. "Why shouldn't I? Even the thought is unworthy of a Christian. Apparently someone heard me make the statement which got back to the individual, and it was specifically requested that I make a public confession or apology. Certainly I wouldn't let a small thing like that hinder the peace of the church. I only thank God that there are no greater evils that the church needs to hear me confess. Here's my confession," he continued, handing Steiner a closely written sheet which he took from his desk drawer. "You'll see that I also added a statement giving my reason for the dissatisfaction I feel concerning the present condition. I'm afraid some folks didn't like that very well. But it had to be said."

"And the others—how were their confessions?" Steiner asked, glancing over the paper John had given him.

"Mostly insignificant. Not the faults that should have been confessed to make things right and bring peace."

It was late Saturday afternoon. The annual business meeting of the Elkhart Institute Association was over at last and the stockholders had gone home. Tired and dejected from the strain of the meeting John slipped into the business office to be alone for a few minutes. Soon there was a light tap on the door and J. S. Hartzler stepped inside.

For a moment neither ventured to speak.

"We—ell, no need to be so glum, is there?" Hartzler finally began, slipping into the chair opposite John. "Seems to me things turned out pretty well in the end. The old board back—most of the old officers, and Mumaw as secretary instead of president as he tried to be. It looked pretty bad, though, for a while," he added, noticing John's tight lips and grim expression. "I was almost afraid we might lose out."

John heaved a sigh so deep it was almost a groan. "Yes, the old board is back, but at what a cost! I expected some opposition. I knew they were up to something, but never, never did I dream of such scheming, such a fight!"

"But we won," Hartzler assured him, trying to be cheerful. "They were smart all right, but not smart enough. You did a good job keeping things going and everything in order."

John shook his head and leaned wearily back in his chair. "Never, never do I want to go through a session like that again. It was quite a shock seeing all those new stockholders coming in."

"Humph, new stockholders! You mean—well, I guess I'd better not say it. But the nerve of them, handing out shares of stock the day before a meeting and expecting holders to have a vote!"

"Anyway, I was glad we had it covered in the constitution," John said.

"Yes, but the way they tried to change the constitution!" Hartzler exploded. "What kind of business is that?"

"Well, never mind. It didn't go through and we're right back where we were, except that we likely have more feeling against us than ever. And we can expect even stiffer opposition."

"I suppose so," Hartzler mused. "None of them looked very happy when they left."

"I'm sorry about it—very, very sorry," sighed John. "I had hoped that things were beginning to clear up a bit. Steiner's meetings seemed to make an impression, and I thought maybe we'd soon see a change. But this puts us right back again."

"Do you suppose Mumaw will act as secretary this time? At least he didn't turn it down."

"No, I'm sure he won't," John replied. "He'll never work with this board."

"So I suppose it'll be my job again."

"Likely," John said, walking over to the window where he stood a moment in silence. "But I've been thinking," he added slowly, "maybe it would be a good idea for me to resign and offer the directorship to one of their men. I know the board is afraid of what Dr. Mumaw might do, but if we handed it over to one of his friends he might stay on and we could all work together again."

Hartzler shook his head. "I don't think it would work. I'm certain neither the board nor the stockholders would accept your resignation. Not just now, anyway. Things are still too critical."

"But something has to be done," John said, "and it will have to be drastic."

For the next two weeks John threw himself wholeheartedly into the work which concerned him most. But it was hard work, he found. Roads in the Yellow Creek area were bad and kept many people from the services. But even more discouraging was the spirit of lethargy which seemed to grip the entire congregation.

> Feb. 25, 1898—The interest was good, but the people seem Gospel hardened. It seems impossible to move sinners in this neighborhood to accept Christ.

But by the time the meetings closed, four young people had made the important decision.

During his stay here John found time to edit a little booklet of outlines of courses given at the Johnstown Bible conference in January. So many people were asking for help in personal Bible study that he decided an inexpensive booklet might help to meet the need.

At home again, John found nothing changed in his absence. Try as he might to ignore them, hard feelings persisted. The hopelessness of the situation almost overwhelmed him. To his diary he confided:

> March 8, 1898—This morning I wrote some letters and then spent the day arranging circulars for the school announcing the opening of the new spring term. Last night I spent the time sleeplessly nearly all night. I do not know any special cause for it unless it is a shadow cast of an event that will bring me great trial. I feel somehow that still greater trial is before me. May God give me strength to stand up for the right.

To M. S. Steiner he also confided his fears for the future:

> March 12, 1898—Your letter came as a sunbeam through a rift in the clouds. The storm has not yet passed by. When we think it has nearly passed, the sky again grows darker and fresh thunder claps terrify us. But the Lord will bring deliverance for the church at Elkhart. . . . Peace and blessing and spiritual life and joy will come. But who knows what it will cost? It may yet cost my life, my removal from Elkhart or my expulsion from the church or silencing from the ministry. So long as requirements do not interfere with righteousness or my conscience they can get me to do almost anything, but when I am assailed in those particulars I am immovable as God gives me grace. I have really felt as though I have been treated like Jeremiah, or John the Baptist or as Joab treated Amasa the captain of David's host. . . . I am told there are complaints against me. I learn that one is for making that explanation which I appended to my confession which I think I read to you. . . . Another is with regard to my course in that school meeting where you were present. Another is against Hartzler and myself for putting out the minutes of that meeting just as we did. We may have to meet all these charges and more besides. It really does not look much more peaceful here than between Spain and the U.S. I do not want to fight. All I ask is "Quiet and be at peace." But if I am driven into a corner and no quarters given me, I will fight for righteousness with all the might God gives me. May He keep me from being carnal.

* * *

"John, is that you?" Bettie called, hearing the front door open and familiar footsteps enter the living room.

"Yes, it's me. Don't get up. I'll come to bed soon."

But in a minute Bettie came shuffling sleepily from the bedroom.

"Why, my dear, it's nearly midnight. You should be sleeping," John scolded, hanging his overcoat on the hook beside the door.

"Well, you know I can't sleep when you're out," yawned Bettie. "And anyway I wanted to fix you some hot milk. How was the meetin'? Get anything settled yet?"

"No, I'm afraid not," John replied wearily. "It seemed to be pretty much like all the rest—charges and more charges, and yet nothing made right. I'm tired of it. Really sick and tired, and I say it's got to stop. All this wrangling! It's unchristian. We've had enough."

Surprised at the sudden change in the tone of his voice, Bettie looked at her husband in wonder. This was a new John, an angry and disgusted John. There was a different lift to his chin, a glint in his eyes that looked almost belligerent.

"Why—why, John, you ain't gettin' mad, are you?"

The muscles in his jaw tightened, and two tight fists were shoved deep into his pockets as John strode over to the stove to warm himself.

"No, not mad," he exclaimed, "but most indignant that God's house should have become a house of wrangling. Tonight's session was most disgusting, and I'm determined it must stop."

"Good," said Bettie, carrying a saucepan of milk to the stove. "And who's to stop it?"

John stood thinking while Bettie watched with continued surprise the formation of a deep frown between the troubled eyes.

"I don't know who, and I don't know how, but I think I'll try a little harder myself. So far I've taken all they've said about me without saying a word. But I see it hasn't done a bit of good. So now I think I'll try fighting."

"Fighting?" exclaimed Bettie in shocked surprise. "Why, John Coffman, that doesn't sound a bit like you."

"Oh, don't worry. I don't mean with fists. Just that I'm going to start defending myself, track down some of those lies and accusations. Perhaps that will put a stop to some of their slander."

"Did they have you on the carpet tonight?"

"No, they took too long with some of the others. My turn didn't come. They say they have some serious charges, but I mean to have a plain talk with a couple of men before another ordeal like this one."

In May, John spent several weeks in Ohio. He wasn't feeling well. The gastric trouble which had seemed some better that spring was bothering him again. Nevertheless he did not let the illness interrupt his vigorous schedule of meetings, and canvassing for funds as well as students for the school. He also attended the Ohio Conference. But the day after the conference he was so sick that he thought for a while he would have to cancel his meeting at the West Liberty Church that night:

> This evening the house was packed. I took for my text I Cor. 1:30, Christ made unto us wisdom, righteousness, sanctification, and redemption. I was quite sick all day of this stomach trouble. I was nearer prevented from preaching than ever in my life, except once in Washington, Ill., on Feb. 26, 1886. God has preserved me so I never missed a sermon.

In spite of illness John got off the train at Ligonier to attend the annual conference of the Indiana Amish churches at Maple Grove before returning to Elkhart. Then he hurried home to be present for the first graduation exercises at the Institute.

There were only two graduates in this class, Robert Martin and Emma LeFevre, but John felt a lift of his spirit that night as he sat on the platform with the faculty members and looked out over the audience. Here was certainly a tangible mark of progress, two young people being graduated from a Mennonite school—the first students to complete a four-year course at the Institute. Next year there would be more, he reasoned, with prospects of a gradual increase in the years to follow.

As his mind went back over the struggles of the beginning years, he felt a thrill of satisfaction in the realization that the school was now an established institution, serving the church. Beginning in the fall it would have for the first time an all-Mennonite faculty. After months of correspondence he had finally lined up a new staff with N. E. Byers as principal.

Of course there was still opposition ahead. The fact was never far from his thoughts. The school was even being blamed for all the trouble in the Elkhart church. But for this night, difficulties, oppositions, threats of ruin—all faded into the background and his heart was filled with thanksgiving to God as he handed out those precious diplomas to the first two graduates.

The summer passed. It was a summer filled with care and worry. Although outwardly John appeared calm, the constant strain took its toll of health and vitality. To his son, Samuel F., who was back again in Ontario, he wrote:

> June 7, 1898—My health is still not good, but I am sleeping better and fortunately I am not worrying as I was about many things. I am taking things that I find impossible to change much more easily. I do not call them right, however. My testimony against them is as strong as ever before. I am glad that I can feel kindly toward all my brethren and toward all men.
>
> Aug. 10—Matters in church and school appear to be going along quietly. Some are saying that we are to have a great bust up here soon. I know nothing of that whatever. Have no idea in

what way it is to occur. I am praying the Lord to lead all things as shall please Him, and shall be for our good. I do not see that anything is going wrong in the school work. I think our prospects are good and all is peaceable. Some say Dr. M. is starting another school with which he expects to crush ours. That is a privilege he has, but I do not fear that he can crush the Institute. He may seriously hinder the work. But I doubt whether he will get up another school. Yet he may.

Rumors concerning a rival school kept increasing during the next few weeks. Then on September 7, a glowing advertisement in the *Elkhart Truth* announced the opening of the Elkhart Normal School and Business Institute in the Blackburn block on Main Street, by Dr. H. A. Mumaw.

John was in the Institute business office looking over accounts when Hartzler came in with the paper.

"Have you seen this yet?" he asked, laying the paper on the desk and pointing to the good-sized ad on the back page.

"No, I haven't," replied John, casually glancing at the announcement. "I'm not surprised, though, after all the talk there's been lately."

"Well, I guess it's not just talk any more. It's to open next week."

"Looks like it," said John. "But let's not worry. I don't think it will hurt us much."

"Likely it'll take some of the town students that might have come to us this fall," said Hartzler.

John nodded. "Yes, we can count on that, but as far as our own young folks are concerned, I don't think they'll get many. That's our big concern."

"Well, just see that you don't worry," Hartzler advised solicitously. "You may say you don't, but it's plain to see that something's bothering you. How many pounds have you lost anyway, this summer?"

"Now don't you start fussing," protested John. "Just because my vest hangs a bit loose. I admit my stomach trouble isn't getting much better, but I don't think it's all worry."

"Are you still doctoring with Mast?"

"Oh, off and on. I haven't seen him for a month or so. I don't think he understands my condition. He's tried a good many remedies but none of them seem to help. I'm getting pretty discouraged with doctors."

"You did go out to Johns, didn't you?"

"Yes, but mostly for Bettie's sake. She thought the sympathetic cure did a lot to help her and Annie when they were sick a few years ago. I'm afraid I don't have much faith in it myself. Maybe that's why it didn't help."

"I certainly hope you find something soon," Hartzler said, looking greatly concerned.

"There's one source of help, you know, that's available to all of us," John replied, rising and walking over to the window. "I've been thinking about it for some time, trying to find God's will. I believe, of course, that the good Lord intends us to do what we can for ourselves with plants and herbs and things He has provided. But I've about decided that medicine isn't going to do me much good. I'm beginning to feel that God may want me to trust Him alone for my healing."

For the next few weeks John struggled in prayer over this matter. Then on Sunday, September 25, he wrote in his diary:

> Today I discarded all medicine and human remedies. Lord, Thou wilt heal.
>
> Sept. 26—I am feeling quite well today and am fully persuaded that my resolve to put away all medicine and trust to God alone for healing is pleasing to Him. I have eaten heavier food and enjoyed a feeling of health that I had not for a long time.
>
> Oct. 8—The Lord has done wondrously for me and answered my prayer so directly that my faith in answer to prayer has again been wondrously strengthened. I do not dictate to God but I take Him at His word when I have a clear impression what His will is and then I pray and act a faith that will not be disappointed.

The first session of the Mennonite General Conference was held in Indiana the first week in November, 1898, at the Holdeman Church. Several days before the historic event people began to arrive at Elkhart. For John it meant the fulfillment of a lifelong dream as well as a season of happy fellowship—something he had missed of late at Elkhart. It was almost like old times again to be able to discuss important affairs with men like Daniel Kauffman, M. S. Steiner, D. H. Bender, and others.

Arriving for the event from Virginia was John's beloved brother-in-law, Lewis J. Heatwole. There were tears in Lewis' eyes and also in John's as they greeted each other at the depot. Neither could speak for a moment. But there was no need for words. Enough that they could feel the bond of sympathy and understanding uniting their hearts. Later, seated in John's study, they unburdened their hearts as they could to no one else.

"So things are beginning to look a little better in Virginia now," John remarked after Lewis had brought him up to date on church affairs. "Thank God for that. I only wish there was some hope for us here."

"Well, I must say I don't quite understand the situation," Lewis said, toying with the end of his long, dark beard. "I know you've written about it several times, but I never could quite see what's at the bottom of it. Why should they be so hard on you? Just how do you figure in all this trouble?"

John was ready with his answer. A faint color crept into his pale cheeks, but he faced Lewis squarely as he replied, "Thank God I have nothing to hide. You know, brother, that bothered me too for quite a long time. It's partly jealousy, of course. And there's the Tract Society and the Institute controversy with me on the wrong side for my own comfort. But I always felt there was more than that, and I think I know now what it is. It came out in a talk I had one day last summer. I haven't mentioned it because I hate to talk about my brethren, but it seems I'm being blamed personally for recent reverses in the publishing business."

"No!" Lewis exclaimed in surprise. "How could that be?"

John shrugged his shoulders. "They seem to think I've been running down the company and turning away business in my travels."

"B—but how could they? Why, you're one of their most faithful employees."

"I guess it's because I've been warning them for quite a while that some of their new business policies might not go down well with our people, and would affect their business. Now that they see it happening, they're unwilling to take the blame, and I'm the culprit. I'm supposed to be at the bottom of a plan to ruin the company and we're using the Tract Society to help do it."

"Hm! I can see you have trouble on your hands," Lewis said.

"I've tried desperately to make them see that such a thought has never entered my mind. I always have and always will work for the good of the house. It's one of our most important institutions. We simply can't get along without it. But I guess they'll only believe what they want to. I'm beginning to think that a full-scale investigation is our only hope."

"Of course a publishing company is a business concern, you must remember," Lewis remarked thoughtfully. "It can't operate like a charitable institution."

"Of course not. No one expects it. That's where the Tract Society fits in, to take care of the charity."

"Yes, there's need for both," Lewis agreed. "But it is too bad some of our ablest leaders have to be tied up so closely with business. It takes too much time and energy that should be given to the church."

"I'm especially sorry Brother Funk can't be freed of this business concern. He has been a leader in the church all these years, and has the kind of exceptional ability that the church needs. But tied up as he is with a business that now seems to be slumping—well, it's too hard on him. He can't give his best to the church, and we're all suffering. I have great esteem for my elder, but it seems he's trying to make up for lack of discipline in business by being overly strict and even harsh in church discipline. All we can do is pray harder that peace may be restored and that the church may become a working church once more."

The conference session at Holdeman's lasted two days, Wednesday and Thursday, November 2 and 3, 1898. At the meeting of the Evangelizing and Benevolent Board on Tuesday, enthusiasm reached such a pitch that the missionary spirit was felt all through the conference.

Chief concern was felt for India. George Lambert, who had returned from his relief mission, was arousing great interest as he presented a vivid description of the tremendous needs of India's starving millions. Even greater than their physical hunger, he reported, was the need of their famished souls.

To the many young people present the concern that the church should be doing something to meet this need was even more important just then than theological or doctrinal problems. It was time for action, they decided, and not content with mere talk, a number formed into small groups for prayer between sessions.

Although the conference ended with the Thursday afternoon session, feeling had mounted to such an extent that an enthusiastic group of young people demanded another meeting, a missionary meeting. Arrangements were soon made to hold this at Elkhart that evening. John was delegated to lead the meeting and missionary-minded Steiner was asked to preach the sermon.

Realizing that this meeting belonged particularly to the younger generation, John invited five young ministers all in their early thirties to sit on the platform with him and take part in the service. They were Aaron Loucks, T. M. Erb, D. H. Bender, A. D. Wenger, and Eli S. Hallman.

Never before had Steiner preached as he did that night. His call to service stirred every heart. It was a call that demanded a response, but the response had to be put off for another day. The church was not yet organized to take care of missionary volunteers.

Not willing to give up until some action had been taken by the church, the leaders of the group asked for another meeting to be held next afternoon. They also appealed to Bishop Funk and other visiting bishops to take some action in case there should be volunteers for service in India. Funk promised to give the problem careful thought.

The meeting next day was quite unlike any other John had ever attended. It was informal. No one was quite sure how to proceed or what to expect. The topics for discussion were rather vague, but finally developed into two major issues—"Shall we commence mission work in India now?" and "If so, who will go?"

It was a solemn, soul-searching hour as these young people faced the issue squarely. One after the other they got to their feet. A few offered themselves for service, among them a young physician and his wife, Dr. W. B. Page from Middlebury, Indiana. But the majority simply expressed great concern, offering to support the work, but excusing themselves from personal service because of other responsibilities.

From the side bench at the front of the room John watched the intense expression on the faces of these earnest young men and women. He particularly noticed young J. A. Ressler of Scottdale, who sat frowning and fidgeting nervously as he listened to some of the excuses being made. Finally Ressler could stand it no longer. "You had better be careful, brethren," he warned as he got to his feet. "It's dangerous to let anything come between you and service to God. He may have to take away some of your blessings as He did for me. I had a wife and a happy home, but He saw fit to take her to Himself. Now I am no longer tied by family obligations. I have no farm to look after or pay for. I am free to go wherever He wants me. And so I am willing to be used in India or wherever He desires to have me."

With only a brief intermission for supper the crowd was back at the church for the all-important final session. The bishops had promised to make appointments for mission work in India if suitable volunteers could be found. The official call for volunteers for foreign service went out that night. And while a tense audience remained in the auditorium singing and praying, a number presented themselves before a fifteen-man committee in an anteroom. Finally around eleven o'clock J. F. Funk returned to the platform and announced that J. A. Ressler and Dr. and Mrs. W. B. Page had been appointed as the church's first missionaries to India!

*God's mercy is most clearly seen when we have passed through severe trials, just as the rainbow is brightest when the cloud behind it is very dark. We can see most distinctly that we are saved after we once clearly see that we are indeed lost sinners and that Christ alone is our Saviour.*—Diary.

# 28

Once more John was back home in Virginia, this time enjoying a longer visit with his mother.

Seated across the table from her son, Mother Frances Coffman barely touched her own breakfast, so intent was she in looking after this boy of hers.

"Ain't you eatin' those taters, John?"

"No, I don't think I'd better. I've been off fried things for quite a while."

"Then I'll fix you another egg," she said, jumping up and heading for the pantry.

"No, Mother, please, I couldn't eat another one. And, anyway, you mustn't spoil me. Anyone that got up as late as I did shouldn't have breakfast."

"Well, you need your sleep too." Frances looked concerned as she studied the face of her first-born. The hollow cheeks and the colorless lips alarmed her. "If you'd only stay here and rest a bit. I reckon we'd soon get some fat on your bones. Now drink another cup of sarsaparilla," she ordered, pouring another cupful from a kettle simmering at the back of the stove.

"But I tell you, Mother, I'm feeling fine. Ever since I quit taking medicine last fall I haven't had nearly so much distress. I'm really surprised how well I stood the trip through Pennsylvania the last few weeks."

"All I can say is, thank the good Lord," Frances said returning to the table. "But I still think you should take things easy for a spell.

All this traipsin' around! It ain't good for nobody."

"I know. But I had to make the trip to see some of our stockholders on urgent business for the Institute. No one else was free to go; so it was up to me."

Frances nodded. "I know. It's always been like that with you, and I reckon it always will. If only a few more of our preachers would be like that. But then you—your name is 'John,' " Frances added thoughtfully. "There's a difference."

John lowered his eyes. He just couldn't meet that soul-searching, loving gaze across the table. A slight flush spread over the thin cheeks as he sat stirring the bit of tea left in his cup.

"I know what you mean, Mother," he said softly. "But I'm afraid—terribly afraid I've fallen short, somehow. The way things are at Elkhart right now—I'm most discouraged. It seems any good I may have done must surely count for little the way things have gone there."

"Now, John," came the sharp rebuke. "No more of that kind of talk. Hasn't God been with you? Hasn't He used you for His own special work? And do you reckon He'd quit usin' you suddenly?"

A wan smile relieved the pained expression on his face as John again raised his eyes. "Thanks," he said. "I needed that. I confess I sometimes feel pretty low when I get to thinking of that impossible situation back home."

"No, not impossible, John. Not with God at the head of things. You've said so yourself, lots of times. Now say it for yourself."

John nodded, gazing almost reverently at the look of devotion in those loving brown eyes. It seemed as if he would draw strength from the unwavering faith of this remarkable woman, his mother.

"And don't you see, John," Frances leaned forward, tapping her spoon on the edge of her cup as she spoke, "you're right now just where God wants you. Right now you're adoin' something extra special just by standin' up for what's right and fightin' the wrong right there in Elkhart."

Frances noticed with relief the look of hope that suddenly swept across John's face.

"Just don't worry," she added. "God will see to it that things turn out right there."

John nodded his assent, silently hoarding up this bit of advice against chilling days ahead.

That week John held meetings for the last time in the old home district. For over a year his brother-in-law, Lewis J. Heatwole, had looked forward to this time. Again and again he had written to John pleading the need of special work among his troubled flock. Although a measure of peace had been restored through the investigating committee, the opposition was still at work, and some dissatisfied members were again spreading their dissatisfaction.

John worked hard and prayed hard during those few days. The future of the Virginia church lay heavily on his heart. He realized keenly how difficult it was for the young people, the sons and daughters of his old friends and relatives, to have any confidence in a church torn by so much strife. Night after night he presented clearly and simply the way of salvation, and also endeavored to bolster faith which had been so severely tested.

Leaving Virginia, John stopped at Baldwin, Maryland, for the first service in a new Amish meetinghouse on Christmas Day. From there he went on to Springs, Pennsylvania, for the Winter Bible Conference. Concerning this conference he wrote to L. J. Heatwole:

> Jan. 16, 1899—The Bible conference was, to my mind, a success. Most of the teaching was able, and the speakers or lecturers, if you would call them such, have improved much with use. The people attended well, and highly appreciated the teaching. No teacher or young preacher within reach could afford to miss that school.
>
> My health improved throughout the whole trip, and I am feeling much better since I am at home, but I am not free of that pain in my bowels at intervals. . . .

Although the church difficulty continued to cause him great concern, there were a number of happy occasions that winter when John could almost forget his troubles.

There was the Sunday in February when Dr. Page and his wife were formally given their charge to serve as missionaries in India. Bishop Funk gave the charge, and for a time all hearts were united in the solemnity of the occasion. J. A. Ressler was in Elkhart, too, that day, and preached the sermon. The three who were to sail soon on their long journey went home with John and Bettie and there was happy fellowship around the dinner table. It was during the Bible conference at Springs that Ressler had received his charge, and had been ordained to the office of bishop.

John's chief interest and possibly greatest joy that year was the Institute. The Christian caliber of both students and faculty was beginning at last to measure up to the standards he had envisioned. To Samuel F. he wrote:

> Nov. 5, 1898—We have the best school we have ever had, and there is a finer religious feeling and zeal than we have ever had in the school. . . . There are about 80 in all classes. . . . I am rejoiced for the missionary spirit we have in our school. The school is so religious that some of the irreligious town boys we still have talk of leaving and going to Dr. M's school. We prefer to have them go rather than pander to their ungodly tastes.

While waiting in a depot in Kenton, Ohio, one February day, John spent the time writing a letter to his mother:

> This morning at 5:25 I left Elkhart to go to West Liberty to

> attend a ministers' meeting that is to last nine days. It is the purpose to make it a kind of school where we build one another up in the Bible truth and the principles and doctrines of the church. I hope we can have a time of blessing and learn much from the Word of God and through His Spirit.

Concerning this meeting he commented in his diary:

> The speaking was able and the subjects well treated. The spirit pervading the meeting is of the noblest kind. I spoke in the forenoon on the minister's relation to the church, and in the afternoon on the relation of the church to her ministers.

The discussion one day was "The mistakes of ministers." John reported in his diary: "I had a list of 45 that I noticed."

Several days after his return from Ohio, John went to Chicago to help with services at the mission. He went on Friday so that he could have a visit with son Ansel, who was still attending Northwestern University. He spent the night with the little group of Mennonite boys at their boarding house. Although Ansel's heavy schedule didn't leave much free time, he did manage to have a talk with him on Saturday morning after he had finished his furnace job.

"How do you like your course this year?" he asked. "Are you quite satisfied with your change from music to languages?"

"Yes, I think so. It's different, of course," Ansel replied, "but I'm enjoying it."

"Don't you miss your music?"

"Not exactly. I still have my voice lessons, choir practice, and an hour's practice every day with the college quartet."

John smiled. "No, I guess you wouldn't miss it much. But have you a career in mind now?" John studied his son thoughtfully.

"Well—" Ansel began, tilting back in his chair. "I haven't made a definite decision. My course this year is rather general. I had thought of teaching, but lately I—I'm just not sure. I suppose you'll think I'm pretty changeable, but some of the boys have been talking to me about—dentistry. And—well, I'm interested."

"Dentistry?" John looked as surprised as he sounded.

"Sure. It's a wide-open field in more ways than one," Ansel quipped. "Lots of room for good dentists all over the country."

"Well, I admit I'm surprised," John finally replied. "But, come to think of it, I guess there must be plenty of opportunity there. Just don't jump into anything like that, though," he warned, "without thinking it over carefully, and praying about it too."

"I have been," Ansel assured him. "I think I can change over quite easily next year, and as far as finances are concerned, I think I'll be able to manage if I can land a good job next summer."

"You're making expenses all right now, are you?"

"Yes, with my furnace job, choir work, waiting on tables, and the job at the printing shop on Fridays."

"Aren't you afraid you're overdoing it a bit?"

"Oh, I manage," Ansel shrugged. "But now it's my turn. How are things going at Elkhart? How's Mumaw's school?"

"All right, I guess," John replied easily. "It doesn't seem to be hurting ours, if that's what you want to know. This is the best year we've had yet."

"Well, I still think it was—"

"Now, son, be careful," John interrupted. "I don't want any member of my family making accusations. Anyone has a perfect right to start a school or any other institution if he wants to."

"Yes, and I have a perfect right to my own opinion—and that is that I don't like what went on over there. It's more like a political hassle than actions of churchmen."

"Please, Ansel, don't!" John pleaded again.

"Don't worry. I don't explode to just anyone," Ansel explained. "But I'm shocked about the situation at Elkhart."

"I know, Ansel. It's hard. But there isn't much we can do. It seems we have to wait and keep praying. Personally I'm learning to take things. They don't bother me nearly so much any more."

"You may say so, but I've got eyes and I can see. I don't like what it's done to you, and I deplore what it's doing to the young folks back home. Where they are looking for strength in the church, they find only weakness. It's bad."

John sighed. "That's what hurts most. For myself it doesn't really matter. But for the sake of the church the struggle must go on."

"All I can say is that it's good you're there. God only knows what would happen if it weren't for you, or what will happen anyway. Do you have any plans at all?"

John shook his head. "Nothing definite, except perhaps bringing up the matter at the spring conference. That may lead to some action."

At the mission on Sunday, John was pleased to see a good attendance at the morning service, with a crowd of about 180 children at Sunday school in the afternoon. With the help of the few workers that had stood by during the crisis, the mission had survived and was beginning to grow once more. Hershey Leaman, a young convert from Pennsylvania, had arrived in the city and was helping to put new life into the work.

* * *

The May sun was pleasantly warm. Flowers were blooming and little back yard gardens looked promising. But John scarcely noticed the row of tiny beets, or the bright red bleeding heart as he sauntered in the garden after dinner. His brother Dan, who regularly ate his noon meal with them, followed John outside and sat on the porch steps watching him.

"Those beans sure are growing fast," Dan said. "Why, you just planted them, was it a week or ten days ago?"

John glanced at the beans and nodded silently.

"Reckon you ain't feelin' so good today," Dan offered.

"Oh, I don't know. Not much different than usual."

"You scarcely touched your dinner."

John shrugged. "I often don't eat much. I wasn't hungry."

"Well, I can't say I blame you today. I wasn't hungry myself. That meetin' yesterday was enough to turn the strongest stomach. Something's got to be done right away, I say. We just can't let things go on like this." Dan's fist came down hard on the top step.

Dejectedly John made his way back to the porch and sank down on the steps beside Dan.

"We've said that before," he said, "over and over again. But what? What are we to do? I thought I had started something when I brought the matter before conference. And I guess I did, but it wasn't quite what I had hoped."

"No, I reckon it wasn't," Dan said. "It kind of backfired. The nerve of them, making an accusation like that against you publicly!"

"Well, I didn't exactly expect it. It was humiliating, but I was glad I could meet it."

"Maybe it would've been better if you'd listened to headquarters and not brought the matter up," Dan suggested.

"No, I had to do it. At least someone had to. We'll never have peace in this church without some outside help. You remember we asked for an outside bishop for our spring counsel meeting. We didn't get it. And what happened? Twenty-two members turn up at the meeting. It's gone too far, and too long. Conference must take action."

"But they ain't doin' a thing," muttered Dan.

"I hardly expected they would, so soon," John replied with a deep sigh. "But at least it's on record. It's letting them know officially that there is trouble, and sooner or later they must recognize it."

"But the trouble is, the bishops control conference. If our bishop doesn't want them to do something, they can't. You know what a stickler he is for bishop authority!" Dan sputtered.

"I know, only too well," John said. "That's the trouble in Pennsylvania too. But there'll be a change someday. God only knows when."

"Well," Dan said, rising and stretching, "all I can say is that for your sake, especially, I wish some folks from these parts were in Guinea."

"Careful now, Dan," John smiled grimly. "That might cost you a confession."

"I reckon it's time to get back to work," Dan said, pulling a watch out of his coat pocket to check the time. "Any ideas about what to do next?"

"I'm afraid not," John sighed. "I've been talking to several men this morning, and I want to see a few more this afternoon. Likely we'll be calling a meeting before I leave for Ohio."

"When's that?"

"Wednesday morning, if I can get ready by then. I have some work to finish at the Institute first."

"I hear they didn't accept your resignation from the board at your meeting last week."

John shook his head hopelessly. "No. I'm sorry they didn't. I think it would have helped relations between the church and school immensely, as well as relieved me. But they wouldn't give in."

"One of these days they'll have to," Dan said sharply as he turned toward the street. "All this work and worry. It's too much for any man!"

Once more John boarded the early morning train, bound for Illinois. This time the destination was Freeport. How many more times would he be making this trip, he wondered, as he settled tiredly into a corner of the seat and closed his eyes. The way he felt just then, it might well be his last. Bettie had tried hard to keep him from going. He had looked very sick the day before when he got back from Ohio. He didn't tell her, but he had suffered severely from pain and gastric trouble almost constantly while he was in Ohio.

But somehow he felt a compulsion about this trip. He had a tender spot in his heart for the Illinois churches. So many of the young people had come into the church through his ministry and he still felt a responsibility for them. It was these same young people who were now launching a Sunday-school conference and they were counting strongly on John's help. As long as he was able to keep going, he decided, he would not disappoint them.

William was accompanying John on this trip to Illinois. He was anxious to visit some old friends as well as to attend the conference. He sat quietly beside his father so that he might get a little more sleep, but John couldn't sleep that morning. Instead, his thoughts raced back over the years to the time of his first visit to Illinois. He was a young man then, full of hopes and ambitions. Plans for his beloved church were just beginning to take form in his mind.

Now at the age of fifty he was old—nearing the end of life's journey, he felt. Ambition was fading fast. True, he still had high hopes and even greater plans for the church. But these would be left for someone else to carry out. A prayer of praise rose in his heart as he thanked the Father for permitting him to see so many of those early plans fulfilled, and for allowing him to have a small part in their fulfillment.

The church at Freeport was crowded right from the start of the conference. All the Illinois churches were represented, John noticed, and a good number of the Amish. The largest delegation came from Metamora.

To John, who was asked to serve as moderator, the enthusiasm of these young Christians was a real inspiration. He also rejoiced to see the spirit of fellowship springing up between the Mennonite and Amish groups. But most inspiring was the deep spiritual tone of the talks and testimonies. Surely, he thought, he had no need to fear for the future of the church with young men and women such as these beginning to shoulder responsibility. In his diary he wrote:

> May 25, 1899—The sentiment is decidedly gaining that the Sunday school conference is a strong factor in gaining acquaintance and bridging up unity between the Mennonite and Amish members. It is doing much to establish young members in the doctrine of the church.

John returned from Illinois actually refreshed. The conference and the week of meetings in Sterling together with his visits to old friends seemed like a tonic to his soul and gave him new zeal as he laid plans for the summer.

Commencement time at the Institute also brought a lift to his spirits. There were ten graduates to whom he handed diplomas this time—ten young men and women going out into the world trained to fill places of usefulness in society and in the church. Yes, it was indeed worth while, he exulted, and suddenly all the work, the worry, and the criticism seemed as nothing.

Meeting with the school board after graduation, John entered enthusiastically into plans for the future. Next year was to be even better. Two men would go out on solicitation during the summer—J. S. Hartzler as well as J. S. Coffman.

Before he started out, however, John had some work to do for the Book and Tract Society. At their spring meeting they decided to issue some seventy-five or eighty tracts in lots of 5,000. They also proposed to get out a circular, "The Book and Tract Messenger," through which to advertise available books and tracts, as well as appeal for funds for the effort. It was John's task to arrange the tracts and to plan the format of the new publication. It seemed his summer would again be a busy one.

*O, sweet sleep, what a blessing! Shall the sleep of death be so sweet? And shall the fair morning of the resurrection be to us as delightful in the brightness of eternal day?*—Diary.

# 29

Bettie noticed the change in John's expression the minute he stepped in the door. He smiled quietly as she ran to him, and grabbing her hands he held them tightly while she searched his face.

"Oh, John," she quavered, "you—you've got things settled?"

"Almost," he smiled. "It was the best meeting we've had in years."

"Thank God, thank God," said Bettie, almost choking on the big lump that suddenly formed in her throat. "So I reckon it paid to fight after all."

"Fight?" John asked, his forehead wrinkling in thought.

"Why, yes, don't you mind? You said you was agoin' to try fightin'."

"Oh, I guess I did, a long time ago. But we soon gave that up. It didn't work."

"Why not?" Bettie asked wonderingly, as she continued to gaze into the calm, patient eyes smiling down at her.

"Just because it made things worse than ever—more words, more bickering. I figured I should be more noble than to quarrel with my brethren. We never would have reached an agreement that way."

News of the meeting with its hopeful outcome spread rapidly through the congregation. Tears of joy and thankfulness shone in many eyes on Sunday morning when John once more took his place behind the pulpit. For some time neither he nor Hartzler had been asked to preach.

Although they could not know that this was to be Coffman's last sermon, everyone listened with the deepest interest that morning. The sermon, based on the story of the lad tormented by a dumb spirit, reflected his own experience as well. From the most trying circumstance of his life had come a fuller revelation of man's helplessness and his utter dependence on God. "Despair may be turned into triumph, even joy," he pointed out, "but only through seeking the help of the Master."

A radiance, almost ethereal, transformed the pallid features as he poured out his heart that morning. The message was simple and clear, reaching many hearts which had also been troubled by the difficulties in the church.

The counsel meeting which had eased tension and brought hope had taken place on Saturday afternoon. It was a meeting for which John had planned and prayed for some time. His diary records the event:

> June 10, 1899—This forenoon I spent most of the time considering plans for procedure to try to get a better understanding in the church here. A number of us finally agreed to hold a council with the other ministering brethren and present our complaints. We met in the afternoon. The meeting so turned out that the charges were not presented and an understanding was arrived at. We feel to thank the Lord that so much has been accomplished in the direction of peace in this brotherhood. May God grant that the good spirit may prevail and bring the long prayed-for peace.

Early Monday morning John sat down to write letters. One of the first was to his mother, for he knew how concerned she was regarding affairs at Elkhart:

> June 11, 1899—My very dear Mother:
>
> May God richly bless and comfort you in this beautiful summer time. This morning I praise my God as I look out at the green grass and the roses and the pinies and geraniums; also at the peas and beans and cabbages, etc. We have a fine season, plenty of rain and pleasantly warm. We have only here and there a fly and no mosquitoes to bother us. Beside this we have good health, all except myself. I am not well yet. I still have some stomach trouble and now I have rheumatism in my shoulder that makes my sleep very restless. In a general way I am much stronger and better than I was a year ago. There is still another reason for which to be very thankful. Our troubles that have been going on for several years have taken a turn toward peace, and we have hopes that we can get everything into good shape in a few weeks and about all go to communion together as we used to do. This will be a time of rejoicing for us. Peace among brethren is a grand thing; but if it is peace without righteousness it is not worth much. We are in hopes that we can get peace on

> a true Gospel basis. The Lord is helping us and answering our prayers that we have so long been sending up to Him through many tears. I often think of my dear Father, how he had his great trials, and had to take unjust censure from unreasonable man, though they may have thought they were doing right. He had his trials and I am sure he aimed to be faithful and he has gone to his reward. I have my trials, and I hope to be faithful and to meet him to join a blessed reward with his. I am growing rapidly old, and my work will soon be over. Yesterday I preached at Elkhart the first time for a number of weeks. Daniel as deacon, Hartzler and Yoder and myself as ministers, had been pushed aside and not asked to preach. But the church had not set us aside. Let us pray that God may settle this matter aright, so that there will be perfect peace.

That afternoon another settlement was made. In response to a call from Dr. Mumaw, John met him in his office. His diary records:

> We had a talk on the situation of the church, and finally I got up the subject of buying his interest in the Institute. We got the bargain settled for $300 for all his interests. . . . I am doing now what I can to talk for the peace of the church which we so much desire.

After another counsel meeting the following Saturday, which proved to be even more satisfactory than the first, plans were made for a communion service with a preparatory meeting to be held the next week:

> June 18, 1899, Sunday—Bro. Funk preached the sermon on examination. A council was held preparatory to the communion. The members nearly all came in and expressed peace and a willingness to observe communion. Yet some made conditions that things should be cleared up and promises faithfully kept.

* * *

"Please, John, you must stop that hoein' and come in out of the sun," Bettie commanded, anxiously watching as he leaned on his hoe handle and mopped his face. He looked thinner and paler than ever under the old, brown straw hat.

"I'll quit just as soon as I've finished these two rows of potatoes," he promised, attacking another weed with slow, weak strokes.

"But you shouldn't be workin' at all this hot weather," she scolded. "Anyone as sick as you was last night!"

"But the doctor wants me to get some exercise," John protested, reluctantly giving in and whacking at an occasional weed as he moved slowly toward the porch. "I admit it does take a lot out of me," he sighed as he settled on the steps beside Bettie.

"You're agoin' to Dr. Spohm for another treatment this afternoon, ain't you?"

"I guess I'd better. The electric treatment seems to be doing more good than medicine. But—"

"Oh, you'll soon see a difference, I reckon, if you just keep on a while," Bettie assured him. "And now that church matters are a little better, you'll be better too. Mebbe we should send to Mother Coffman, though, for some more sarsaparilla."

"No, Bettie, I'm afraid nothing will do me much good any more. But I'm leaving it to God. I—I don't want to worry you," he said, taking her hand in his, "but sometimes I feel that my work is about done here."

"Please, John, don't—don't talk like that," Bettie said huskily. "Why, you're young yet, just fifty, and they still need you here so bad, the way things are."

John sat quietly stroking the hand that trembled between his own. "These things are in God's hands, of course," he said, admiring a fluffy white cloud floating across the blue summer sky. "And if my Father has more for me to do here, He will give me strength to do it. But we must face the fact that our time will come. Life and death are His to decide. Only He knows what is best. And, oh, how wonderful it would be just to be at rest—with Him!"

Wearily John laid his head on his arms, while Elizabeth rose quietly and, brushing tears from her eyes, disappeared into the house.

It was plainly evident to both his family and his friends that John's health was failing, and failing rapidly. But in spite of weakness and pain he tried hard to keep on his regular schedule, attending meetings, looking after Institute business, working at tracts, and preparing "The Book and Tract Messenger" for publication. Also there was a daily stint in the garden and a trip to Dr. Spohm's office for the electrical treatment. Only to his diary did he confide his growing distress and weakness:

> June 20, Tuesday—I feel as though I am getting worse each day, but still I propose to keep good courage. I am utterly unfit for work, yet I put in some time in the garden in order to get exercise.
>
> June 21—I feel weaker today than I have yet. Still the doctor tells me to keep up courage and he assured me that conditions are changing favorably. This evening the young people went to the Institute Literary society and report a good time. It is a great pleasure to have Ansel at home with us again for a while.
>
> June 22—Today I went down to the doctor and felt almost exhausted till I got back. This is the weakest I have ever felt in my life. Appetite is gone and I have very distressing pain in the stomach. God knows whether He desires me better. If so He will in some way help me. If my work is done, I am glad to leave the field of my labors. I leave it all with my dear Master. This evening I did not feel able to go to the Bible Reading.

On Monday, June 27, John was admitted as a patient to the Battle Creek Sanatorium in Michigan. His decision to enter the hospital for observation and treatment brought relief and hope to his family and friends as well as to himself. He had been impressed by the hospital on several visits and had confidence that if human help were possible, he would get it there.

A little note to his family the next day stated:

I am cheerful. It is pleasant to have one hundred people around you all intensely interested to have you well.

William took advantage of the Fourth of July holiday to visit his father at the sanatorium. He found him sitting outside in a wheel chair enjoying the coolness of the morning air and the beauty of the lovely gardens.

"Well, good morning, Father," he called softly as he approached the secluded shady spot where John was sitting. "Getting your fresh air and sunshine?"

"William!" John jumped in surprise at the sound of the familiar voice and, stretching out his hands, drew his son close. "This is a surprise! How could you get away on a Monday morning?"

"It's the glorious Fourth, don't you know? Surely they keep it around here."

"Keep it? Just listen. They've been firing those cannon crackers all night. I guess I just forgot they celebrate at Elkhart too. How's everybody?"

"Fine," William replied, "but anxious to know how you're getting along."

"Well, I think I'm a little stronger. As strong as one can expect to be on baby food, anyway," smiled John. "But I'm afraid the pains aren't much better."

"What are they doing for you, anyway?" William asked, drawing up a chair beside him.

"Oh, hot fomentations, electric baths, massage, salt glow, hot and cold spray to my spinal column, galvanic treatments, and I don't know what all."

"And what's the diet you were talking about?"

"Well, for breakfast every morning it's gluten gruel and almond cream."

"Hm! Doesn't sound too bad," William observed. "But I think I might like a few pancakes once in a while. Has Dr. Kellogg looked you over yet?"

"I saw him yesterday," John replied.

"And what did he say?"

"Not too much. He did admit that cases like mine are rather—well, uncertain. But he felt I would soon start to improve and likely improve rapidly."

"So—o, that sounds encouraging," William said, forcing a cheerful smile. "Oh, some mail for you," he added quickly, seeing a nurse approach with a handful of letters. "Do you want to read them now or wait till I'm gone? I have to leave at twelve to make connections back to Elkhart."

"Pick out one or two and read them to me," John suggested, leaning wearily back in his chair while the nurse rearranged his pillows.

"Here's one from the Publishing Company," William said. "Maybe we'd better look at that."

"Likely about next quarter's Sunday-school lessons," John said.

William glanced quickly over the letter. "They say they want the fourth quarter soon so they can get them out during the dull part of the season. 'If you have not already prepared the copy,' he read, 'we presume that you are not in a position to do so owing to the fact of your illness. Please advise us at once as we are in a position to make arrangements for them and it is necessary that we have the desired information.' "

"Well, they are in a hurry, aren't they?" commented William, returning the letter to the envelope.

"It's only businesslike," John said. "Of course they have to know soon. I wrote to D. F. Janzen to see whether he might take over this quarter. It would be something he could do during the summer vacation."

"I doubt whether he will. He's in summer school in Chicago. I saw him the other day and he said he'd be writing to you."

"What else have you got there?"

"Here's one from a Miss Ellen Haines. Wants to know whether there'd be a possibility of a position at the Institute next fall, and whether you'd address their township Sunday-school convention in Adamsville in August."

"You'll look after that for me, won't you?" John asked. "I'm afraid I'll have to decline. How about our own conference? Is everything settled now? Last I heard we had forgotten to appoint choristers."

"Yes, I think everything's lined up. And you'll have plenty of time to prepare your talk on the International lessons."

"Yes, I've been thinking about it," John said. "If I'm well enough to get there."

"Oh, you'll be fine by then. You've got about six weeks yet," William replied quickly as he continued to sort through the letters. "Here's a letter from John Horsch. Would you like me to read it?"

John nodded agreement and William began:

> I will not weary you by a long letter but will tell you this evening that my thoughts are with you and I am earnestly praying the Lord for your restoration. Bro. Coffman is needed here below, there is yet so much work for him, and I will try to do my

> part in praying the Lord to restore him to us, and to help him to bear what He sees best to lay upon him. I know that the Lord answers prayer, and that our trials and sufferings are only for our good and that He will help us to bear them.
>
> Let us hope for some more changes for the better in our church. The Lord be with you to bless and comfort. May you taste much of His love and goodness. Do not answer this letter.

"That was nice of him," John smiled wanly. "Tell him I really appreciated it when you get home. Maybe you'd like to answer a few other letters for me too. I thought I'd get at the job sometime, but after I've written a card home every day it's about all I want to do. I got such an interesting one from A. D. Wenger in Palestine. I tried to answer it, but my hand was pretty shaky. You can take both letters home for Mother to read if you like."

On the train on his way back home, William looked through the packet of letters his father had given him. On top lay the letter addressed to Wenger. As he read it, he seemed to be hearing again that clear, ringing voice he had heard so often behind a pulpit. It seemed almost like the poetic utterance of one of the prophets, those words penned by his father. Deftly they summed up the past and revealed what he knew the near future held for him:

> May you go up into Mount Zion, worship at Bethel, be guided by Jehovah, and may our watchword be Mizpah. . . . I think I never felt so much that I would like to be in the Holy Land as when I read your letter. Your good wishes for the church and her institutions were encouraging to me. . . . Yes, I feel that I am living for the church which maintains the doctrines of Him whose feet pressed the valleys and hills of Palestine, who wept over Jerusalem, who lived in the spirit of sacrifice which would make this world glorious, who died for the sins of the world, who is waiting in glory for the time when He shall come to take us to Himself. I am glad that the church has wakened up to the necessity of establishing her institutions and doing vigorous evangelistic and mission work. I think I have lived for this, and if He could use me just a little I am satisfied. . . . I am willing to stay and work, but have also a desire to depart. If the Lord has work for me I will do it cheerfully. . . . Your journey is a great one indeed. God be your strength. He will be with you to the ends of the earth. No, I shall never look on the Holy sepulchre, Mount Calvary, Cedron, Gethsemane, Olivet, but I expect to see Him who made these places sacred. Beholding Him I shall be satisfied when I awake in His likeness.

William sighed as he folded the letter and tucked it in the envelope. Was it possible that his father might not get well? He hated to admit it, but obviously his condition was very serious, and he was even weaker than when he had entered the hospital. But the doctor had said there was a chance, he assured himself. Desperately he clung to this hope as he journeyed homeward to make his report.

For the next few weeks letters kept pouring in for John S. Coffman. The usual stack of business and personal correspondence almost doubled as friends in many places learned of his illness and wrote to cheer and encourage him. In spite of his illness, requests of all kinds kept coming in, including requests for meetings later in the year.

> South English, Iowa—Bro. John, as we did not get to hold meetings at the time I wrote you we want to hold a meeting say to begin long the first of October. . . . Could you come and conduct the meeting for us at that time? Please write me at once. When is Fred (S. F.) coming home? If you can't come we would like to have Fred if possible.

J. B. Smith, one of his converts at Berlin, Ontario, who had graduated from the small college at Ada, Ohio, and was now in charge of the Bethel congregation at Garden City, Missouri, wrote to suggest a Bible conference in Missouri that fall. Jonathan Kurtz of Ligonier was anxious to have him come for Sunday services soon. A friend in Ipava, Illinois, wrote:

> I would like to know if there is or likely to be a place open in the publishing house so that I could get a position to work. By fall I need to work to keep soul and boddy together. I have had a longing for a number of years to move some place where we would have church home. We have been here for 22 years without that privilege. . . .

From C. K. Hostetler, secretary of the Evangelizing and Benevolent Board, came an appreciated note in which he assured him:

> We are praying for you. Anna B and Miriam have your name on the catalogue among those they ask God to bless every evening after they are through with "Now I lay me."

A long newsy letter from J. M. Shenk in Ohio also warmed his heart, as did those from many other friends.

In a few weeks John returned home, his condition unimproved. There was nothing more the doctors could do. Everyone realized that the time left would be short.

When the pain wasn't too intense, the little bedroom in the house on Eden Street was a cheerful place, and it became a hallowed spot where differences were forgotten and where friends encouraged each other and prayed together.

Samuel F. came home to be with the family at this critical time. He spent as much time as possible with his father, relieving and assisting the male nurse who had accompanied him from the hospital.

Alone in the room, sometimes late at night, sometimes in the early morning, the two enjoyed deep spiritual discussions. The world of the spirit was becoming more and more the real world to John, while S. F. caught a new vision of the life beyond. There were times when pain made it difficult to talk and impossible to sleep. Then it was that S. F. heard his father pray. Sometimes he could scarcely hear the words, but again they came strong and clear. It wasn't for himself he prayed, but for the work which had been on his heart for so many years—the churches he had served; individuals who had not yet found Christ; the peace of his beloved church at Elkhart, and so often for the welfare of the Institute he had helped to establish.

At John's request Bishop Funk and Bishop D. J. Johns called one morning to anoint him. It was a solemn service, one which he had frequently conducted and which on several occasions had resulted in healing. There was a smile on his lips, a gleam of trust and hope in his eyes, and he seemed to be talking to a close personal friend as he whispered, "Not my will, Father. You know best."

"More letters for you," S. F. said, coming into the room one morning as John roused from a fitful nap. "One from Pandora, Ohio."

"Oh, Steiner, God bless him. Another one of my boys," John exclaimed, smiling weakly.

"Shall I read it to you, or would you like to sit up and read it for yourself?"

"You read it, please. I don't feel like sitting just now. Maybe you'd prop me up just a little with another pillow."

My dear brother, In His name greeting:

> I hear that you are not well, and have for that reason thought often of you these days. Last night I could not sleep for several hours, so I spent the time in meditation and prayer. I recalled many blessed experiences with you and that, of course, makes me lonesome for you.
>
> I wondered how I might be able to help you or send you relief of some kind. I know you do not lack for friends if you need their presence or attention. They no doubt gladly do all for you they can. But you know we naturally love to do something for those who have done so much for us. . . . I wish, however, that you may know and feel assured of my heart-felt sympathy and of my daily sighs and prayers and longings for your health and happiness and for your usefulness to the church and your worth to the Christian cause—the deeper work of grace in the soul you have so earnestly defended and greatly extended.
>
> There are ties that bind us like cords, ties we cannot tell why or how—but we feel them rooted down deep in the soul. And we never fully know their strength nor their influence over us until we begin to entertain thoughts of their severing. . . .
>
> Our lives have been knit together in service and in purpose. You have "begotten" me in the faith and very largely helped to make me what I am. If the Lord can use me to any advantage or success in the advancement in His cause and Kingdom it is

largely due to the fact that He used you as an instrument to break up and crush my heart to loving obedience in that "little white church" at New Stark. So I do not wish to worry you by these thoughts, but, if possible do my humble duty and "honor those who have the rule over us." I want you to know that I love you and praise God for you and for your concern for my well being and my soul. . . .

Some of my friends at Elkhart keep me informed as to your state, and we all pray for you. Only be "calm in the soul" knowing that the Lord in whose hands our lives have been placed and to whom our souls have been committed knows best how to use us to the greatest glory.

The Lord of power and of love be with your body and watch over your soul. In His Name. One of your sons in the faith, tenderly

M. S. Steiner

P.S. Clara wants me to acknowledge her concern for you and her kind remembrance these days of the blessing your life has been to her. I had thought only of our relation in the light of personal experience, so failed to recognize my own dear one in the few moments of pouring out my inner feelings for you. Accept it as a word of encouragement and comfort. M. S.

John's eyes were closed when S. F. finished reading the letter, and he lay there relaxed and motionless, with a trace of a smile on his lips. S. F. was beginning to think he had fallen asleep when suddenly he drew a deep sigh.

"Maybe that was it," the words came softly and slowly from the pale lips. "Maybe that was the special purpose, to get a few good men like Steiner started in the work."

"That's part of it," S. F. remarked, rising to smooth the pillow and straighten the sheet. "There are quite a few men working for the church who would likely have been doing something quite different if it hadn't been for your interest and influence. But you have done a lot more than that—a great deal more."

"No, Samuel, not me. It was the Lord. If He has used me, I'm thankful. I don't feel so concerned about leaving the work with men like them ready to go ahead."

S. F. noticed his father wince as a sudden spasm of pain once more shook his body.

"Maybe you'd better just rest now," he said, tenderly wiping beads of perspiration from his forehead. "The pain's getting worse?"

John groaned. "It—it's bad. But, Samuel, I—I just want to say I'm glad you're going to carry on, too. I'm finished now, but you—you're just starting. God has a special purpose for you too, the same as He had for me or anyone else He calls."

It was Saturday evening, July 22, when John died. After a night and day of sheer agony that no medication could relieve, he was finally permitted to enter that rest for which he had yearned so long.

That night telegrams went out to relatives in Virginia and to ministers in various states where John was especially well known and loved. The announcement of his death was received with great sorrow in many congregations on Sunday morning.

On Tuesday they came for the funeral, a host of friends from Michigan, Illinois, Ohio, Pennsylvania, and other parts of Indiana.

Plans for the service were not too difficult. John himself had requested that his Amish friend and associate, D. J. Johns, should preach the sermon. Since the Prairie Street Church was far too small to hold the crowd, arrangements were made to take care of the overflow at the Institute. M. S. Steiner was asked to address this group.

Both ministers used John's favorite text for their sermons—Galatians 2:20, "I am crucified with Christ: nevertheless I live." A number of other ministers also took part, including Reverend Townsend, representing the Elkhart Ministerial Association, who attended in a body. It was estimated that over one thousand attended the service.

Miles away in the old Bank Church in Virginia, where Coffman had been ordained, a third service was held at the same hour. It was a memorial service for the boy from the valley who had given his life in serving his Master in many ways and in many places. Here, too, a large crowd assembled, showing love and sympathy for the mother, brothers and sisters, and other relatives who could not make the trip to Indiana.

Back at the little house on Eden Street that evening supper was served to the many visitors. But eventually the crowd diminished and only a few close friends remained. Among them were two ministers from Ohio—M. S. Steiner and John M. Shenk.

"Let's go out on the porch and cool off," S. F. suggested to the small group who sat talking with Bettie in the stuffy little parlor.

"Not a bad idea," said Steiner, rising and leading the way to the door. "Come on, Brother Shenk, you look as if you could use some fresh air. And what about you, Mother Coffman?"

"Oh, you folks just go on out," said Bettie, looking pale and exhausted as she leaned back in her rocking chair, fanning herself. "I'll just set here a spell and then go to bed."

Seating themselves on the porch steps they were soon joined by William and Ansel, who came walking down the street from William's home.

"Are the little girls in bed?" S. F. asked, making room for William on the bottom step while Ansel sprawled on the grass beside Jake and Daniel.

"I got them home," William replied, "and I imagine Lydia will soon finish the job."

"They will miss their grandfather," Shenk remarked wistfully. "They seemed very fond of him."

"A lot of folks will miss him," observed Steiner, gazing up at the darkening sky where a few stars were beginning to appear. "I just don't see how we're going to get along without him."

For a moment no one spoke. Only the rattle of dishes and the low voices of women in the kitchen broke the evening stillness.

"I've been thinking a lot about that," S. F. finally ventured. "We can't help wondering why he was taken so soon. It does seem as if he could have accomplished a lot more. But it must be in God's plan. His work must have been finished."

"I wonder about that," Ansel spoke up. "It seems to me he might have lived a little longer if he hadn't had quite so much to worry about the last few years. What do you think, Steiner?"

"Well, Ansel, I agree with your brother," Steiner replied quietly. "But I know how you feel, too. It is too bad your father had to suffer all that mental anguish. But who are we to question God's ways? He does hold the power over life and death. To question that is to question His very nature—to limit the power of the Omnipotent. Don't you see that?"

"Y—yes," Ansel replied slowly, "but it's pretty hard to believe that Father was really finished, just when he was at his—his prime, you might say."

"His work isn't finished," Steiner replied. "The work he was doing is the kind of work that goes on. He helped get this church of ours out of a deep rut, and helped put a lot of us on the right track so we wouldn't slip back again. At least we hope to keep working, don't we, Shenk?"

"Amen," came Shenk's response. "I'm sure your father's influence will be felt, maybe long after the man has been forgotten. Why, I heard just today of several young people who accepted Christ after they heard of your father's death."

"One was a boy in Sterling, Illinois," William said. "We stayed at their home a few months ago and he said he heard Father pray in the middle of the night. It made a great impression on him. Really started him thinking."

"Did you ever hear about his mother's experience when he was born?" S. F. asked, turning to Steiner. "About a revelation she had that God had some special service for her son?"

"He never mentioned it," Steiner answered, "but your grandmother told me about it one time when I visited her."

"And what do you think?" S. F. continued. "Can you see any really special accomplishment in his life? Has the prediction been fulfilled?"

"Well, boys," Steiner said, "maybe I'm prejudiced. J. S. was closer to me than any man I ever knew. I've been watching him for years and trying to evaluate what I've been seeing. I'm not a prophet, but I think I can see great things ahead for the Mennonite Church. There will be more schools, more city missions, more foreign missions. I also see Sunday schools and young people's activities throughout the entire church and we must admit that he had a lot to do with this awakening. Is that special enough?"

"I know what he'd say," S. F. replied quietly, "Not I but Christ."

"Yes, 'I am crucified with Christ: nevertheless I live . . . and the life which I now live in the flesh I live by the faith of the Son of God, who loved me, and gave himself for me.' That wasn't just a favorite text," Steiner said quietly. "It was the actual pattern for his life. I'll never forget a sermon I heard him preach on this. He made it so clear and simple."

"You know," Shenk interjected thoughtfully, "I think right there you have the key to that awakening you've been talking about—and right there is the special mission J. S. performed for the church, that emphasis on the new life. That's what helped so many people and strengthened so many congregations."

Again there was silence. S. F. picked up a little twig and sat peeling the bark from one end. "Well, brethren, if that's the case, then our duty is clear," he mused, snapping the twig and glancing from Steiner to Shenk. "If that's the teaching that has caused the awakening, then it will have to be our main emphasis, too, if the work is to go on."

Both men nodded thoughtfully. "Right," said Steiner, while Shenk agreed with another hearty "Amen."

"What a wonderful text it is for a sermon—a good many sermons," S. F. continued, his eyes fixed on a bright star on the horizon: "New life—a new life in Christ."